CW01266398

John
Pascoe

for
Dorothy Pascoe

Published with the assistance of

CREATIVE NEW ZEALAND

NEW ZEALAND HISTORY RESEARCH TRUST FUND

D.O.W. HALL MEMORIAL TRUST OF THE NEW ZEALAND ALPINE CLUB

MOUNTAIN AND FOREST TRUST OF THE FEDERATED MOUNTAIN CLUBS

WELLINGTON SECTION OF THE NEW ZEALAND ALPINE CLUB

John Pascoe

CHRIS MACLEAN

Craig Potton Publishing

in *association* with

The Whitcombe Press

First published in 2003 by

Craig Potton Publishing
Box 555, Nelson, New Zealand
www.craigpotton.co.nz

in association with

The Whitcombe Press
39 Bruce Avenue, Brooklyn
Wellington, New Zealand

© 2003 The Whitcombe Press

ISBN: 0-473-09443-6

All rights reserved. No part of this publication
may be reproduced, stored in a retrieval system
or transmitted in any form, or by any means, electronic,
mechanical, photocopying, recording or otherwise,
without the prior written permission of the publishers.

Edited by Anna Rogers
Designed by
Margaret Cochran & Geoff Norman
Production by Geoff Norman
Printed in China by Everbest Printing Co. Ltd

Contents

OVER THE WHITCOMBE PASS

Jakob Lauper
1863

edited by
JOHN PASCOE

John the Evangelist

John Pascoe's 16 books reflect his love of the mountains and his passion for the history of his own country. He discovered both as a young man, while exploring the Whitcombe Pass (left) at the head of the Rakaia River.

Inspired by the peaks he and his companions had come to climb, he was also fascinated by the exploits of the men who first explored the area, and determined to make their stories familiar to others. His earliest newspaper articles, for instance, recalled Samuel Butler and John Baker who discovered the pass in 1861. Later, when Pascoe came across Jakob Lauper's account of his and Henry Whitcombe's extraordinary journey in 1863 across the pass to the West Coast, he edited it, wrote an introduction and got it published. He also brought to light the achievements of explorers in other areas, both Maori and European, most notably Charlie Douglas, whose writings he edited and published in 1957 as Mr Explorer Douglas.

Pascoe wrote his books between 1937 and 1972, a time when New Zealand was still evolving from a distant British colony to an independent Pacific nation with its own distinctive character. Initially the colony was slow to make the transition: although New Zealand became a dominion in 1907, it did not formally adopt the Statute of Westminster, granting full independence to former British colonies, until 1947. In this period of national adolescence, Pascoe played a vital role by helping New Zealanders to understand who they were. Like a kaumatua, he told of forebears and their deeds, encouraging Pakeha to see their place in a new land. In doing so he helped New Zealanders to gain a sense of themselves and the magnificent country they inhabited.

Unlike many of his contemporaries, John Pascoe never visited England, and never wanted to, although he made two trips to the United States. In a 1969 letter to his eldest daughter, Anna, he wrote: 'As one who is nearly untravelled I have always sought and found consolation in the knowledge that in my writing I have tried to interpret my own country to my own countrymen'. It was a task he tackled with zeal. 'I have made myself a kind of evangelist,' he told a climbing friend, 'hence my steady output of books, which I hope will interest and influence young jokers.'

His distinctive collection of photographs of New Zealand life during and after the Second World War has also made an important contribution to New Zealanders' sense of their past. Taken together, his books, articles and photographs are a memorial to a man who was, above all, a New Zealander.

MY INTEREST IN JOHN PASCOE began in the early 1990s when I was researching a book on the Tararua mountains and came across his provocative, uncomplimentary remarks about them in his book *Land Uplifted High*:

> For sheer miserable monotony of contour, rigour of weather, and bleakness of outlook it is hard to beat the Tararuas. They are to Wellington trampers what oatmeal is to Scottish people; dull solid fare which gives them staple virtues. It is no defence for the Tararuas to say that they have their fine days. As with shrews, their nicenesses are unpredictable. Some give these ranges their affection, but this presupposes lack of knowledge about other regions and at least an enviable optimism. Then again some winters have given the Tararuas an even coating of snow, but the icing on the cake seldom remains long enough to be tasted. The two passable rock climbs on the range are inaccessible and often hidden in mist. There are no glaciers. The tributaries of the rivers are barred with gorges and waterfalls, and to the insult of a dreary grass line is added the indignity of vicious sub-alpine scrub.[1]

As a Tararua enthusiast I found this description galling and I wanted to know more about the man who had written it. I visited his widow, Dorothy Pascoe, who said that the passage was typical tongue-in-cheek Pascoe prose intended to rile some of the dour local trampers he had met through the Tararua Tramping Club.[2]

I knew little of John Pascoe beyond his wartime photographs, and had read only one of his books, but talking to Dorothy quickened my interest. She showed me a metal box, the size of a cabin trunk, which was filled with John Pascoe's papers. A quick reading of some of his letters (he kept carbon copies of them all) showed the same opinionated writing that had damned the Tararua Ranges. The big box was full of letters in manila folders, arranged by subject or by year; here was a legacy for any future biographer. Dorothy was looking for just such a person. 'Would you be

Dorothy Pascoe

interested?' I was, but with another book underway, I could not consider it. I forgot John Pascoe.

In 1994 one of John's four daughters, Sara Pascoe, began researching a biography of her father. She regularly sent me copies of items such as photos and newspaper articles as well as copies of letters she had received from John's surviving climbing friends. I encouraged her to continue her correspondence with 'the ancient mountaineers', as she called them, but at the same time, because she had such a tremendous admiration for her father, I feared her account might be rather uncritical. I knew little about biography, but enough to understand that a book by one family member about another (particularly a child about a parent) should be treated with caution. I was also concerned because Sara seemed to focus almost entirely on her father as a mountaineer. Even with my limited knowledge, I realised that, apart from some notable ascents and exploration of little-known country, there was a lot more to John Pascoe. What of the photographer who had documented New Zealand life in the 1940s? Or the man who had tried so hard to be a poet? Or the archivist who had battled to introduce new ideas, such as an oral history archive, to the conservative civil service of the 1960s? If I did not like the kind of biography Sara might write, perhaps I should do it myself.

So, in 1999, having finished my other book, I began work on a biography of John Pascoe. Sara agreed to help, as did Graham Langton, an alpine historian who had also shown an interest in writing Pascoe's story. My first sustained examination of the tin trunk revealed even more useful material than I had imagined. Here were copies of Pascoe's correspondence, both personal and official, from the 1930s to the 1970s. He had moved from Christchurch to Wellington in 1937 and from then on had kept copies of almost all the letters he wrote. Better still, most were typewritten so his barely decipherable handwriting would not be a problem. The trunk also contained numerous negatives, loose photos and albums full of photos that had never been publicly seen before. Of particular interest were the Pascoes' holiday albums which recorded the activities of a post-war New Zealand family in the mountains, the bush and at the seaside. Pascoe's documentation of his own children's development was as impressive as his earlier, well-known photographic collection of New Zealanders in wartime. The trunk was a treasure trove, a biographer's delight. I soon realised that its contents would reduce the element of speculation that often underpins, and weakens, a biography.

I also examined John Pascoe's substantial collection of papers held by the Alexander Turnbull Library. These were of a more public nature, and included correspondence with his publishers, but were just as opinionated as the tin trunk material. A typical example was a letter Pascoe wrote in 1952 to the editor of the Pegasus Press, Robin Muir. 'Have you had time to listen on radio to poets reading their own work?', he asked, then gave his own detailed response to the series:

> I liked R.A.K. Mason fine – he was unemotional and even too matter-of-fact, as tho a plumber had toddled into your room, grabbed R.A.K. Mason from the shelf, and started to read it in a flat voice. But his dynamic subjects seemed enhanced by his prosaic delivery. Allen Curnow, on the other hand, emoted

in his usual verbal-orgiastic way; not intolerable, but at times irritating. Fairburn gives a good flick to his wit, and also Vogt, but both are rather smart-alecky to reach deep. Alistair Campbell last night was very good – in the way that Mason was. Baxter I find superb tho some people here reckon his vowels are overdone but I find it satisfying to listen to him, as he has the rich benignity of bar-room bonhomie. I would liked to have had Denis [Glover] in this series, but whoever organised it (I suspect Baxter-Vogt) left him out, also Witheford, Spear and Johnson. Poor Lou is still in the wars. Why will the poets rush to the *Listener* columns – why not leave it all to the disciples to make fools of themselves.[3]

I resolved to include enough excerpts from Pascoe's letters to give a sense of the man and to ensure that his voice could be heard. Nevertheless there was the danger that if I relied too heavily on Pascoe's own words the story of his life might become self-serving and inaccurate. To gain a more balanced view I recorded interviews with a number of Pascoe's contemporaries, most of whom were now in their 80s and 90s. Because of their age I made them my top priority. Sara Pascoe's collection of 'Letters from Ancient Mountaineers' was also invaluable, as many of them had died since she began her correspondence. At the same time Graham Langton trawled through numerous publications to make a chronology of Pascoe's expeditions and writing. The results of his research revealed a remarkable number of articles in a variety of magazines, alpine journals and newspapers.

My most valuable source of information, however, was Dorothy Pascoe. As her initial reticence in the presence of a tape recorder diminished, I gathered much useful information from a series of interviews. But before I was even ready to write, Dorothy, too, seemed destined to die. A deteriorating cardiac condition, which restricted her circulation and gave her a waxy pallor, reminded me all too clearly of my own father in the months before his death.

In June 2001, at the age of 83, she courageously chose to undergo open heart surgery, partly 'to keep an eye on Chris'. One night soon after the operation, I kept her company while she battled demonic dreams brought on by too much morphine. As I sat there beside her hospital bed, I realised the extent of her commitment to this book. I had thought that writing John Pascoe's biography would be a detached exercise, largely a matter of reading and analysing books and papers; as it turned out, my relationships with Dorothy and her daughters have been equally important.

At an early stage I made two decisions that have determined the nature of this book. The first was to emphasise that John was a twin. He and his brother, Paul, were born only three hours apart. Furthermore, as 'mirror twins' their genetic material had been split in two at conception, producing two people with complementary characteristics. For example, John was left-handed, Paul right-handed; John preferred to do things while Paul liked to design or dream; Paul had sons, John had daughters. Here, I realised, was an unusual situation for a biographer. John would always be centre stage, but Paul would appear whenever his activities seemed relevant to John's. To include Paul Pascoe meant, of course, that I also had to gain the confidence and cooperation of his sons and their families. Fortunately they gave it. I am grateful to Jonathan and Simon Pascoe, in particular, for their willingness to expose their father and his life to public scrutiny.

The second decision was to give equal weight to John Pascoe's public and private lives. The account could have been limited to his work, books and mountains climbed, but his letters gave me the opportunity to chart changes in New Zealand society after the war as seen through the lens of a family. This has been possible because his letters give revealing insights into the vortex of emotions that is family life, or as Pascoe called it, 'the turmoil of living'. I have been able to adopt this approach because Dorothy and her daughters have been willing to disclose details of their private lives, and I am grateful for their courage.

In 1953 a Timaru schoolboy, Rob McCullough, wrote a profile of John Pascoe for a school project. He sent Pascoe a copy for comment. In his reply, Pascoe was positive and encouraging, then remarked, 'Your main fault is one that is common to all biographers; you are too kind to your subject. That is a human fault. You do so much work on the joker about whom you write that he becomes even more able and virtuous than he is.'[4] Keeping this in mind, I have reported Pascoe's foibles and mistakes as well as his attributes and achievements.

Pascoe had one characteristic that interested me above all others – his unquenchable zest for life. He never lost his enthusiasm. Even during his nadir, the family crises of the 1950s and 1960s, he remained positive. He would take his daughters into the beech forest that surrounded their Eastbourne home and encourage them to talk freely, before reiterating his own philosophy: find strength in your situation whatever the circumstances, keep going one step at a time towards your objective and you will eventually reach it. This was apparent in Pascoe's own climbing record and in his books; as Dorothy said 'he had an extraordinary tenacity in everything he did'. Some saw this striving as evidence of an inferiority complex and, given his uncertain start in life, that seems plausible. 'John was always proving himself,' recalled Dorothy. 'In the mountains he was testing himself, and long distance running [at which he did well] was another way of testing yourself.'[5] Both John and Paul worked tirelessly to objectify their lives, Paul in buildings, John in books. In the end, when the detail of their lives has fallen away, that is what remains.

A friend of John Pascoe's, Frank Fitzgerald, regularly commuted to and from downtown Wellington with him, first on the ferry, later on the bus. He recalls that while others chatted or read the paper, Pascoe was always busy writing a review or an article, or planning his next book. To Fitzgerald, who was also a climber and photographer, Pascoe deserved his success because he worked so hard and in doing so made an invaluable contribution to his country. 'Never before or since,' Fitzgerald recently wrote, 'has anyone been such an energetic, enthusiastic and consistent recorder in prose and pictures of interesting events in the back country and mountains of New Zealand.'[6]

CHRIST'S COLLEGE

J H Pascoe. School House .... Form .

		MONDAY	TUESDAY	WEDNESDAY	THURSDA
MORNING	1	ENGLISH. A.G.G.	LATIN. J.M.	GEOMETRY E.G.H.	ENGLISH J.M.
	2	FRENCH. A.G.G.	ALGEBRA. E.G.H.	FRENCH. A.G.G.	ALGEB E.G.H.
	3	GREEK. E.J.	FRENCH. A.G.G.	GREEK E.J.	FRENCI A.G.G
	4	LATIN. J.M.	DR...	LATIN	LATI ..M.
AFTERNOON	5	HISTORY J.M.	DIV... O....		...TOR ..M.
	6	TRIG. E.G.H.	Gre... E....		...EEK .J.
PREPARATION	1	Latin.	M		...tin
	2	French.		3. English.	...eek English
	3	Greek.			
		Nets.	Day off.	Harmony.	Nets.

TIME TABLE

3rd Term, 192**6**

FRIDAY	SATURDAY
TRIG. E.G.H.	FRENCH A.G.G.
LATIN. J.M.	LATIN. J.M.
ENGLISH. A.G.G.	ENGLISH J.M.
GEOMETRY. E.G.H.	HISTORY J.M.
GREEK E.J.	
FRENCH. A.G.G.	
Latin. French. History. Drill.	Orchestra.

CHAPTER ONE
'A Skinny Stammerer'

During the 1950s, John Pascoe wrote several letters to students who had asked for information about his life. They may have been surprised to find that the veteran mountaineer and author had a physically unpromising childhood.

'I was a weakly infant,' he wrote, 'and very skinny and herring-gutted as a kid. Enjoyed Sumner Primary School but didn't like Christ's College much as I was bullied there.' This may have taught him endurance, but it did little for his self-assurance: 'As a skinny stammerer, I had not much confidence in myself at school and was earmarked as an oddity'.

In this photo John (left) and Paul (right) flank their friend, Walter Ollivier, during the school's annual picnic at Corsair Bay on Banks Peninsula. All three boys look happy, but the train journey to the bay was traditionally an ordeal for the younger boys because the long tunnel between Christchurch and Lyttelton provided bullies with an ideal opportunity to prey on others without detection.

DOROTHY PASCOE COLLECTION,
INSET – JONATHAN PASCOE COLLECTION

T HE PASCOES LIVED ON CLIFTON HILL, overlooking the seaside suburb of Sumner, to the southeast of Christchurch. At first, the twins, John and Paul, enjoyed the daily routine of going up the steep track behind their house to get milk from the hilltop farm. If the day was clear it was exciting to look westwards and see the distant, serrated line of the Southern Alps lit up by the rising sun; or northwards, where the faint outline of Tapuae-o-uenuku rose like a pyramid above the wide sweep of Pegasus Bay.

But one morning when it was John's turn, the farmer's wife stared at the unusually thin boy and said, 'I wish you wouldn't come here – I can't bear to look at you!' This stinging reproach was so clearly remembered that he recounted it many years later to his wife.[1] Other, more kindly observers, were concerned rather than repulsed by the twins' frail physique. When Fanny Whitcombe, who lived on nearby Richmond Hill, watched John and Paul climbing the Aranoni Track on their way home from school, she wondered how their legs – 'as thin as a stick insect's' – could carry them up the hill.[2] Yet, within a few years, those spindly legs took the twins to the top of many of the Canterbury peaks they had seen in the distance from the slopes above Sumner.

The twins' frailty was the result of their early entry into this world. Born on 26 September 1908, the boys weighed only 1.4 kilograms each.[3] Because Sir Truby King's innovative ideas on infant welfare had yet to be implemented, there were no Karitane Hospitals to give intensive care to premature babies. The twins' survival was so far from certain that their mother, Effie, was advised to choose one child to nurture – and leave the other to die.[4] The same question was put to their father, Guy, by a friend: 'Which rat are you going to drown?'[5] But Effie wanted both her sons. For weeks they were patiently fed at home by a nurse using an eye dropper, until they were strong enough to suck milk through a teat.[6]

It must have been a worrying time for the Pascoe parents. Their daughter, Alice, born five years earlier, had developed in the normal way. Now it

Clifton Hill, above Sumner, was developed at the beginning of the 20th century by the architect Samuel Hurst Seager. The Pascoes bought one of Seager's finely crafted houses near the top of the Aranoni Track (below, far left), a zigzag pathway still used today. Above the houses, farmland rose to the summit of Mount Pleasant.

WILLIAM PRICE PHOTO,
ALEXANDER TURNBULL LIBRARY

As children John and Paul Pascoe were familiar with this view from Clifton Hill of the Canterbury Plains and the distant Torlesse Range. Years later, at the age of 17, Paul sketched the same view in his diary. He was sufficiently knowledgeable to be able to mark all the peaks and features of the Torlesse Range (A-F) as well as other landmarks such as the Waimakariri Gorge (J) and the river's path across the plains.

SIMON PASCOE COLLECTION

was as though a hoped-for son had been split into two before birth. This was exactly what had happened: the boys were identical twins, created when an egg was divided at conception.

Identical twins are psychologically as close as two people can be, closer than fraternal twins who develop from separate eggs. Because identical twins are so alike, they can be very competitive, but those distinguished by complementary characteristics, such as the Pascoe boys, have less cause to vie with each other. Like all twins, they share a private world, particularly as young children, and have a rapport that is, perhaps, most apparent in speech. Each learns from the other and this mutual influence can cause difficulties such as stuttering.

Research has shown that a sibling of a stutterer has a 20 per cent chance of having the same handicap. This increases to 32 per cent with fraternal twins and 77 per cent with identical twins.[7] Since it is known that twins are more likely to stutter than other people, and young males are more likely to do so than young females,[8] it is not surprising that John and Paul Pascoe both stuttered. They were also slow to walk.

At the age of five, John developed a hernia that was probably caused by a descending testicle becoming stuck in his abdomen. An operation was necessary. He remembered little of his stay in hospital but recalled that when he came home he was 'spoilt till I was well again'.[9] For the rest of his life he guarded the remaining testicle with extra care, especially when crossing cold rivers.[10]

These problems might suggest a miserable childhood but the twins were loved and secure, and soon displayed the same determination that characterised their parents. Effie Pascoe had a morning bathe in the sea all year round, and Guy Pascoe was also a keen swimmer. Sometimes the twins accompanied him when he swam from Sumner to New Brighton across the Heathcote Estuary, where there was sometimes a strong current. This is a tradition that continues in the Pascoe family today.[11]

Effie Pascoe was the daughter of Edward Denham, then mayor of Sumner. She was a redoubtable character, sure of her Victorian values and not to be contradicted – and she passed on her strong sense of self to her sons. All his life, despite his stammer, John was quick to express his opinions in any company and Paul had a similar confidence, as an incident at Sumner Primary School showed. During an art class the teacher said to him, 'Poplars don't look like that', to which Paul replied, without hesitation, 'Ours do.'[12]

Guy Pascoe was a confident member of Christchurch society. As the son of a clergyman, he had a firm sense of right and wrong and was a churchman all his life. As a lawyer, he was known for his 'unshakeable integrity', a virtue colleagues sometimes found difficult because 'with his clear perception of what was right and just in the matter in hand, he found compromise, though sometimes inevitable, always repugnant'.[13] As a schoolboy at Christ's College he excelled academically and on the sports field. He was head of school and played in the first XV for three years. Later, he played rugby for Canterbury. In 1900 he completed his legal studies and joined George Harper's law practice, which then became Harper, Son and Pascoe. Guy Pascoe expected that John – who was the elder twin by half an hour – would join the firm. John accepted this without question and from an early age saw himself as a lawyer.

As it turned out, however, his father's interest in exploration was a more lasting influence. Guy Pascoe was the New Zealand solicitor for Robert Falcon Scott's polar expedition which sailed from Lyttelton in 1910. He received letters from Scott and other members of the party and John collected the stamps.

Scott took with him a prefabricated hut for use as a meteorological station. When the supply ship returned to New Zealand with surplus equipment (including the hut) on board. Scott's agent, Joseph Kinsey, erected it in his garden at Sumner. The twins, visiting Kinsey with their father, would play in the hut, which reminded them of the heroic story that gripped New Zealanders for years to come.[14]

Above all, it was his father's own exploration that impressed John. The few photos of Guy Pascoe that survive include a sequence taken in 1914 when he and two companions explored the upper Waimakariri during an unsuccessful attempt on Mount Rolleston.[15] Years later, writing about his own lifelong passion for the mountains in his book *Great Days in New Zealand Exploration*, John Pascoe recalled his father's adventure and the effect it had on him at the time: 'As a young man I was not alone in a romantic hunger for seeking new horizons. Had not my father, Guy Pascoe, been in the first climbing party up the Crow branch of the Waimakariri? He too had pointed to the Main Divide and told me how Samuel Butler had written a book about an undiscovered race on the other side; these Erewhonians captured my childish imagination.'[16]

John Pascoe dedicated *Great Days in New Zealand Exploration* to his father, an appropriate gesture since the book recounts the achievements of Guy Pascoe's generation and earlier pioneers as they explored a new country. Some of them were known to the young John and their exploits influenced his later life. Among them was George Harper, who was one of the first to drive sheep from Canterbury over the mountains to Westland.[17]

Retracing George Harper's route today, it seems remarkable that sheep could be taken through such steep terrain: from Lake Coleridge up the

Effie Pascoe (née Denham) with her daughter, Alice (right), and sons Paul and John (on her lap), c.1910.

Effie's family emigrated from Somerset to Canterbury in 1859. Her father, Edward Denham, was a solicitor. In 1874 he married Emily Nalder, the daughter of a solicitor in Akaroa. Effie, the youngest of their seven children, was born in 1880.

ROSEMARY WATT COLLECTION

Guy Pascoe

JONATHAN PASCOE COLLECTION

Paul (left) and John Pascoe, aged eight. The twins grew up at a time when the British Empire was still powerful, its virtues personified by heroic figures such as the polar explorer, Robert Falcon Scott. Effie Pascoe's hero was T. E. Lawrence, 'Lawrence of Arabia', the young Englishman whose exploits in the Arab revolt against the Turks made him famous.

JONATHAN PASCOE COLLECTION

Wilberforce River towards the divide. At the headwaters of the Wilberforce, a seemingly vertical rock slope guards the approach to Browning's Pass. Yet this was Harper's route. George Harper became not a sheep farmer but a lawyer, and years later when John Pascoe was a law student working in his firm, the old man told him how 'at the last steep pinch to the pass, where the way lay up a narrow rocky gut, he had to push each sheep bodily'. Once they reached the pass, Harper and his helpers followed a crude path hacked and blasted out of the slopes above the Arahura River, to reach Westland. Here they were well rewarded for their exertions as sheep fetched 5 shillings a head in Hokitika – big money in those days.[18]

Had Harper not described these pioneering adventures to John Pascoe (who later wrote them down) they might have been forgotten. Pascoe was also impressed by Harper's other achievements, such as his efforts to relieve unemployment, for which he was knighted, and most of all perhaps, by the discovery that Harper had been taught Greek by Pascoe's boyhood hero, Samuel Butler, the author of *Erewhon*.[19]

The enigmatic and versatile Butler – author, explorer, musician and runholder – was to become one of Pascoe's favourite subjects. He wrote numerous articles about him and he appears in many of Pascoe's books. But the person who probably taught the young John most about how to tell a story was his father's friend, Judge O. T. J. Alpers, whom John later described as 'the doyen of raconteurs'.

The twins came to know Alpers during the summer holidays when the Pascoes and other Canterbury families would gather at the small settlement near the mouth of the Rakaia River known as Rakaia Huts. Here they stayed in cottages clustered on the northern bank, not far from the sea. Unlike Sumner, however, there was no inviting stretch of sand but a great mound of shingle thrown up by stormy seas. Behind this barrier, the trapped waters of the Rakaia flowed across the low-lying land, creating a large lagoon and a network of waterways – a perfect world for children. Swimming, sailing, picnics on the shingle bar, rabbit shooting on the riverbank and camping on the Island – a low rise marooned by the river – introduced the twins, their sister, Alice, and their friends to the outdoors. Only the jokes and stories of Judge Alpers kept John indoors.[20]

Alpers took an avuncular interest in the twins. In 1921, when John and Paul were about to start at Christ's College, he gave each of them a large scrapbook entitled 'College Days' in which he encouraged them to keep mementos of their school years. In an accompanying 12-page letter he offered advice ('It is not life that matters – it is the courage you bring to it') as well as his ideas of what the twins might become at the end of their schooldays: Paul would be an art student at the Slade School of Art, while Alpers envisaged John as a young barrister at the Middle Temple, London's legal hub, preparing his first brief.[21]

Alpers had great hopes for the boys and a fondness for Christ's, which he was confident would transform them into fine young men. A photo of the twins, taken as they were about to leave for their first day at the school, shows them proudly smiling in their new uniforms, but the smiles did not last long. They were the target of bullies who picked on them because they were small and because they stuttered. John also wore braces on his teeth.

They were subject to the initiation rituals typical of such schools in those days and were also bullied by boarders because they were day boys (then a minority at the school). It was a miserable time. John later told his family a little of what he and others endured. He mentioned, for instance, his friend Arnold Wall being forced into a bath made murky with ink and dangerous with broken glass – a practice discontinued, according to the school's official history, when a boy cut his bottom and the wound became septic.[22] John and Paul also suffered that perennial humiliation of new boys, 'blackballing', in which their testicles were coated with shoe polish.

Fortunately for the twins, their cousin, Bill Day, who they knew well from family holidays at Rakaia Huts, was also at Christs's. Three years their senior and of much more robust physique, Day took them under his wing – a kindness John remembered all his life. Only those boys who had obvious self-assurance, however, were likely to entirely escape the bullying. One who did stand up to them was future Second World War hero Charles Upham, recalled by Paul Pascoe as being completely fearless. His biographer describes how:

> As a mere new boy at Christ's, [Upham] intervened between three louts who were teasing a little fat boy, shouting at them:
> 'Leave him alone, you pigs!'
> He drove them back, not with the threat of his fists – for they would have availed him nothing – but with a passion that flowed from his icy-blue eyes. It was something that indicated a force of personality lying deep within him. They desisted, worried and frightened by the look that blazed from him.[23]

The lagoon at Rakaia Huts.
Inset: John and Kim, the Pascoes' pet dog, among the driftwood on the boulder bank at the rivermouth.

ALICE PASCOE PHOTO, JOHN PASCOE ALBUM, DOROTHY PASCOE COLLECTION

Bloy's Banjo Band was well known in Christchurch in the 1920s, often entertaining returned servicemen and the residents of old people's homes.

Because John Pascoe (seated, middle front) was by far the youngest member of the band, he was their mascot — and was indulged accordingly. He did not always keep time with the others and would sometimes be still playing well after they had come to the end of a piece. They would politely wait for him to finish.

JOHN PASCOE ALBUM, DOROTHY PASCOE COLLECTION

The Pascoe twins, 1922.

Despite the bullying, the young Pascoes had moments of fun at Christ's. For instance, some masters found it difficult to distinguish John (left) from Paul, so they would mark one of the boys' blazers with chalk. But, as soon as an opportunity arose, the twins would swap blazers to perpetuate the confusion.

JONATHAN PASCOE COLLECTION

Another pupil who also tolerated no nonsense was Denis Glover, later to become well known as a poet, printer and wit. Unlike Upham, Glover did not hesitate to use his fists if he felt it necessary. Nor did he come to Christ's as a skinny, stuttering new boy but as a solid sixth-former, an experienced boxer, who had spent his earlier secondary schooling at one of New Zealand's top schools — Auckland Grammar. There Glover had learnt to work hard, to respect others and to look after himself: 'It was my first introduction to democracy, to freedom, to the inviolability of the individual provided he could look after his own rights'. His shift to Christ's College in 1929 was a shock:

> To move from a school of nearly a thousand boys, none of whom took any immediate interest in the mad swarm around them, to a small closed circle of just over three hundred was an enormous shock. They demanded not only your name but also all your initials' names. They were not content just to call you Glover, they wanted to know what the D was for, the J was for and the M was for. They observed whether you picked your nose with your right or left fingers, whether your hair was brushed the right way, whether you had an affectation, or wore your cap on one side of your head; and above all they were suspicious if you showed any interest in study. I remember that the headmaster, the Rev. E. C. Crosse, congratulated the school on having got 45 per cent of entrants through Matric — a school record. Well now, at Auckland Grammar, if they didn't get 98 per cent through, masters would resign.[24]

Glover was perceptive. Although he arrived two years after the Pascoes had left the school, little had changed. During the 1920s Christ's had reached the lowest point since its foundation in 1851. When Guy Pascoe was at the school in the 1890s, its academic record was among the best in the country, but by the time his sons were there pride in scholarship had given way to academic mediocrity and a preoccupation with tradition.[25]

In 1921 a new headmaster had been appointed to revitalise Christ's. An Englishman, the Reverend E. C. Crosse (who was also appointed school chaplain) set out to improve the academic performance, stamp out cheating and limit extreme bullying. But being something of a bully himself, and unable to work with others, he had little success. There was constant friction in the staffroom and he was hobbled by a permanent stand-off with his deputy, the popular A. G. Flower, who had been acting headmaster before Crosse's appointment. There was also conflict between Crosse and the Old Boys' Association, as well as with some members of the board of governors. Guy Pascoe, who was on the board, attempted to mediate but Crosse's inflexibility sabotaged his efforts and bitterness remained until Crosse resigned in 1930.[26]

The Pascoe twins were at the school for most of Crosse's tenure. As they grew older, the bullying lessened and they settled into the school's monastic routine of drill (cadets), sport, prayer and prep (homework). In the classroom they showed some promise. Of the two, John was the more able, showing a consistent aptitude for English and history. His best subject, however, was Latin – essential for an aspiring solicitor – for which he received the form prize three times in his first four years. Both John and Paul also did well in divinity reflecting, perhaps, the influence of their grandfather, Canon William Pascoe.[27]

The twins did not enjoy team sports such as cricket and rugby, although they showed some ability as swimmers and, eventually, as long-distance runners. To be able to swim was invaluable, because it enabled them to escape one of Crosse's first innovations – and humiliations: a new school cap with a distinctive blue top, to be worn only by those boys who could not swim.[28] In hindsight, their running ability was also important. John later wrote: 'When in my last year at school I found I could run long distances without fatigue I seized on that to restore my self-respect'.[29]

Looking back on their school life, John acknowledged it to have been a difficult time. He maintained an 'intense distaste' for Christ's and never forgot those who had tormented him. As the smaller of the twins, John may have been bullied more than Paul, and even at this early stage of life, his non-conformist nature may also have made school difficult. On the other hand, although Paul told one of his sons that 'the happiest day of my life was the day I left school', he seemed less affected by the bullying.[30] He made lasting friendships with some of his schoolmates and was involved with Christ's for the rest of his life. His first job, as an apprentice to the well-known architect Cecil Wood, found him assisting with the design for a new classroom block at Christ's.[31] Later he sent his own sons there and also designed an extension to the chapel and new gates for the school's main entrance.

When they were 15, both boys were given diaries by their parents. John does not seem to have kept his for long but Paul, who was more conscientious, wrote in his for two years. The entries give an invaluable insight into his life, revealing that his interests revolved round his family, his preoccupation with painting and his fascination with the distant peaks of the Canterbury mountains which he observed each day and often sketched.

Canon William Augustus Pascoe, the paternal grandfather of Alice, John and Paul, was sometimes regarded as an eccentric because of his beard.

One of his contemporaries, E. C. Studholme, described him as 'a slightly built man of medium height with a long red beard – in fact it might have been called a "super" beard, for in later years it reached nearly to his waist. He was a splendid country parson, for he was keen on riding and swimming and other outdoor sport, thinking nothing of riding to Hakataramea and other outlying districts. When Mr Pascoe rode fast, as he frequently did, his beard streamed over his shoulders like two red pennants, and my earliest recollection was of him swimming in a pool at the Waimate end of the Gorge, with his long red beard looking like a piece of seaweed being propelled along by a pair of legs.'

Waimate was his first parish. Later he was in Hokitika and in 1880 he became vicar of Holy Trinity Church, in Avonside, Christchurch, where he remained until he retired in 1912. He died six years later.

SIMON PASCOE COLLECTION

Although the Pascoe twins did not excel in sport at Christ's College, they had some potential as distance runners. In this photo, taken shortly after the start of the half-mile handicap, Paul is second and John fourth.

JONATHAN PASCOE COLLECTION

The diaries also include glimpses of his life at Christ's, his opinions of masters, his comments on sports events as well as gossip – all expressed in the schoolboy slang of the day. For example, the superlative 'stunna' or 'stunner' was a favourite expression for anything that impressed him (often food) and the verb to 'scrooch' had a variety of meanings such as to dominate, or appropriate from another. A bike was a 'grid'; if you crashed it the result was a 'kag'.

As an adult John, too, took a delight in language that may have had its origins in the slang of his schooldays. For instance, he coined the term 'to salube' to describe relaxing – especially sunbathing – in the hills, and also popularised 'hencackle' to describe an easy walk or climb considered suitable for women.

Late in 1923 the Pascoes' lifestyle changed when they bought their first car, a Dodge, which gave them a new freedom to explore. Previously the family had relied on public transport. To reach Rakaia Huts from Sumner, for example, they took a tram into Christchurch, then 'a sooty and slow train to Southbridge, and eight miles of springless dray and plodding horses to the huts themselves'.[32] In the Dodge, this journey of 90 kilometres took only two hours.

Now Canterbury's mountains were within the Pascoes' reach. Early in January 1924 the family drove the new car to Springfield where Effie performed the tricky feat of driving the Dodge up onto an empty railway wagon. The train then took the family and the car through the mountains to Otira, on the recently completed railway that now linked Christchurch with the West Coast, avoiding the rough and difficult drive over Arthur's Pass. When they returned to Springfield they stayed at Kowai Bush, a small farming settlement a few kilometres to the north. To reach it, they had to ford the Kowai River in the Dodge and once again it was Effie, not Guy Pascoe, who drove. When the family returned to Christchurch John had

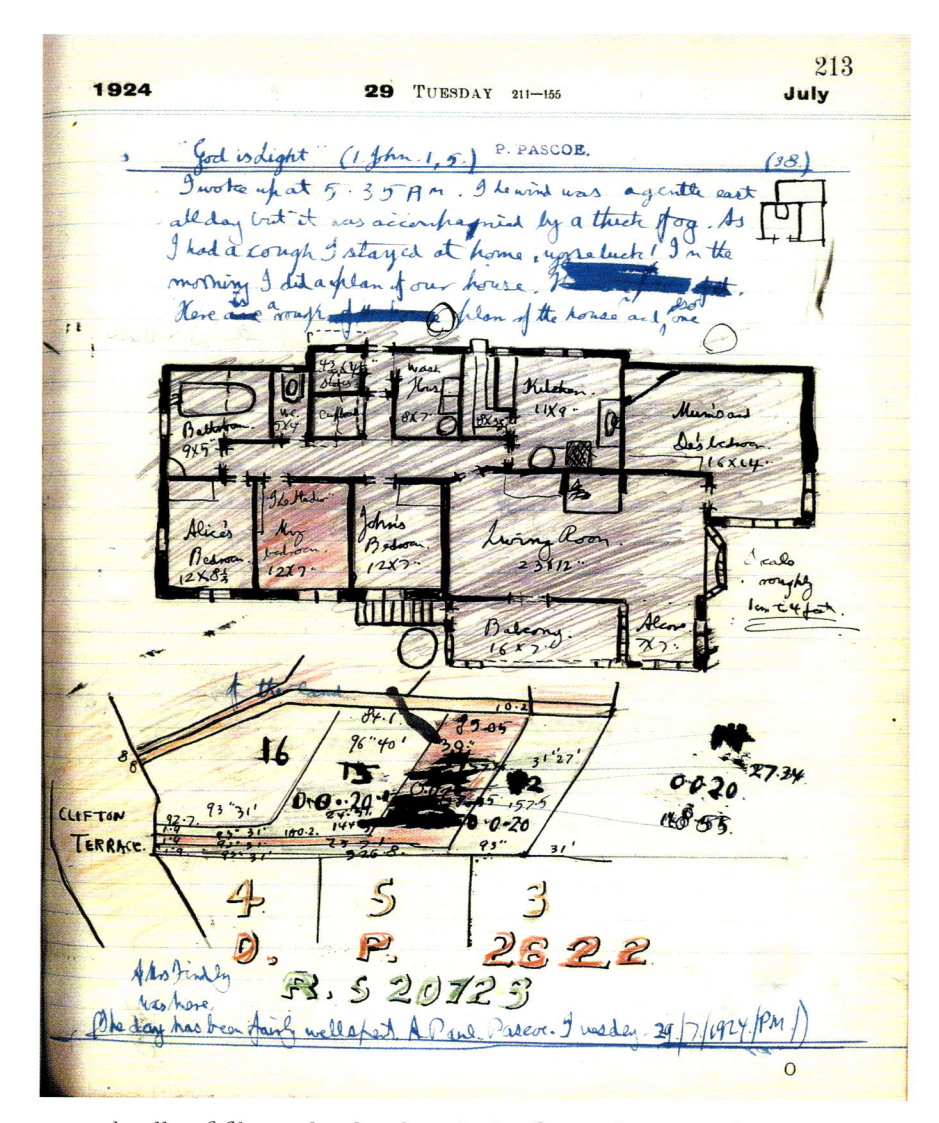

Between 1902 and 1914 the architect, Samuel Hurst Seager, built eight wooden bungalows on Clifton Hill. The Pascoes lived in one of them and Seager's sense of design, strongly reminiscent of the Arts and Crafts style, probably influenced the young Paul Pascoe.

From an early age, Paul expressed an interest in becoming an artist but his mother warned him against the idea, saying there was no money in it. His sister, Alice, suggested he consider architecture instead and Paul took her advice. At home from school with a cough, Paul spent the morning drawing a plan of the house in his diary.

SIMON PASCOE COLLECTION

several rolls of film to be developed, the first indication of his interest in photography. After all its exertions, the Dodge was cleaned and spruced up with Noble's piano polish.

Next summer's activities carried on from this foray into the mountains. In December they stayed at Kowai Bush again, and were so taken with it that they began negotiations to buy a section there. Paul was now firmly focused on the dominant peak in the vicinity, Mount Torlesse, which he had painted the previous summer. On 3 January 1925, he recorded that: 'At 4.28 a.m. exactly I got out of bed and ran over to the warry [washing house and spare room] to see the sunrise giving rosy hues to Mount Torlesse. It was stunner.' The same day, the family took the train to Otira and Paul was excited by the 15 tunnels the train passed through on the way. Between tunnels, he was delighted to catch glimpses of Mount Torlesse.

Guy Pascoe stands beside the family's first car. Effie is at the wheel with John beside her, Alice is in the back.

PAUL PASCOE ALBUM, DOROTHY PASCOE COLLECTION

Alice and John at Rakaia Huts, c. 1926.

When they were children Alice was particularly fond of John. As adults their lives diverged when Alice went to live in India and then England, but their affectionate relationship endured despite the distance.

PAUL PASCOE ALBUM, JONATHAN PASCOE COLLECTION

They stayed the night at the Otira Hotel, where John took part in an impromptu concert. He played his banjo, the hotel's cook accompanied him on the piano and another guest played a set of spoons placed in the neck of bottles. According to Paul, 'the combination sounded stunner – especially in the distance'. Next day the Pascoe family travelled on, by train, to Moana, on Lake Brunner. The weather was fine and the ride exhilarating but Paul was not impressed by the company at Moana. Beneath a sketch in his diary of the view from the hotel he wrote, revealing his sheltered and religious upbringing, 'The view is lovely but only man is vile. The hotel is quite clean but the bar is open at all hours (against the law), there are drunkards on the premises and such words as bl.... and bu.... are flying around. It is disgraceful.'

On their return journey to Kowai Bush from the intemperate West Coast, Paul sketched various routes by which Mount Torlesse might be climbed. Starting at sunrise the next morning, Alice, her father and his friend, Major Howell, climbed the Torlesse Range by a route Paul had seen from the train, and reached the top of Rubicon Peak, adjacent to Mount Torlesse.[33]

Usually the end of January meant a return to Christ's College, but because of the infantile paralysis (polio) epidemic then sweeping the country, the twins stayed at Rakaia Huts. All schools were closed for the first term of 1925 but when Christ's resumed, John and Paul remained at Rakaia, in the relative safety of an isolated settlement, for a second term. Paul's diary reveals that the previous December, at Sumner, the boys had been to see the family doctor, who prescribed a year's rest – though Paul does not say why. This may explain why the twins – now aged 16 and presumably becoming more physically active – did not go with their father and sister to the top of the Torlesse Range.

During their long stay at Rakaia Huts they were supervised by Alice, who was five years older; their parents also made regular visits to ensure all

In *August 1914* the Midland Railway from Christchurch reached *Arthur's Pass*, making it readily accessible for the first time. It was not until *1923*, however, that the railway to the *West Coast* was completed.

The key to its completion was the 9-kilometre Otira Tunnel. Boring through the mountains was an engineering feat that took 10 years. At the time, as the text of this Railways brochure proudly emphasised, the Otira Tunnel was the longest in the British Empire and the seventh longest in the world. New Zealand Railways promoted the Christchurch to Hokitika route as the ideal way to see the Southern Alps.

The Pascoes were quick to take advantage of the opportunities it offered. Within a few months of its completion, the family used the train to transport their car from *Springfield* to *Otira*, then set off to explore the *West Coast*.

ARCHIVES NEW ZEALAND

Paul's painting of his room at Clifton.

When he was a boy his interest in art was fostered by the artist, Cranleigh Barton, a neighbour at Clifton. In 1920, aged 12, Paul entered one of his paintings, 'Scarborough Head from Clifton Hill', in a local show and won first prize.

In 1925, on the twins' return from six months isolation at Rakaia Huts escaping from the infantile paralysis (polio) epidemic, Paul unpacked his possessions. 'I put my pictures etc up again today. I have put all our school books up over my wardrobe,' he wrote in his diary.

'The view out of my window is lovely. My panorama is right to left — Scarborough, the sea horizon, the Kaikouras (seaward and inland), all the coast along to Mount Grey and then the beach along to the Estuary.'

SIMON PASCOE COLLECTION

was well. Fortunately for the twins, they were taught by a neighbour, a very competent retired schoolteacher, Miss Granville, who helped them prepare for their forthcoming Matriculation (University Entrance) exams. Both boys passed. Paul's results are not known; John passed in English and Latin but failed in French, history, maths and science. Nevertheless, the two passes were sufficient to gain his Matriculation and Solicitors General Knowledge, which

Following Guy Pascoe's death, his widow donated a bell in his memory to the chapel at Christ's College.

JOHN PASCOE ALBUM, DOROTHY PASCOE COLLECTION

was an essential prerequisite for a law student.[34] More valuable in the longer term, perhaps, was Miss Granville's love of literature and language. Later, John recognised that she inspired him with her passion for prose and discussion. Another neighbour, the eccentric Charlie Milne, had an extensive library which John said 'sated even my appetite for books, as stimulated by Miss Granville'.[35]

It turned out to be an eventful year. In June 1925, the twins returned to Christ's. In November the Pascoes sold the house at Sumner ('the Fells have scrooched us down to £1,400', wrote Paul in his diary) and moved to a large house with a tennis court at 195 Antigua Street in Christchurch. On their final day at Sumner, Paul walked up to the farm on the hills above the house to enjoy the views for the last time. It was a relief to find that the mountains were also visible from their new home. He wrote: 'From Mum's window one can see Mount Torlesse and part of Mount Hutt. From Alice's window you can see the Castle Hill Peak, Mount Torlesse and part of Mount Hutt.'[36]

He enjoyed the tennis court, especially after the end of year exams: 'I play tennis most evenings now, it clears my head'. As usual, the family spent Christmas at Kowai Bush and the twins' growing maturity was recognised when they were allowed to take the Dodge for short journeys on their own.

In April 1927, quite unexpectedly, Guy Pascoe died of a heart attack at the age of 48. That he might have had a heart condition was realised only after his death, when Alice recalled once walking with her father and noticing his face had turned a curious shade of green.[37] Effie was devastated. Although she had dominated the family, it was Guy's quiet, gentle presence that had given her confidence. He was her rock – and now he was gone. Effie had a nervous breakdown, and although she recovered, her grief was apparent for the rest of her life.[38]

The effect on the twins was less obvious. While their father was alive they were protected, cossetted even, by their parents because of their difficult start in life and their continuing frailness. Guy's death, which occurred during their last year at Christ's, marked the close of their childhood. Freed from the restrictions of school and of their parents, John and Paul soon matured to become energetic young men whose exploits in the Canterbury mountains during the following decade would have made their father proud.

CHAPTER TWO

The Intelligence Officer

During the late 1920s and early 1930s John Pascoe (far left) discovered mountaineering. For five years he did little else, to the detriment of his legal studies. Although he was not as robust as his climbing companions, he had great courage and stamina which enabled him to carry a heavy pack over long distances and to meet the inevitable physical and mental challenges.

Pascoe's interest in the mountains coincided with the transformation of the Christchurch Tramping Club into the Canterbury Mountaineering Club. He and other adventurous young members were excited by opportunities to explore unknown alpine areas and to climb virgin peaks. His interest in history and early maps made him an important member of many CMC alpine expeditions. He was, he later wrote, 'the intelligence officer'. In turn, he was assisted by stronger companions who helped him cross flooded rivers and led on difficult climbs.

Among the many peaks John Pascoe scaled in this period were 25 that had never been climbed before. One of these, Mount Evans (left), became a personal obsession for which he was prepared to risk all. 'It was,' he later told one of his daughters, 'a do or die effort.'

In describing his adventures in the Canterbury Alps, Pascoe found his vocation as a writer. Initially, he wrote for newspapers and also sent his photos to magazines. Towards the end of the decade he melded these accounts together to form the backbone of his first book, Unclimbed New Zealand. Written in a laconic, colloquial style, it was refreshingly different from earlier alpine literature. Twice reprinted, it became a classic.

H. M. SWENEY PHOTO, DOROTHY PASCOE COLLECTION

'JOHN WAS BORED with law studies – the only time I knew him to be bored with anything he did,' recalled Jean Bertram, a family friend who had known the twins since primary school.[1] Exam results confirm this: in his first year as a law student, John Pascoe failed all four subjects and did not even sit the contracts exam.[2] Had his father been alive, he may have been more motivated. Nevertheless, he continued to study law, working by day in his father's legal firm and attending lectures at Canterbury College in the evening. In his spare time, he enjoyed cross-country running with the Christchurch Harrier Club.

Running competitions were held in winter. During the summer, John maintained his fitness by walking. In 1928 he was invited to join members of the newly formed Christchurch Tramping Club on an outing to New Brighton. The walk was not particularly strenuous, but it was a significant occasion because he made the acquaintance of Roger 'Boney' Chester and Ivan Tucker, then 'the leaders of youthful Canterbury trampers'. Their accounts of adventures in the mountains encouraged him to join them on expeditions further afield. In *Unclimbed New Zealand* he acknowledged their influence.

> Further trips with Chester and his friends on the Port and Peninsula Hills, accessible from Christchurch, led me to appreciate to the full their capacity for hill climbing and I listened avidly to their tales of the Whitcombe Pass and Mount Rolleston in winter. We visited the outer ranges. I learnt that a coating of firm snow can transform a tedious shingle trudge into an ascent of mature delight. Whereas at first I tramped to keep fit for cross country running, I later retained cross country activity merely to keep fit for climbing. In this, the ranges came to exercise an attraction I could not resist.[3]

As his photo albums show, he went tramping in the Canterbury foothills at least once a month, sometimes more often. Not surprisingly, his studies suffered. In his second year, he again failed all subjects and still did not feel sufficiently confident to sit the contracts paper.[4]

John (left) and Paul wearing their first suits, 1928.
DOROTHY PASCOE COLLECTION

John Pascoe represented Canterbury as a harrier between 1929 and 1931. In this race through Christchurch streets, he is on the outside in second place.
DOROTHY PASCOE COLLECTION

John Pascoe (centre) with members
of the Christchurch Tramping
Club at New Brighton, 1928.
From left to right: Chris Fenwick,
Mehrten Stace and Roger Chester.
The following year John and Paul
Pascoe joined the club.

IVAN TUCKER PHOTO, JOHN PASCOE COLLECTION,
ALEXANDER TURNBULL LIBRARY

The Pascoes' cottage at Kowai
Bush was designed by Paul. Its
large, partially enclosed verandah
was ideal for sleeping during the
summer, and could accommodate
groups such as the Christchurch
Tramping and Mountaineering
Club.

JOHN PASCOE COLLECTION,
ALEXANDER TURNBULL LIBRARY

In the meantime, his brother Paul was pursuing his architectural career with far more enthusiasm. As an apprentice to Cecil Wood he did not, at first, even receive a wage but he found the work stimulating and enjoyable. In 1929 Paul received his first commission: to design a holiday bach for his mother at Kowai Bush. Immediately it was built, the twins used it as their base to fulfil a long-held ambition: a two-pronged attempt to climb and traverse the nearby Torlesse Range.

On 30 November 1929 members of the Canterbury Mountaineering and Tramping Club (CMTC), as it was now known, gathered at the cottage. Early next morning John led the fast party – 'Boney' Chester, Ivan Tucker and Bert Mabin – along the Midland Railway towards the Waimakariri Gorge. At Staircase Creek they scrambled up to a long ridge leading to the Torlesse peaks. In the meantime, Paul Pascoe, accompanied by Carrick Bloxham, Geoff Flower and Charlie Wood, set off to climb the range by a more direct route from Kowai Bush. The two groups met on the top. For the Pascoe twins, this was an especially satisfying moment as they stood on the summit of the range they had admired from afar for so long.

Returning to Kowai Bush, Paul's party found the descent difficult down steep snow slopes and shingle slides, and Charlie Wood sprained an ankle. 'Fools trod where angels fear to tread,' wrote Paul in the family visitors' book. John's group meanwhile, carried on along the tops in an attempt to traverse the range. As they neared Castle Hill Peak, they relished the challenge of negotiating the ridge that led to 'the Gap', a distinctive feature of the range. An anonymous account of their adventure, published in a Christchurch paper the following week, described this section.

Shortly after 3 pm the party found themselves on the top of a sheer wall of rock overhanging 'the Gap'. This is one hundred feet wide and can be seen distinctly from the plains below. The only access to the foot of the wall was via a tricky 'chimney' some 180 feet high. After this was negotiated some easy rock-climbing led to Castle Hill Peak around which an easterly mist was swirling. After a brief rest, a descent was made.[5]

The author was probably John Pascoe and, if so, this was his first published article. In the next few years he was to become well known for his regular newspaper accounts of CMTC achievements.

The Torlesse trip, the twins' first significant foray, showed their different attitudes. John was clearly more ambitious. Paul was content to reach the top and contemplate the view, and he was cautious on the difficult descent. John thrived on the challenge and danger of 'the Gap'.

John could not have successfully traversed Torlesse, however, without companions who shared his ambitions. He was fortunate to have joined the CMTC at a time when its most energetic members were looking for new, more demanding climbs. The Pascoes had suggested the Torlesse Range, and from its peaks many more mountains were visible. In the past, these distant ranges had been difficult to reach and trampers and climbers only visited areas such as Arthur's Pass, which was accessible by rail. Now the club benefited from the growing popularity of motor cars and could reach mountains throughout Canterbury. Stuart Meares, Nui Robins and Ivan

The shingle peaks of Canterbury's Torlesse Range are linked by a rocky ridge with a distinctive notch, known as 'the Gap', which is visible from the West Coast road. The CMTC's trip in November 1929 was John Pascoe's first challenging climb, and the first traverse of the range. Years later Pascoe recalled, 'we ran 8 miles from Kowai Bush to the Staircase up the railway line, ran up the spur to Otarama Peak, ran to the back peak, ran along the raggedy ridge to the Gap and over the Castle Hill Peak, ran down to Porters Pass and ran down to the Kowai River. As I remember it, we had a marathon of about 14 hours.'

ORIGINS OF THE CANTERBURY MOUNTAINEERING CLUB

Organised tramping in New Zealand began in 1919 when the Tararua Tramping Club was formed. It was followed in the 1920s by many other clubs.

The Christchurch Tramping Club started in 1925 after the Canterbury Progress League organised an expedition to the head of the Waimakariri. The trip had been suggested, in a letter to The Press, by an energetic 18-year-old, Gerard Carrington, who was keenly interested in exploring and mapping the area. It was then agreed to form a tramping club. The CTC's first outing was on 10 May when a group climbed Mount Herbert, on Banks Peninsula. Soon after, plans were made to build a hut at the head of the Waimakariri River.

'Charlie' Carrington, as he was known, was the first secretary and treasurer. His father was Dean of Christchurch and early meetings were held at the deanery. Almost immediately Carrington began packing building material up the Waimakariri to the proposed hut site. Returning from one of these trips in August 1926 he, William Brassington and John Shannon decided to raft down the Waimakariri Gorge. While negotiating rapids in the gorge their raft capsized. Brassington survived, but Carrington and Shannon drowned.

Their deaths shocked the fledgling club, which struggled without Carrington's leadership. It was not until 1928, when Chris Fenwick took on Carrington's vision of a hut

Carrington Memorial Hut, 1933.
JOHN PASCOE COLLECTION, ALEXANDER TURNBULL LIBRARY

in the Waimakariri, that the CTC again flourished. At the end of that year the partially built shelter was officially opened and named the Carrington Memorial Hut. At the same time Mount Armstrong, which dominates the head of the Waimakariri, was renamed Carrington Peak and the CTC changed its name to the Canterbury Mountaineering and Tramping Club to reflect its growing interest in climbing.

Once completed, Carrington Hut provided the CMTC with an invaluable base. It was from here that the club launched what John Pascoe called 'The Waimakariri Invasion' at Easter 1930. Thereafter the CMTC was simply known as the Canterbury Mountaineering Club (CMC).

Tucker owned cars which they made available, as did some of the members' parents.

By the end of 1929, club members had explored all the outer ranges and were keen to tackle the higher mountains further inland, close to the Main Divide. The fact that some of these peaks had never been climbed made them even more enticing. How long they would remain so was uncertain, as the keenest climbers began to probe the Southern Alps. Soon after he had led the Torlesse traverse, 'Boney' Chester, for instance, took another party to the top of Carrington Peak at the head of the Waimakariri.[6]

At Easter 1930, a large contingent from the CMTC headed for the upper Waimakariri, and from there parties dispersed in all directions. For two of the groups, the objective was to make a first ascent of the pyramid-shaped Mount Gizeh. Each party selected a different route and it was agreed that neither would set off before 6 a.m. on Saturday. If bets had been taken, 'Boney' Chester's more experienced group would have been at shorter odds than the party of Christ's College old boys led by John Pascoe, of whom only Dick 'Gran' Clark had much climbing experience. But an error on a map led Chester to the wrong peak and it was the unfancied Christ's trio who reached the top of Gizeh, much to their delight.[7] It was a lesson that taught both Pascoe and Chester the value of thorough research before any trip.

The first party to reach the summit of Mount Gizeh (2162m) consisted of (from left to right) Geoff Flower, Dick 'Gran' Clark and John Pascoe. This, their first virgin peak, was an important moment for all three. Pascoe later sent a copy of this photo, and nine others taken at Easter 1930, to the New Zealand Free Lance which featured them in a full-page montage. These were probably his first published photos.

JOHN PASCOE COLLECTION, ALEXANDER TURNBULL LIBRARY

During the remainder of the Easter break, Chester showed his prowess in a series of prodigious physical feats. On Easter Monday he, Evan Wilson and Sid Milne made the first traverse of Mount Rolleston, and two days later the trio climbed three peaks – Mounts A. P. Harper, Murchison and Speight – in a single day. Pascoe's party could not match Chester's efforts, but they did climb Mount Davie and Carrington Peak.

Nevertheless, Gizeh was the only virgin peak attained and in being among the first to reach its summit, John Pascoe acquired a taste for 'bagging new peaks' that was to become addictive. Other members of the CMTC also realised that there were various alpine prizes in the offing. After Easter the term 'tramping' was no longer used, and the organisation was known simply as the Canterbury Mountaineering Club, or CMC.

The summits and passes explored during the long weekend led the club to contemplate even greater challenges further afield. 'These three days out

CMC members and their cars lined up in Happy Valley, at the foot of the Torlesse Range, December 1930.

A. MACKIE PHOTO, JOHN PASCOE COLLECTION, ALEXANDER TURNBULL LIBRARY

Paul Pascoe, 1930.

Although Paul did not attempt to match his brother's rapid development as a climber, the twins continued to tramp together in the foothills and outer ranges.

Paul's interest in the mountains took other forms. In March 1931, for example, he completed the first map of the Arthur's Pass alpine area, which was published by the Lands Office in Christchurch. A few months later he and John wrote an alpine song, 'Bergschrund Bill', to be sung to the tune of 'Casey Jones' from 'Transportation Blues'.

PAUL PASCOE ALBUM ,
JONATHAN PASCOE COLLECTION

John Pascoe at Mount *Algidus* Station, December 1930, en route to the head of the Mathias.

The generosity of station managers in making packhorses available to CMC members allowed them to move quickly up the Rakaia and Wilberforce Valleys to the peaks, reducing a two- or three-day trudge to a one-day journey.

JOHN PASCOE COLLECTION,
ALEXANDER TURNBULL LIBRARY

on sunlit snow gave the confidence of experience,' Pascoe later wrote. 'Mountains came to mean much more than citadels placed in rows merely for the conquest of guided parties and the admiration of passing trampers. The citadels became objects of inspiration and solace. Panoramas from Mounts Gizeh and Davie gave us a vision of the distant southwest, where the Wilberforce, Mathias, Rakaia and Rangitata ranges lay.'[8]

There was the difficulty, however, in knowing which of these faraway citadels remained unclimbed. In the early 1930s, maps were usually so incomplete that large areas of mountainland had not been recorded in any detail. Nor was there a register of first ascents (although the New Zealand Alpine Club was soon to start one). The only way to find out was by laborious research, and this is where John Pascoe came into his own. Although he failed all four law papers for the third time in 1930, his experience as a law clerk, which involved searching title deeds and examining registers, taught him how to find old records and maps.

John took it upon himself to study the reports of the early surveyors who had probed the Southern Alps in the 1860s and 1870s in their quest to find passes to the gold-rich West Coast. He also found the maps of the provincial geologists who followed the surveyors, and he wrote to the runholders and musterers whose knowledge of the high country was unsurpassed. Pascoe's information was crucial, as Chester later acknowledged. 'In our mountaineering trips it was his research and organising ability before the event which was mainly responsible for any success we achieved. Personally, I just put on my pack and went along, depending on John to have all the maps and knowledge of the country which was essential and so hard to find in those early days.'[9]

In the winter of 1930, after the CMC invasion of the Waimakariri, the club secretary, Cuth Thornton, suggested to John that he examine the alpine area at the head of the Mathias River. He accepted the idea with alacrity. Replies from deer cullers and musterers revealed that the Mathias Pass had not been crossed for 30 years. The little exploration there had been in the vicinity was secondary to a futile attempt in the 1880s to build a packhorse route up the Mathias River to the pass, and over into Westland. A benched track had been laboriously hacked out of the steep slopes of the upper Mathias, but had gone no further.[10]

After Pascoe's research suggested that a number of unclimbed peaks lay to the north of the Mathias Pass, a CMC party, led by Chester, set out to investigate. The members were Brian Wyn Irwin, Allan Willis and, of course, John Pascoe, whose knowledge guaranteed his inclusion. On 28 December they made camp at the head of the Mathias amid the surrounding glaciated bluffs. It was up one of these that Chester led them next morning. Irwin did not go with them, but instead explored the head of the valley. Meanwhile Chester, Pascoe and Willis reached the top of the buttress and followed a steep, razor-edged spur they named Treachery Ridge to the Main Divide.

Perfect snow conditions enabled them to quickly reach the first of a line of unclimbed summits, which Pascoe called Gerard Peak, in honour of the musterer who was a member of the first party to cross the Mathias Pass. From

John Pascoe on the Mathias traverse, December 1930.

One of John Pascoe's most important contributions was his photography, which complemented the incomplete maps used by climbers in the 1920s and 1930s. His seven-volume photographic archive, arranged by locality, was often consulted by other climbers.

ALAN WILLIS PHOTO, JOHN PASCOE COLLECTION, ALEXANDER TURNBULL LIBRARY

there, they could see an arc of virgin peaks around the head of an unnamed glacier. Soon afterwards, they ascended a second unclimbed peak.

Pascoe's laconic account in *Unclimbed New Zealand* barely hints at the excitement the climbers must have felt:

> Details of the climb are unnecessary. We kept an even pace on the steep sound rock and snow ridges, whipping across many cornices and revelling in the work. We traversed the new peaks of Notman, Stout, Ballance and Kensington. More tricky rockwork took us up to Shafto Peak. We had traversed seven virgin peaks of the Mathias Divide.
>
> We had to decide whether to continue this interesting traverse, or to return content by descending the south ridge of Shafto Peak. Beyond us lay Mts Harrison, Kai-Iwi, Mystery and Bryce – the latter a fine conical peak. From these mountains descended an unmapped glacier, source of the Mathias River. Chester's determination was to keep traversing.

Willis and Pascoe followed Chester, but the pace was exhausting and eventually led to Pascoe's first alpine accident:

> After crossing over Mt Harrison we made a slow detour to avoid an unbridged crevasse. The Mystery Ridge was sharp, like a baby Silberhorn, and at the Mystery col we looked up at the final thousand feet of Mt Bryce. All went well till we were in a loose rock chimney. A pillar of rock gave way as I wearily tugged for a handhold. At that time I had not heard of the principle of 'balance climbing', and was too tired to observe technical niceties. The rock pillar brushed me aside, bruised my arm and rocketed down to the glacier, but the rope held taut.

While he recovered on top of Bryce, evening mist gathered. A steep glissade took them down to the foot of the glacier. As they trudged down the upper Mathias, they discussed their achievement and realised others would find it hard to believe. 'Had we only climbed three of the eleven peaks, our contemporaries would have agreed that the mountains were reasonably formidable, and not all bumps on a ridge. As it was, Chester's fitness and dash had carried us far beyond our hopes.'

This caricature of John Pascoe, with his trademark red spotted handkerchief and habitual pipe, was drawn by his cousin, Cuth Denham. It captures something of his character, which made him so well known among climbers. His enthusiasm, love of the mountains and remarkable physical stamina, combined with an effervescent sense of humour and a love of storytelling, made him a rewarding companion in even the most adverse conditions.

MARTHA PASCOE COLLECTION

Next day they climbed the Agassiz Range, south of their camp. Problems with snow goggles meant Willis and Irwin did not go far along the tops, but Chester and Pascoe continued and climbed two more virgins, one of which Pascoe named Comyns Peak after the leader of the sheepmen who found the Mathias Pass. As Chester was the faster and more adept rock climber, Pascoe sat on a ledge under the virgin Mount Marion to wait while Chester traversed the peak and went on to climb Mount Frieda, his third first ascent of the day. As he did so, John Pascoe contemplated the view of 'a maze of Westland ranges' and was particularly impressed by distant Mount Evans and the roar of an avalanche cascading from one of its glaciers.[11]

On their return, John sent a selection of photos to the pictorial weekly, the *New Zealand Free Lance*, and was rewarded when eight of them appeared in a full-page feature. A similar spread also appeared in the *New Zealand Railways Magazine*.[12] Seeing his work in print was a thrill and the payment was a useful supplement to his £1 a week wage, helping to pay for food, transport and climbing equipment. He also wrote a detailed account of the Mathias trip for the *New Zealand Alpine Journal*.[13] But, as they had anticipated, the number of first ascents meant some of the climbing fraternity dismissed the Mathias trip as inflated 'peak bagging'.

How riled Chester, Pascoe and Willis were by these comments is unknown, but they may have encouraged the trio to contemplate more credible challenges. If so, this may explain why Chester decided that they should spend Easter 1931 exploring the headwaters of the Rakaia to search out likely routes to the summits of Mounts Whitcombe and Evans, the two highest unclimbed peaks in the Southern Alps. No one could claim that they were bumps on a ridge. As schoolboys, John and Paul Pascoe had been fascinated by the chance discovery of an 1870s geological survey report in the school library.[14] Now the report provided John with the only real map of the head of the Rakaia.

Faced with a nor'west gale and heavy rain, a more experienced party might have abandoned the trip. Chester's father drove them up the Rakaia Valley and at the end of the road they had to ford the river on foot to reach Manuka Point Station, their base for the mountains beyond. Chester and Pascoe were accompanied by two other CMC members, 'Gran' Clark and Basil Honour. All four realised that the rapidly rising river would be difficult to cross, but Chester was determined to try. Not for the first time Pascoe found that his friend could place him in situations beyond his capability. Nevertheless, Chester's charisma was such that, like the others, he accepted the decision. Pascoe's account of the Rakaia crossing in *Unclimbed New Zealand* is sobering:

> The flood surged past the bank in yellow waves. We were at the main stream. Chester shouted that our only hope of fording lay in working upstream until the river forked. A strata of moving boulders continued to thud under the water. Of all the macabre sounds of alpine travel in Canterbury, the worst is the thud as boulders are rolled over in the river as if they were pebbles. After half an hour's work we reached a slim shingle bank, which was rapidly becoming submerged by the rising river.

There was little chance of retreat. As always, Chester took the lead and after a struggle, succeeded in swimming across. As he swam he pulled a rope which

ROGER 'BONEY' CHESTER

Chester's climbing career was brilliant but brief. He was one of the first to join the CTC only weeks after its inception in 1925 and went up the Waimakariri with Carrington, but he did not become especially active until 1928, when he began to study engineering at Canterbury College.

For the next six years he spearheaded the CMC's exploration of the Southern Alps, leading parties to the top of many unclimbed peaks, including the much-coveted Mount Whitcombe. His stamina and determination made him a natural leader. According to his friend, Allan Willis, people would follow him anywhere.

Chester also enjoyed other sports, including wrestling and boxing. He is remembered for one particular fight when he met Denis Glover in the ring to decide who would represent Canterbury at the Universities Tournament. 'Glover fancied himself as a pug', recalled Allan Willis, but 'Chester cut him to bits' – a verdict Glover endorsed in his autobiography Hot Water Sailor. 'Chester, tough, formidable, heavy-fisted, gave me the most terrible hiding I've ever had in my life.'

In 1933 Chester left for Australia where he later became the manager of the Warragamba Dam, Sydney's water supply. He never returned to New Zealand, but his memories of Canterbury's mountains and his fellow climbers remained clear. John Pascoe he remembered as 'always making a greater effort than he should have been physically able to manage and somehow coming out on top by the sheer ascendancy of his spirit'.

JOHN PASCOE COLLECTION, ALEXANDER TURNBULL LIBRARY

he tied to a log further up on the other side. Pascoe's turn was next. The impossibility of crossing upstream into the full force of the current must have been apparent, yet he accepted the challenge.

> With my pack strapped on I began the crossing. Unfortunately the river had swept a deep hole in the line that I took. The pack forced me under the surface of the water. The river forced my hands from the rope. I hurtled down in the current. The pack held me under. Two hundred yards downstream the river curved. Struggling blindly I was spewed into a shallow. Bruised and sodden I gulped for air till Chester ran down and dragged me to the bank.

Watching Pascoe nearly drown convinced Clark and Honour there had to be a better way. It was futile to fight the river. Instead, they used the current to carry them over, taking turns to tie themselves to the end of the rope while Chester and Pascoe pulled them across.[15] They were lucky to have made it: those with more experience would have waited for the Rakaia to subside. Without Chester's strength the other three might all have died.

'Bit wet, aren't you?' was the greeting they received when they arrived at the Manuka Point homestead. Laurie Walker, the farm manager, thought

'Gran' Clark, Basil Honour, John Pascoe and 'Boney' Chester on Lauper Peak, Easter 1931.

John Pascoe made a habit of photographing himself and his companions on various summits. To include himself in the photo, he would place his camera on a rock, set the time release, then dart back to the group which was bunched together to fit into the frame.

The unusually low camera angle often showed footwear as clearly as faces. Here Clark (left) is wearing crampons, which gave much better footing on ice than the hobnailed boots worn by the others. Crampons were first used in New Zealand in 1895 by the English climber, Edward FitzGerald, and his Swiss guide, Mattias Zurbriggen, in the Mount Cook region. Although they were clearly useful, few local climbers wore crampons because they were considered 'unsporting' and a threat to the work of alpine guides, one of whose jobs was to cut steps in icy slopes.

The spread of guideless climbing in the late 1920s, however, prompted a new interest in crampons. The first CMC member to use them was Andy Anderson in 1928. John Pascoe bought his in 1931, soon after this photo was taken. With the greater security they provided, Pascoe and his friends could contemplate climbing major mountains such as Whitcombe and Evans.

JOHN PASCOE COLLECTION, ALEXANDER TURNBULL LIBRARY

them extremely foolish. As they spent the next two days at the station sheltering from the rain, there seemed little point in having taken such a risk. When the weather finally cleared there was insufficient time left to consider either Evans or Whitcombe. Nevertheless, they raced up the Rakaia to the Whitcombe Pass in a day, a journey that usually took at least twice that time, and made camp there.

Next morning they set out in cloud and rain to climb Lauper Peak, which rears above the pass.[16] It had been scaled only once before, in 1915. As they climbed, rocks loosened by the rain ricocheted down the steep slopes. John Pascoe was struck on the head and was lucky not to be seriously injured. Ten years later, he still had a lump on his skull.[17] On the summit they relished the view of the surrounding peaks, rising above the cloud:

> Sinuous mist concealed the Bracken Snowfield. The serrated Red Lion Peak and the rugged battlements of Mt Evans pierced the stormy Westland turmoil. To the west Mt Whitcombe rose sheer from the Ramsay Glacier, and so held our attention that we were unwilling to dwell on the view of the lesser mountains of the Lyell Valley. With a last glance at the immense Whitcombe buttresses we began the descent.[18]

Back in Christchurch, Pascoe, realising he could not continue to fail exams forever, devoted himself to his legal studies with new vigour. For the rest of 1931 he did fewer climbs, although he still managed some quick trips by train to the peaks at Arthur's Pass, including a first ascent of Mount Oates. At the end of the year his application resulted in his first exam passes – in history (50%) and jurisprudence (53%).

But he was seldom content to stay in the city for long and his desire to return to the mountains was partly a result of his awkwardness in conservative Christchurch society. As a schoolboy he had found it difficult to fit in at Christ's, unlike the more chameleon Paul, who had also adjusted to the unwritten rules of the city's social life. John found it much harder, however, and had little interest in succeeding. At social events he would often leave early and Paul, covering for his brother, would thank their hostess twice.[19]

The east face of Mount Whitcombe (2650m) from the summit of Lauper, Easter 1931.

In 1863 the discovery of gold on the West Coast prompted the Canterbury Provincial Government to send the surveyor, Henry Whitcombe, to find a route through the Alps to Westland. He was accompanied by a Swiss surveyor's assistant, Jakob Lauper. After they crossed the low pass at the head of the Rakaia discovered by John Baker and Samuel Butler, their trip became a struggle for survival as they battled their way down a succession of gorges. The two-week journey to the coast was marked by incessant rain, lack of proper equipment and hunger. Eventually, starvation led them, against Lauper's advice, to try crossing the swollen Taramakau River. Whitcombe drowned while Lauper clung to a log and survived.

JOHN PASCOE COLLECTION, ALEXANDER TURNBULL LIBRARY

John's impatience to return to the Rakaia was fuelled, too, by the knowledge that climbers from further afield were also preparing to attempt Whitcombe and Evans. Generously, he had supplied one Wellington group with eight pages of information about Rakaia routes, and in 1931 he began a correspondence with Ian Powell, a Wellington climber of considerable skill and determination who had climbed Mount Murchison and planned to return to the Canterbury mountains.[20] Pascoe made it clear to Powell that no one should have exclusive rights to an unclimbed peak:

> Personally I dislike the old English Alpine Club theory of a man putting a ring round a virgin peak and keeping others from trying it. It is very unsporting. It is far more sporting to give all possible information to others desirous of entering the contest. To hell with people who want a 'virgo' kept 'intacta', you might as well have a half-mile race with only one starter. Nor'westers and floods give enough trouble to climbers after new peaks, without having hoary old gentlemen wanting certain peaks left alone for their convenience. Anyone with intentions of Whitcombe and Evans will be welcome to all we can tell them.[21]

John Pascoe also wrote about mountaineering in general in an article for *The Press* entitled 'Climbers and Guides – A Plea for the Amateur', in which he argued strongly against the use of guides. 'Can there be true satisfaction in knowing that you have paid a man to secure a peak for you? When this is done, it comes that "every peak has its price".' He seems to have been more concerned with this issue than his fellow climbers, some of whom gratefully accepted advice from alpine guides. Pascoe, perhaps, saw guides as an extension of the gentlemen's world that prevailed in Christchurch. His hostility to guided climbing reveals as much about John Pascoe's prejudices as it does about the established alpine fraternity. In his *Press* article he boldly allied guideless climbing, as exemplified by the CMC and other youthful enthusiasts, with the country's favourite game:

> The national sport of New Zealand is rugby football. The public have taken every endeavour to see that this sport is kept untainted by professionalism. The greater sport of mountaineering will give sweet reward to those who set their experience such as it is against rotten rock, and blue ice, and the inevitable danger of the flooded river as it roars down to the lowland gorges.[22]

As always, 'the greater sport' beckoned and on Christmas Day 1931, Chester led a party of six CMC members, including Pascoe, up the Rakaia with Mount Whitcombe in mind. Once again the weather was against them. A nor'wester was blowing and boulders could be heard rumbling down the flooded Rakaia. Remembering his near drowning, Pascoe approached the river cautiously, mindful that his slight physique was a real disadvantage when crossing rivers:

> Chester led us to an island in the main river. Honour slipped in a side stream but Willis, Mirams and Chester rescued him. The final stream was the worst, which Willis, Chester and Mirams forded safely, and dragged Honour, Barnett and me through by turns on the rope. It was noon on a blazing December day. Yet the ice water of the river was so cold that three hours later I was still shivering, abjectly miserable.

LAND INFORMATION NEW ZEALAND (NZMS 260 SERIES – 1KM GRID)

Mount *Whitcombe from the Kinkel Ridge, December 1931.*

Basil Honour (left) and Wyn Barnett may not have looked so happy when John Pascoe took this photo, had they known that at that moment Chester, Mirams and Willis — supposedly reconnoitring a route by which they would all climb Whitcombe the next day — were in fact well on their way to its summit.

JOHN PASCOE COLLECTION, ALEXANDER TURNBULL LIBRARY

While they made camp near the toe of the Ramsay Glacier, a group of Tararua Tramping Club climbers stopped for a chat. That very day they had tried to climb Mount Whitcombe by the north-east ridge, but had to turn back because icy rocks on the razor-edged route made it impassable. One of the Wellington climbers taunted Chester, asking him (with an implicit reference to the Mathias traverse of the previous summer) if he was intent on climbing 'some cheap virgins'.[23]

Next day rain forced the CMC to postpone their attempt on Mount Whitcombe, and they intended to use the day to reconnoitre various possible routes. They split into two groups: Pascoe, Honour and Barnett would climb Mount Kinkel to examine the southern ridge of Whitcombe, while the stronger, faster party of Chester, Mirams and Willis would go up the Ramsay Glacier to investigate the 'impossible' north-east ridge. By mid-afternoon the Kinkel group had returned to camp, but when the others had not returned by nightfall they became uneasy. At dawn, Pascoe and Honour started up the Ramsay Glacier to look for them. Halfway up, they heard a shout and saw three specks glissading down the slopes of Mount Roberts, well to the south of the summit of Mount Whitcombe. Clearly, the fast party had climbed Mount Whitcombe, then traversed its serrated summit – there could be no other explanation for their presence on Mount Roberts.

Chester was the first to reach Honour and Pascoe. He explained that the previous day's reconnoitre had changed to an assault when they realised the Tararua party's 'impossible' ridge was 'within the capacity of mere mortals'. The following excerpt from an account of their climb, written by Allan Willis, suggests that if the Tararua group had been prepared to wait for a day, they might have been the first to climb Whitcombe, as much of the ice had melted by the next afternoon:

Bill Mirams climbing a steep section during the first ascent of Mount Whitcombe, December 1931.

ALLAN WILLIS PHOTO, JOHN PASCOE COLLECTION, ALEXANDER TURNBULL LIBRARY

> There had been a heavy thaw since the last big snowfall, and the rocks were reasonably clean, except for masses of ice crystals, which swept down the rock face with a musical tinkle when swept off with the axe. We were not long in coming to grips with the ridge and were very thankful to find it composed of solid reddish-coloured rock. On the Ramsay Glacier side, the ridge fell away sheer for thousands of feet. The other side, however, was better and the rock was riven by longitudinal cracks which provided perfect handholds and footholds. Chester was leading, and struck a sticky piece without a handhold; so we undid the rope, and after several attempts, because of the strong nor'-west wind, he managed to lasso a pinnacle some distance above him. With the aid of the doubled rope while I belayed him, he soon dragged himself on to a safer spot, to which he hauled Mirams and me.
>
> For some distance after this the rock was not far off the perpendicular, so we had the rope out most of the time, though the security it afforded was more tangible than real. Most of the time the nor'-wester was swirling mists over the divide and we were not sure how far ahead lay the high peak. As it was getting on for six o'clock, we were getting a little anxious: however, after three or four false alarms we crawled on to the high peak of Whitcombe about 6.30 pm. The view was magnificent – we seemed on top of the world. For miles and miles to the west lay a billowing carpet of mist, broken only by the summits of ice-capped peaks, looking for all the world like coral islands. To the north lay Evans and the Red Lion, and beyond them the Mathias Peaks, with the wedge-shaped peak of Bryce particularly outstanding. Turning east, we could look down on Louper Peak, and beyond Louper, the Arrowsmith Range. South again reared D'Archaic and Cook and many others we could only guess at. After a round of photos, and having built our cairn, we capped it with a brandy bottle containing our names.[24]

Willis and Mirams soon joined Chester, Honour and Pascoe on the Ramsay Glacier and described how, after reaching the top of Whitcombe the evening before, they decided not to return by the precipitous ridge of their ascent, but to push on across the summit in the hope of finding an easier way down.

DEATH IN THE MOUNTAINS

John Pascoe's first experience of death in the mountains came in 1932 when he joined searchers scouring the alpine area behind Carrington Hut for two missing trampers.

Harold Smith, Bernard Robbins and Keith Loney set out to cross from *Westland* to *Canterbury* via the well-known 'Three Passes' route. On 9 January they crossed Browning Pass and reached Park-Morpeth Hut on the *Wilberforce*. The following day they intended to cross *Whitehorn* and Harman Passes to Carrington Hut. When they reached

Whitehorn Pass it was misty and raining. Instead of descending towards Harman Pass, they wandered onto the slopes of Mount Isobel, became separated and spent a miserable night in the open. Robbins fell while trying to descend a steep creek at the head of the Taipo River and Smith died of exhaustion during the night. In the morning, Loney found Smith's body and crawled back to Park-Morpeth to raise the alarm. Several days later the bodies of Robbins (pictured) and Smith were retrieved by searchers.

JOHN PASCOE COLLECTION, ALEXANDER TURNBULL LIBRARY

An anxious descent in mist and gathering darkness was followed by a long, cold night spent wandering about with little idea of where they were. It was so cold that Chester, Mirams and Willis walked all night to maintain circulation. At dawn the trio climbed up from a glacier in Westland to reach the Main Divide. Soon after, while cautiously descending ice cliffs below the summit of Mount Roberts, they saw Pascoe and Honour.

Pascoe later wrote, without bitterness, that 'Willis and Mirams joined with Chester in wishing we had been with them'. Pascoe accepted this with good grace, but it was very disappointing. With more than a year's research and planning devoted to climbing Whitcombe, he had every right to feel let down. Willis and Mirams felt bad about his absence, but when Chester, their leader and guide, had said as they set off up the ridge, 'We're going to crack this damned thing', they accepted his decision. Still, Willis remained

John Pascoe's 'golden road', the east ridge of Evans.

JOHN PASCOE COLLECTION,
ALEXANDER TURNBULL LIBRARY

remorseful. More than 60 years later, he wrote 'I have always had regrets over John not being with us that day, as he had more right to be on that climb than either Mirams or me. He had done all the topographical and historical research which was invaluable.'[25] Others were more critical. When CMC member Andy Anderson heard about the ascent, he regarded it as a 'breach of contract' because John Pascoe had done 'all the planning, the organising, everything'.[26]

To Chester's credit, he immediately looked to make amends. At dawn next morning he, Barnett and Pascoe set off to climb Mount Evans, a remarkably ambitious plan as it lay 12 kilometres north of their camp on the other side of the Main Divide. To reach the base of Evans, they first had to climb the Ramsay Glacier and cross the Erewhon Col, then negotiate the Bracken Snowfield.

It was noon when they began to climb the precipitous east ridge, which they soon found extremely challenging. At intervals there were large rock outcrops with steep, icy cornices between them. After three hours of careful climbing they could see the low peak of Evans, but it was guarded by a sheer ice cliff, topped by an overhanging cornice. They could go no further. Even Chester accepted that the final section was beyond them. As they retreated, the evening sun lit the surrounding peaks and the east ridge of Evans with golden light, which profoundly impressed Pascoe. Later, reading James Elroy Flecker's play, *Hassan*, he thought of the east ridge of Evans as 'the golden road to Samarkand'.

The first attempt on Evans had failed. 'This experience quite startled me out of the idea that I could get new peaks easily; somewhat of a contrast to the previous season in the Mathias when we had cleaned up thirteen virgins in two days,' Pascoe wrote. It also gave him a clear purpose. 'I absorbed the necessary humility and my imagination, already a susceptible one, fired a love for a grim mountain. Whether Mount Evans gave us mercy, kindness or hardship did not concern me much. All I knew was that I must climb it.'[27]

The Pascoes' home in Antigua Street was sold in the Depression.

JONATHAN PASCOE COLLECTION

Paul Pascoe and his fiancée, Helen Ferrar, in Tyrolean fancy dress, 1933. The Ferrars, like the Pascoes, had a holiday home at Kowai Bush and it was there that Paul and Helen probably first met.

Helen's father, Hartley Ferrar, studied geology at Cambridge. After graduating, he accompanied Scott on his first expedition to the Antarctic (1901–04). He then worked in Egypt and served in Palestine during the First World War, before settling in New Zealand where he joined the Geological Survey.

JONATHAN PASCOE COLLECTION

From then on, Pascoe took every opportunity to publicise Evans, especially its east ridge. For example, the major achievement of the CMC's Rakaia expedition that year was undoubtedly the first ascent and traverse of Mount Whitcombe but, as John was not there, he had to leave that story to others. Instead, he sent descriptions of the first ascent of Mount Kinkel (a 'hencackle', by his own admission), and the failure of the first attempt of Evans, not to *The Press*, but to the *New Zealand Herald* in distant Auckland. He also sent photos to the *Auckland Weekly News*. These articles, the first published under his name, are coloured by heroic language, poetic allusions and the bold contention that the east ridge of Evans, like the western ridge of Mount Tasman and the southern ridge of Mount Cook, was impossible.[28]

Returning from the mountains meant resuming the Pascoe routine: 'swotting of a sort, a lot of long-distance running and energetic trips to accessible foothills'. But life in New Zealand in 1932 did not proceed smoothly, as the Depression continued and there was rioting in the big cities. In the previous year unemployment had risen rapidly and those lucky enough to keep their jobs had to accept wage cuts. Less than a fortnight after Pascoe returned from Evans, a hungry crowd in Dunedin attacked a grocery shop, a minor outburst compared with the rioting in Auckland in April when 250 shops were attacked. In May angry crowds rampaged through Wellington's streets looting shops, overturning vehicles and fighting with the police.[29] In Christchurch, as elsewhere, young men were urged to sign on as 'special constables' to assist the police, and John Pascoe was one who joined, though he later regretted the decision.[30] But he was lucky: Christchurch was the only major city to escape the rioting, and he was not needed.

The Pascoes did not escape the impact of the Depression, however. Guy, their breadwinner, had died in 1927, two years before the global wave of prosperity generated by the American stock market collapsed and the Depression began. For a time Effie, Alice and the twins continued to live at Antigua Street, but in December 1931, while John was preparing for the Whitcombe trip, they moved to a smaller house in Peterborough Street. After only a few months this, too, was sold, and they shifted to Oxford Terrace where they rented part of a large house.[31]

Architects were among the first to see their work evaporate: in 1932 Paul was out of work for nine months.[32] John kept his job but, despite this, his life was not progressing as well as Paul's. The twins lived in the same house, shared a common interest in the mountains and often went tramping together. Nevertheless their lives were diverging. Unemployment did not erode Paul's confidence; it simply gave him more time to study architecture. As one of a group of Christchurch students working towards extra-mural degrees from the School of Architecture in Auckland, he helped to establish the Christchurch Architectural Atelier, where the students refined their designs and discussed the latest trends from overseas. Visitors to the studio often included senior members of the profession who would comment on the students' work and contribute to the stimulating discussions.

In March 1932 Paul addressed his student colleagues on 'The Quality of Charm in Architecture', citing examples from home and abroad – no easy feat for a stutterer. His talk was later published in the *New Zealand Institute of*

Members of the CMC at their annual Sports Day, Lake Rubicon, 1933. From its inception, the CMC struggled with the contentious issue of whether to admit women as members. At the inaugural meeting in 1925 it was agreed that 'membership be refused to women until the total membership is considerably larger'. This was briefly relaxed in 1927 and one woman, Miss H. Claxton, joined, but had to resign six months later when the original ban was reinstated. The restriction on female membership was not repealed until 1977.

W.A. TAYLOR PHOTO, JOHN PASCOE COLLECTION, ALEXANDER TURNBULL LIBRARY

Architects Journal.[33] By the end of the year he was once again working with Cecil Wood. Paul showed his familiarity with the latest overseas trends by refurbishing the Tivoli Cinema in Cathedral Square in the successor to the Art Deco style – 'jazz moderne'.[34]

Paul also had a girlfriend, Helen Ferrar.[35] They soon became engaged, with the blessing of his mother, who wished her children to succeed both professionally and socially. John, by contrast, was a less promising prospect. He cared little for his appearance, did not have a girlfriend and was making very slow progress towards a law degree. Nor did his alpine achievements count for much in Christchurch society at a time when the relatively new recreations of tramping and climbing were still regarded with a certain amount of suspicion.

In spite of his lack of experience with women, John was developing a reputation as a raconteur. Allan Willis recalled that when they went up the Rakaia to climb Whitcombe 'John weighed everything meticulously to cut down weight. He even cut the handle off his toothbrush. In spite of this he found room for a bound volume of the *Satyricon of Petronius* which filled in many a wet afternoon and gave us an insight into practices none of us had ever heard of.'[36] John was also an enthusiastic singer of the bawdy songs that were popular among Canterbury climbers (and he never stuttered when he sang). But his lack of any actual familiarity with sex was apparent, at least to the publican of the Bealey Hotel, Fred Cochrane, who was heard to say to John after a session in his hostelry, 'You've got more fuck in your head than your ass.'[37]

Paul Pascoe's diary shows that John was determined to learn to yodel, and his persistence was rewarded when he suddenly mastered the call of the European mountain dwellers.[38] 'He wanted to do what he thought mountaineers did,' recalled Priestley Thomson, who knew John through cross-country running. 'He thought mountaineers yodelled, so he learnt to yodel and he'd yodel at the drop of a bloody hat.'[39]

Betsy Blunden, John Pascoe and Bryan Barrer after their first ascent of Mount Oates, February 1931.

John Pascoe did not share the CMC's bias against women: he invited Betsy Blunden to join him and Bryan Barrer in an attempt on Mount Oates, near Arthur's Pass.

Betsy, aged 21, was the world's first female alpine guide, having spent the previous three years working at the Hermitage. Nevertheless, her presence on the train to Arthur's Pass caused comment. In her autobiography she wrote: 'The CMC was a male-only club and when we took off on the goods train for Arthur's Pass I was the only female among the climbers. John had to take a barrage of snide remarks about burdening himself with a female who would hold him up, etc, etc.'

In fact, Betsy was as capable and fit as John. Although he led the trio, in darkness, up the Mingha River and through bush to the ridge leading to the summit, it was Betsy who found a better route down. On their return to Christchurch, Pascoe was again ribbed about climbing with a woman. According to Betsy, he simply ignored the remarks and sat puffing on his pipe.

JOHN PASCOE COLLECTION,
ALEXANDER TURNBULL LIBRARY

Thomson and Pascoe shared an affection for tobacco. Thomson smoked 40 cigarettes a day and a pipe on occasions, yet still managed to win the Canterbury University 3-mile race in record time.[40] Pascoe preferred a pipe and became well known for his habit of continually sucking on it, even when crossing rivers or while climbing hills. In time it became his most distinctive trademark.

Climbing, smoking, telling stories and yodelling were all part of John Pascoe's campaign to create an identity for himself, arguably, at least in part, as a response to brother Paul's achievements. In hindsight, this process had begun the previous year, when John wrote his article for *The Press*. He followed this with 'Climbs in the Rakaia Hills', which was published in the *Christ's College Register* – the only time he ever wrote for it. Although the article begins with a brief history of Rakaia exploration, the greater part is devoted to a description of John's unsuccessful ascent of 'the golden road'. Once again, he placed Evans among New Zealand's greatest peaks: 'Evans refuses access by this route with as incisive a mien as the southern ridge of Cook'.[41]

Evans was crucial. If John could be the first to reach its summit, it would prove his ability as a climber beyond doubt. But he knew he must be quick, because other climbers were keen to have a go at the Southern Alps' most prominent unclimbed peak. Foremost among them was Ian Powell. In May 1932, Powell and two other members of the Hutt Valley Tramping Club came south to climb Evans. They chose the extremely difficult north-east ridge, which offered the most direct, but the steepest approach to the summit, and they were within 150 metres of the top when a sudden blizzard forced them to retreat.[42]

The near success of this audacious ascent made it clear to Pascoe that he must not delay. He devoted 1932 to preparing for his next attempt, the following summer, when he hoped the weather would be kinder.

> All that year I trained for the task. Successive Saturdays of long distance racing and running, successive Sundays of climbing, often waist-deep in rigorous winter snows, and eager bouts of crampon work on ice-clothed ridges had hardened my skinny 8½ stone to wiry fitness. I knew that storms, rivers and exposure to cold and to steep slopes would be on the cards. All my spare time activities were oriented towards Mount Evans.[43]

There was also a problem that no amount of training could overcome: this time Chester was not coming. He had seen enough of Evans on his first foray and planned, instead, to reconnoitre a route from the head of the Rakaia to Mount Cook. Allan Willis was overseas. So, unexpectedly, Pascoe was thrust into the role of leader. To replace Chester, he recruited two athletic men. The first was Priestley Thomson, who had experience in the North Island ranges but had only climbed Tapuae-o-Uenuku in the South Island. However, his enthusiasm and stamina compensated for his lack of alpine experience. The second was Gavin Malcolmson, a natural athlete who excelled at whatever sport he chose. As a West Coaster with alpine experience, Malcolmson was familiar with the kind of weather that made Evans so difficult. Finally there was Wyn Barnett, who knew what to expect because he had been with Chester and Pascoe on 'the golden road' the year before.

Mount Evans from the Bracken Snowfield.

Mount Evans was named by early Westland surveyors after Jimmy Evans, a pioneer who farmed cattle in the Waitaha Valley. Adjacent Red Lion Peak was named after the Hokitika hotel built and run by by Evans and his wife Jane. Both mountains could be seen from the hotel.

The serrated north-east ridge of Mount Evans (centre), first attempted by Ian Powell's party in 1932, requires the climbing of five large rock towers. The rock is, however, firm and today this spectacular ridge is the preferred route to the summit.

JOHN PASCOE COLLECTION, ALEXANDER TURNBULL LIBRARY

On Christmas Day 1932 they made their way up the Rakaia to the Whitcombe Pass. Rain flooded the Whitcombe and Wilkinson Rivers, made travel difficult and forced them to shelter for days in a cave until, on 31 December, a fine dawn lured them onto the McKenzie Glacier. In a few hours they reached the north-west ridge of Evans. At this point their luck ran out: the rain returned and they had to retreat. Two days later, a second attempt seemed to infuriate the weather god guarding Evans, provoking a sudden storm that chased them back to their cave. On both attempts, Pascoe photographed their route through the McKenzie Icefall for future reference. Their holiday time was up, and they had to return to Christchurch.

In the next few months four other parties took advantage of the summer to attempt Evans, but they, too, were frustrated by bad weather. Among them was Ian Powell. After 10 years work with the Public Trust in Wellington, he had three weeks long service leave which he spent, in February 1933, up the Rakaia in 'what was supposed to be the best mountain weather of the year'. But the reality was different: 'Admittedly, it didn't rain the first afternoon, but in the next 20 days it either rained, hailed or snowed at some stage every day. We spent a week below Mount Evans ... When we arrived we had to go down a bit to get water but, after the first day, we just put the billy outside the tent.'[44]

Cave Camp, beside the Wilkinson River, Westland. Various parties used this natural shelter during attempts on Evans in the early 1930s, most of which were defeated by bad weather.

Mountaineering often involved periods of intense physical activity interspersed with long spells of enforced relaxation. Smoking, eating and talking helped to pass the time. In January 1933, Wyn Barnett, John Pascoe and Priestley Thomson (pictured) spent a week in a cave sheltering from the rain. Pascoe later wrote, 'We bunched together in the cave, as we tired of the cramped quarters in the tent. Thomson produced a tin of homemade meat paste from his swag. White specks in the paste [maggots] increased. We threw the living pottage into the stew of rice and beans. I doctored a broken pipe stem with plaster. Keas screeched their sad hakas in the rain. We argued about subjects ranging from crevasses to eugenics, university life to the Odyssey.'

DOROTHY PASCOE COLLECTION

These failures gave Pascoe new hope, and the next summer he set out again with the same friends. This time they decided to approach Evans via the Ramsay Glacier, rather than the Whitcombe Pass, to avoid flooded rivers and, perhaps, the worst Westland weather. But again, they had no luck:

> Mostly everything went wrong. Our jinx was a bit of a dag. He pelted rain into the Rakaia River and the extra swagging was horrible. Instead of sitting out a storm in a bivouac based on rock, what must we do but push on regardless up the Ramsay Glacier, camp where we did not want to, and get almost buried in a wind-drift. I awoke in the early hours fighting for air, and thought my heart had given out. What a paradox to have more guts than heart; something like an abattoir. I thought dolefully of gloomy prophecies of family friends who reckoned my heart would never take the strain of carrying half my weight over rough country. How relieved I was to find it was lack of air, not heart failure, that troubled me. We soon got air.
>
> And then, the retreat down to the Lyell Hut, minus all of our most essential camping equipment. The hare that another party cooked while seven men sniffed the fug of the hut interior. And my heart, not failed, but heavy with sorrow, because my loyal second man, the accountancy student [Wyn Barnett], had strained an arm and had to abandon the trip. That left Gavin, Priestley and me. New snow fell. Rocks would be glazed. Our tent, crampons, rope and billies were still buried up the Ramsay Glacier. A week gone by and we had got nowhere fast. If the game was snakes and ladders, we had gone down more snakes than were on the board.[45]

When the weather finally cleared the other group of CMC climbers went up the glacier with Pascoe's party, helped them to retrieve their buried gear, then plugged a trail in the soft, deep snow up to the Erewhon Col at the head of the Ramsay Glacier. Their generous assistance sparked a recovery in Pascoe's spirits as his party trudged across the Bracken Snowfield, before descending to their familiar cave beside the Wilkinson River. It had been an exhausting day but their attempt on Evans was back on track.

The following day, the last of 1933, dawned fine, but with uncharacteristic nonchalance Malcolmson, Pascoe and Thomson spent the day sunbathing:

I cheered up, just to be back in the company of the beloved mountain. I relaxed, as did the others, had a sacrificial bathe in a pool of ice-water, and got the great task in perspective. Our attempt was overdue. What matter? Our party was well-knit and our foibles immaterial. Gavin was a born leader, Priestley as capable on steep rock, I was happy on ice, and intelligence officer by sheer necessity.

Before dawn on New Year's Day 1934, they left camp and found their way through the McKenzie Icefall in the dark. Malcolmson was anxious but didn't let it show. Only later did Pascoe learn that:

Gavin had dreamed that we would be killed on the climb, but wisely kept the premonition to himself. I was stripped of sloth by the knowledge that the climb was on. Priestley was confident and efficient. We passed known ledges and gulleys and gained the sheer rock ridge that rose to a low peak. Mist and avalanches swept below. Above there rose rock beyond my capacity, but Gavin overcame it with deft competence and Priestley followed. They helped me up with the rope. With this obstacle below I knew that nothing could stop us, save lack of time.

By midday they were close to the top of Evans's low peak:

We moved with zest, knowing that each step took us close to our goal. Our eyes were used to the exposed faces below; there was no terror in the contemplation of death, for we were making height, not falling off it. Lean, sweaty and sure, we traversed the low peak, took a gap with nonchalance, and made the last pitches to the summit in the middle of the afternoon. The top was a cornice, overhanging to the Shelf Glacier. It would not take the weight of a man, so I gave it an accolade with the shaft of my ice-axe. I tore a strip of blue handkerchief to leave in a cairn on the nearest rock.[46]

Priestley Thomson recalls that on reaching the summit his overwhelming feeling was one of relief: 'Thank God that it had been climbed', and 'Thank God

On the summit of Evans (2620m), New Year's Day, 1934. From left to right: Priestley Thomson, Gavin Malcolmson, John Pascoe.

JOHN PASCOE COLLECTION, ALEXANDER TURNBULL LIBRARY

Bert Mercer's aerial photo of Evans and environs shows the eastern approaches to the peak. Pascoe's 'golden road' (top, centre) climbs from the Bracken Snowfield to the southern end of the summit ridge and the north-east ridge is also clearly visible.

Mercer took this photo while flying over the Whitcombe Pass in 1933. He gave a copy to Pascoe who noted on it the names of various features such as the Ramsay Glacier (left), Amazons Breasts (centre), Bracken Snowfield, Barron Glacier (lower right) and Red Lion and Col, on the skyline.

JOHN PASCOE COLLECTION, ALEXANDER TURNBULL LIBRARY

that Johnny Pascoe had done it!' Pascoe's response was surprisingly muted. He didn't yodel, 'he certainly made no speeches'. According to Thomson, 'there were no congratulations. He muttered something like "well that's that – at long last", or some remark like that.'[47]

Pascoe's low-key response may also have been due to weariness, the sense of deflation that sometimes follows the attainment of a long-held objective and his preoccupation with how they would get down. The others soon realised he had a tough agenda in mind. Thomson suggested that they return down the ridge they had climbed, but Pascoe was keen to traverse Evans and find some other way down. It was up to Malcolmson to decide. At this point Pascoe produced aerial photos of the unknown terrain beyond Evans, which had recently been taken for him by Captain J. C. 'Bert' Mercer, the pioneer West Coast pilot. Malcolmson agreed to the traverse. Again, Pascoe's superb research proved its worth. But the decision was not taken lightly: all three knew that to carry on across Evans would inevitably mean a cold night out in unknown country.

After half an hour on the top they set off and were soon standing on the cornice which had blocked access from 'the golden road'. A dangerous descent to Red Lion Col, a low point between Evans and an adjacent peak, focused attention on survival. It was here that they chose to spend the night.

The careful climbing required to cross the summit of Mount Evans safely is apparent in this 1979 photo and explains why it took more than four hours for Malcolmson, Pascoe and Thomson to traverse Evans and descend to Red Lion Col.
ERIC SAGGERS

'Our food was limited to dates and lumps of cheese,' recalled Pascoe. Like the party benighted on Mount Whitcombe, they found it too cold to stay put for long, so they walked to restore vital circulation. 'The col was broad and flat, rather like a running track. We would trot around the track till our numb feet regained feeling, and then we would sleep against a rock till our feet woke us up again. The instalments of sleep averaged half an hour.'[48]

At dawn they found a steep route down to the County Glacier which curves round to the north-west beneath the ridge they had climbed the previous day. Their descent was made possible by crampons. From the lower glacier they climbed to the north-west ridge of Evans, above the McKenzie Icefall, as rain clouds gathered, and at 10 a.m. they reached their cave camp. They had been away for 30 hours.

The rain that fell while they slept marked the end of the good weather that had allowed them access to Evans, and made their exit from the mountains more challenging than Evans itself. As they crossed the Bracken Snowfield, a snowstorm became a blizzard. With no visibility and a broken compass they had little idea of where they were. As it grew dark they put up the tent, but the gale tore the canvas, leaving them exposed in their sleeping bags. All they could do was smoke and hope: 'We sucked grimy pipes for comfort, and found warmth in glowing bowls'.

Pascoe worried that if they froze to death, as Scott's party had done on their return from the Pole, no one would know that they had climbed Evans. In his diary, the last entry had been made on their day of relaxation before the climb:

> Accordingly, I found a pencil stub, and in the dark with numb fingers, relying on sense of touch wrote 'Climbed Evans 3 Pks. Benighted Red Lion Col. Returned County McKenzie Col. Rain in McK camp. Tough climb. Gavin and A. P. lead finely. A cold benightment on Red Lion Col. These scratched notes are written in snowbound tent in sleeping bag and terrific blizzard on Bracken Snowfield. We are having an eventful trip. Hope to get out of this camp O.K.'[49]

Simply entitled 'Satisfaction', this self-portrait was taken by Pascoe in Duncan's Hut after his successful ascent of Mount Evans.

DOROTHY PASCOE COLLECTION

Next morning, a break in the storm allowed them to escape. Abandoning the tent, they found Erewhon Col, crossed it and followed the Ramsay Glacier to Lyell Hut. Finally safe, Pascoe began to revel in their achievement. While his companions pushed on over the Mathias Pass to return to jobs in Westland, Pascoe walked down the Rakaia Valley on his own. Joy lightened his step and he made good time, despite the rain. With Evans behind him he was unstoppable, twice fording the main channel of the Rakaia, his former nemesis.

His solo crossings were evidence of the new confidence Evans had given him. Being in the first party to climb Evans was undoubtedly a turning point in his life. Relieved of his obsession, the 25-year-old was now free to think of the future. Climbing Evans proved Pascoe was a capable mountaineer, but where to climb next? He had stood on the summits of almost all of Canterbury's significant mountains. Further south lay the higher peaks of the Mount Cook region, but Pascoe considered them to be the preserve of the guided climber. The answer was provided by his boyhood hero, Samuel Butler, whose experiences as an explorer were to inspire Pascoe to seek out unknown territory.

ANGEL COL   GUARDIAN PEAK   ADA

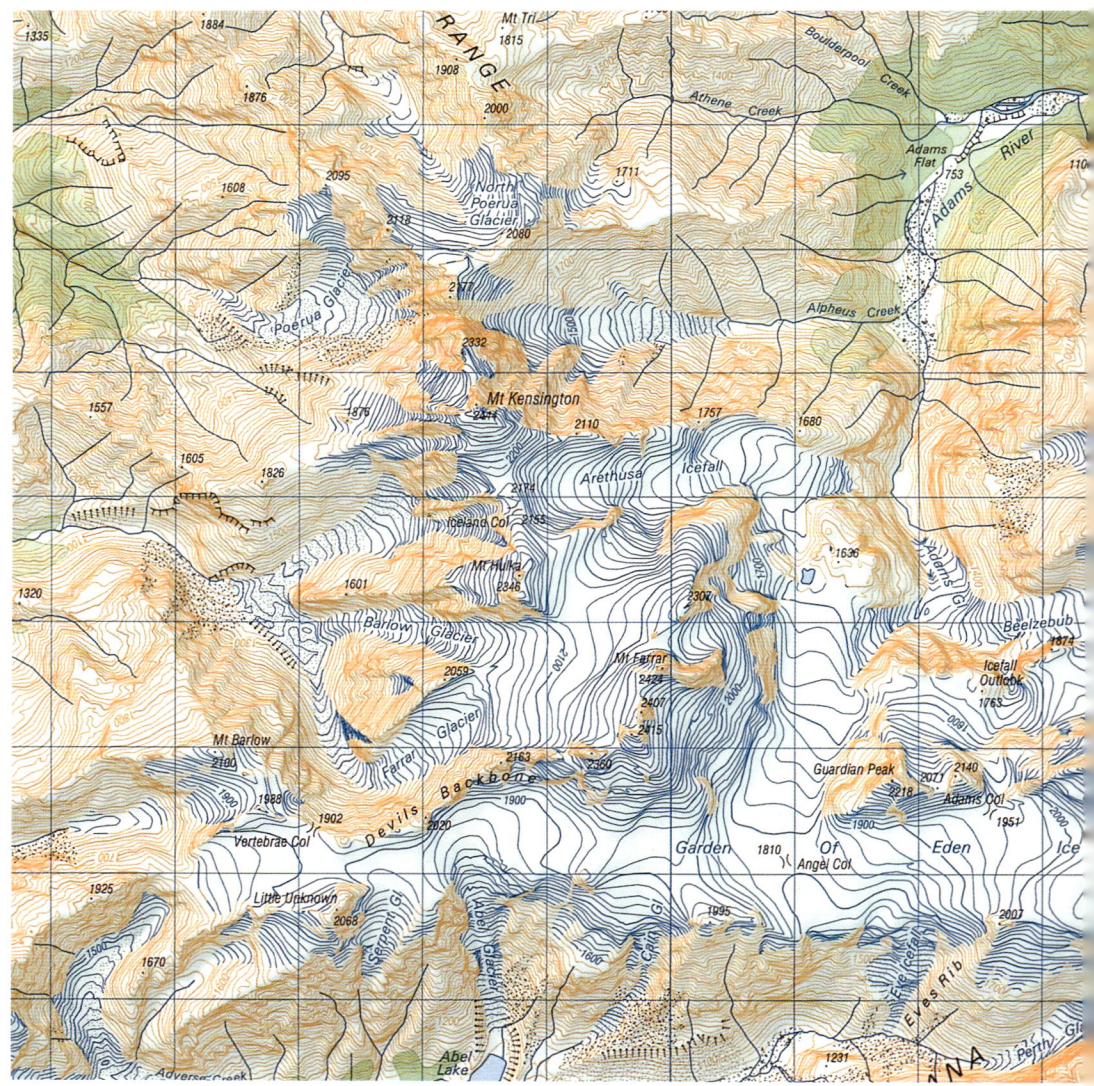

BAKER PEAK   PERTH COL

PERTH GLACIER

The Explorer

John Pascoe started mountaineering when many of Canterbury's peaks were unclimbed. He and the CMC took full advantage of this opportunity which, in hindsight, was brief. Within five years even remote mountains such as Evans had been climbed.

Canterbury's climbers then looked for new opportunities elsewhere. Some went to Mount Cook to try higher peaks. Pascoe chose instead to seek out unknown country on the Westland side of the Main Divide, where he was rewarded with the discovery of an extensive alpine ice plateau which was named the Garden of Eden. Pascoe and his companions also gave biblical names to the adjacent icefalls. Later he went to the Mount Cook region, where he made two unsuccessful attempts on Mount Tasman.

In describing these adventures in articles, and later in Unclimbed New Zealand, John Pascoe showed a growing interest in history, especially the journeys of the early explorers and pioneers. Towards the close of the 1930s, this interest and his increasing confidence as a writer, led him to reassess his life and take a new direction.

Above: John Pascoe's five-part panorama of the Garden of Eden, taken from the top of Eve's Rib on 26 December 1934, gives a 270 degree view of the ice plateau and surrounding peaks.

JOHN PASCOE COLLECTION, ALEXANDER TURNBULL LIBRARY

LEFT: LAND INFORMATION NEW ZEALAND (NZMS 260 SERIES – 1KM GRID)

S AMUEL BUTLER IS REMEMBERED most vividly as the high country runholder who played Bach on the piano amid the sheep and tussocks. That incongruous image has endured while other aspects of Butler's life have receded from public memory – or so it seemed to John Pascoe, who made it his mission to promote Butler's lesser-known achievements. Although Pascoe was not the first to write about Butler, it was largely because of his interest in Butler's exploration that Pascoe's contemporaries came to know more about this unusual pioneer whose progressive ideas provoked such mixed responses. Some admired him, others were suspicious of the young Cambridge graduate turned runholder. One sheepman considered Butler to be 'very nearly if not quite an infidel' because of his Darwinian views. Another neighbour, Ellen Tripp, a daughter of Bishop Harper, did not approve of him at all. In her diary she wrote: 'His was a peculiar nature, and full of wild theories. My husband enjoyed talking to him, but I thought his views very upsetting, and we did not like it when he tried to convert our maid to his ideas.'[1]

Pascoe had no such reservations. To him Butler was 'a man of the mountains', an explorer whose work 'is an inspiration to the present generation of mountain travellers'. He had been the first European to explore the upper Rakaia, an alpine area Pascoe had come to know well during his three attempts on Mount Evans. No doubt Butler's non-conformity also appealed to Pascoe, who was never entirely at ease in conventional Canterbury society. But it was Butler's exploration, and the novels it inspired, that prompted Pascoe to write a number of articles and a chapter of *Unclimbed New Zealand* about him.

As a boy, Pascoe had been excited by his father's accounts of Butler's strange civilisation on the other side of the mountains. Later, when he read Butler's satirical novel, *Erewhon*, it added detail to these stories. Then in the early 1930s, when Pascoe began to explore the upper Rakaia, he learnt about Butler's exploration in that area. Soon the student became the advocate, as Pascoe began to publicise his hero.

Pascoe's first article, published in *The Press* in 1933, described Butler's journey in the summer of 1861 to the head of the Rangitata. From a high

So strong was John Pascoe's interest that he illustrated his copy of Erewhon *with photos of the Whitcombe Pass and other scenes which he inserted in the book beside relevant passages and also annotated the text with his observations. Similarly, Paul Pascoe enclosed copies of John's photos in the copy of* Erewhon Revisited *he had inherited from his father.*

DOROTHY PASCOE COLLECTION

Although Baker and Butler's discovery of the pass at the head of the Rakaia was not acknowledged when it was named, Butler's exploration in the area was remembered when the surveyor G. J. Roberts later gave Butler's name to this peak.

Like Butler, Pascoe learnt to respect the Rakaia River after making perilous crossings of it when in flood. In Erewhon Samuel Butler described it as 'an awful river, muddy and horribly angry, roaring over an immense river-bed'.

point overlooking the next valley to the north, the Rakaia, Butler and his companion, the surveyor John Baker (the 'Chowbok' of *Erewhon*), saw a low pass that looked as though it led through the mountains to the West Coast. A week later they ventured up the Rakaia on horseback, forded the river and crossed the pass, but they did not go much further because they could see no useful grazing land on the Westland side.[2] On the pass itself, Butler sensed a pervasive, menacing melancholy which he described in *Erewhon*. Two years later, the Canterbury Provincial Government sent the surveyor, Henry Whitcombe, and a surveyor's assistant, Jakob Lauper, to investigate. They crossed the pass and continued on to the West Coast where Whitcombe drowned. Subsequently, his name – not Butler's or Baker's – was given to the pass, and Lauper's was bestowed on the stream that gives access to it. Whitcombe also had a major peak in the vicinity named after him.[3]

Seventy years later, Pascoe took the opportunity to mark Butler's contribution. In 1931, he was asked to advise on a suitable name for a newly discovered saddle at the head of the Ramsay Glacier, near the Whitcombe Pass, and his suggestion, Erewhon Col, was accepted.[4] A year later, friends of Pascoe's continued this theme when they named the saddle on the southern side of the upper Rakaia, from which Baker and Butler had first seen the pass, Chowbok Col.[5]

Pascoe's article 'Samuel Butler in the Rakaia' was his first historical piece; previously he had written solely about climbing. The change of subject may have been deliberate, as *The Press* had recently criticised climbers in the wake of Edgar Russell's death on Avalanche Peak. Pascoe had more reason than most who were on the mountain that day, to take the censure personally. Like the rest of the large group that reassembled beneath the peak after the avalanche, he did not realise that Russell was missing. Had he known that Russell lay buried in the snow, he would not, of course, have gone on to the summit. In a letter to a friend Pascoe described Russell's death as 'a hell of a bad business and all the more from whichever point of view it was looked at'. He went on to describe the difficulty he had in writing Russell's obituary: 'it was the hardest job my pen has ever had to do. Brevity had to follow on the heels of sincerity. If I had not known and liked Edgar it might have been easier, but it was very hard because you can feel so much and yet express so little.'[6]

The editorial in *The Press* was based on the coroner's findings that the Avalanche Peak party lacked 'adequate organisation and leadership' and took 'grave and unnecessary risks'. If climbers did not follow guidelines for mountain safety, the paper suggested they might need to be regulated:

> In the last few years better roads and cheaper fares have brought the mountains within easy reach of many hundreds of young men and women who know nothing of the hazards of climbing. It is unfortunate that such persons have in their hands the future of mountaineering in New Zealand. If they, or even a small minority of them, elect to learn wisdom through disasters, the generous freedom now given to climbers will be severely restricted. If they are wise enough to learn from those with experience and to realise that the art of mountaineering lies not in taking risks but in avoiding them, the pleasures of climbing in New Zealand will continue to be enhanced by an absence of regulations and formalities.[7]

Arthur's Pass from the slopes of Avalanche Peak.

During the 1930s, John Pascoe and his friends made many climbs at Arthur's Pass thanks to the regular train service. 'Our debt to the railways was incalculable,' he later wrote, 'and we all made friendships with guards and drivers and station officials that last until this day.'

The timing of the trains set the schedule for many an exhausting alpine weekend. 'Some of us ran cross-country races or played football on Saturday afternoons, tore home to change to climbing clothes, and slept on the "perishable" goods train that left Christchurch in the late afternoon. As there was no climbers' hut to use [until the CMC built one at Arthur's Pass in 1936], we made do with the waiting room at the railway station as a cookhouse, but left for our mountain before dawn, plugged a snowy trail to the top, and returned in time for the return excursion train at 4.30pm. The journey home was enlivened with songs, and we heated our bacon and brews on spirit cookers or a primus.'

THE DEATH OF EDGAR RUSSELL

On 30 July 1933 John Pascoe and several other CMC members joined a large group of Canterbury University College students on an ascent of *Avalanche Peak at Arthur's Pass. Above the bushline the weather was bad, with a strong nor'wester and driving snow. A few of the students turned back. Those who went on were soon joined by several other people, not known to them. Conditions were so difficult that instead of following the usual route up the ridge to the summit, the combined party crossed a sheltered snowy basin beneath the ridge, and began to climb a steep slope to Avalanche Peak.*

Peter Maling was just behind the leader, when he and the rest of the group were swept down the slope by an avalanche. Some were buried in the snow but others were left with limbs sticking out. Maling was one of the lucky ones: his face was exposed so he was able to breathe. Quickly he and others pulled the rest of the group out of the snow. A check was made, and the students descended to Arthur's Pass while John Pascoe and another climber went on to the summit, then rejoined the group. It was not until they were on the train back to Christchurch that someone realised Edgar Russell was missing. Pascoe stopped the train at Springfield and returned to Arthur's Pass to get help. The next day a large CMC contingent arrived to help search for Russell.

BRIAN WYN IRWIN PHOTO, JOHN PASCOE COLLECTION, ALEXANDER TURNBULL LIBRARY

Left: Searchers endured blizzard conditions above the bushline for several days after Russell was reported missing.

Above: His body was found a week later when, on Pascoe's initiative, a second trench was begun (in the foreground) further down the slope below Avalanche Peak.

WEIGEL PHOTO, JOHN PASCOE COLLECTION, ALEXANDER TURNBULL LIBRARY

The threat of regulation was real. In the early 1930s a series of alpine deaths cast climbing in a poor light, even though most of the fatalities were caused by freak events. In 1930 five people died on the Tasman Glacier during a sudden, severe electrical storm, probably after being struck by lightning.[8] The following year a large group of Auckland University students went missing on Mount Ruapehu and when they were found, one was dead.[9] Both incidents occurred at a time when the government was being urged by the president of the New Zealand Alpine Club, A. P. Harper, to introduce a licensing system for alpine guides. At the time of Russell's death, a bill had been passed by the House of Representatives but had not been approved by the Legislative Council. In fact, it went no further. Even if it had become law, the proposed legislation would not have restricted guideless climbers such as the CMC, but that was not clearly understood by Pascoe, *The Press* or the public.[10]

Russell's death was also embarrassing for Pascoe, because he had previously written about independence and safety in the mountains. His *Press* article, 'Climbers and Guides – A Plea for the Amateur', was intended to rebut the government's proposed regulations, but Pascoe had concluded with a romantic reflection on the dangers of mountaineering. Under the heading 'Safety not Everything', he had illustrated his contention with an excerpt from a poem which depicted death as a drowsy descent into sleep – not the choking suffocation in snow that must have been Russell's end.

> The guided climber will say that his safety and success are of paramount importance, and laymen will criticise the young fools who go guideless into the high ranges. The guided will never know the delight of a self-won peak. The mountains will teach their craft to those who are willing to learn and if
>
> 'Some are let fall from knee or shoulder
> Footslip or spit of stone or avalanche.
> They are quiet at last and life ceases to camber
> Or wandering the snowfield in darkness and doubting
> Will sapp'd and joint and sinew melting
> They despair of the way and will wait for the morning
> And they breathe the drowsy breath of the ice-wind
> … Then sleep a little, then sleep for ever.'
>
> they will have paid the price of a mistake. It is this keen struggle with these odds that provides the fascination of mountaineering.[11]

Fortunately for John Pascoe, newspapers can change their tune remarkably quickly – and the public's memory is often short. A few months after the inquest into Russell's death, when Pascoe returned to Christchuch with news of the first ascent of Mount Evans, *The Press* was quick to praise climbers. An editorial celebrated the CMC's achievement and listed the attributes of mountaineers, which it considered were an antidote to 'the increasing urbanisation of modern life'. It also described their 'invaluable' contribution in clarifying confusing alpine topography and their correction of errors made by the early surveyors.[12]

Such public recognition was welcomed by climbers, particularly Pascoe, who enjoyed acknowledgement of the achievement that had obsessed him for three years and, in particular, the editorial's specific endorsement of the CMC. His identification with the club was intense, more so than for other members, perhaps because it filled the void created by his father's early death. If the club was criticised in print, as it had been in the past, Pascoe had often been the first to reply – and always with vehemence. It was his second family, to which he gave fierce loyalty.

John Pascoe asleep on Mount Enys, Craigieburn Range, February 1934.

Climbing a peak in Canterbury's outer ranges on a hot day can be hard work. To beat the heat, Pascoe sometimes climbed at night, then slept on the summit during the day. Years later he recalled night climbing: 'With a handful of other crazy people I would leave the camp at the foot at 8 p.m. when the others were turning into their bunks. We knew the range so well we needed no moon to help us. Climbing steadily to keep warm, but not so fast that we became tired, we would plod up to the summit of the range in the dark. But when we saw the first light of dawn from Mount Enys, or Mount Olympus, or Hamilton Peak, we would not count ourselves crazy. Then we would gloat over the panorama of distant acquaintances on the Main Divide from Mount Rolleston to Mount Whitcombe, and laze in the sun and melt snow with a little primus cooker. I have been on most of the outer range summits by dawn, and can understand the satisfaction that musterers get from being early on their top beats in the autumn muster.'

STAN FORBES PHOTO, W. A. KENNEDY COLLECTION, CANTERBURY MUSEUM

John Pascoe (top) and Basil Honour by James Cook, who was briefly married to the painter, Rita Angus, in the early 1930s. Angus, like Pascoe, wrote for The Press Junior, contributing the occasional article on how to draw and paint.

DOROTHY PASCOE COLLECTION

In the meantime, his actual family was dispersing in pursuit of individual interests. His sister Alice left for India in 1933, and soon after John's return from Mount Evans, Paul went to England to further his career as an architect.[13] As adults all three had remained close, with friends and interests in common. Now only John remained at home with his mother.

But the void created by their departure did not last long. Soon after his success on Evans, he was asked to write a regular column for The Press's younger readers about life in the mountains and for most of 1934 and 1935 'In Mountain Ranges' was a prominent part of The Press Junior. Each week, John Pascoe described a different aspect of alpine life, invariably illustrated with one of his photos. In doing so, he showed an inventive ability to extract stories from his own experiences. Topics varied from the predictable such as 'Tracks', 'Guides' and 'Unclimbed Peaks' to descriptions of walks on the Port Hills and at Arthur's Pass. But he also wrote about 'Schoolboy Mountaineers' (for example, Charles Hilgendorf, who made the first ascent of Carrington Peak, aged 14) and the 'Kitchens and Cooks' of high country sheep stations. His resourcefulness was perhaps best illustrated by 'Space' – an account of jumps, dives and falls from high places, accompanied by a photo of a naked Boney Chester diving into a river from a high bluff.

This period was Pascoe's apprenticeship as a writer; it taught him the discipline of regular writing to a specified length on subjects that had to be made interesting for a general readership.[14] It also gave him valuable experience of illustrating stories. For example, what makes a photo interesting? How can an image add to a recollection? As he looked through his alpine albums, he saw familiar photos in a new light. An early picture of friends fooling around on the bonnet of a moving car, for instance, was now used to illustrate an account of different ways of reaching the mountains.

"FEEDING THE BABY" at 30 mph: Geoff Derbridge, Allan Willis, & Gavin Malcolmson.

JOHN PASCOE COLLECTION, ALEXANDER TURNBULL LIBRARY

IN MOUNTAIN RANGES
SPACE
(By John Pascoe)

A Mountaineer's Dive

Science teaches us that a body falls through space at 32 feet a second. Caution, involving the use of the rope, will bind hillmen to their hills so that the risk of falling will be reduced to a minimum. Modern technique by Continental climbers has attained such a pitch that gravity is defied by their ways and means. Ingenious engineering feats with pulleys and swivel-hooks, the latter welted with hammers into crevices of hard rock or blue ice, have become the fashion in Europe. The Bavarian mountaineers are primarily responsible for these amazing tactics, which are as yet unknown to New Zealanders. An enterprising British cragman, however, has studied the art of falling, and he claims that he can fall 30 or even 40 feet without serious injury. His gift, if indeed it can be called a gift, is a rare one, and should never be sought by ordinary mortals.

Being used to heights, some mountaineers do not fear depths. Nimble jumps have sometimes saved trouble in areas of deep crevasses and broken ridges. One of the ablest of the Canterbury mountaineers was R. R. Chester, who led many expeditions before he left for Australia. Chester was as sure-footed as any goat. A characteristic high dive into a mountain pool is illustrated by the above photograph. This daring leap was made with accuracy and grace from a narrow ledge.

John Pascoe, June 1935.
During the Depression, many
young climbers had little money to
spend on outdoor clothing, so they
made do with old coats and
trousers. John Pascoe was the
original 'grunge' mountaineer.
He took great pride in his ragged
appearance and identified himself
and the CMC with the band of
pilgrims in Hassan. Pascoe's dress
was deliberate, to symbolise his
rejection of European alpine
traditions, which he thought were
exemplified by the gentlemen
climbers at the Hermitage. When
he eventually came to know some
of them, he modified his views.

PAUL PASCOE ALBUM,
JONATHAN PASCOE COLLECTION

'The Golden Road' on Mount
Evans by Jean Stevenson.
DOROTHY PASCOE COLLECTION

The Spirit of the Pilgrim

"The Golden Journey to Samarkand"

JAMES ELROY FLECKER—the poet—is well remembered in terms of his play—'Hassan.' The tribulations of the rise and fall of the Baghdad confectioner are traced with the warp and weft of subtle Eastern design. From greasy merchant of odorous sweetmeats to exalted friend of the Caliph Haroun—the transition is sketched with glamour. Attendant upon adventure by night is adventure by day. Rebellion, torture, romance, and lust are woven into the changing hours.

Hassan becomes surfeited with riches, pomp and power. The Caliph's desire for cruelty repels the peacable confectioner. Ishak, the tempestuous poet whirls Hassan away to the Gate of the Moon, whence starts the caravan for the 'cities of the Far North East.'

Thus do the dazzling flares of four Acts become focused to the pin point of brilliance in the final Pilgrim's scene:

> "Away, for we are ready to a man!
> Our camels sniff the evening and are glad."

Pilgrims are not confined to eastern lands alone. Rendered fanatical by their faith and relatively impervious to discomfort, their passion for travel and hazard is not to be reduced to terms of mere masochistic or religious enterprise.

Compare the Pilgrims of Hassan with a band of high-level hillmen in the Southern Alps.

> "But who are ye in rags and rotten shoes,
> You dirty-bearded, blocking up the way?"

asks the Master of the Caravan, and he receives the answer:

> "We are the Pilgrims, master: we shall go
> Always a little further; it may be
> Beyond that last blue mountain barred with snow
> . . . . But surely we are brave
> Who take the Golden Road to Samarkand."

A party of Southern mountaineers returning from a traverse of the glacier country at the head of their native rivers would not look so very different from their Eastern brethren. Beards may grow in Bokhara. Beards may grow in a Westland cave. Rags may rot anywhere.

Arid deserts sometimes lie in plateaus in the Orient. Symmetrical snowfields may lie at the head of a hanging valley in the Southern Alps. As Hassan says:

> "Sweet to ride forth at evening from the wells,
> When shadows pass gigantic on the sand,
> And softly through the silence beat the bells
> Along the Golden Road to Samarkand."

The giant outline of some of the South Island's mountains will cast so deep a shadow that snow glinted by evening sun is soft, and snow chilled by twilight is frozen. Yet these two varieties of snow may lie on the same slope, in the same plateau.

A visit, for instance, to the Full Moon Saddle and the delicate symmetry of the Bracken Snowfield, that alpine desert of the hinterland on the Westland side of the Rakaia Divide, would strengthen justification for such a fantastic conception. An eastern ridge of a mountain in the vicinity was christened the 'Golden Road to Samarkand,' because the irony of the situation disclosed that a pilgrimage along that turreted route was a matter of no lush carpets. The cloud of imagination allied with the silhouette of suggestion, and the name of the ridge has remained.

To the average lowlander a hillman is an individual to be discussed in the same breath as a moron. Deliberately to forego the delights of a sea side resort in the summer months of the nor'wester period, in order that an inhospitable pass may be crossed, or a mountain fastness explored, is indeed incomprehensible, save to those who have been lured up rivers to their sources by our goddess of the snows. Let Ishak explain:

> "We travel not for trafficking alone;
> By hotter winds our fiery hearts are fanned:
> For lust of knowing what should not be known,
> We take the Golden Road to Samarkand."

In his play Flecker emphasises the lengths to which his pilgrims carry their wanderlust—they desert their wine and women for the journey from the Gate of the Moon.

> "O turn your eyes to where your children stand.
> Is not Baghdad the beautiful? O stay! . . . . .
> "Have you not girls and garlands in your homes,
> . . . . . Seek not excess: God hateth him who roams!"

The Watchman at the Gate of the Moon is sardonic about it all. He asks:

> " . . . . For what land
> Leave you the dim-moon city of delight?"

but has to console the bereft wives. His comforts are like Job:

> "What would ye, ladies? It was ever thus
> Men are unwise and curiously planned."

A woman laments:

> "They have their dreams, and do not think of us."

and in the still distance sing the Voices of the Caravan:

> "We take the Golden Road to Samarkand."

JOHN D. PASCOE

The Press Junior also provided Pascoe with his first romantic experience. Although he had known its editor, Jean Stevenson, since they were children, it was not until he began to write regularly for the paper that they knew each other as adults. Jean was impressed by his 'succinct style and good photographs' and it was probably her suggestion that he write a weekly column.[15] As their relationship developed, she introduced him to her literary friends, which gave him a different view of his city at a time when Christchurch was considered to be the most vibrant cultural centre in the country. But John Pascoe was not always comfortable among poets, socialists and writers, some of whom were vegetarians. On one occasion he was invited to Jean's flat for dinner and was shocked to be served salad.[16]

For her part, Jean reciprocated by taking an interest in the mountains, although she did so vicariously, rather than by actually going into the hills with John. For instance, on his 26th birthday she gave him a copy of Flecker's play *Hassan* with a pen and watercolour sketch of 'the golden road' on Mount Evans, which she had drawn from one of his photos, tucked inside. Jean also encouraged him to broaden his horizons as a writer, to consider submitting

Christmas Eve, 1934. From left to right: John Pascoe, Priestley Thomson, Duncan Hall and Gavin Malcolmson resting in the Frances Valley at the head of the Rangitata, on their way to the Garden of Eden.

The extensive ice plateau to the west of the Main Divide was discovered in 1911 by Dr Ebenezer Teichelman, Alec Graham and Jack Clarke when they made the first ascent of Mount Tyndall. From its summit they looked down on the plateau which extended far to the west. Further exploration did not take place, however, until a new generation of young climbers took an interest in the area more than 20 years later. In the summer of 1933–34, groups climbed to the east and south of the snowfield and their descriptions of it excited other climbers, especially in the CMC. As had happened with Mount Evans a few years earlier, a race developed to be the first to explore the area and climb its peaks.

JOHN PASCOE COLLECTION,
ALEXANDER TURNBULL LIBRARY

articles to literary magazines and to read a wider range of books. In the past he had written for newspapers and climbing journals, but had looked no further. Now, with her support, he reworked his favourite theme, the likeness of the CMC to the pilgrims of *Hassan*, into an article, 'The Spirit of the Pilgrim', which he sent to the *Canterbury University College Review*.[17]

Pascoe was once again among fellow pilgrims in December 1934, when he and the veterans of Mount Evans, Gavin Malcolmson and Priestley Thomson, set out to explore an untrodden alpine area in Westland. The fourth member of the party was Duncan Hall, another CMC member. Their intention was to explore an extensive ice plateau recently seen from a distance by several CMC parties climbing at the head of the Rangitata. As this was to be a journey of exploration, sufficient supplies for 16 days were required and because they were all smokers, tobacco was also needed. Before their departure, they found that they had between them 420 cigarettes, 17 cigars, 23 ounces of cigarette tobacco and 20 ounces of pipe tobacco which, in total, equalled the weight of the group's dried meat.[18]

Their journey up the Rangitata Valley was evocative for Pascoe, as this was the area of Butler's run. On Christmas Day the quartet crossed the Main Divide to reach the Perth Glacier in Westland, which they were the first to traverse. At its base, the group found a ridge that took them to their objective, and as they were the first to reach the great ice plateau, it was their right to name it. Priestley Thomson suggested a biblical theme, his idea inspired by a play on the name of the nearby Adams Range. His companions agreed. So the great expanse of snow and ice became the Garden of Eden, and the rivers of ice spilling over its southern edge were named the Eve Icefall and the Serpent, Cain and Abel Glaciers.[19]

Pascoe was impressed by the size of their discovery: 'The Garden of Eden is on a giant scale and the alpine pastures must be miles long, containing an area of snow and ice equivalent to the névés of the Rakaia and Rangitata put together'.[20] More surprises lay in store when they crossed the plateau to a high saddle they named Angel Col. From there they looked down on the Adams Glacier, which they found was fed by two valleys choked with ice. But further opportunity to explore was denied by the worsening weather, which forced them to hurriedly retrace their steps. From the edge of the plateau they descended Eve's Rib to reach their campsite in the upper Perth just as the rain began in earnest.

On Friday 28 December Pascoe
wrote: 'Gavin got another kea. We
washed ourselves and cleaned up
camp, and vice versa. Gavin [left]
and A. P. [Priestley] plucked the
keas and they went down the hatch
nicely for dinner, seeming as tender
as turkey, and we didn't even have
to waste time in picking our teeth
with the feathers.'

JOHN PASCOE COLLECTION,
ALEXANDER TURNBULL LIBRARY

It rained for the rest of the trip. For several days they sheltered in their small three-man tent, made bearable by a flysheet that gave them more room. Entertainment was provided by keas who tried to eat their equipment. This was, they decided, sufficient provocation to allow them to emulate the early explorers' habit of eating native birds. On 27 December Pascoe recorded that 'It rained off and on, mostly the latter. Duncan felled a kea with a rock. The coon keas were obstreperous and chewed pack straps, so Duncan hung the bird upside down outside the tent pour encourager les autres.' The next day another was caught. 'The keas ate our belongings. We ate the keas.'

Tent fever eventually forced them out into the rain. Further down the valley they climbed a side stream to attempt the first ascent of a high peak standing apart from the rest, which was christened The Great Unknown. Relentless rain made the climb unpleasant and by mid-afternoon they were still some distance from the summit. To Pascoe the conditions were 'unpleasantly reminiscent of the tragic day on Avalanche Peak when my friend Edgar Russell lost his life'. This time sounder judgement prevailed and they retreated.[21]

With no let-up in the rain, further climbing and exploring was out of the question. Instead they continued down the sodden Perth Valley. At one point they found an old blaze on a tree; nearby lay tins of meat, relics

Gavin Malcolmson prepares
a meal beside the tent in which
he, Duncan Hall, John Pascoe and
Priestley Thomson lived for a week
at the head of the Perth Valley.
Most of the time it rained.

JOHN PASCOE COLLECTION,
ALEXANDER TURNBULL LIBRARY

During the Depression of the 1930s, a number of people lived in remote West Coast valleys. While following the Perth River down to the coast, Pascoe's party came across Gamble's Hut, a typical prospector's home with a well-tended vegetable garden. Gamble had a six-hour walk to reach the main road.

JOHN PASCOE COLLECTION, ALEXANDER TURNBULL LIBRARY

of Dr Teichelmann's exploration 10 years before. Only Thomson was game enough to open one and try the preserved tongues which he said were 'delicious'.[22]

On reaching the coast, the group dispersed. John Pascoe remained at Whataroa for a few days, staying with the Gunns, a local family. They told him about the legendary explorer, Charlie Douglas, who spent 30 years exploring South Westland during the latter part of the 19th century. Pascoe was intrigued. He knew nothing about Douglas, but noted: 'Everywhere on the Coast the name of Charlie Douglas is treated with deep respect'. Conversations with the Gunns and others gave him a new sense of the West Coast. Here, he realised, was a self-contained community, isolated by mountains and rivers with its own history and heroes, like Douglas. Until then Pascoe's ideas of the past had been drawn from Canterbury, but his stay on the Coast gave him a more detached view of his own province.

Back in Christchurch, Pascoe and his three companions had every reason to feel satisfied. They had found a new route across the Alps and had discovered the Garden of Eden. From Angel Col, they had had tantalising glimpses of the Adams Glacier and its icefalls, sufficient prospects for further exploration to sustain John Pascoe through another year of 'the monotony of ill-paid work'.[23]

In reality, his life outside the law office was far from dull. His relationship with Jean Stevenson seems to have stopped early in 1935, but if he was heartbroken it was shortlived, because before long he was out walking on the Port Hills with a new female friend. John met Joan Singleton in the back of a truck taking a group of Canterbury University College students to Arthur's Pass; he and some other CMC members had joined them to share the cost.[24]

Joan had recently moved from Wellington to Christchurch to attend teachers' training college. She was also studying geography at Canterbury University College under Professor George Jobberns, whom she found inspiring. Before coming to Christchurch she had been one of the leading

During the 1930s, John Pascoe developed a keen interest in photography. In 1935 he purchased a new Rolleicord camera and tested the sharpness of the lens by photographing a collection of climbing equipment. This image was used to illustrate one of his articles for The Press Junior.

JOHN PASCOE COLLECTION, ALEXANDER TURNBULL LIBRARY

John Pascoe and Joan Singleton at the Rhodes Memorial on the Port Hills, 1935.

JOHN PASCOE COLLECTION,
ALEXANDER TURNBULL LIBRARY

young members of the Tararua Tramping Club. Not surprisingly, John found her enticing. So did other young climbers. According to Austen Deans, 'John wasn't the only student in those days who harboured romantic fantasies about Joan Singleton. She was a very attractive personality, quite apart from her remarkable ability in the mountains, with quite a literary turn of mind.'[25]

Deans remained a distant admirer, but John and Joan soon became close friends and spent much of their spare time together walking to get fit for trips into the mountains. John's mother did not approve of the pair going into the hills on their own, so they invited the male climber, Merle Sweney, to come along as a chaperone and to make up a threesome for safety. During the winter of 1935, they made several ambitious trips. In May they crossed the Main Divide from the Waimakariri to the Taipo River in only two days without a rope, tent or sleep. Not even a snowstorm on Campbell Pass deterred them. Then, in August, they did a demanding traverse of Mount Rolleston, tough enough to test any courtship. Pascoe later described this journey in *Unclimbed New Zealand*. Once again, they ignored the need for sleep:

> We left Arthur's Pass at 11 p.m. one Saturday and followed the route via the upper Otira Valley. At 2 a.m. we lashed on crampons and had no trouble in reaching the Goldney ridge at 6000 ft. Thence soft snow delayed our progress. At 10 a.m. we left the low peak to begin the more interesting climbing. The rocks were glazed, and the glaze was sheathed in turn with two inches of soft snow. Crampons were invaluable. By dint of interminable scraping and acrobatics we arrived at the summit three hours later. Descending a steep couloir, we plunged down into the deep snow of the Waimakariri glacier.

From there, the usual route followed the Waimakariri River to the road: a long, shingle trudge that the trio had done just a few months earlier. Instead, Joan suggested that they cross the col at the head of the Waimakariri and find a way down the Rolleston River to the Otira-Arthur's Pass Road. Pascoe and Sweney were keen:

> No one had crossed the col before, but we believed it to be a reasonable route. At 3 p.m. we crossed the col and descended to the snow wilderness below. Following a minute stream we had difficulty in a minor gorge, and using crampons had to climb up through a tunnel of rock with an ice floor. Darkness fell as we entered the bush. A chill winter moon lit up the sombre gorgeline ahead. There was no time to fossick for a possible route in the steep bush. We put our faith in the river. It was running low. At one place the main stream cascaded over a boulder into a pool. We roped down the rock, waded the pool navel deep, and shivered round the bluffs. At 9 p.m. we reached the Otira railway line. Our train was due to leave Arthur's Pass at 5 a.m. We walked through the five miles of the Otira tunnel. Very sleepily we emerged at Arthur's Pass at 1 a.m. The twenty-six hours of continuous travelling had given us every variety of ice, rock, gorge and river work.[26]

When summer returned, Pascoe planned to go back to the Garden of Eden. Whether Joan was invited is not known, but it was unlikely given the CMC's staunch refusal to include women. Neither Priestley Thomson nor Gavin Malcolmson, veterans of the past three summer trips with John, was

The *Arethusa Icefall* from the Icefall Outlook.

JOHN PASCOE COLLECTION,
ALEXANDER TURNBULL LIBRARY

available, so Pascoe had to find new companions. Merle Sweney was an obvious choice, as they had been climbing together for much of the previous year. As always, the CMC was a reservoir of keen adventurers and provided Hector McDowall and Arthur Pearson to make up a party of four – the minimum needed for safety on such a trip.

'While other friends in the club were girding their loins for objectives such as stalwart Cook and D'Archaic', Pascoe intended 'to return over the key "Angel" Col to the Adams country.' [27] During the year he had done considerable research and, as he told *The Press*, through 'information gleaned from authoritative Lands Department sources, mountaineering journals, mining, and other records it appeared definite that the Adams headwaters were literally unvisited. Even Charles Douglas, the great West Coast explorer, had not penetrated the valley.' [28]

Setting off on Christmas Eve, the four followed Pascoe's route of the previous summer to the Garden of Eden and Angel Col. Here they camped on a promontory overlooking the Adams Glacier which they named Icefall Outlook. From their eyrie, they looked down on the icefalls that fed the glacier and named them the Arethusa and Beelzebub.

Next morning they rose early to attempt the first ascent of Mount Kensington, the highest unclimbed peak in the vicinity. But hopes of views from its summit, which would give them the opportunity to clarify the complex country to the west, were frustrated by mist. Despite the poor visibility and a rising nor'wester, the quartet also climbed Mount Hulka – another first ascent. Despite having 23 virgin climbs to his credit, Pascoe was pleased to stand once again on a previously unclimbed peak. Hector McDowall was experiencing this pleasure for the first time:

Arthur Pearson contemplates the Beelzebub Icefall from the Icefall Outlook campsite.

JOHN PASCOE COLLECTION,
ALEXANDER TURNBULL LIBRARY

John Pascoe (pictured, leading) did not usually enjoy rock climbing — he was more confident on snow and ice — but he relished the final approach to Mount Hulka. After leaving the low peak they found 'a delectable surprise in the shape of 180 feet of sensational, steep and super-firm rock comprising the true top of our objective'.

JOHN PASCOE COLLECTION, ALEXANDER TURNBULL LIBRARY

A growing interest in documentary photography is apparent in these portraits which John Pascoe took in January 1936, at the end of the Adams Valley trip.

From left to right: John Pascoe, Merle Sweney, Arthur Pearson and Hector McDowall.

JOHN PASCOE COLLECTION, ALEXANDER TURNBULL LIBRARY

Politely we asked Hec to stand on the summit splinter as it was his first virgin peak. Hec leapt to the narrow rock and Arthur noted a movement in the peak. On the descent we noticed the top splinter was split and could actually have been pushed over. If Hec had gone over, with us roped, how curious to relief parties we would have looked, festooned from the gibbet-like needle.[29]

The following day it rained. Pascoe's trip diary, later worked into an article for the *Canterbury Mountaineer*, described their Sunday in a way that suggested he was exploring both new territory and new writing styles:

> SUNDAY 29th DECEMBER — Apparently the Satyr nor'west whipped the Daughter of Dawn to a torrent of tears, or it rained, or something. Anyway the empty billy left out overnight had collected 6 inches of water. The low tent pitch kept us safe, and we could not growl at not having the weather in hand, because when we had seen a 'hog's back' (storm cloud) the day before we had not grabbed it by the tail. The storm blew itself out and in the evening we were released from the bondage of the tent to sit outside and cook listening to Hec's droll humour, Arthur's wit and Merle's wisdom.[30]

From their high camp, the explorers descended the Adams Glacier to reach alluring river flats. 'For two miles the Adams flats are half-a-mile wide and sweep with the serenity of golden corn, under the shadow of Speculation Hill. Flowers, bell-birds, avalanches, keas, cliffs and unruffled space blend with peace and contentment,' wrote Pascoe. Immediately below the flats, however, lay a gorge none of them liked the look of. Pascoe's literary aspirations, particularly his fondness for classical allusions, were apparent in his later description:

> In this gorge, which we named Eblis, the river is chocked with giant boulders and the fall is terrific. Above, the bush appears to interlock the sky, and below is chaos as of *Paradise Lost*, noise, and a series of obstacles to human progress. I should explain that Eblis was a monarch of spirits of evil. Refusing to worship Adam he lost his high estate as an angel of light. Vathek wrote in 1784 Eblis was 'tarnished by malignant vapours' and caused the 'powers of the abyss to tremble'.[31]

Assessing Eblis as impassable, Pascoe persuaded his companions to climb over Speculation Hill. Beyond it the terrain was difficult, but with no alternative available the quartet struggled on through dense scrub, across steep hillsides and down narrow gorges towards the coast. For Canterbury climbers

used to walking through open beech forest and on the shingle flats of wide river valleys, the West Coast bush was a punishing experience.

A year earlier Pascoe's party had endured persistent rain; they now faced a lack of water. At one stage, the group went 36 hours without a drink, including a thirsty night perched high above Hot Springs Creek:

> At dusk we camped on an earth hollow scooped out of the hillside. The aneroid showed 2900 feet – 1500 feet above the gorge. No water available as there were no creek gulches. The corrugations in the canyon side were not holding running water, a quaint welcome from the West Coast. We could have taken Dr Teichelmann's advice and squeezed handfuls of earth and moss to a semblance of black coffee. Instead of this we dined off bacon and supped from a weird mixture of raw rolled oats, butter and brown sugar.[32]

After 12 days they were relieved to arrive on the West Coast, but at Hari Hari their high spirits were flattened by news of the death of Max Townsend, a friend and fellow CMC member, drowned in the Rakaia. Once again Pascoe stayed on the Coast and visited Dr Teichelmann to discuss early Westland exploration. On his return to Christchurch via Arthur's Pass, he climbed Rolleston (his eighth ascent) 'for exercise and as a prelude to work the following morning'.

With his exploration of the Adams Glacier-Garden of Eden area accomplished, Pascoe as usual wrote an account for the *Canterbury Mountaineer*. In the past his articles had had touches of humour and the occasional literary allusion; now he pushed this style to the limit with numerous excerpts from a variety of cultures: Irish fairytales, poetry by Whitman and Shelley, and Greek mythology.[33] The description revealed, for those who had the patience to read it to the end, rather more about his literary aspirations than the territory traversed.

Soon after finishing his florid account for climbing colleagues, he began to write a more prosaic version, perhaps at the suggestion of Joan Singleton, for the *Journal* of the Royal Geographical Society. It was indicative of Pascoe's remarkable self-confidence that he submitted this article to such a prestigious publication. At the same time he applied for membership of the society and was accepted. But being entitled to write FRGS after his name did not come cheaply – the £5 entrance fee and the £3 annual subscription added up to a princely sum.[34]

At the same time Pascoe sought to secure the names he and his companions had given to features of the Garden of Eden and the Adams Glacier. A map showing them was made and sent to the Geographic Board of New Zealand for formal approval, but the board was not impressed. Its members, including the experienced explorer, A. P. Harper, who had sometimes accompanied Charlie Douglas, accepted several but rejected all the biblical ones. Pascoe defended their choice of names, arguing that Milton had combined biblical and classical allusions in *Paradise Lost*. Not surprisingly, his advocacy had little effect. But, as he later explained:

> Because our map was the only one for a few years, and my report was published in the *Canterbury Mountaineer*, *Unclimbed New Zealand* and the *Journal* of the Royal Geographic Society, and one of my friends wrote a long account of the

A climber approaches the top of the Wee Macgregor Glacier en route to the Garden of Eden, while the early morning sun lights up the John Pascoe Ridge in the distance.

SHAUN BARNETT, BLACK ROBIN PHOTOGRAPHY

trip for the New Zealand Alpine Club, our names caught the imagination of the men who followed us, who adopted them without question, thus our rejected names became firmly established with local usage, as it were, and persist to this day.[35]

Some years later, Pascoe received personal recognition as an explorer when the line of peaks that separates the Garden of Eden from the Garden of Allah was officially named the John Pascoe Ridge.

It is not clear who followed Pascoe's example by naming the Garden of Allah and Satan's Saddle as counterpoints to Angel Col and the Garden of Eden, or even when the northernmost plateau was first explored, but it must have been soon after Pascoe's trips because these new names were in use by 1940.[36] It is curious that Pascoe did not return for a third time, to explore the Garden of Allah, as he and his parties had seen it in the distance from their Icefall Outlook campsite. Perhaps, after successive summers of exploration with the daunting difficulty of finding a route down Westland rivers to the coast, he had satisfied his urge to explore – at least for a while. Also their ascents of Mount Kensington and Hulka had reminded Pascoe that the mountains offered other challenges. It was now two years since his last really difficult climb when he made the first ascent of Mount Evans. He had climbed in the outer ranges and at Arthur's Pass, but his main focus had been on exploration. The final pitches on Mount Hulka, in particular, seem to have reawakened his interest in climbing. His plans for the summer of 1936 certainly suggest this, as he had quite a different prospect in mind: climbing at Mount Cook.

A few years earlier this would have been unthinkable. In the early 1930s John Pascoe was the most vehement advocate of guideless climbing and never missed a chance to criticise those who were assisted by guides. In particular, he persistently portrayed climbing in the Mount Cook region in pejorative terms. As late as 1935 he was still suggesting that a tough Canterbury peak climbed without a guide was as demanding as the higher peaks to the south. In September of that year, he had written an article for the Victoria League's *Monthly Notes* in which he reiterated this view:

> It is a fact that the young men of Canterbury seek the adventurous expeditions into the comparatively unknown ranges rather than climb, with guides, the more spectacular peaks further south. The camps have not been stocked with cakes nor the streams flavoured with ale; and in many instances sudden storms have robbed parties of deserved objectives. Yet the joys of struggle have been so attractive that a peak snatched after trouble with floods in the low levels, and gained after trials with difficult conditions in the high levels, is as valued as a row of ten-thousanders.[37]

By 1936, however, it was apparent, even to John Pascoe, that his dismissive view was out of step with other climbers' aspirations. As early as 1932, Boney Chester had forsaken a second attempt at Mount Evans to reconnoitre an alpine route from the Rakaia to the Hermitage. He was followed in the next few years by other CMC members who made a number of successful climbs of the high peaks, some with the help of guides. By the mid-1930s a new, younger group of climbers in the CMC was tentatively considering climbing overseas.[38] Clearly, Pascoe's adherence to his oft-stated view meant he was in danger of being left behind. If he had not climbed some of New Zealand's higher peaks, he could hardly expect to be invited to join a Himalayan expedition.

Also, experience showed that guides and amateur climbers could amicably share peaks. The two groups got on well and the only cause of tension was accommodation, especially the sharing of mountain huts. The Hermitage was a tourist hotel with traditional standards of dress that all guests – including climbers – were expected to observe. Some of the amateur climbers found the Hermitage expensive and too formal and would have preferred plainer accommodation, but the only alternative was the small Sealy cottage which was often full, and the only restaurant was at the Hermitage.[39]

Unless they were prepared to camp on snow and ice, climbers in the mountains had little choice but to stay in the existing huts, most of which were maintained by the Mount Cook Company. Amateur climbers were made welcome so long as they recognised that the guides and their guests had priority. Harry Ayres worked as a guide at Mount Cook in the late 1930s, and his biography shows that the guides:

This sign in the Tasman Valley at Mount Cook shows why John Pascoe objected to the pervasive presence of the Mount Cook Company which, because it leased the Hermitage, acted as if it owned the area.

JOHN PASCOE COLLECTION, ALEXANDER TURNBULL LIBRARY

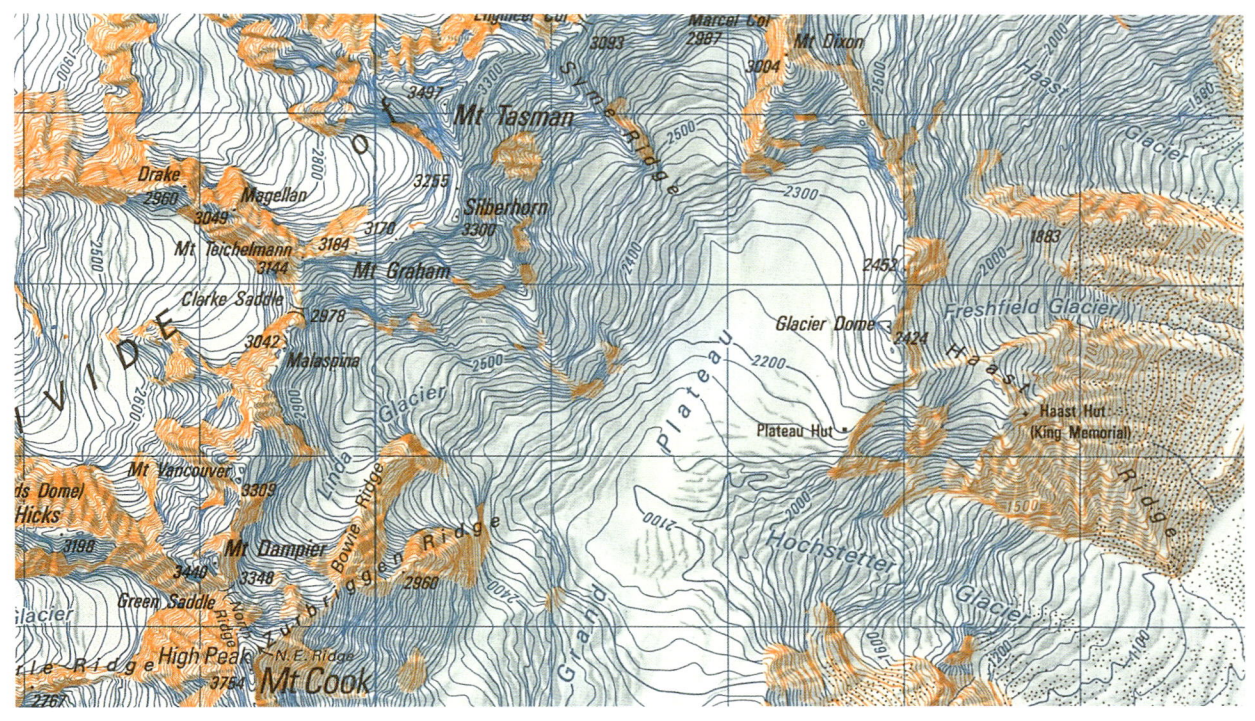

LAND INFORMATION NEW ZEALAND
(NZMS 260 SERIES – 1KM GRID)

… had no hard feelings about these young climbers, at least while their numbers were small. The problems between the two groups arose not over climbing but over the use of huts. The huts were all owned by Mount Cook and were in excellent condition and always well stocked with food. When a guide left a hut it was with the expectation that he or one of the other guides would be the next to use it. But as the number of amateur climbers increased the huts became overrun and problems arose when amateurs and guided parties arrived at the same huts.[40]

In October 1936, Pascoe wrote to Ian Powell: 'At Xmas I am alping, I hope, with David Hall of Wellington and hope to do something stupid from Haast Hut'.[41] Powell was familiar with Mount Cook and his example was probably another factor in Pascoe's decision to climb there. In 1934 Powell had climbed Mount Cook with Bert Mabin from the Haast Hut in the record time of 11 hours and 5 minutes — a feat that was not bettered for many years.[42] Climbing Cook was not, however, an option for Pascoe because of public perceptions about the peak. Five years earlier, in his article 'Climbers and Guides — A Plea for the Amateur', he had written: 'Every man of the mountains will know the question: "Have you climbed Mount Cook?" If you haven't, well, you haven't climbed. So thinks the public.'[43] Pascoe and Hall chose, instead, to climb Mount Tasman which, although 300 metres lower than Cook, was considered to be the more difficult. It still is. The Alpine Club's centennial publication *Great Peaks of New Zealand* rates Tasman as 'the mountaineer's mountain'.[44] Pascoe and Hall were joined by a third climber, Duncan Hall (no relation), who had been with John Pascoe on his first visit to the Garden of Eden.

The trip did not begin well. At the Hermitage, Pascoe failed to dress for dinner, as Tom Newth, another CMC member, later explained:

> Dinner in those days was a dress affair with gowned ladies and tuxedoed escorts. We managed sports coats and ties. Johnny presented himself in a khaki shirt and trousers tucked into red socks. A bandana around his neck completed the outfit. Dinner passed safely, but at coffee and liqueurs afterwards in the lounge the manager approached Johnny:
> 'Haven't you got any clothes, Pascoe?'
> Johnny: 'Yes, I'm wearing them.'
> Manager: 'Lounge clothes, Pascoe.'
> Johnny: 'I'm here to climb mountains, not to be a lounge lizard.'
> Manager: 'Very well, Pascoe, kindly leave the lounge.'

Pascoe left. Next morning he had breakfast in the staff dining room, before joining a large CMC group heading for the Haast Hut.[45]

When they arrived, guide Mick Bowie and his client H. K. Douglas of Wellington were already in residence, preparing to climb Tasman the next day. So were Pascoe and the two Halls. Bowie and Douglas planned to take the usual route up the Silberhorn Ridge to Tasman, which was a problem for Pascoe who would not consider walking in a guide's footsteps. Instead, his party chose to attempt Tasman by another route, climbed for the first time by the Taranaki ice specialist, Rod Syme, and Dan Bryant in 1931.[46] On Boxing Day both parties set off early. The extremely steep angle of Syme Ridge meant Pascoe and his companions had to cut steps in the ice all the way up. By late morning they were within 100 metres of Tasman's summit ridge, but as the slope ahead looked inclined to avalanche, they decided to cut across the east face. Had they continued to follow Syme's route, they would almost certainly have made the top but, as Pascoe recalled later, 'we thought it would be cunning to work a diagonal course up the steep east face and sneak up under a cornice to the summit ridge'.[47]

Did they feel it necessary to pioneer a new route to prove the mettle of guideless climbers? Whatever the reason, their planned shortcut was a radical departure from the usual approach of New Zealand mountaineers at that time.[48] Peaks were climbed by ridges, not up faces, which were simply too steep and too dangerous. In Europe, however, some face-climbing had recently been attempted.

Their attempt to traverse the upper east face of Tasman was not a success. The trio made slow progress and were continually forced to detour round crevasses and huge blocks of ice. Eventually they reached a point where it was evident that they could not reach the summit because it was cut off by long crevasses stretching across the face of the peak. Nor could they climb down, but they could at least travel sideways to join the summit ridge. Tiredness may have affected their judgement for, once again, they made a strange decision. In *Unclimbed New Zealand* Pascoe explained why they chose to descend the icefall that spills down the east face:

> We could have retraced our steps and completed the Syme line of ascent, but it was about 2 p.m., and we had been told that a night out on Tasman would not be moral. Descent of our route on Syme's ridge didn't attract us, nor did we want to cut across the east face and use Bowie's steps on the Silberhorn, though it would be feasible.[49]

David Hall had made a similar descent in the Swiss Alps. On that occasion he had been lucky to escape injury when he and his companions had glissaded down an icefall only to end up in an avalanche triggered by their descent.[50]

Tasman was tougher and higher than the Swiss mountain. The trio were weary, out of their depth and in real danger. Pascoe knew it: 'It was exposed and steep. The packing up the ridge the day before [to Haast Hut] had rather taken the edge off our energy, and we had rather a listless spell on the lower lip of a crevasse when we had a bit of food. I was sick.' What he did not mention was that one of them fell, but was saved by the rope. In arresting the fall David Hall wrenched his shoulder. Priestley Thomson and Tom Newth were about 2 kilometres away on Glacier Dome, watching Pascoe and the Halls' descent. Both were, in Thomson's words, 'shocked speechless'.[51] Later Newth wrote of seeing 'three horizontal dots suddenly become three vertical dots. "Did you see that?" said Priestley to me. I was holding my breath so hard I could only nod. They descended straight down the face.'[52]

The trio spent the next few days recovering at Haast Hut. David Hall's injury did not improve, so he left for home. In the meantime, Newth and Thomson climbed Mount Cook, and Pascoe and

Mount Tasman from Glacier Dome.

Pascoe and the Halls' route followed the Syme Ridge (far right), then across the upper east face to the 'schrunds that beat us'. The trio then made their dangerous descent down the east face through the icefall to the Grand Plateau.

TOM NEWTH PHOTO, JOHN PASCOE COLLECTION, ALEXANDER TURNBULL LIBRARY

The schrunds beneath the summit ridge of Mount Tasman which prevented Pascoe and the Halls climbing any higher on their first attempt.

JOHN PASCOE COLLECTION, ALEXANDER TURNBULL LIBRARY

Duncan Hall, John Pascoe and David Hall at Haast Hut after their demanding descent of the east face of Mount Tasman.

JOHN PASCOE COLLECTION,
ALEXANDER TURNBULL LIBRARY

Duncan Hall still had hopes of another attempt on Tasman, but had to wait for the weather to improve. When they did finally set out again on 2 January, they were accompanied by Tom Newth.

This time they intended to follow the standard route up the Silberhorn Ridge, since there were no guides present. But, as Pascoe and his companions soon discovered, even this approach was not easy to follow. Ironically, the services of a guide would have been helpful. Pascoe later described the difficulties:

> The step cutting on the Silberhorn Ridge had been hard work, and as we left the ridge to steer a diagonal course past the deep crevasses ahead Duncan Hall took over the work from me. We were so intent on avoiding a line of séracs [pillars of ice] we missed Mick Bowie's route to the Silberhorn summit, and

Duncan Hall and John Pascoe spent a week in Haast Hut waiting for the weather to improve so they could have another go at Mount Tasman. Pascoe later recalled: 'The time passed pleasantly enough in the stormy weather. Cooking grand feeds is always good fun for hungry men. We varied this with long short-story sessions of varying virtue. We watched three of our friends put into practice their shaving doctrines; the rest of us cherished grubby whiskers of different hues. The architect, the carpenter, the forester and the sharebroker gave us a diligent debate on the ramifications of forest ventures from all angles.'

Left to right: Jack Hayes, Andy Anderson, John Pascoe and Duncan Hall.

JOHN PASCOE COLLECTION,
ALEXANDER TURNBULL LIBRARY

The southern and eastern slopes of the Silberhorn and the east face of Mount Tasman (centre) showing the routes of Pascoe's two attempts to reach the summit. On the right, the ascent on Boxing Day: up the Syme Ridge, then across and down the east face.

On the left, the attempt a week later: up the Silberhorn Ridge, across to Clarke Saddle, then a night on the upper Linda Glacier (X).

D. THEOMIN PHOTO, JOHN PASCOE COLLECTION, ALEXANDER TURNBULL LIBRARY

began a lot of up-and-down steep face work. Each time we attempted to gain the divide a cornice cut us off, and we found our course had veered along the southern slopes of the divide till we were half-way between the Silberhorn and Mt Teichelmann. Ruefully we smoked pipes and noticed a sheath of cloud envelope the summit of Mt Cook.[53]

By now they were on the wrong side of the Silberhorn and each step took them further away from Tasman. By the time they reached the Main Divide it was noon, cloud had come down and a strong nor'westerly wind made conditions unpleasant. Any thoughts of Tasman had to be abandoned. The challenge now was to find a way down. Rain and snow began to fall when suddenly three figures appeared out of the murk. Pascoe's party were greeted by their fellow climbers at Haast Hut, Chris Johnson, Eric Miller and Arch Scott, who had just completed a traverse of Mount Teichelmann and now found themselves in the same predicament. 'They said they'd burnt their boats, and we explained we'd sunk a whole fleet,' recalled Pascoe, as the two groups conferred and agreed that their most likely route to safety lay down the Linda Glacier on the north face of Mount Cook.

To reach it, the combined group had to climb to the top of Teichelmann, descend to Clarke Saddle, then cautiously traverse across steep ice slopes to reach the glacier. As they came to the saddle, Miller slipped. Arch Scott anchored the rope and stopped his fall, but the accident delayed them. 'Our descent from the Clarke Saddle was painfully slow; it was a tortoiselike race against a benightment,' wrote Pascoe. Luckily the high summer daylight lasted until 10 p.m., but an hour later all six were 'still floundering in an area of deep holes which overlooks the upper Linda Glacier'. When Tom Newth, who was leading, twice fell into crevasses, it was obvious they could not continue. Newth found a small ice cave which he shared with Scott and Johnson, while Pascoe, Hall and Miller stamped out a ledge in the snow on the edge of an adjacent crevasse.

Ropes were fed from Pascoe's party to those in the ice cave to stop them if they fell from their perch. He later wrote of that long, cold night: 'We sat shivering like Brave British Boys and snivelled to ourselves while the storm swirled snow'. When dawn finally came their limbs were numb – 'legs leaden and lifeless, feet swollen without sensation'. In the light of the new day, their decision to stop there was vindicated for just 10 metres below them was an immense crevasse, into which they might all have fallen. They had to climb up to avoid it, and the work restored circulation. Daylight made their descent easier and faster than the night before, and they soon reached the Grand Plateau. Here they were met by Priestley Thomson and other climbers from Haast Hut who had come to look for them.

Pascoe made light of the experience, calling it the 'Teichelmann Nocturne', but to Tom Newth 'it could easily have been the Teichelmann disaster'.[54] There was, however, a positive aspect to their night out. In the past, Arch Scott and John Pascoe had disliked each other: Pascoe thought Scott a snob and Scott, in turn, disapproved of Pascoe for his criticism of guided climbers and had been irritated by his provocative behaviour at the Hermitage. But after their benightment on the Linda Glacier they became friends, and remained so for the rest of their lives.[55]

Tasman defined Pascoe's ability as a climber. Tom Newth thought that 'Johnny could not adjust to the scale of the high alps'.[56] The episode also suggested that Pascoe and the Halls were victims of his determination to avoid any association with guides. Other climbers were more flexible: some took advice from guides; others, including Arch Scott, had climbed with them. But Pascoe was so determined to prove himself as an independent climber that his party took unnecessary risks.

Back in Christchurch, Pascoe reassessed his future as a mountaineer. If he was not likely to achieve distinction among the high peaks, the Tasman episode did at least clarify what he had already achieved elsewhere. Among the unclimbed mountains of Canterbury and Westland his knowledge, rather than advanced climbing ability, had been crucial, but at Mount Cook there was no need for an 'intelligence officer'. The mountains were familiar and it was the guides – not Pascoe – who had the specialist knowledge of the terrain. Realising now that the first ascent of Mount Evans was likely to be the zenith of his climbing career, Pascoe wrote a number of articles about it. If Tasman indicated he would never become a top mountaineer, the flurry of features he wrote for magazines in early 1937 showed that his literary inventiveness and flair for publicity were without equal. Several years earlier, while writing for *The Press Junior*, he had developed a talent for writing about alpine themes, and he now polished this in articles published in New Zealand and England.

'Memorable Nights above the Snowline' appeared in one of the first few issues of *The Monocle*, a stylish new local magazine established in 1937 to

Mount Cook and the Linda Glacier, photographed from the Silberhorn Ridge during the second attempt on Tasman before the weather deteriorated.

JOHN PASCOE COLLECTION,
ALEXANDER TURNBULL LIBRARY

TEICHELMANN – NOCTURNE OR DISASTER?

Pascoe's account of this adventure was written soon afterwards.
Tom Newth's version, printed below, recalls these events almost 60 years later:

John invited me to join his rope because he favoured the safety of a three man rope. I gladly accepted. He had great confidence in Duncan Hall as anchor man, so I was for the middle of the rope.

We left in good conditions for Silberhorn with Tasman via the 'Horn ridge as our ultimate objective. It was plain cramponing through to, and up the lower section of the Silberhorn ridge. It steepened a little but was still comfortable for crampons. John decided to start step cutting. He cut one rope length and gave it up as too hard. We changed places on the rope. I suggested we push on with crampons. After about 100 feet John asked me to cut steps as he felt insecure. A further 100 feet up we left the ridge to follow Bowie's route which avoided the very steep hard ice prevailing on the top 600 feet of Silberhorn. I felt sure we had left the ridge a few feet too soon. This later proved correct as a big crevasse forced us to traverse much too far across the slope.

Time was lost and it was midday when we topped out on the divide. It began to snow and it was obvious Tasman was out but Silberhorn was only 10 minutes away. Out of the mist Arch Scott's party appeared, they had climbed Teichelmann and were proceeding towards Silberhorn with the intention of descending using our route of ascent. John and Arch had a 5 minute discussion and a decision was made to get down to safer levels using Archie's line of ascent via Clarke Saddle. On reflection this decision was the wrong one. Our line of ascent was right at hand, it was sheltered from the nor'west and was much shorter.

We walked along the easy ridge over a snow bump that a month later was to be called Mount Graham. As we approached Mount Teichelmann Scott's party who had already climbed it sidled around to avoid a small rock section. We only had about 200 feet to go to grab Teichelmann and after missing Silberhorn I decided that for the effort already expended, Teichelmann would only take a few minutes and was not to be missed. I quickly climbed a rope length up moderate rock – when the rope tightened I looked for John. He called to me 'Where is Arch?' I replied 'Out of sight around the corner'. John said 'OK boy pull.' I pulled and kept pulling until John was alongside me. John said 'Sorry boy, I am a bloody fool on rock'. I was surprised but said 'No sweat, come on'. Another rope length and we were on top. We

traversed on and down, and in a few minutes overtook Archie's party. Eric Miller was their anchor man and when I came within a few feet of him I quickly saw he was spreadeagled in an icy shute and in difficulty. Arch was a rope length below looking up. At that moment Eric gave a small groan and shot off. I yelled 'belay' to Arch, who got his axe in just in time as Eric slid a double rope length and hit the end with a hell of a jolt. He managed to get on his feet after a while but was badly shaken. Because of this, progress from then on became pitifully slow. We were, of course, obliged to stay with them and I feel sure had I taken the lead at this point we may just have got into the Linda before dark and followed Frank Gillett's trail down to the plateau and on to the hut. We carried on and daylight deserted us. Arch asked us to take the lead as his party had 'had it'. I asked him 'Is this where you came up?' He said: 'No, we were hundreds of yards further to the left'. I was plainly shocked and replied 'then what the bloody hell are we doing here?' I quickly repented, apologised and said 'Let's go'. The situation became very awkward. The snowfall had built up to about 4 inches over the frozen slopes. Crampons balled up at every step. John did not have the weight to stamp through the snow cover to get the crampons to bite in the frozen surface below. He went off his feet several times. Duncan Hall did a tremendous job of fielding him time after time. It was so dark one could not see one's companions on the rope and we were dependent on voice contact. I tried to sidle out onto the Upper Linda and made some progress until I broke through a crevasse – fortunately small. I brought John and Duncan over. Carried on about 100 yards and sensed I was on a convex slope – this meant big 'mines'. I prodded every step ahead with my axe – even so I broke through again up to my armpits. I felt all around with my feet, I just trod air – it was a big one. With a lot of effort I got out on my back. I called a halt, and we waited for the Scott party to catch up. My opinion was further movement was not justified. I thought some shelter could be found by backtracking to where I had broken through the first time. We did this. I worked hard with my big axe to enlarge the hole enough to make room for three. At this stage while I was mining below the surface John, Duncan and Eric stamped out a platform and sat down on it. They told me to cease chopping holes in the mountain, they would be OK.[57]

emulate the success of *Life* magazine overseas. It began with a spirited defence of the occasional night out which, wrote Pascoe, was 'not the scandalous or sensational choice of naughty boys that it is often made out to be'. He then catalogued a number of famous benightments including his own experience on Red Lion Col, but made no mention of his long cold night on the edge of a crevasse on the Linda Glacier only a few months earlier. At the same time an account of alpine rescues entitled 'Relief Expeditions in the Mountains', with the byline 'Written and Illustrated by John Pascoe FRGS', was published in the *New Zealand Railways Magazine*, the equivalent of today's airline magazines.[58] Both articles included photos of the first ascent of Evans and references to it in the text. Railway passengers learnt, for instance, of the successful climbers' anxious night on the Bracken Snowfield, lost in a blizzard, while *The Monocle's* columns included his now familiar assertion that Mount Evans was in the same league as Mount Cook.

Later in the year, the English journal *Tobacco* featured John's 'Tobacco in the Mountains', an account of the contentment it had given him and others in the outdoors.

> To those who cherish a glowing pipe, the tang of tobacco reeks well in camp, of calm or of storm. From personal experiences, any New Zealand mountaineer whose briar is as indispensable to him as the shaft of his ice-axe, may recall the pleasant hours when tobacco smoke was merged into the luxurious image of a perfect view or set in relief against the savage banners of a nor'west cloud bank.[59]

Again, the text was illustrated with his photos.

Undoubtedly his greatest coup, however, was the appearance of 'First Ascent of Mount Evans, Southern Alps of New Zealand' in a most unlikely publication: the 1937 special Christmas edition of *Blue Peter*, an English magazine specialising in 'dramatic stories of the seven seas'. Sandwiched between descriptions of the Submarine Service, harbours of interest and notable master mariners was Pascoe's detailed account of the ascent of Evans, accompanied by nine generously reproduced photos.[60] Whether readers were surprised by the incongruous inclusion is not known, but Pascoe's confidence and initiative were well rewarded. He received £11 for the *Blue Peter* article, the equivalent of one month's salary.[61]

The money was useful, but these published articles were worth far more to Pascoe because they also gave him hope of a new career. By 1937 it was obvious he would never be a lawyer. It was three years since he had passed an exam and in the nine years he had been studying law he had failed all but six papers.[62] Even if he had passed the necessary exams, his speech impediment would have made life as a lawyer difficult. Clearly, he could not contemplate court work, and even as a solicitor his stutter would not help him win the confidence of his clients. With friends and family he stuttered only occasionally, but when he was nervous or in formal situations it became more frequent. Paul Pascoe, on the other hand, had succeeded in managing his stammer to the extent that he could disguise it as a thoughtful pause, and this had made it easier for him to succeed as an architect.[63] Also during the Depression the harsh measures lawyers sometimes had to mete

Pascoe was delighted that his article about the first ascent of Mount Evans was published in Blue Peter, especially since it had been turned down elsewhere — or, as Pascoe put it in a letter to his mother, 'had received raspberries internationally as it were. I think it has been rejected in Canada, Aussie and England.'

RAY CHAPMAN COLLECTION

out disturbed John. Later, looking back, he had no regrets leaving the profession he described as 'a bunch of pox doctors'.[64]

Instead he decided to apply for a job with the government, hoping to write guidebooks about the mountains and tourist resorts. J. H. Upham, senior partner of the law firm that had employed him since he left school, was sad to see him leave, but thought it would be for the best: 'He has worked under me for many years and I have received most valuable assistance from him, in fact if it were not that I feel that he is probably entering into a larger sphere of duties, and may in such way be of valuable service to the Public, I should be much more unhappy at his leaving the firm'.[65]

Others were equally positive. The editor of *The Press*, Hugo Freeth, wrote in his testimonial: 'Mr Pascoe has the rare capacity for remembering what he has seen and for writing about it accurately, clearly and with fine descriptive style'. Professor H. G. Denham, the acting rector of Canterbury University College, also endorsed his ambition to write guidebooks, as did C. G. Ellis, a former Chief Draughtsman of the Lands and Survey Department in Canterbury, who noted: 'He has many virgin ascents to his credit and his work, be it climbing or reconnaissance, preparation or writing, bears a thoroughness and an individuality which is unique'.[66]

His most original supporter, however, was H. E. Hart, the superintendent of the Lake Coleridge Power Station, who had come to know him well, as John was in the habit of calling in for a chat on his return from his many trips to nearby Mount Oakden, and the Matthias and Rakaia headwaters. The superintendent revealed that John Pascoe's knowledge of the Southern Alps had been crucial when deciding on the route for the trans-alpine transmission line: 'The Browning's Pass route was marked at the time, but Mr Pascoe's information regarding snow conditions, difficulties of patrol, etc led to this route being abandoned in favour of the Arthur's Pass route'.[67]

These testimonials were sent with his letter of enquiry to government departments. Clearly he was qualified to write about the mountains, but was there a need for such a writer? As it turned out, one department was interested in Pascoe, but not in the mountains. What it had in mind was, however, even more appealing and would extend and excite Pascoe just as much as the alps of Canterbury and Westland.

I owe it to you to tell you

conscription. If I was conscripted I'd

resist it to the extent of trying

... series of hide-outs I

... made a real attempt

... "Bush Rangers" for Ne...

being conscripted for such a secre... Home Defen...

Duff has influenced me; on

himself satisfied that conscrip...

& desirable (... dai...

& I call him a " bloody old

hatred of fighting for

self - preservation & I hope) -

do than get shot or sick in P...

problems never have to be faced. J

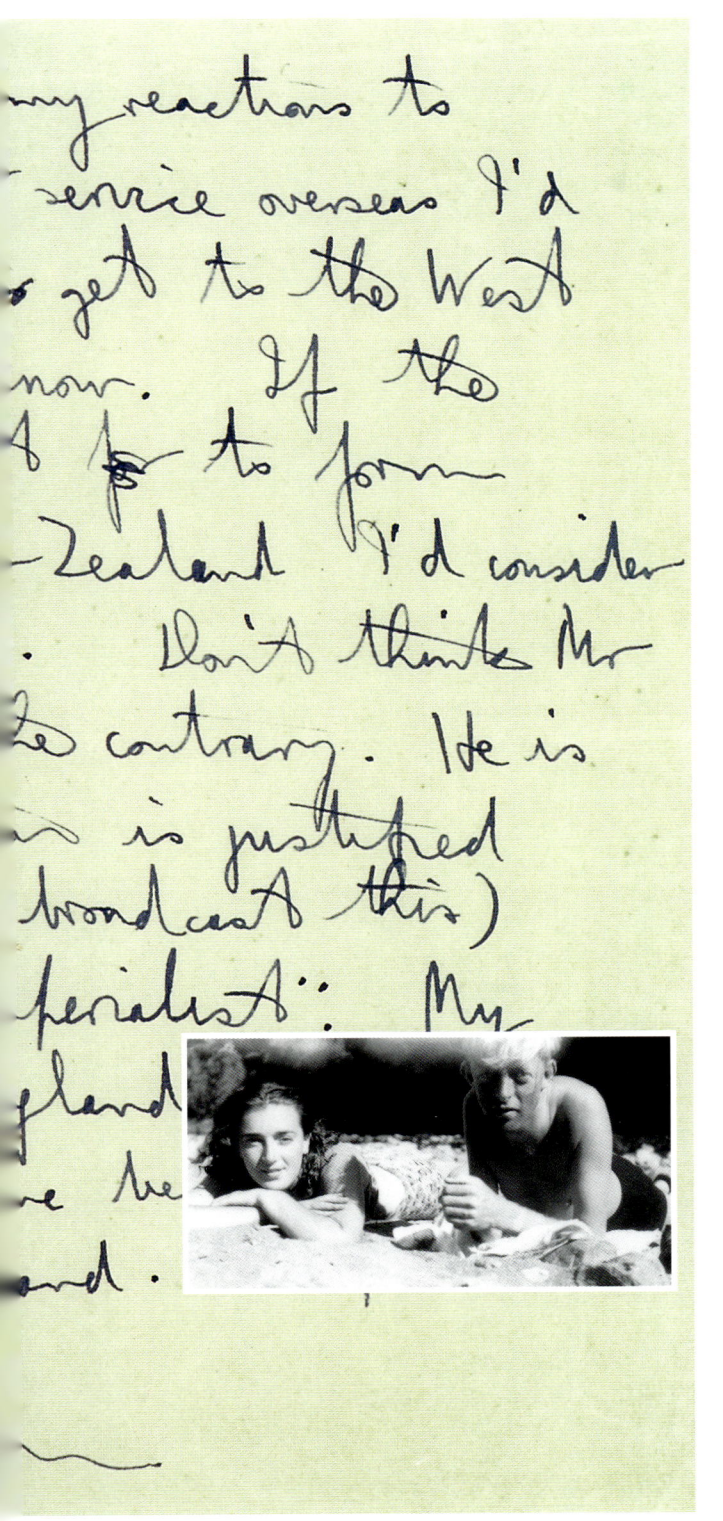

CHAPTER FOUR

Love and War

In 1937 John Pascoe moved to Wellington to work for the Department of Internal Affairs and soon became the illustrations editor for the centennial project Making New Zealand. He enjoyed regular contact with intellectuals such as Eric McCormick, John Beaglehole and Oliver Duff, later first editor of the Listener, with whom he shared a cottage in the bush at Days Bay. These people, Pascoe wrote, 'raised my standard of self-criticism, made me think and gave me objectives in scholarship of which I had barely dreamt'.

Later he also met Dorothy Harding, a left-wing idealist who shared his enthusiasm for the outdoor life. Together they explored Wellington's coastline and hills which, Pascoe was delighted to discover, offered many opportunities for exercise and 'salubing' in the sun. In 1940 they married. She was a pacifist and he had no interest in volunteering for active service overseas. In a letter (left) to his mother, he outlined his attitude to conscription.

At the same time Pascoe became involved in a controversy when some members of the New Zealand climbing fraternity took strong exception to his opinionated comments in The Mountains issue of the Making New Zealand series. Fortunately the outbreak of the Second World War meant that the furore was only briefly a public matter, but the bitter divisions it caused lingered for some years.

TOP LEFT: FRANK FITZGERALD COLLECTION
BOTTOM RIGHT: DOROTHY PASCOE COLLECTION

NO ONE LIKES TO BE REJECTED, and John Pascoe was no exception. He clearly remembered Mr Collett, the Tourist Depart ment's Assistant Manager, who invited Pascoe to come to Welling-ton in May 1937 for a job interview, then 'turned me down flat'. Two years later, when Pascoe's book *Unclimbed New Zealand* had just been published to widespread critical acclaim, Collett wrote to Pascoe asking him to present a copy to the Tourist Department's library. 'I replied all dignified but gave him the works properly,' he told his mother. Before he mailed his letter he showed it to the man who did give him a job, Joe Heenan, the Under-Secretary of Internal Affairs, who said 'Collett had a "bloody cheek" to ask for a free copy'. Pascoe also showed the letter to Oliver Duff, the editor of *Making New Zealand*, 'who compared my reply to Samuel Johnson's rebuke to Lord Chesterfield'.[1]

Nevertheless, Pascoe probably had reason to be grateful to Collett, for his rejection by the Tourist Department may have encouraged him to con-sider writing a book to enhance his employment prospects. Pascoe has left no record to indicate this was so, but he began to write *Unclimbed New Zealand* the same month he met Collett. There were other reasons too, for becom-ing an author. If he were eventually successful in getting a job in Wellington, it would mean leaving the mountains and climbing friends who had made the past decade so exciting. Looking back, he could see that it had been a crucial period in New Zealand's alpine history when the CMC, in particular, had made an important contribution to exploring the alpine regions of Can-terbury and Westland. Their exploits should be recorded, and he was the man to do it.

To anyone else the idea might have been daunting, but John Pascoe had already done a lot to publicise the club's activities. If he were to stitch some of his existing writings together and fill in the gaps, he could make a book. Better still, by adding his articles about Samuel Butler to the accounts of climb-ing and exploration, the proposed volume would also have an historical aspect. By day he continued with his legal work in Christchurch; at night he wrote. Notes in the margin of his manuscript book show that by the end of May 1937 he had written the first two chapters, which encouraged him to think he could also complete the remaining 20. With remarkable confidence he sent a synopsis of the book, with copies of several of his recent articles, not, as might have been expected, to a local publisher such as Whitcombe & Tombs (who published many New Zealand authors and were based in Christchurch), but to John Barclay, a literary agent in London.

John St Francis Barbe Barclay was English, but from 1916 to 1921 had attended Christ's College where he distinguished himself both as a scholar and a sportsman. In his final year he was a prefect, captain of the shooting team and a member of the first XV. The Pascoe twins began at Christ's in Barclay's last term and this slender connection was enough for Pascoe, 16 years later, to approach the Englishman about his book.

By 1937 Barclay was a rising star in the British literary firmament. After completing an MA at Canterbury College in Christchurch he had gone to Eng-land where he had a novel published, became editor of *The Columnist*, assistant editor of *Pearson's Weekly* and also worked as a literary agent for John Paradise. In his spare time he was a keen climber and adventurer who had explored parts of Bolivia, and had an understanding of New Zealand climbing.[2] His reply gave Pascoe hope:

> Dear Pascoe,
>
> I remember you and your brother very well, and I was very glad to get your letter.
>
> I am a keen Alpinist myself and I feel sure that we would be able to sell your proposed book on Alpine Travel and exploration in New Zealand, especially as no similar book has appeared for a long time.
>
> As an agent I am habitually pessimistic, but I think that you evidently know how to write and to take photographs, and you obviously know what you are writing about, and so I am inclined to be enthusiastic about your proposed manuscript. I think this should be not less than 80,000 words − longer, if possible − and profusely illustrated with your excellent photographs.
>
> I shall look forward to hearing from you about your book again, and needless to say am always interested to hear Christchurch and Christ's College news. Most New Zealanders with literary ambitions come to us, but few of their ambitions are realised, I am sorry to say. Donald Cowie and Ngaio Marsh are two notable exceptions, and I feel sure you are going to be a third.[3]

Fuelled by this encouragement, Pascoe's pen flew across the pages of his manuscript book and by July 1937 he had completed 18 chapters. Margin notes show that he sometimes wrote an entire chapter in a single evening.[4] Instalments of the first draft were sent for appraisal to his friend David Hall, then teaching in Wellington. Hall had been educated in New Zealand, then at Cambridge, and had climbed in New Zealand and Europe. Pascoe considered him ideal for the job and told Barclay: 'his constructive criticism is very useful both in presentment of material and questions of grammar and style. Being a New Zealander who has lived in England and climbed abroad he can help me hit the happy medium between colonial exuberance and gutless purism, more briefly, between impudence and dignity.'[5]

Meanwhile in Wellington, Eric McCormick, another New Zealander who had studied at Cambridge, was appointed Secretary of the National

Samuel Butler's homestead in the Rangitata Valley, drawn by Paul Pascoe at John's request for reproduction in his book.

John was so impressed by this drawing and another of Mungo Pass which was also included, that he asked Paul to design the cover: 'Looky here, young feller, a cover on these lines in black and white would suit "Ice Axe, New Zealand", down to the ground. If you feel in the mood, a combination and permutation of New Zealand, [Mounts] Evans, Cook or Torlesse, Pipe, Crampons (even a beer "Stein" or Handle), Boots, Ice Axe on a tent or sleeping bag would be swell.' Paul agreed and John was pleased with his design. Allen & Unwin were less impressed and chose instead to use one of John's photos for a simpler, more dramatic cover.

The first page of John Pascoe's manuscript 'Ice Axe' which he wrote between May and July 1937. Published two years later as Unclimbed New Zealand, it was virtually the same as the initial draft, with the exception of the opening sentence.

MANUSCRIPT AND ARCHIVES COLLECTION, ALEXANDER TURNBULL LIBRARY

Paul and Effie Pascoe, Hampstead Heath, 1936.

Two years earlier Paul had travelled to England to further his architectural studies and to meet his fiancée, Helen Ferrar, who had travelled ahead of him. Just before his departure, however, Helen broke off their engagement – by letter.

In London, he was employed first by Brian O'Rorke, an expatriate architect, then by the Architectural Press. This work, Paul wrote in his diary, brought him 'into direct contact with the leading architects in England'. In 1936 he joined the Tecton Group which he considered 'perhaps the most advanced of young modern architects in London'.

Working on some of the most innovative architectural projects in Britain was stimulating but stressful and he began to show signs of nervous exhaustion. His mother travelled to England and they returned together to New Zealand. Paul spent several months at Hanmer Hospital recovering from a nervous breakdown which he preferred to call a 'breakthrough'.

From then on he was careful not to become overtired. Each day he would leave work, lunch with his mother, then have a quick nap before returning to work; he also made a habit of going to bed early.

DOROTHY PASCOE COLLECTION

Centennial Historical Committee. Already Dominion Archivist, McCormick now had the additional job of planning a series of publications to mark the nation's first 100 years of European settlement. He realised that 'If the committee's aims – and the Government's – were to be achieved in a reasonable time, there was an urgent need for assistance. None was in sight, while the burden of secretarial work showed no sign of slackening.' In July 1937 when McCormick visited Christchurch, one of his tasks was

> to call on a man named Pascoe who was seeking a job in the department. When I did so I was touched by the applicant's eagerness and impressed by his accomplishments. He was working as a clerk in his late father's legal firm, not at all happily, for his interests lay elsewhere. He had just had a book, *Unclimbed New Zealand*, accepted by the English firm of Allen & Unwin – something I had yet to achieve. He was also an expert photographer, as a selection of his work demonstrated.[6]

This recollection, written years later, was coloured by hindsight. At the time, Pascoe's partially completed manuscript, then tentatively entitled 'Ice Axe', had yet to be seen by any publisher – let alone accepted – as Barclay wisely intended to wait until he had a finished typescript before hawking it around London. Barclay did not receive it until December 1937, five months after Pascoe and Eric McCormick met. Nevertheless, Pascoe's implication of imminent acceptance, based on Barclay's encouraging initial response, did the trick. On his return to Wellington, McCormick recommended that Pascoe be appointed his assistant. In August 1937 Pascoe moved to the capital to become the second member of the centennial publications team.[7]

It was a good time to leave Christchurch. For several years John had been the only one of his siblings living there and had shared the family's flat in Oxford Terrace with their mother. But as Paul had recently returned from England to resume work in Christchurch he would keep Effie company. A job in Wellington also gave John the opportunity to escape Christchurch society and the considerable influence of his mother, who was a redoubtable character, certain of her beliefs and her expectations of others. Even then, the connection was not entirely severed. He wrote to her each week and also sent her parcels of dirty clothes which she would wash and iron and send back to him.[8]

Within a few weeks of his arrival in Wellington, John was sure he had made the right decision. In a letter to Barclay he was enthusiastic about his new job:

> For the next three years I'll have a wonderfully interesting time. New Zealand have a Centennial or something in 1940. The Labour Government have organised a historical survey. Honorary provincial boards of academic distinction ferret out material which is collated by a central committee in Wellington. The Secretary actually has to do most of the work and take editorial responsibility. My job is to help the Secretary. I get better pay here than I did as a law clerk and although I've only been in Wellington for two weeks am finding it most varied and interesting. My work extends from research in archives to selection of pictorial matter with routine work such as correspondence thrown in. It will be a great education for writing as I don't specialise but have to delve into Maori lore, fish, forestry and God knows what unorthodox aspects of history. I'll have no time for writing articles for newspapers as I work most

nights in the week on the job. The Secretary is a bloke called McCormick and is a very efficient and able historian, and also is very good to work with.[9]

The idea of a historical survey came from Joe Heenan, Under-Secretary of Internal Affairs, who was charged with organising the commemoration of the centenary. Heenan's genial manner masked an iron will. As the friend and confidant of Peter Fraser, one of the most powerful figures in the first Labour government, Heenan enjoyed great influence which he used to further his particular projects. As early as 1936 he had set his sights on the 1940 centenary, and succeeded in outmanoeuvring a number of other aspirants to gain control of its planning. But it was not until the Director of the Council for Educational Research, Dr Clarence Beeby, showed him a series of illustrated publications called *Building America*, that Heenan found the format he wanted for a popular history of New Zealand's first European century. *Building America* was a series of magazine-style periodicals, each devoted to a particular subject, which could be collected and bound into volumes. Heenan resolved to produce a similar series on New Zealand, using the relatively new offset printing process which allowed text and illustrations to be presented on the same page. It was to be written in a clear, simple style with a range of illustrations to realise his vision of an accessible history that would reach a wide, general readership.[10]

On first meeting Pascoe, Heenan was not impressed. According to McCormick, he was 'put off by his unprepossessing appearance, his retreating chin and skimpy moustache, and his stutter (always at its worst in moments of stress)'. Within a few months, however, Heenan had revised his opinion, convinced by the South Islander's industry and enthusiasm.[11] To test Pascoe's research and writing skills he asked him to prepare an account of the purchase and early development of Auckland based on some of Governor William Hobson's recently discovered personal papers. Although Pascoe had never been to Auckland and was awed to be the first to use the new material, his account pleased Heenan, who was also finding Pascoe's skill as a photographer useful.[12] As John told his mother, 'Heenan has been getting all impressed with my photos lately. He wants me to take a colour one of a swell begonia tree (me degenerating to a plant photographer) and also to better a press photographer's view off Rona Bay of the harbour, so that he (Joe) can have a 100% Xmas card done for himself this year'.[13]

In February 1938 Pascoe was made illustrations editor for *Making New Zealand*, a position almost as important as the editor's, given the proposed pictorial emphasis. Soon after, Oliver Duff, an experienced journalist, was appointed editor.[14] Pascoe had already made an inventory of photos held by various government departments and he now supplemented this by creating a card index of illustrations held by the General Assembly Library and the Alexander Turnbull Library. This laborious job might have overwhelmed a less determined person; John Pascoe not only completed it but went further afield in his search for illustrations. As he later wrote:

> The searcher got greedy – wanted to see what else existed in New Zealand. So one by one the leading libraries, museums and private collections in the towns and provinces were inspected with curiosity. Parallel with this activity was the

Alice and Rosemary Morgan, 1937.

Alice Pascoe attended Craighead School in Timaru and was head girl in her final year. In 1933 she travelled to India to stay with an old school friend. There she met David Morgan, a captain in the Green Howards. Later she joined her mother and brother Paul in London. In 1936 Alice married Captain Morgan in India and the following year she returned to Christchurch to give birth to their first child, Rosemary.

Alice shared the itinerant life of a professional soldier, travelling extensively before settling in England. Like Paul, Alice had a talent for drawing.

DOROTHY PASCOE COLLECTION

SIR JOSEPH HEENAN

Joe Heenan was one of New Zealand's most unusual civil servants. His outstanding administrative ability was complemented by a shrewd understanding of his staff: he allowed them great independence, at the same time insisting on excellence, and the result was mutual respect and affection.

John Pascoe photographed Heenan at his desk – the only existing picture of him at work. From his office in the old Government Buildings opposite Parliament, Heenan wielded great influence. His achievements reflected his upbringing. Born on the West Coast in 1888, he inherited from his bootmaker father a passion for sport; his mother, a school-teacher, bequeathed him a love of literature. When Joe was four the family moved to Wellington where he later went to Wellington College and Victoria University. By day he worked in the Department of Internal Affairs drafting legislation; at night he studied law. His experience as a draftsman gave him an invaluable understanding of government and he also came to know many politicians well.

In 1935 he was appointed Under-Secretary of Internal Affairs. Respected by the new Labour government, he formed a most effective partnership with leading ministers. Over a cup of tea with Peter Fraser following Cabinet meetings, Heenan discussed how best to implement Labour's policies. During the 15 years he was in charge of the department, he achieved a great deal. He considered the organisation of the 1940 centennial celebrations, and the successful Making New Zealand pictorial series, his most notable contribution.

DOROTHY PASCOE COLLECTION

Heenan was a horse racing columnist for the New Zealand Free Lance and also wrote regularly for the Sydney Bulletin on literary matters. He himself had greater literary aspirations which were never realised, partly because he was busy assisting other writers. He helped to fund the inaugural New Zealand Writers' Week in 1936 and arranged financial support for Frank Sargeson as well as Denis Glover. He was a keen supporter of Landfall, established the New Zealand Literary Fund and also created an arts fund in Internal Affairs, the forerunner of Creative New Zealand.

selection of topics, and writers to handle them, the method of printing, and location of amateur and professional photographers who would be asked to pitch the salt into the contemporary savouries. Material came from England, from Australia, and, often when it was least expected, from pioneer families' descendants who had heard of the project and wanted to encourage it.[15]

In the little spare time he had, Pascoe took to the hills. Excited by the prospect of new mountains to explore he had climbed Mitre, the highest peak in the Tararua Ranges, only three days after arriving in Wellington. Thereafter he spent many energetic weekends in the local mountains which reminded him of more familiar South Island territory. 'The Tararuas are like Westland,' he wrote to his brother, 'but without river danger. The Wairarapa Plains are very reminiscent of Canterbury around Kowai [Bush], the rivers are like the West Coast, a salubrious combination. I am getting very attached to the Tararua hills and will certainly have new trips to do for years.'[16]

In February 1938 he received disappointing news from London. John Murray, Barclay's first choice of publisher, had rejected 'Ice Axe' as 'rather bald and lacking in continuous narrative'. Barclay, however, reassured John that he would keep trying: 'We have sent your manuscript now to George Allen and Unwin, who like books about New Zealand'.[17] When he told his mother she, too, was disappointed but he was soon able to lift her spirits with good news about Paul. While in England, Paul Pascoe had completed his thesis, entitled 'The Study of the Early Buildings in the Canterbury Settlement of New Zealand', and presented it to the Royal Institute of British Architects (RIBA), as a requirement for associate membership. When Professor F. L. W. Wood of Victoria University visited England in 1937, he was shown the thesis by the librarian at the RIBA and recognised it as a valuable work that should also be available in New Zealand. He brought a copy back to Wellington and arranged with Eric McCormick for additional copies to be sent to all the New Zealand university libraries as well as the Mitchell Library in Sydney. Another copy was retained by McCormick as a reference for *Making New Zealand*.[18]

More good news followed. On 24 March Barclay sent a cable: 'Publication arranged Allen and Unwin usual royalty terms ten pounds advance writing airmail'.[19] John Pascoe was thrilled. The acceptance also impressed Heenan, who told him the next day that when the national centennial work finished in 1941, he intended to make Pascoe a permanent member of the department.[20] When Barclay's letter of confirmation arrived a few weeks later it was a mixture of congratulations and caution:

> Mr Unwin does not like the title *Ice Axe* which, he says, means nothing. I agree with him, and suggest *Unclimbed New Zealand*, which he will accept and likes, unless you can think of a better one. It must be a title that says what the book is about.
>
> Mr Unwin has climbed a lot at Mount Cook and knows New Zealand. One of his nephews, who you probably remember at school, was, curiously enough, my fag.
>
> Mr Unwin is probably the most important and respected of all publishers, and I consider that you are fortunate in getting him to publish your book. I think you should have a book to be proud of, and you deserve it as you have taken great pains with your MS.

But Barclay also warned against excessive optimism:

> Mr Unwin today gave me a copy of *The Conquest of Mount Cook* [by Freda du Faur] and told me that it took him 20 years to sell 750 copies of it. Your book will be produced in the same way, but I hope it won't take all that time to sell an edition of it![21]

Publication of *Unclimbed New Zealand* was scheduled for the spring of 1938 to coincide with the Christmas market. Pascoe promptly got this news into the *Dominion* and *The Press*, and it also appeared in the *New Zealand Herald* and the *Otago Daily Times*, much to his delight.[22] He noted Barclay's reference to the slow sales of *The Conquest of Mount Cook*, and set to work publicising *Unclimbed New Zealand* through tramping and climbing clubs. With typical optimism, he reassured Barclay that 'Whitcombe's quota of 200 copies won't last long', and 'provided that there is no war in the next ten years I hope I'll be running to a second impression by 1948 – the Centennial interest in 1940 will of course help me'.[23]

Soon after John Pascoe received the news that Allen & Unwin would publish Unclimbed New Zealand, *he arranged for these studio portraits to be taken for publicity purposes.*

DOROTHY PASCOE COLLECTION

John Pascoe working on Making
New Zealand c.1938.
Paul Pascoe's painting of the
Torlesse Range hangs on the wall
behind him.

DOROTHY PASCOE COLLECTION

The centennial was very much on Pascoe's mind. Preparation of the pictorial series was now in full swing, and there were only 18 months left to produce the 30 issues scheduled to begin appearing at the end of 1939. Oliver Duff soon realised that he needed more help and Pascoe's climbing friend, David Hall, was hired to assist with editing the texts and to write some of the issues. Hall had recently left teaching to try to earn a living as a freelance writer, so his appointment to the staff of Making New Zealand could not have been more timely. The arrival of Duff and Hall gave the project a greater presence. In the first few months, when only McCormick and Pascoe were employed, they worked in cramped conditions in the attic of the General Assembly Library; now they moved to an old wooden building in Sydney Street which was named Centennial House. The surveys Pascoe was to illustrate were written by expert contributors, or sometimes by a member of the centennial staff. On occasions John was asked to write a particular section (for example, an account of the Reverend Samuel Marsden's work, for the Missionaries survey) and his work was scrutinised by various people. This process might have deterred a less confident writer, but Pascoe recognised it as 'wonderful training'. If his stint for the Press Junior five years earlier had been an apprenticeship, this was the equivalent of post-graduate study. In a letter to his mother and brother he described the rigorous appraisal of his Marsden article:

> Dr [Guy] Scholefield [the Parliamentary Librarian], Mr Duff, Mr Heenan, McC [Eric McCormick], and Dr Beaglehole all had a piece of it. The criticisms were all interesting, and not much alteration had to be made. It is a wonderful training in writing. Having to pass such a Committee; a Librarian, a Press Editor, an Under-Secretary, and a Professor and a Scholar is the most rigid test. They'll quibble at anything. If a sentence is too long, it must be 100% logical. If it is short; it must have 'snap', not be 'bald'. Talk about literature by vivisection, it is amusing having your work carved into neat slices for microscopic examination.[24]

For most of the time however, John Pascoe's concern was with pictures rather than words. It was his job to find illustrations for all the surveys, a daunting task given the variety of topics. His comprehensive card index proved invaluable, but sometimes even he was stumped when an appropriate illustration could not be found. However, his experience as the author and illustrator of numerous magazine articles helped him to overcome such difficulties. Several years after the publication of Making New Zealand, Pascoe described the work and his bold solution to fill the inevitable gaps:

> The fifteen 'spreads' of the letterpress were pansied up with headings and rechecked for accuracy. Then cards flew out from the index, so eager were they to alight on to likely positions. At least, animate cards would have done that. Some spreads would be jostled by a crowd of a dozen possible pictures, where decency of appearance would ask for only three; other spreads would be forlorn without the ghosts of pictures. But the editors grabbed cunning and beat it into a tool. Where, so they argued, you have an abstract idea, and cannot illustrate it even by dragging the distant relation of a glimmer along by the short hairs, then don't worry – just illustrate the abstract with something that has no relation, and write your caption boldly with the statement that this is not the idea but it is a so-and-so, and don't you reckon it is interesting, as such, and what a cow it is that the idea cannot be illustrated.[25]

Each issue was laid out by John Pascoe under the watchful eye of John Beaglehole from whom he learnt a great deal, not only about design and typography, but also about history and politics. Beaglehole first became interested in book design while working for Whitcombe & Tombs after he had left school. With a confidence beyond his years, he persuaded the firm to import books notable for their design and typography. Later, when he came to know Joe Heenan, he found they shared an interest in both literature and fine books.[26] Heenan, recognising Beaglehole's invaluable talents, brought him into the *Making New Zealand* team as typographical adviser. In the past, Beaglehole had been viewed with suspicion because of his radical ideas and, as a result, had been passed over for the position of Professor of History at Victoria University.[27] He remained unrepentant and when the first Labour government was elected in 1935 he was brought in from the cold. As Heenan's adviser he had great influence; together they raised state patronage of the arts to an unprecedented level.

Pascoe was politically naïve when he arrived in Wellington. 'John didn't really have a political idea in his head,' Eric McCormick later recalled. 'I remember having a discussion with him and he was saying things such as, "those socialist buggers", so I quickly pointed out to him that I was a socialist myself.' McCormick and other colleagues at the Centennial Branch and his historical work quickly broadened Pascoe's thinking. Attracted by his enthusiasm and interest in learning, a number of older people became his unofficial mentors. Both Heenan and Beaglehole challenged Pascoe intellectually while also helping him in other ways. Heenan, for example, arranged for the Department of Internal Affairs to buy him a new Rolleicord camera and also gave Pascoe a cherrywood pipe.[28] An older friend was the draughtsman, Guy Harding, who had drawn the maps for *Unclimbed New Zealand*. Soon after Pascoe arrived in Wellington, Harding took him home to meet his family. They stopped at a pub on the way and John found he had to watch his loosened tongue in the family's company. Dorothy, one of the daughters, remembered the impression he made: 'Our visitor was a strange young man. Windblown sun-bleached hair, blue watery eyes, and his face tanned a deep mahogany brown. All this was explained when we heard he had just returned from a failed attempt to climb Mount Tasman. John was so different to the other young men I knew.'[29]

Guy Harding and John Pascoe shared an enthusiasm for the outdoors. A few weeks later, on a summer Sunday morning, they biked from Wellington to Paremata Beach. After a picnic lunch Harding entertained the friends who had joined them while John went for a swim that quickly became an adventure reminiscent of his youth at Sumner, when he and his brother crossed the Heathcote Estuary. In a letter to Paul he described what happened:

> A strong tide was ripping out to sea from the Porirua Harbour. It didn't look far to the Titahi Bay Peninsula over the way so I gave it a go, and got over after losing a lot of ground. It was swift like the Rakaia, but such warm blue salt water I've never been in before. Coming back I walked upstream a long way before I took off to the deep water and let the tide do most of the work. It was a corker swim.

During the summer of 1937–38 John Pascoe returned to Haast Hut with the Wellington climber, Bert Hines, to complete his unfinished business on Mount Tasman. True to the vow made on his earlier visit, Pascoe avoided any involvement with the Mount Cook Company. He and Hines camped in the Tasman Valley rather than stay at the Hermitage, and also camped outside the hut.

But it was not a good year for climbing. Insufficient snow had fallen to cover the crevasses on the Grand Plateau, so access to Tasman was difficult and uncharacteristically large expanses of rock were exposed on the mountain itself. As these areas were covered with ice, an attempt was out of the question. Instead, Hines and Pascoe climbed the Anzac Peaks and made an ascent of a minor peak, Novara, on the Malte Brun Range on their way down the Tasman Valley. They arrived at their car to find it had been damaged by keas.

JOHN PASCOE COLLECTION, ALEXANDER TURNBULL LIBRARY

From the summit of Novara in the Malte Brun Range, John Pascoe took this photo of the Hochsetter Icefall and Mount Tasman. Bert Hines stands on the cliff-edge in the foreground.

JOHN PASCOE COLLECTION, ALEXANDER TURNBULL LIBRARY

Other, similar letters show John's delight in weekends spent exploring the coastline. 'Wellington has it over Christchurch for salubrious marine architecture and environs,' he told Paul, 'and there are billions of good private picnic places.'[30]

He also found that the hilly city offered endless possibilities for a fit young man. On the day he received his new camera, he celebrated by riding his bike to the top of Mount Victoria where he took 'candid shots of oblique wireless masts, and experimented with screens' (filters) to test the new equipment. 'It was sunny and perfect. Wellington is a beautiful city.' A month later he was out exploring the hills with the Brooklyn Harrier Club but found the pack he was with 'irritatingly slow. So I must be in a state of perennial hill-fitness,' he told his family in Christchurch. 'It was exhilarating to be loping over the hills with the wind in the hair and plenty of good speed in reserve.'[31] Enchanted as he was with his new surroundings, Pascoe still had other places in mind. Each payday he banked some of his earnings in the hope that, by 1940, he would have about £200, which might be enough to join the proposed CMC trip to the Himalayas. 'I'm saving my pennies for remote possibility of Kanchenjunga (not Everest),' he reassured his mother, who may have thought he was by now safely weaned from dangerous pastimes on high mountains.[32]

At Easter 1938 John was shocked by the death of a friend on Mount Evans. Norman Dowling was one of a party of three Tararua climbers who made the second successful ascent of Evans, but on the way down he fell to his death. Not for the first time Pascoe found himself writing an obituary for a companion killed in the mountains. He showed it to Dowling's parents 'who liked it very much'.[33] The earlier deaths of fellow climbers Edgar Russell on Avalanche Peak and Max Townsend in the Rakaia had not deterred Pascoe, and nor did Dowling's now. John and Stan Conway, the architect of the CMC's Himalayan plans, founded a new branch of the CMC in Wellington to keep in touch with other Canterbury climbers and to plan further alpine adventures. In the meantime, Pascoe and Conway explored the Orongorongo Ranges and also the Terawhiti coastline where they stayed in a cave, once the 'hide-out of the artist Nugent Welch'. From there they could see familiar territory. 'Splendid view of the Kaikouras and miles of the South Island. Sunrises and sunsets very fine,' he reported home.[34]

Oteranga Bay was one of John Pascoe's favourite places on Wellington's south coast. He enjoyed staying in a cave once frequented by the artist, Nugent Welch.

DOROTHY PASCOE COLLECTION

While most weekends were active and social, Pascoe occasionally chose to do something different. In July 1938 Oliver Duff introduced him to an American sociologist, Dr Kolb, who was visiting the Centennial Branch. In conversation with Pascoe, Kolb 'lamented that he couldn't raise photos or descriptions of *people* in all classes'. Pascoe understood what he meant, and told Kolb 'that in the weekend I'd take a cross-section of back country life, and give him a written account of musterers, their work, life, pursuits, conversation, reading, tobacco, etc. Painting characters with words is a job I've been wanting to do but haven't tried.' By Sunday night Pascoe had completed an 8000-word article and was pleased when Kolb told him he would take it back to the United States and show it to a colleague at the Carnegie Institute.[35]

In hindsight, John Pascoe was fortunate to have written this article when he did, in a brief hiatus between checking the proofs of *Unclimbed New Zealand* and his next major writer's job, a 5000-word survey of tramping, hunting and climbing for *Making New Zealand*. Although he knew these subjects well, *The Mountains*, as it was titled, nevertheless took up most of his spare time. 'I was up till 12.30 a.m. one morning on it and last night till 11 p.m.,' he told Effie and Paul. 'I enjoyed the problems the work raised, and am glad I did it, even if it has to be re-written.'[36]

Just how thoroughly Duff scrutinised the text of *The Mountains* is not known; what is clear is that both he and Pascoe were under tremendous pressure to complete the bulk of the proposed series before November 1939 – now barely a year away. In that time authors had to be engaged, and drafts checked, edited and illustrated. *The Mountains* was to be number 10 in the sequence; a further 20 were yet to be done. At the same time Duff and Pascoe were required to edit and illustrate a series of book-length historical surveys. As it turned out, a number of these never came to fruition, but their uncertain progress simply meant more work and worry.[37] Whether because of overwork, or simply because he thought John Pascoe was a mountain expert, Duff seems to have approved the draft text without realising that it contained opinionated, inflammatory material not usually found in government publications.

Musterer, Glenthorne Station, Wilberforce Valley.

As he made his way to and from the mountains during the 1930s, John Pascoe became familiar with the lives of station hands in the Canterbury high country. He often photographed them and his albums are an invaluable record of their activities.

Living in Wellington sharpened his appreciation of their lifestyle which he described in an article for a visiting American sociologist. Later it was published in the New Zealand Geographer. Paul Pascoe also wrote about the high country. His acclaimed thesis, 'The Study of the Early Buildings in the Canter-bury Settlement of New Zealand', included descriptions of the homestead at Glenthorne Station and a number of other houses.

JOHN PASCOE COLLECTION, ALEXANDER TURNBULL LIBRARY

The frenetic pace of the *Making New Zealand* series was in sharp contrast to the funereal pace of the production of Pascoe's own book. It was now almost a year since he had sent the completed typescript to London: 'it requires as much patience to see this book through as it did to wait for the top of Evans'. Publication had been promised for the antipodean spring, but in November Barclay told Pascoe it had been delayed – 'so that shoots me in the pants for Xmas sales'.[38] The delay was embarrassing since he had arranged extensive publicity, compiled lists of likely buyers through various alpine and

Oliver Duff stoking the copper for the washing at 'The Caboose', Days Bay.

When Duff was appointed editor of Making New Zealand in 1938, he came to know John Pascoe well. They worked together, often shared an evening meal and enjoyed their discussions. Duff soon invited Pascoe to share his cottage in the beech forest at Days Bay.

'The Caboose', as it was known, reminded John of the Pascoes' bach in Canterbury: 'It is just like Kowai [Bush],' he told his mother, 'but is handy to the office. Moreporks hoot at night, two owls sit on a branch by the verandah. Plenty of bush around, yet no dampness and the harbour outlook is corker. It is wonderfully contented in the evenings; we just sit and yarn, smoke and read.'

DOROTHY PASCOE COLLECTION

tramping clubs and promised copies to friends and family. Now the delay had to be explained to everyone including Miss Granville, his old teacher from Rakaia Huts, who was to review it on National Radio. But it was too late to withdraw Unclimbed New Zealand from Whitcombe & Tombs' Christmas sales pamphlet as it had already been printed.[39]

Further delays meant the book did not finally appear in Britain until January 1939, and John had to wait another month before it reached New Zealand. In the meantime his English clipping service sent him the first reviews by airmail. The Scotsman highlighted the campaign to climb Evans and the chapter on Butler, but made no attempt to evaluate Unclimbed New Zealand. The London-based New Zealand News offered more. Under the headline 'A Great Book', an expatriate praised Pascoe's evocation of 'the glorious forest and mountains of Westland which seem so remote from the square miles of streets which we call London'. The only criticism of the 'superb volume' was the absence of the index which, while listed on the contents page, was not included – presumably an oversight.[40] The Manchester Guardian's reviewer thought it 'a tantalising book', but found some of the colloquial expressions incomprehensible: 'Mr Pascoe's lively pen lacks clarity; one cannot always follow his choice of epithets'.

Pascoe was lucky that another of Barclay's authors, New Zealander Donald Cowie, reviewed the book for several English literary journals and

John Pascoe, Days Bay, c.1938.
DOROTHY PASCOE COLLECTION

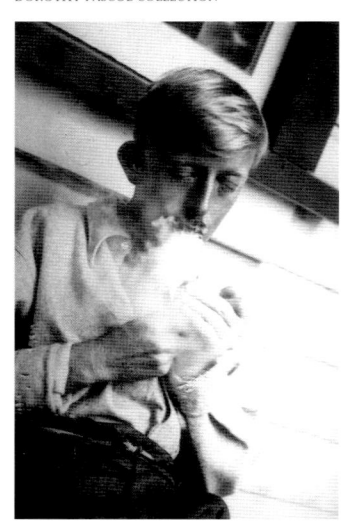

From 1906 to 1948 the harbour
ferry, the Cobar, sailed from
Eastbourne and Days Bay to
downtown Wellington. The regular
service was used by some of the
Centennial Publications staff
including Eric McCormick, Oliver
Duff and John Pascoe, who had
houses in the bush at Days Bay,
and Joe Heenan, who lived at
Eastbourne. Their stimulating
early morning conversations often
drew in other commuters who
enjoyed the erudition and banter.
ALEXANDER TURNBULL LIBRARY

was enthusiastic. In the *London Mercury* Cowie concluded: 'The book only wants a better title, an index and a short account of North Island climbing to be, like Evans before Pascoe, quite impregnable to human assault. But later editions – of which there should be many – may see to that.' In the *Fortnightly Review* Cowie highlighted 'the description of Mr Pascoe's traverse of Mount Evans after unsuccessful attempts on three consecutive years. This has the epic quality of Himalayan misadventure.' [41] The *National Review* saw *Unclimbed New Zealand* in the context of the deteriorating political situation in Europe. Pascoe's book, its reviewer suggested:

> ... should convince many people that this British Dominion, now within a month of London, and with a currency depreciated 25 per cent in terms of sterling, offers more attractions for a sporting holiday than many much-vaunted Continental resorts. And New Zealand is almost, if not quite, beyond the range of potential aggressors. A seasoned mountaineer, Mr Pascoe writes in direct and muscular English prose, and illustrates his letterpress with a batch of the best alpine photographs since Smythe.[42]

When the book eventually reached New Zealand, the newspaper reviews were all enthusiastic. Unlike the *Manchester Guardian*, the *New Zealand Free Lance* had no difficulty with Pascoe's penchant for the vernacular: 'The author has a talent for the exact epithet and the descriptive phrase'. But the paper whose verdict probably meant most to Pascoe was *The Press*, his hometown daily. In it, Dr George Jobberns, the influential Professor of Geography at Canterbury University College, expressed his delight. Under a picture of Pascoe with Mount Evans in the distance, Jobberns noted that the author 'has such a gift of simple and vivid description of landscape as gives his book high value as a piece of geography'. This must have pleased Pascoe

A FALL ON MOUNT ROLLESTON

Unclimbed New Zealand included two colour photos by John Pascoe: rata in flower on the Mungo Pass and Mount Rolleston, Arthur's Pass (right). It was probably the first New Zealand book with Dufay slides, a recent invention, the forerunner of the modern colour transparency.

At Easter 1939, soon after the book's arrival in New Zealand, John Pascoe made his ninth ascent of Mount Rolleston with a group of friends. They camped on the low peak. Next morning they climbed the high peak and had just begun their descent down in a steep, icy couloir when a nasty accident occurred. He later described what happened:

> *We had no crampons. I patiently scratched slight steps down the steep slope. I had no sense of danger and was enjoying the work. Then I heard an ominous bump; Bert Esquilant had slipped. Dyson, as anchor-man, saw what I had heard, and rammed in his pick as belay. When the strain came on his end of the rope, the knot untied and he was left in his steps while gravity took its toll of us. I had also anchored with my pick, but Bert was a heavy man, and his weight and impetus were great. He pulled me from my steps, and down I went. As I shot past him I saw that with the trained reactions of good technique he was fighting to check his fall by scraping his pick into the slope. By the time my rope whipped taut he was pulled again out of control. Then it was my turn to fight with my ice-axe to hold us. But this see-saw only increased our speed, and soon we were going full pelt down the frozen snow, sometimes in the air, other times on the slope, always clinging with the pick wherever possible. But to no avail. The snow basin below seemed to leap up as though to meet us. A shoulder of rock from the divide ridge threatened to batter us, in which case we should have been killed or seriously injured. I do not*

> *remember being frightened, but thought 'this is it!'. In a few minutes we had fallen some thousand feet to where the snow was less frozen, and the slope had eased to a basin, where at last we gained control. We got to our feet, looked wryly at each other, and checked for injuries. Bert's shirt sleeves had been rolled up, and his arms were burnt badly with the friction of fall. Otherwise he was unhurt. I had no injury. We signalled to the others far above that we were alive, and sat down to watch them cut steps slowly down the slope over which we had tumbled.*[43]

as it was one of Jobberns's students, Joan Singleton, who had encouraged him to think and write as a geographer and this, in turn, led to his membership of the Royal Geographical Society. Jobberns concluded a generous review with this appraisal: 'I have found his book of absorbing interest. By it he has revealed himself to the world as a unique character, and has made a notable contribution to New Zealand literature.' 'What a nice review Dr Jobberns gave me in *The Press*,' John wrote to his mother.[44] But, at the same time, he must have known that the most rigorous reviews, those of his fellow climbers, were yet to come; in the meantime he basked in the success of his book and its publication on both sides of the Tasman as well as in England — a heady experience for the young man who until recently had been a lowly law clerk.

Unclimbed New Zealand was well supported by the country's leading bookseller, Whitcombe & Tombs. In September 1939, the Lambton Quay branch displayed Pascoe's book in its window and when he visited Christchurch later that month the managing director, Bertie Whitcombe, took him to lunch at the Canterbury Club. 'I got on well with Bertie W.,' he told his mother, 'and saw quite a lot of potentates I knew.'

Whitcombe & Tombs' support was rewarded. In the first six months after publication, two-thirds of the first edition of 1260 copies of Unclimbed New Zealand were sold, most in this country. Sales elsewhere, of course, were much smaller: 159 in England, 98 in the United States and 45 in Australia.

DOROTHY PASCOE COLLECTION

Predictably, the Australian *Bulletin* paid particular attention to the chapter on bushrangers and ended its review with the following perceptive comment: '*Unclimbed New Zealand* gives a very vivid picture of the mountaineer, a man who boils the billy, battles with blizzards, is always about to be drowned in the turbulent rivers of the south, and who quotes very good and extraordinarily bad poetry with equal fervour upon the mountaintops'. The *Sydney Morning Herald* emphasised Pascoe's photographic skills and included his photo of 'the golden road' on Mount Evans.[45]

Soon after its Australian release, *Unclimbed New Zealand* was also published in the United States by Macmillan of New York. Pascoe was delighted by this rare honour and his pleasure was heightened by several positive reviews, one in *Appalachia*, the journal of the Appalachian Mountain Club, and another in the American Geographical Society's *Geographical Review*. The latter's reviewer concluded: 'I know hardly another book on the mountains in which the illustrations are so satisfactory'.[46]

But Pascoe's long run of accolades came to an abrupt end with a searing review in the prestigious *Alpine Journal* of the English Alpine Club. In it the Otago climber L. V. (Dan) Bryant was fair and generous in describing *Unclimbed New Zealand*'s contents, but went on to make a scathing assessment of Pascoe's judgement and experience as a mountaineer:

> His two unsuccessful attempts to scale Mount Tasman, which mountain he refers to as 'the most notoriously difficult New Zealand ice peak', reveal faulty judgement and a lack of knowledge of the conditions obtaining in the Hermitage region. His party left Syme's ridge because it 'looked inclined to avalanche'. But the party courted greater disaster on the face of the mountain. If Syme's ridge was likely to avalanche no attempt on Tasman that day could be justified and certainly not a descent by the E. [East] face.

The attempt by the Silberhorn arête ended in a night out in a very treacherous place. Here again the ridge was forsaken, this time because of its excessive steepness, although the party had hardly started on the really steep section of the arête. The author treats the spending of nights out in this area with a levity which displays a complete ignorance of conditions. He would be well advised to gain more experience and reach some summits in this part of the Alps before he speaks so dogmatically about it.[47]

Bryant knew what he was talking about. With Rod Syme, he had been the first to ascend Tasman by Syme's Ridge, the route of Pascoe's first attempt. A few years later Bryant became the first New Zealander to climb in the Himalayas when he joined the British reconnaissance on Everest in 1935.[48] Bryant also had other concerns:

The book is slightly marred by his excessive fondness for quoting second-rate poetry, often without any particular point, and by the enormous number of strings of names of parties who made the first ascents. These disfigure many pages and should have been worked in by footnotes. And in parts his book is far too incoherent and disjointed, a fault which could have been avoided had he devoted a little more time to polishing it.

A month later, much the same criticism appeared in the *New Zealand Alpine Journal*. Jock Sim was gentler than Bryant, but he also drew attention to the author's Tasman escapades: 'The peaks of the Grand Plateau are exacting in their observance of routes, and cannot be forced or tampered with in bad or doubtful weather conditions. They require the curbing of impetuosity and fabian tactics, characteristics of but rudimentary development at that time in Pascoe's make-up.'[49]

If Pascoe was unnerved by the verdict of his fellow climbers, he made no mention of it in his usually very candid letters home. To an extent, he may have been able to shrug off these criticisms because he was now immersed in a different world where few people read mountain club journals. He was also very busy as the pace of *Making New Zealand* continued to quicken, and he had new company to occupy him. In July 1939 Paul Pascoe came to Wellington to write the text for the housing title in the series, and

After his two frustrating visits to the Mount Cook region, John Pascoe turned his attention to the more accessible mountains of the central North Island. In January 1939 John and David Hall (right) enjoyed 'a perfect four days at Ruapehu.... We camped at 6000 feet all the time and had corker weather. First day we went to the top of Ruapehu. Second day traversed a Pinnacle Ridge of loose rock (very sticky, not often done). Third day, climbed Ngauruhoe. Fourth day, sunbathed.'

DOROTHY PASCOE COLLECTION

John Pascoe (left), Oliver Duff and Eric McCormick (right) at Wilson & Horton's Auckland factory as the first issue of Making New Zealand *is printed.*

DOROTHY PASCOE COLLECTION

the brothers enjoyed living and working together. At the end of the month the first issue of *Making New Zealand* was printed. Heenan was delighted and gave a copy to Prime Minister Michael Joseph Savage. John Pascoe, in turn, was pleased when Heenan rewarded him with his second rise in less than a year, which took his annual salary to £425 – far more than his meagre wage as a law clerk. Heenan bought a bottle of champagne and they celebrated after work on Friday night.

A few hours later John was at Otaki Forks, en route to the Tararua tops. '12.30 a.m. up the bush to the snow in the dark. The snow deep, wet, mushy and soft. The wind keen. Later a storm. Nearly continuous travelling and snow plugging in a gale, retreat in rain, a thunderstorm, and wasn't I glad to get a good night's sleep again.'[50]

If his infatuation with the 'salubrious' Tararua Ranges was being tested, so was his rapport with Joe Heenan. 'I had an argument with Joe about "Navigators and Explorers" for which I'd written the text,' he told his mother.

> Heenan was all reproachful because I'd left the North Island with little space. I pointed out that by 1840 the Maori had covered the interior and that white men had little work in the North that was comparable with the South. And that I'd argue with any professor in the world that I'd got the story of NZ exploration in perspective. So he had to take that. I also pointed out that because 'The Maori' Pictorial deals mainly (98%) with the North Island, the South Islander wouldn't have cause to complain.[51]

By far the greatest interest in John Pascoe's life at this time was his growing romance with Dorothy Harding. It had begun at the Tararua Tramping Clubrooms. Dorothy recalled entering the hall and noticing 'a group around a young man who was entertaining them with a tale of obvious wit in a stammering voice and I recognised John'. She, in turn, was noticed by the raconteur:

In February 1939 John Pascoe visited New Plymouth to hunt out illustrations for Making New Zealand. He did not allow time for an ascent of Mount Egmont (Taranaki) but was persuaded to climb it at night with two local mountaineers, Trevor Wright and Dave Rawson.

They set off at 11 p.m. Pascoe later wrote: 'We paced each other up the scoria, and steered by starlight as there was no moon. Nocturnal prowls in the Southern Alps had inured me to night climbing. Here on Egmont my companions knew the route. We reached the top in well under three hours, cracked a bottle of beer, and romped down the mountain again. We reached the car at 4.20 am, and I returned to my hotel for a short sleep before I took the train home.'

Later in the year he returned to Egmont and climbed it with a Tararua Club group. As it was icy, most of the climb was done with crampons and on reaching the summit he photographed this ice-covered rock.

DOROTHY PASCOE COLLECTION

Seeing me he came over and sat beside me while we watched the slides. Before the evening was over he had persuaded me to go on the club trip to what was then known as Mount Egmont the coming weekend. Again he sought me out and we sat in the bus together laughing and talking through the night. After a few hours sleep at the mountain hut John was off with a climbing group while I skied and wandered about the lower slopes of the mountain. On the journey back to Wellington I told him of my preference for going with small groups into the hills. 'Right! Come with me next weekend and we will go over to the Orongorongo River.'[52]

When John described the trip to his mother and brother as 'One of the most perfect weekends alping I've ever had', he made no mention of Dorothy Harding, who was soon his regular weekend companion. She remembered that first trip to the Orongorongo Valley clearly: 'John leading the way through the bush track, puffing at his Petersen pipe. With his rhythmical lope, long red socks covering sinewy legs, he set the pace.'

This became the pattern of the months that followed. We were both working hard at our jobs and almost every weekend we would choose a different area of the Wellington hills to explore. John lived in Days Bay so it was often the better weather and the hills towards the Wairarapa that attracted us. We would climb Mount Matthews – finding a spot with some outlook and sun to salub – have a lunch of smoked oysters on hunks of bread washed down with a bottle of beer. Then we would travel down the Hinakitaka Ridge to Palliser Bay where we would pitch a tent for the night. Sometimes we would return to Days Bay by a pass over the range or walk around the coast.[53]

Dorothy Harding was no stranger to the hills, having grown up in Khandallah playing with her brothers on the slopes of Mount Kau Kau, then, as she grew older, accompanying them as they explored the hills behind Wellington's northwestern suburbs. 'Eric and Peter would go off to wander the hills that stretched from Khandallah to Ngaio. Sometimes they would take me with them. To be included in the party, I knew the unspoken rules: one – I must not complain, two – I must not lag behind. Consequently I developed

John Pascoe competing in the Tararua Tramping Club's marathon. This annual endurance race is tough. Every contestant must wear boots as they race from the start in the Catchpool Valley, along the Five Mile Track to the Orongorongo River, which they cross. After running down the riverbed for a short distance they recross the river before making the steep climb up to Cattle Ridge, which brings them back to the Catchpool Valley.

John Pascoe relished the challenge and took part in the annual marathon six times after coming to Wellington. But the race itself was only part of an energetic weekend in December 1939, which he described in a letter to his mother: 'A field of 28 started. I got 4th place, and improved on my last year's time by 2 minutes. As usual it was a tough race. Altogether I had a lot of exercise. I walked from Days Bay to the race start (say 9 miles), then ran the 10 miles. Dorothy Harding was due to come from Muritai by the late bus so I walked out to meet her about midnight which covered 12 miles. And, of course, we walked back to the caboose [at Days Day] on the Sunday, about 9 miles. Am feeling very fit and well.'

DOROTHY PASCOE COLLECTION

a technique to keep pace with them by stretching my stride to the utmost then taking quick little runs to keep up.' By the time she met John such tactics were no longer necessary. 'Fortunately,' John told his mother, 'Dorothy can move fast and carry her own swag independently so I don't have to go round like a beast of burden as some blokes have to do when they travel in duplicate.'[54]

Theirs was a companionable courtship of conversations and comfortable silences. From Dorothy, John gained a different view of the world. She was an artist working at the Centennial Exhibition in Kilbirnie where she painted models for the New Zealand display. She was also a socialist whose idealism reflected the influence of her father, Guy Harding, a longtime member of the Communist Party. When she and the other artists realised that they were being underpaid by their employer, she represented them in meetings with the management and eventually won a wage increase.[55]

From John, Dorothy learnt about the mountains of the south and the interesting people he met while working on *Making New Zealand*. He, too, had to deal with challenging situations at work. The relentless pressure of illustrating the series was unavoidable; less predicable was the public reaction to each issue. The inaugural pictorial survey, *The Beginning*, was published on 1 November 1939 and thereafter a new issue appeared each fortnight. The generally enthusiastic response was reflected in steady sales, especially in the main centres.[56] Ten-year-old Graeme Maxwell, the son of Auckland school teachers who recognised the educational value of *Making New Zealand*, was one who read each issue avidly, especially those about trains and aeroplanes. And the whole family perused and discussed each title.[57]

Sometimes, however, people with knowledge of a particular subject were critical. John discovered this when the third issue, *Navigators and Explorers*, which he had written, was published. Heinrich von Haast, the son of the 19th-century explorer and scientist, Sir Julius von Haast, wrote to the *Dominion* 'disappointed and grieved' that 'the writer gives one the impression that my

Dorothy Harding painting models for the Dominion Court display at the Centennial Exhibition, Rongotai, Wellington, 1939.
DOROTHY PASCOE COLLECTION

Paul Pascoe worked closely with his brother on Making New Zealand. He did a number of drawings for various issues and also wrote the text for Public Buildings and Houses.

Joe Heenan was impressed. At a public meeting he said 'he had one of the most brilliant young architects in New Zealand' on his staff, and he told John Pascoe 'Paul beats my record for being fast on the job'.

Photos by John Pascoe appeared on the covers of two issues of Making New Zealand: the Railways and The Changing Land, which shows the Putangirua Pinnacles on the South Wairarapa coast. Sometimes he also used photos taken by friends, such as Frank Fitzgerald's shot of sheep on a hilltop above Cook Strait for Squatters and a close-up of a dredge, taken by his climbing companion Merle Sweney, for Gold.

father did no serious exploring, but almost made a "picnic" out of it. He also speaks of my father "scattering German names" about, the true fact being that he commemorated, in naming the Southern Alps, the great scientists of all nationalities, not forgetting the English ones, as the names of Tyndall, Hooker, Owen, Darwin and others testify.'[58]

The next day the newspaper printed a letter from A. P. Harper in support of von Haast. Pascoe was already aware of Harper's sense of grievance. A month before, the 'grand old man' of New Zealand exploration had written to congratulate him on the publication of *Unclimbed New Zealand* (which had appeared nine months earlier), but also to point out that his own achievements had not been adequately acknowledged. Instead, Harper claimed Pascoe had emphasised his partner in exploration, Charlie Douglas, at his expense.[59]

Pascoe was unmoved. He told his mother: 'von Haast and A. P. Harper have started a correspondence sniffing at my text of the pictorial survey of "Navigators and Explorers", this in the *Dominion*. I don't intend to reply.'[60] A few weeks later, in late December 1940, Harper's anger was again roused by Pascoe because of comments in an interview with the *New Zealand Free Lance*. Beneath the headline 'Deep Affection for Mountains – John Pascoe Chats about Their Interest', the paper accorded Pascoe the title of New Zealand's 'No 1 mountain man', a position Harper had long regarded as his:

> Johnnie Pascoe, as his friends call him, has a deep affection for mountains and pipes, and before he can talk mountains he must light his pipe. And what pipes they are! When he was contentedly puffing away, he said suddenly, 'shoot'.

HEINRICH VON HAAST

Heinrich von Haast, son of the 19th-century explorer and scientist Sir Julius von Haast, was offended by several comments in Navigators and Explorers, particularly John Pascoe's remark that Sir Julius had 'sprinkled German names liberally all over the landscape. These guttural legacies survive on the map to this day.'

Heinrich von Haast wrote first to John Pascoe who replied: 'Actually I feel that I gave your father a most interesting space in the letterpress. And I think the newspaper correspondents read the wrong interpretations into my text if they thought I was anti-German.' Haast then wrote a six-page, closely typed letter to Internal Affairs Minister Bill Parry, pointing out a number of errors and requesting a page of corrections in a subsequent issue. Parry usually relied on his Under-Secretary, Joe Heenan, for guidance but Heenan was ill and the overworked Eric McCormick was left to deal with the matter, though there was little he could do as Pascoe was not prepared to acknowledge his prejudice. Meanwhile Heinrich von Haast continued to write to the minister until Parry eventually asked him to stop as 'no good can be served by further correspondence'.

S. P. ANDREW COLLECTION, ALEXANDER TURNBULL LIBRARY

'Well, Mr Pascoe, New Zealand knows you as its No 1 mountain-man. So what we want to know is something about yourself.'

'You ask,' said the mountain-man, 'and I'll do my best to answer.'

'What was your original vocation in life?'

'I first started out as a law-clerk.'

'Did you like law-clerking?'

'No, I certainly did not.'

'How did you become interested in mountains?'

'I first became interested in mountains through my association with the Christchurch Harrier Club and since then I have never let up.'

'What was the greatest obstacle in your early years of climbing?'

'My main difficulty was to overcome inferiority-complex. Twelve years ago it was often hammered into the youth of the country that only mountain-guides or European climbers could reach the top without any risk. Happily, a band of young men in the Canterbury Mountaineering Club opposed this idea and were able to prove that New Zealanders can use their heads as well as their boots.' [61]

Harper was incensed. Beside the interview in his copy of the paper, he wrote: 'What rot. This is surely a record for conceit? "No 1 mountain man" who has had only one successful season in the big stuff – 99½ % of his work is in small peaks. The statement about guides 12 years ago is simply untrue.' [62]

There was some validity in both Pascoe's and Harper's comments: the conflict between them represented the different viewpoints of the old and new generation of New Zealand climbers. When John Pascoe started climbing in 1929 he had been assisted by the Canterbury Mountaineering Club which had thrived in the province in the absence of the New Zealand Alpine Club (NZAC). From 1914 onwards, successive attempts to revitalise the near-dormant NZAC had only limited success, mainly because its president, A. P. Harper, required applicants to have had some alpine experience. His preoccupation with creating an organisation like the Alpine Club of London effectively alienated some of the rising generation.[63] This was particularly evident in Christchurch. In 1915 W. A. Kennedy had made attempts to establish a Canterbury branch of the NZAC but his letters to the club had been ignored. Not surprisingly, he and other local men such as Edgar Williams considered starting their own club, but it was not until 1925 that it became a reality. W. A. Kennedy was the CMC's inaugural president, a post he held for 15 years. Even though he was hurt by Harper's rudeness in ignoring his letters, Kennedy nevertheless joined the NZAC when it finally formed a Canterbury-Westland Branch in 1932. John Pascoe also joined, as did many other members of the CMC. But less than a year later, Pascoe wrote to Doug Knowles, an Invercargill climber and photographer, 'This NZAC section is a joke and should be in liquidation. I was much relieved to resign from it the other day. There is only one first-class club in Canterbury. That is the Mountaineering Club.' Pascoe was in no doubt as to who was to blame for the tension between the two organisations. 'A. P. Harper has two sides,' he told Knowles. 'One: he is an affable old-timer who can tell yarns about the old days in a fascinating manner. Two: he is the stern veteran and "finger of doom" who writes in Truth about the foolishness of the present generation and who still holds to his fetish of bloody stupid ideals. We in Canterbury

A. P. HARPER

Arthur P. Harper was president of the New Zealand Alpine Club between 1914 and 1932. His interest in the mountains began in the late 1880s when he was a law student in London. A friend introduced him to climbing in the European Alps and when he returned to New Zealand he made a number of trips in the Southern Alps. In 1891 Harper, George Mannering and Malcolm Ross founded the New Zealand Alpine Club. It was based on the Alpine Club of London which catered for the gentleman climber.

The New Zealand club adopted similar membership rules at a time when there were few climbers, irrespective of their origins, and as a result the club did not prosper. Also, the founders were preoccupied with other matters. Harper, for example, first had to deal with his father's financial failure, then spent two years far from society exploring South Westland. He preferred exploring to climbing but by the turn of the century he had little time for either. His work as a lawyer and mine manager on the West Coast, as well as the demands of family life, kept him busy and he did not return to the mountains until 1912, when he explored the upper Waimakariri Valley. Later that year he moved to Wellington.

In 1914 a Canadian climber, Otto Frind, visited New Zealand and was surprised to find the NZAC in hibernation. He agitated strongly for its revival but the restrictions on membership and the outbreak of the First World War stymied Harper's efforts to build up the club.

It was not until the 1920s that the NZAC finally became effective as Harper recognised the need to be more egalitarian and relaxed the membership criteria. He also encouraged young climbers. At the same time, he regarded himself as the preeminent authority on exploration and alpine matters. His public pronouncements irritated some of the rising generation of climbers, in particular John Pascoe, who knew how little climbing Harper had done since the 1890s. Pascoe respected other senior climbers such as W. A. Kennedy and George Mannering because they 'never patronised us but encouraged us, and, having personal contact, we liked these men for their kindness and stimulus'. Their contact with Harper, however,

S. P. ANDREW COLLECTION, ALEXANDER TURNBULL LIBRARY

was unfortunately by way of club rivalry, he later recalled. 'Had we climbed with him, I have no doubt we would have been won over by his best qualities; that of the old explorer in the field, game as Ned Kelly, and enduring in storm and cold.'

Mutual mistrust culminated in Pascoe's aspersion against the NZAC in The Mountains issue of Making New Zealand. For the next decade daggers were drawn but towards the end of Harper's life the two men were reconciled. When Harper died in 1955, John Pascoe was one of his pallbearers: 'I said prayers from my heart as we buried him'.

never see side number "One", but get fed to the back teeth with "Two". Hence we think he has done more to harm climbing than any other living N.Z. alpine authority.'

Years later, Pascoe admitted that 'When the NZAC started a branch in Christchurch we regarded it as a rival to the CMC, and decided that while the CMC was of the people for the people, the NZAC was for the nobs and for the guided tonks. Thus we became noisier, wrote more articles, extolled our virtues as tough guys, and thought of the NZAC as more genteel, even snobby.'[64]

Further south in Otago, organised climbing had evolved differently. The upsurge of interest in the mountains in the first quarter of the 20th century had culminated in the establishment of an Otago branch of the Alpine Club, which flourished because there was no local alternative such as the CMC to compete for members. Harper did all he could to facilitate the birth of the Otago branch to prevent the NZAC being eclipsed by a local club, but was unable to do the same in Canterbury. This might seem surprising since Arthur Harper was born in Christchurch and spent the first 28 years of his life there. But he could never forget the shame his family suffered when his father, Leonard Harper, was alleged to have embezzled £200,000 from the family law firm in the early 1890s. Leonard fled the country, leaving Arthur to sort out the family's finances. Once he had done so, A. P. went into exile. He explored the West Coast for two years and later worked as a lawyer in Greymouth, then Thames, before finally settling in Wellington. He never returned to Christchurch.[65]

In Arthur's absence his uncle, George, revived the family law practice and was soon joined in the partnership by Guy Pascoe, John's father. In hindsight, had the scandal not occurred, the evolution of the NZAC might have been different and A. P. Harper would probably have welcomed John Pascoe as a protégé, if not his heir apparent.

Tensions between the two erupted again in February 1940 when The Mountains was published. It contained a condensed historical outline of mountaineering, tramping, hunting and skiing in New Zealand. The 5000-word text was illustrated with 65 sketches and photographs, one-third of which were either taken by John Pascoe or came from his personal collection. As most of his photos were of Canterbury climbing scenes, the issue had a distinctly parochial flavour which was reinforced by Pascoe's partisan prose. One section in particular caused controversy. In introducing the section entitled 'A New Zealand Generation of Climbers', Pascoe credited the Englishman H. E. L. Porter (who had written the introduction to Unclimbed New Zealand) with reviving interest in climbing in the Southern Alps after the First World War, and the Tararua Club (of which Pascoe was a member) with the fostering of tramping in the North Island. Both assertions were only partly true. He then continued with a barely disguised eulogy to the CMC:

> From another quarter, hill-less Christchurch, a new army moved to the mountains. A handful of clerks, students and shop workers sprinkled with experienced men in their prime, and some old timers, formed the Canterbury Mountaineering Club. The adolescence of this club, a major force to-day in the Southern Alps, was not without its growing pains. Abetted by cheap

The cover of The Mountains shows the eastern slopes of Mount Cook from the air, with the ice cliffs of the Caroline Face in the foreground and the long ridge to the summit in the distance.

FYFE – 1894
GREEN – 1882
MANNERING – 1890

Paul Pascoe's drawing of Mount Cook, seen from the north-east, was based on a photo taken by John Pascoe (page 82) which John used in The Mountains *to illustrate the first three attempts to climb New Zealand's highest peak.*

A. H. MCLINTOCK COLLECTION, ALEXANDER TURNBULL LIBRARY

excursion trains and cheaper petrol for decrepit motor cars, its members thrust their noses into the more accessible valley nooks and glacier crannies. Carrington, its founder, was drowned in an attempt to follow on a raft, an old canoe trail of Mannering's in the Waimakariri Gorge. The Club did not aim high, but built up its membership slowly and without restrictions for new men, who were not required to send in a list of achievements or ascents. A wide circle of juniors came to like the back-country. They slept in rude huts, looked at the Main Divide from the foothills, talked with awe of Mount Rolleston in winter, and formed life-long friendships. At distant Mount Cook, Porter was performing stupendous traverses of the giants with Marcel Kurz, a cartographer and mountaineer destined to Himalayan fame. The Tararua Club in the North Island pursued its active course. The New Zealand Alpine Club, alas, rested on past laurels, and left isolated men to carry on its tradition.[66]

Within a few days of *The Mountains* publication an outraged A. P. Harper was marshalling support among the climbing community to publicly rebut Pascoe's account. He first wrote to the editor of the *New Zealand Alpine Journal*, Jock Sim, noting angrily that 'This man and his persistent publicity is becoming a danger to New Zealand alpine history. There was SOME climbing done before J. P. and the CMC came into this world!' [67]

The Mountains was not yet in the Dunedin shops when Harper's letter reached Sim. Nevertheless he was familiar with the account because John Pascoe had sent him a copy when it was first released, presumably for him to review in the *Journal*, which suggests Pascoe was oblivious to the furore it would provoke. Sim read *The Mountains* and replied to Harper 'it is the most deplorable publication that has ever appeared'.[68] He also gave Harper a précis of what he had said in a letter to Pascoe:

> I wrote Johnny with my comments on the work and said he had let himself down as an historian. That what he had written in the past had been only the personal opinion of J. D. P. and therefore not worth becoming entangled in controversy over, but that an official publication like this cannot be allowed to pass and that as Editor I will probably be forced publicly to join the lists against him.
>
> The conceited young ass! Isn't there some fable of Aesop about an ass who thought he had a golden voice and brayed unceasingly!

In the meantime, Harper had written a restrained but forceful letter to John Pascoe listing a number of errors in the text of *The Mountains*, and also referring to the beginning of guideless climbing which 'most emphatically did not originate only 12 years ago in Canterbury, as you said to the *Free Lance*'.[69] Pascoe wrote him a brief, breezy reply the same day:[70]

Dear A. P.,

Thanks for the letter. It is good to get other points of view. The point about guideless climbing is that it only developed in a big way in recent years. You and Mr Mannering have often told me how hard it was to get companions in your day, whereas today the problem is to keep the size of the party to reasonable limits.

I'll see you on Saturday. Again my thanks for your interest in our work. The 'Free Lance' story still has me blushing with shame.

Yours sincerely

Johnny Pascoe

On Saturday, however, Pascoe was sick, so missed the Alpine Club meeting and did not have to face Harper. A letter to his brother makes it clear he was busy and had other things on his mind:

> In the weekend I nursed my cold on Saturday; stayed in bed till 4 p.m. which cured me. In the evening I worked on the Pictorial of 'Manufacturing' till 10 p.m., read till 11 p.m. Met Dorothy on the late bus at Moana Road at 11.15 p.m. We walked up the hill to that old hut on the ridge and then pitched sleeping bags (plural) outside the hut at 12.30 a.m. I did nothing to merit hellfire or eternal salvation.
>
> We talked a bit, then slept soundly until 8 a.m. on Sunday morning. Later we walked along to Lowry Trig and sunbathed all day.[71]

The next day at work Pascoe and his colleagues met the English documentary filmmaker, John Grierson, who was visiting New Zealand to advise the government. It seemed that there would be jobs for David Hall, Eric McCormick and John Pascoe in a new documentary unit. Pascoe also had another offer of work to consider when the centennial was over, from Wilson & Horton, the printers of *Making New Zealand*, who were most impressed with his layout skills. His real preference, as he told his mother, was for 'A hut in the back country and an attempt at novel writing which would suit me better than £500 p.a. and of course the war complicates any ideas or plans of any kind'.[72]

Perhaps because of these distractions, John Pascoe seemed surprised when the *Otago Daily Times* published a lengthy letter criticising *The Mountains*, signed by the editor of the Alpine Club *Journal* and the secretary of the Otago section, Scott Gilkison, who had contributed three photos to the pictorial survey. Their opening salvo, 'For a Centennial publication we suggest that there are too many inaccuracies, too unbalanced a treatment of the subject, and too many slighting statements which are the result of club rivalry and personal animosity', was supported by a long list of errors and omissions. Throughout, they took every opportunity to attribute the defects to Pascoe's bias and to mention him by name.

The attack hurt Pascoe. In a letter to his brother he explained his response: 'The *Otago Daily Times* published a most vituperative personal attack on me by Jock Sim and Scott Gilkison à propos *The Mountains* but just reverberating with jealousy and parochialism. Nasty work. But I cannot reply to the paper as I am a Civil Servant, and I don't want to. Have written amiable personal letters to Jock and Scott separately. However I suppose I must lump the brickbats with the bouquets.' [73] His response, like his earlier reaction to criticism of the *Navigators and Explorers* issue, suggested either that he did not understand that he had made factual errors, or that criticism caused him to 'close up' and ignore it.

When a similar letter appeared in the *Evening Post* from the vice-president of the New Zealand Alpine Club, it was clear to Pascoe that he was the subject of an NZAC campaign. The official response from his editor, Eric McCormick, stoutly defended Pascoe and reminded his critics that 'the purpose of *The Mountains* is to give a brief survey in the severely limited space of 5000 words of the development of mountaineering in New Zealand, not a list of names and achievements which would have been meaningless to the public', but McCormick did not know enough about the subject to be able to defend the veracity of Pascoe's account.[74] Ill health had prevented Heenan attending the centenary celebrations at Waitangi earlier in the year and he was still absent when controversy caused by *The Mountains* needed attention. Had Heenan been at the helm, the situation might have been managed differently. When he eventually returned to work, Heenan was furious with Pascoe, but as Pascoe remained resolutely certain he had done no wrong, little could be done.

The whole controversy was probably meaningless to the public, who would not have bothered with the lengthy letters of complaint and reply, but to the protagonists it was important. John Pascoe and David Hall immediately resigned from the New Zealand Alpine Club and they were later followed by other members of the CMC. In the end A. P. Harper recognised that his campaign would only hurt climbing: 'An inter-club feud will do the sport harm, the NZAC will survive it but the whole sport will stink in the nostrils of the public. J. D. P will get the publicity he loves and he won't worry about the sport – he cares nothing for that, it comes second to, or as useful medium for, his personal vanity.'[75]

To Dorothy Harding, the furore was bewildering. As she and John walked Wellington's hills they talked about it. She sensed that he was hurt by the criticism but also that he did not really understand why he was being

During the Second World War, Guy Harding, who had drawn the maps for Unclimbed New Zealand, *and his youngest daughter, Judy, painted a series of evocative murals on the walls of the Unity Centre in Cuba Street, Wellington. Judy did most of the painting while her father provided most of the ideas.*

Several murals showed the benefits of communism, others depicted the workers' contribution to the war effort and the sort of society the triumph of socialism would create. But first the fight against Nazism, graphically illustrated in 'Onward, Through Victory over Fascism to World Peace', had to be won.

DOROTHY PASCOE COLLECTION

Dorothy Harding, Fitzroy Bay, January 1940, watching the First Echelon of New Zealand troops depart from Wellington Harbour.

The previous evening John and Dorothy left Eastbourne to camp at Fitzroy Bay despite a Defence Department notice warning that access along the coast was prohibited.

As they walked along the ridge above the coast, searchlights from the gun emplacements at Fort Dorset and the radar station on Palmer Head picked out the pair and followed them.

The next morning John and Dorothy understood why, when they saw a troopship leaving the harbour. Dorothy found it very moving and climbed onto the rock to be alone. Both she and John had friends in camp who could be sailing away to war, perhaps never to return.

DOROTHY PASCOE COLLECTION

targeted and would not admit any culpability.[76] It may be that his school experiences of bullying taught him to simply endure the behaviour of others, rather than to try and understand why he was being picked on.

But they did not dwell on it because there were far more significant matters to worry about. The world was following Hitler's march across Europe. Britain had declared war on Germany the previous September after Hitler invaded Poland, and New Zealand had immediately followed suit. In February 1940 Paul Pascoe volunteered for active service. Pleased by his patriotic example, Effie Pascoe wrote to her other son with the news. John realised that he owed his mother an explanation for his reluctance to follow Paul. First, he told her that even if he did volunteer, Joe Heenan would not allow him to go until *Making New Zealand* was finished. Then he outlined his reasons for wanting to stay in New Zealand.

I reckon I'd be foolish to put my nose into the military machine and be transported to places where I'd be no use other than as a vague sacrifice. If there is ever a real threat of invasion to N.Z. I could be of more use than as a foot slogger on the other side of the world.

All your beliefs lead you to do what you honestly think is right; so do mine. I'll admit that I haven't got the guts to take the punishment that the Christian Pacifists seem to be heading for. Nor do I attend their meetings. But then if I'm willing to be of real use (and that doesn't include territorial drill), I'm not a Pacifist.

Here in Wellington there isn't half the feeling against non-enlisters that there is in Canterbury. If it is a long war, there'll be conscription, but maybe by that time I'll have a better idea where my use lies. I could be a better hand for England if I worked on a farm in New Zealand.

I'm not scared by the horrors or discomfort of war – my experience in the least tough of the back-country has shown me how to keep a wry grin when it is unpleasant and how to get on well with other people. But if I do anything, I want it to be practical and not a symbol of heroics where I dash away at the first call.

Each one to his own feelings. For Paul's sake, I'm glad he enlisted. Only time can tell me what I do.[77]

The same day he received a letter from Paul, telling him he had been rejected by the army doctors. 'Thank God you were turned down from Khaki,' replied John, then added, 'I hope Eff was satisfied with my War Letter – I couldn't have met her more than I did'.[78]

What John had not told his mother was the strength of his feelings for Dorothy Harding. Earlier, Effie Pascoe had written seeking clarification of the nature of their relationship and John had assured her:

You have nothing to worry about in my weekend habits. Whether the tramping partnership between me and Dorothy matures into anything more lasting, I cannot yet say. I shall do nothing that causes Dorothy harm, or cause worry to her people or you. We like each other's company better than other people's and that is why we go out together; I don't think the guardian angel has had to work overtime on us from a moral point of view.[79]

Six weeks later, however, he was more deeply involved with Dorothy. For many young couples the prospect of war quickened courtship to marriage. But before John could even consider a wedding, Dorothy would have to meet his mother, so he suggested that at Easter they should do the 'Three Passes' trip from Canterbury to the West Coast. This would allow her to meet Effie and, at the same time, he could show her the Waimakariri mountains where he first discovered climbing. But to Dorothy's surprise John, knowing his mother would not approve of their journey without a chaperone, invited Dorothy's father, Guy, to accompany them.[80] It proved a bad idea. While changing trains at Christchurch railway station, they were met by Effie and Paul. As John organised the transfer of their swags, Dorothy talked to Paul, which left his mother and Guy Harding together.

Effie told Dad what a wonderful man Chamberlain was. Dad challenged her opinion – Effie burst into tears – and was led away by Paul. Leaving me furious with Dad and John displeased that Effie had ignored me.

The train stopped at the Klondyke Corner [near Arthur's Pass] for us to alight with our packs. Soon we were trudging up the Waimakariri riverbed, breathing the fresh mountain air, and delighting in the mountains in the distance. We both put the tensions created by war aside and resumed our easy companionship.

Guy Harding and his daughter, Dorothy, after their transalpine tramp with John Pascoe at Easter 1940.

In his youth Guy Harding had been a champion athlete and distance runner. He was capable of great endurance; for example, he ran cross-country to climb Mount Egmont and back to his home town, New Plymouth, a distance of 70 kilometres, in less than 20 hours — a feat he repeated several times. By 1940, however, he was middle-aged, a smoker and far from fit. He was also beginning to have hip trouble. As a result he found it difficult to keep up with John and Dorothy, whom he was meant to chaperone.

DOROTHY PASCOE COLLECTION

Guy Harding remained a liability. Thinking he still had the athletic prowess that made him a champion runner in his youth, he had not bothered to train for the trans-alpine trip and now found he could not keep up. But he could not devise a strategy as his daughter had done to keep up with her brothers, so the younger pair often had to wait for him. On the second day, they left him at Park Morpeth Hut and climbed Mount Marion together. It was Dorothy's first mountain and she found it wonderful. 'I liked the way my body responded – inching up rock faces – choosing safe foot and hand holds – each step taken with rhythm and purpose. Sometimes my eyes on some alpine plant growing from a rock crevasse – then my focus would stretch to absorb distant mountains – clouds – range upon range stretching into the distance.'[81]

On their return to Christchurch, she and John stayed with his mother. Both hoped this second, longer meeting would be more successful, but

Opposite: While he was illustrating Making New Zealand John Pascoe's photography improved rapidly. He took photos on the wharves for Shipping, documented the reconstruction of the Ngauranga Gorge road in Wellington for Tracks and Roads, photographed signals in the Wellington railyards for Railways and buildings such as the Waterloo Hotel, Parliament and the Wellington Railway Station for Public Buildings. Most of these images became part of the Making New Zealand collection now held by the Alexander Turnbull Library but some, such as these shots of the Ngauranga Gorge, were retained by John and put in his personal photo album.

DOROTHY PASCOE COLLECTION

Dorothy's bad luck continued. While climbing out of the tin bath in Effie's small kitchen she accidentally knocked a piece of fine china to the floor, breaking it. She apologised and offered to replace it, only to be curtly told by Effie that it was irreplaceable. Nor did Dorothy's lack of a recognisable pedigree, in Christchurch eyes, impress Effie who resorted to the faint compliment 'She's so good with her hands' when introducing Dorothy to her friends.[82]

Back in Wellington, John was incensed to find that Harper was still intriguing against him and was told by a family friend that the older man was spreading the rumour that he was a communist – no doubt prompted

by his association with Dorothy Harding. Harper had also written to the *Evening Post* complaining about *The Mountains*, which raised doubts in the mind of Joe Heenan. 'Oh how the brickbats fly,' John wrote to Paul. 'The worst of it is that Joe is beginning to look for the cloven hoof under my clinkers. I can take it. I know I wrote a fair story and rest happy in my conscience.'[83]

Harper was also finding the controversy difficult. Several CMC supporters wrote letters in Pascoe's defence to the *Otago Daily Times* and the *Evening Post* and, as Harper had feared, the issue had become one of inter-club rivalry, obscuring his initial concerns. In an attempt to halt the purposeless war of words, Harper wanted to enlist the help of W. A. Kennedy, the immediate past president of the CMC, but his earlier arrogance returned to haunt him. Unable to write to Kennedy because he had repeatedly snubbed him in the past, he wrote instead to an ally in Dunedin who wrote to a friend in Christchurch who knew Kennedy. By this circuitous route, Harper hoped he might persuade the CMC to desist.[84]

Harper had the time for such convoluted scheming, but Pascoe was simply too busy. He and Eric McCormick still had 13 issues of *Making New Zealand* to produce, as well as eight books from the centennial series to edit and illustrate before the end of 1940. 'The reality of keeping to such a programme is rather gruesome,' he told Paul, who had been engaged to write two of the pictorial surveys. The situation was made worse by Heenan's close scrutiny, probably as a result of *The Mountains* controversy:

> I had another argument with Joe the other day because he insisted on last minute alterations in two Pictorials on which I had been busting my boiler to get them to the printers in time. It is such a neck and neck struggle with time that additional obstacles are a real pain – like running a race behind time and having to stop and change shoes half way around the course. Joe told me I'd have to get out of my attitude of saying 'No' to all his suggestions – personally I'd rather be a 'No-Man' than a 'Yes-Man'.
>
> Mac [Eric McCormick] went back afterwards and told Joe that I wasn't unreasonable but that I was thinking of progress first, last and all the time. Joe said he'd given me the works because of his affection and respect. The 'whom he loveth he chasteneth' touch. However, it is all serene now, but I know that future occasions will arise when I'll have to put forward my views, even in opposition. However I'd never get another boss as good as Joe and I can take anything from him and never lose my admiration for his personality that lets his workers use their imagination and enterprise.[85]

John still found time at the weekends, however, to go walking with Dorothy. She later recalled a Sunday when they tramped along the coastal track to the Pencarrow lighthouse: 'We talked about the people we knew and how the war was changing their lives, when John expressed the thought that maybe it was wrong to marry in the time of war, leaving the young wife to cope with life on her own at home'. Dorothy didn't agree and said so: 'To marry was a belief and stake in the future and that in itself was important. When so much was against it – life must go on.' The next day John rang her and suggested lunch on top of the Tinakori hill. 'Sitting on top, munching our sandwiches, he suddenly blurted out his deep love and wish to marry. He was impatient and would have been happy for me to marry that week. I

Dorothy Harding had her 23rd birthday the day after she married John Pascoe who was nine years older.

DOROTHY PASCOE COLLECTION

persuaded him I would need at least three weeks. And so the date was set. Hand in hand we ran down the hill.'

On 22 June 1940 John and Dorothy were married at St Barnabas Church in Khandallah, Wellington. In keeping with their wishes, only immediate family were invited. Even so, Dorothy was anxious at the prospect of another meeting between John's mother and her father, but she was saved by the war. The previous night a German submarine sank the SS *Niagara* off the coast of Northland and as a precaution all shipping movements in New Zealand waters were suspended. Effie and Paul were booked to come to Wellington on the inter-island ferry but were unable to sail and the ceremony went ahead without them. Oliver Duff was John's best man. Afterwards they took the ferry to Days Bay and shared their wedding breakfast with Oliver and his wife in the Pascoes' new home, a small shabby cottage in a large neglected section, known as 'The Garden of Holidays'.[86] John later told a colleague at Internal Affairs: 'We chose the shortest day of the year to marry, to give us the longest night'.[87]

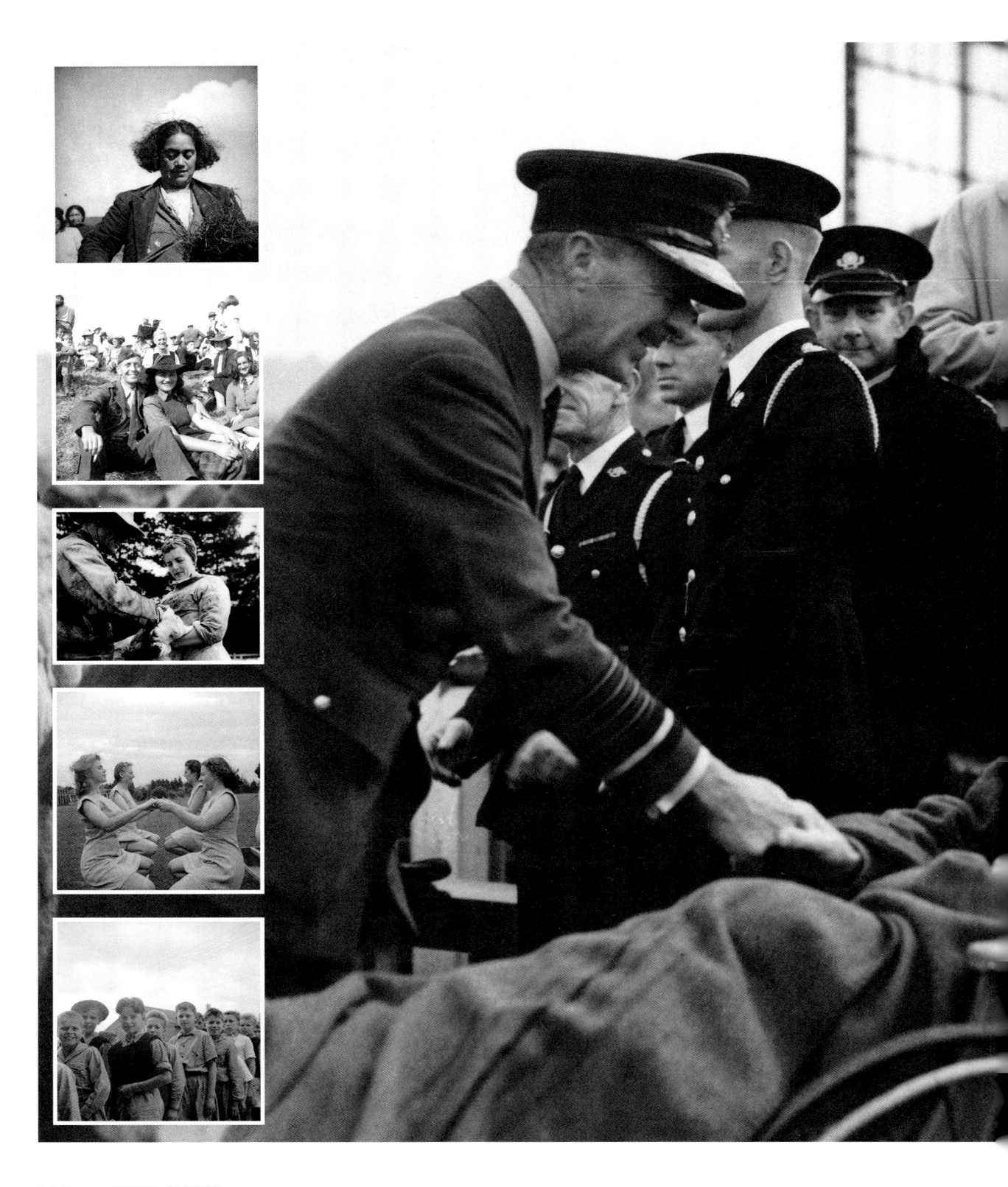

CHAPTER FIVE

'Traveller with a Camera'

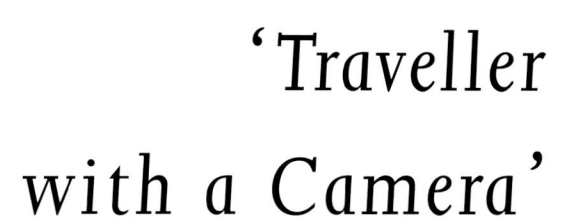

John Pascoe (centre, top) with his Rolleicord camera c.1943, during an investiture ceremony for wounded American servicemen who received Purple Heart medals from the Governor General, Sir Cyril Newall.

When Making New Zealand was completed in 1941 John Pascoe became eligible for conscription but was pleased to be rejected by army doctors as 'unfit for military service'. He saw this as an opportunity to serve his country in a different way. As official photographer for the Department of Internal Affairs, his brief was to record New Zealand in wartime. He took up the task with typical enthusiasm, travelling widely to photograph a variety of activities, many of which were performed by women in the absence of men overseas.

During the war a number of his photos were published at home and abroad and his wartime collection has been regularly used ever since. At the time John Pascoe was known chiefly as an author and climber; today he is equally well known as a photographer. His reputation as one of New Zealand's earliest and most influential documentary photographers derives mainly from his wartime work.

DOROTHY PASCOE COLLECTION

Left: Photos by John Pascoe and his accompanying captions from the War Effort Collection, Alexander Turnbull Library:
- Maori girl trims roots of pine seedlings at a State Forest nursery, Pongakawa, 1941.
- Marine and Maori girl, Ngaruawahia, 1943.
- Ear-marking a lamb, Porongahau, 1943.
- Instructors trained for spare time fitness, Hutt Valley, 1944.
- Polish refugee boys, Pahiatua, 1945.

'IF I HAVE TO GO TO THE WAR OVERSEAS it will be as a poor bloody individual become one of a mad crowd, it will not be as the stalwart champion of liberty and fraternity,' John Pascoe wrote to his brother. *Making New Zealand* had protected him from conscription but as the series finished the likelihood of military service overseas seemed imminent. Joe Heenan had said as much. He told Eric McCormick and John Pascoe that if they were called up in 1940 he would appeal, but the following year he said they could be 'bloody cannon fodder' for all he cared.[1]

McCormick did not wait for his marble to be drawn but volunteered, much to the surprise of those who thought he was a pacifist.[2] He saw little alternative:

> I was of military age (in my early thirties), unmarried, an anti-fascist, and would soon complete the editorial job I had undertaken in 1939. Clearly it was my duty to join the thousands of fellow-countrymen already serving in the armed forces. True, I had been a pacifist since school-days, but not for religious reasons, the only ones that counted before an official tribunal. In the last war, I recalled, Hemingway had driven an ambulance, while my Cambridge friend F. R. Leavis had been a stretcher bearer. Perhaps I might find some similar niche. What finally prodded me into action was the announcement that late in July voluntary recruitment for the New Zealand army would be replaced by periodical ballots for eligible men – conscription, in short. Wishing to avoid the uncertainties and anxieties of the new system, I decided to enlist.[3]

John Pascoe did not share McCormick's sense of duty and his recent marriage underlined how much he had to lose. He had found immediate contentment in wedded life and when Paul Pascoe announced his engagement to Ann Sellars in October 1940, told his brother, 'Ann will be to you what Dorothy is to me'. John's recipe for a happy marriage was 'the simple requirements such as sun, sea and hills'. Or, as he put it in language reminiscent of Damon Runyon, one of his favourite American authors: 'Money, cars, furs, social parties and palaces mean nothing to our dames'. For Dorothy, still coming to terms with her mother's recent suicide (after suffering bouts of depression for many years), marriage was like 'coming in to a safe harbour'.[4]

At the time of their wedding John had been too busy for a honeymoon but in December 1940 he and Dorothy spent three weeks at the head of the Waimakariri enjoying what he called their 'Alpine Honeymoon'. With only one wet day 'we took with delight to a routine,' wrote John, 'whereby we climbed a peak one day and sunbathed in the valley or on the grassline the next'. They climbed Mounts Isobel, Campbell, Murchison, Mottram and Stewart, then followed the Taipo River to the West Coast. In the Taipo valley they stayed with the Dillons, who had gone up the river during the Depression in search of gold and instead had found a contentment that kept them there. John was taken by their pioneering spirit: 'Their ingenuity was boundless. They made their own slab huts. Nothing went to waste. When a plane crashed several years ago in their valley, the family made cooking gadgets from oddments left behind by the salvage parties.'[5]

Yet even in the remote Taipo the war in Europe was never far from their thoughts. It was, according to Dorothy, 'a dark shadow in the background

When Eric McCormick volunteered to join the army he hoped for a non-combatant role but at Trentham Military Camp he was put in the infantry. After a few months, however, he was transferred to a medical unit. As an archivist, he was mindful of the need for someone to organise the collection of military papers for future use, so he wrote to Heenan from Trentham to suggest he be given the job. Heenan agreed and obtained the Prime Minister's approval. Soon after arriving in Egypt, McCormick was made a lieutenant and transferred to the Public Relations Office of the Second New Zealand Expeditionary Force. In a letter to Heenan, he described his archival job: 'I'm doing precisely the sort of work I had wanted to do after the Centennial, and except for my mode of dress and other such details, I might very well be working in some obscure corner of a government building in Wellington; in fact our office has a very close resemblance to the G.A.L. [General Assembly Library] office where John [Pascoe] and I worked for the first few months — dust and all.'

DOROTHY PASCOE COLLECTION

John and Dorothy Pascoe began their 'Alpine Honeymoon' in December 1940 by walking up the Waimakariri riverbed to the Southern Alps. Along the way they passed several abandoned cars, casualties of various attempts by Nui Robins and other CMC members to drive to Carrington Hut at the head of the valley. In his photo album, John Pascoe described this wreck as 'bait for kea'.

DOROTHY PASCOE COLLECTION

Dorothy Pascoe on the summit of Mount Murchison, one of the many peaks she and John climbed during their 'Alpine Honeymoon'.

DOROTHY PASCOE COLLECTION

of our lives'. John hoped he would be turned down by the army: 'Maybe the doctors will look askance at my one testicle and call it a day!'[6] But if that did not happen and he had to go overseas, Dorothy was determined to have the company of their child in his absence. While in the Waimakariri they had decided to try to conceive, and on their return to Eastbourne they received news of Ann and Paul's plans to start a family: 'I wonder whether Ann and Dorothy will be having a race for the baby event,' John mused in a letter to his mother.[7]

In anticipation, John and Dorothy took steps to find a home of their own. 'The Garden of Holidays' was small and the rent might be better spent repaying a mortgage. 'After looking at a lot of depressing bungalows we at last got the cottage we want.' His Himalayan climbing fund now became the £200 deposit on a property at 75 Main Road, Eastbourne, and in January 1941 they took possession of their first home.[8] Now the energy that had taken them to the Orongorongo Ranges and elsewhere at weekends was spent on renovations. John was delighted to discover he had the makings of a home handyman. 'Am I a carpenter now! I have just put in a door lock; and am now on the ambitious project of making a cupboard,' he boasted to Paul, who was even less adept with tools. Dorothy cleaned and made new curtains and John's mother sent them some furniture. With new carpet on the floor 'and Mount Evans on the wall', it was home.[9]

Within a few weeks Dorothy was having morning sickness. 'I want a girl; Dorothy a boy,' John told his mother. 'However we must wait till the chicken is hatched.' At the same time, John was surprised by the unexpected publication of his article about his exploration of the Garden of Eden and Adams Icefalls in the *Journal* of the Royal Geographical Society: 'They have hatched this material for 3½ years and I had given up hope of it ever appearing. But I suppose the war has killed exploration for young Englishmen and they have to fall back on the poor bloody Colonials to fill their pages.'[10]

Life could not have been better for John Pascoe. Even Heenan's threat to let him become cannon fodder now seemed to have been a bluff: by the time the final issue of *Making New Zealand* appeared in February 1941, Heenan had already begun to press for Pascoe's continued employment in his department. He had applied to the acting Prime Minister, Walter Nash, for a dispensation from war service and had reinforced this in a letter to his own minister, Bill Parry. In it, Heenan traced the evolution of *Making New Zealand* and described the contributions made by each member of the Centennial Publications team. Heenan reserved his biggest bouquet for Pascoe:

> The pictorials are the outstanding work they are generally admitted to be principally on account of Mr Pascoe's genius for selection and layout of the illustrations. I remember when he sent his first layout to Wilson and Horton, Mr Dennison, the Works Manager, was almost lyrical in his praise. He stated that never had such layouts ever been placed before him; without further ado he and his assistants could proceed straight away without, as was too often their experience, having to make considerable alteration and adjustment in measurements. It is difficult to give anyone who has not worked closely with Mr Pascoe over the whole period of production, any clear realisation of the vast work entailed, first of all in visualising the range of illustrations, then

When Paul Pascoe married Ann Sellars at Avonside Church on 30 November 1940 his brother was his best man. The officiating clergyman asked the groom: 'Do you, John, take Ann to be your wedded wife?', to which Paul replied: 'I'm not John, I'm Paul'.

DOROTHY PASCOE COLLECTION

Dorothy and John Pascoe's first home at Eastbourne.

DOROTHY PASCOE COLLECTION

collecting from all manner of obscure sources, the necessary pictures and photographs, and then making a final selection of all the material gathered. Mr Pascoe's work did not cease with all that. He himself had to go into the field with his camera, and some of the finest photographs in the whole series were taken by him. I would draw your special attention to the cover picture of No. 30 [see page 108], the final issue of the series. To say more about Mr Pascoe's outstanding work would be little more than gilding the lily.

Truly the pictorials as a whole are a monument to Mr Pascoe.[11]

In March, Dorothy Pascoe received news that her sister-in-law, Ann, was also pregnant — 'It is really thrilling that we are making it a Derby'.[12] Dorothy's pregnancy proceeded normally until the fourth month when, at short notice, she was taken to hospital for an operation to remove her still-born baby.[13] She was devastated.

After a few days rest, she returned to Eastbourne. John was sad and solicitous, but following their evening meal he returned to his typewriter. For the first time in their marriage, Dorothy felt distanced from him. 'How could he write at such a time?' she wondered as she lay crying on the bed while he tapped away in the next room.[14]

John's apparent insensitivity may have been a predictable masculine response for the time, but it was also due, in part, to his preoccupation with the novel he had begun as soon as *Making New Zealand* was finished. For the first time in five years he was free to experiment with fiction, a welcome respite from the historical accounts he had been writing almost continuously since 1937. His reading of contemporary American authors may also have encouraged him to try a different genre. The untitled novel, the story of an attempt by three climbers on the virgin peak, Scimitar, draws heavily on his own life. Their decision, taken on the summit, to traverse into unknown territory and their cold night out on an icy perch, echo Pascoe's experience on Mount Evans.

The characters lack depth but their language is lively and colloquial; their soliloquies are broadsides aimed at a variety of targets, especially Canterbury high society. The influence of American authors such as John Dos Passos, Damon Runyon and John Steinbeck is apparent in the gritty dialogue which portrays, in the bawdy argot of the CMC, the climbers' fascination with, and fear of women . The central character, Pete (John's nickname for his brother Paul), has a developing relationship with a young woman in the office where he works. Before he leaves for the mountains Pete says goodbye to her:

> Pete had said 'I'll miss you,' to Sadie with a sudden revelation of feeling that it was as well that he wasn't taking her places over the holidays. Of course, he had taken her to movies, to dances, for walks, but no what have you. Sadie seemed lubricious enough, as they went, but he hadn't come at it yet. And didn't intend to. He hadn't with anyone. Not that he didn't want to. But too many jokers were seeing sheilas wobble nappies in the sink.

Pete and his friends were also relieved to leave Christchurch:

> Mac secured the swags under the swathe of ropes. Snowy started the lorry.
> The route lay down Rolleston Avenue, past the Gothic arches of the University attempting to capture a mellow history beyond their reach, past flatulent luxury houses in Park Terrace, and by Avon willows whose green shrouds seemed to mourn their inability to compete with the beauty of the New Zealand bush. Snowy collected some bottles from a pub in Papanui Road. Taking a short cut through a suburb of houses with pleasing sun porches they left behind this atmosphere of genuine home life at last to hit the bitumen of the main south road. Snowy huddled over the wheel. 'Good to be out of that bloody city,' he said.[15]

John Pascoe's opportunity to write fiction lasted barely four months. In July 1941 Heenan sent him to Rotorua to write a film script about, and a history of, trout fisheries in thermal regions. When Dorothy had recovered from her operation she joined him. They lived in a motor camp beside the lake and used thermal steam for cooking. 'We can also bathe in a corker hot natural bath in our backyard,' he told his mother. His research took him all over the geothermal region and sometimes Dorothy went with him. It was an ideal way to revive their spirits. 'On Sunday we both biked 12 miles away and walked through Maori property to a secluded spring on the edge of Lake Rotoiti. We could lie in the bath in the sun with a full view of the beautiful lake and all the time have a spout of spring water playing on our shoulders. I reckon we are having our second honeymoon now.'[16]

Heenan was pleased with John's work on thermal fisheries and also had other projects in mind for him. John hoped he might have a break in order to return to his novel, especially since his brother was now also working on one. When Paul was about to visit Wellington, John suggested he bring his 'and we can read each others' or what there is of them'.[17] Paul's novel which, like John's, was largely autobiographical, was soon abandoned because he considered it 'too corny'.[18] John never got the chance to get back to his, because as soon as he had finished his 'History of thermal fisheries' Heenan told him his next task would be to write a history of the Department of Internal Affairs. 'Oh boy what a job,' he confided to Paul. 'Properly done it might take years. The Dep't. is the oldest one of all and I'd have to go back to 1840 and trace the course of Government Administration (seems a job for a Leicester Webb or Beaglehole rather than me).'[19]

Heenan did not confirm the project, perhaps because he realised John could be called up at any time. Paul Pascoe had been rejected as 'unfit for military service' and Heenan wondered whether John might be too. 'It would be a touch of irony if he, who takes the Southern Alps in his stride, were turned down as medically unfit,' he wrote to Eric McCormick, now on active service in Egypt. Heenan was encouraged by a recent example: 'More unlikely things have happened. I was reading in "Time" the other day of a famous American athlete who within the space of a fortnight or so, had reduced both the two and three mile world records by some seconds, and was then turned down as physically unfit for the American Draft.'[20]

In August 1941 John was called up. But when he paraded before the army examiners he was graded CIII and turned down. No reason was given but it may have been because of his stutter. According to Oliver Duff, the rules of war (codified in the Geneva Convention) exempted stutterers from war service on the grounds that they might find it difficult to say that vital phrase: 'I surrender'. John Pascoe was so pleased that he ran from the Buckle Street barracks to the ferry at the other end of downtown Wellington and crossed the harbour to share the news with Dorothy. She was delighted. In the First World War two of her uncles had been killed and she had seen the devastating effect of their deaths on her family, especially her grandmother who would weep when war songs were played on the radio. Dorothy believed 'that mankind must find other means of solving conflicts'.[21]

When news of John's rejection eventually reached Eric McCormick in Egypt, he was entertained. 'You will have been as diverted by the result of Johnny Pascoe's medical examination as I was,' he wrote to Heenan. 'I had not suspected the health-giving properties of a sedentary life (my own) or the debilitating effects of sunbathing and mountain climbing. However, I feel that Johnny's special talents can be made better use of in New Zealand than here and that it was the right decision for the wrong reasons.'[22]

Finally freed from the prospect of service overseas, Heenan promptly appointed Pascoe official photographer for the Department of Internal Affairs. His first assignment was to escort a *National Geographic* reporter, Howell Walker, on a three-week tour of the South Island.[23] On his return, John was delighted to discover Dorothy was pregnant. He was not at home for long, however, as his next job soon took him back to the mountains of the South Island. The Minister of Internal Affairs, Bill Parry, a tireless advocate of the benefits of physical exercise, had established a Physical Welfare Branch within his

'SOUTHERN TOURABOUT'

In October 1941 Pascoe accompanied Howell Walker, a National Geographic reporter, on a tour of New Zealand. The editors had asked him to write an article on 'The Making of an Anzac' and suggested he spend three months in Australia. When Walker pointed out there was a 'NZ' in Anzac they responded by offering him a week in New Zealand. Pascoe met him in Auckland and was appalled: 'This was the usual approach of special correspondents,' he explained, 'to make a quick flit from Auckland to Rotorua, thence to Wellington, and then back to their own country, where they wrote a chapter about New Zealand without having ever been in the South Island.' Walker agreed that he should spend six weeks in New Zealand with equal time in each island.

Pascoe's account of their travels makes no mention of the North Island and he may not have accompanied Walker there, but in the South Island they covered more than 2000 miles together: 'To my relief he was keen to avoid tourist conversations,' wrote Pascoe. 'Where possible we would stay with families on the route. He wanted to see industrial and social life, and his work was to be more than a travelogue.' From Blenheim they drove to Nelson, down the West Coast and crossed Arthur's Pass to Canterbury and Otago. For Pascoe, the highlight of their journey was a visit to Milford Sound. They walked through the Homer Tunnel, then under construction, to Milford. Walker accepted a ride down to the sound but Pascoe preferred to walk. 'I wanted to approach Milford Sound humbly as a pilgrim in a sweaty and pedestrian manner,' he wrote in 'Southern Tourabout':

> I walked down the nine odd miles of road, passed temporary camps and bridges, swapped experiences with some of the hard cases working there, plotted climbing routes up fearsome spurs and bluffs each time a new series of them loomed around the next corner, and generally absorbed the atmosphere of primeval New Zealand. For Milford Sound and its approach is one of those places that no overstatement can spoil. The sheer magnificence of giant cliffs, with enticing glaciers perched on shelves untrodden, and rising to jagged summit ridges gave me the impression of awe I had longed to experience. I was glad to be alone.

DOROTHY PASCOE COLLECTION

They returned to the North Island through Central Otago and the Mackenzie Country. Despite Walker's desire to see 'industrial and social life' their tour took them to the least populated parts of the South Island.

When Walker's article was published it was very disappointing. The 47-page illustrated essay still reflected his editors' bias, for most of the text and photos were about Australia, while New Zealand featured only in the final few pages. Even then, the sole evidence of their two-week journey in the South Island was the inclusion of three photographs. Nevertheless, the journey was instructive for it showed Pascoe how a reporter-cum-photographer went about his work.

department. One of its initiatives had been to build a series of huts on the route over Harper's Pass, from the headwaters of the Hurunui to the upper reaches of the Taramakau River in Westland. In November, John led a group of Physical Welfare staff and travel consultants over the pass, and at the same time, made notes for a route guide. He enjoyed the trip but realised that, as the leader, he could not leave the party to climb some of the adjacent peaks, although he was tempted to do so.[24]

Within days of John's return to Wellington the world situation changed abruptly. On Sunday 7 December 1941 the Japanese air force attacked the United States fleet lying at anchor in Pearl Harbour, Hawaii. Many ships were sunk, 3500 sailors were killed and thousands more wounded. This assault (by a country that had a peace delegation in Washington DC at the time) struck at the United States, the world's most powerful nation, in much the same way as the destruction of the twin towers of the World Trade Centre 60 years later. Pearl Harbour also changed the whole scale of the war, turning it into a global conflict.

The new direction of the war posed a problem for the New Zealand government as many people thought the New Zealand troops should be brought home. Churchill, however, requested that they remain in the Middle East and Prime Minister Peter Fraser, after careful consideration, agreed – a very difficult decision to make. In the following months the islands of the Pacific became stepping stones for the Japanese forces as they moved relentlessly southward. To many New Zealanders an invasion seemed to be only a matter of time. Others thought the Japanese lines of communication and supply were already stretched so far that they would only be able to make hit-and-run attacks. John Pascoe was one who feared an invasion. He joined the Home Guard and was assigned to the Eastbourne Signal Unit. He described his first exercise in a letter to his mother: 'The patrol work on Friday night was amusing. The Army undertook to provide food, blankets and transport, but although we did our stuff from 7 p.m. to 5 a.m. there was no transport, food or shelter. So we provided our own. I spent all Saturday sleeping on the lawn to recover.' Home Guard duties soon became all-consuming as John

The possibility of a Japanese invasion of New Zealand prompted the construction of a large air raid shelter in Parliament's grounds. John Pascoe photographed its installation in 1942 (right) and subsequent removal three years later.

WAR EFFORT COLLECTION,
ALEXANDER TURNBULL LIBRARY

was away with his unit for three nights of each week and often for much of the weekend as well. 'I'm getting to be a Home Guard widow,' Dorothy told Paul and Ann Pascoe. 'John has just left for his flag-waving practice while I write letters and sew napkins.'[25]

Her adjective 'flag-waving' was descriptive rather than pejorative, as John's signal unit practised a variety of methods of communication from Morse code to semaphore. But what he really enjoyed was the exercise and the challenge of negotiating routes through the bush-clad Orongorongo Ranges, usually at night. 'I'm very fit because of bivouac-material swagging for the H.G. [Home Guard] Signal Station on the inevitable "Sugarloaf" about 1,100 ft above the valley of the Wainui-o-Mata, which gives a view of the Rimutakas, Kaikouras, Wellington Harbour and hills. I find it hard work and great fun,' he told Paul and Ann. In the same letter he described in detail his Home Guard activities:

> Now I know the Morse code, it only remains to get up a bit of speed; as it is I can pick out words here and there when the lamps begin to flicker in the distant night. We get damn-all daylight parades. But the routine we seem to have got into to our enjoyment, is to rendezvous at the end of the Muritai road at 4 p.m. on Saturdays, go to a rubbish dump, and add to our load of shovels, axes, spades and slashers more loads of old lino and corrugated iron, and then to lug it all up to the top of the hill station miles away. Then while some of the crack signallers open up communication with other distant hill-tops, I get water from a secret supply, boil up, and the other blokes begin the bivouac building. After dark the signalling and the work continues to after midnight; then we sneak home making as little noise as possible (I horrified them by getting all exuberant in the moonlight last week, and yodelled) and not using torches. Last Saturday it was pitch dark, and I had to mosey the way along a scrub ridge, and managed not to lose the way. Apart from nearly losing one chap down a disused 30ft mine shaft, it went well.

This hilltop shelter near Eastbourne was built by John Pascoe's Home Guard unit with material salvaged from the local rubbish tip.

PASCOE COLLECTION,
ALEXANDER TURNBULL LIBRARY

Two nights a week were spent practising parade ground drill which John did not enjoy, but he was fortunate to be part of a unit that was more informal than most. 'The unit are a good lot, and real dags. All the other H.G.'s but our unit have uniforms, but I hope ours will be postponed, because they will be hellish hot to run round hills in.' Cadet training at Christ's College was now useful. 'Last week we had rifle practice and I found the Old School training had stuck, and I knew all the exercises required. But I find it hard to adapt my lambs tail to military step, and the other chaps say "Pascoe's gears aren't built that way".'[26]

At the start of the war, John had baulked at military service overseas because he did not want to die for what he saw as no useful purpose on some European battlefield. Ironically, it was his habit of sleeping off nights with the Signal Unit on the lawn the next day that nearly killed him. On one occasion he had woken, lunched with Dorothy, then wanted to linger on the grass in his sleeping bag. But Dorothy insisted they do the dishes, which was just as well 'for halfway through there was a terrific crash on the roof – we ran outside to see what it was. The chimney pot had blown off and one big jagged piece lay on J's bag just where his head would have been.'[27]

On 15 February 1942 the 'impregnable' Singapore fell to the Japanese. It seemed now that nothing could stop their advance. John, like many others, was convinced that 'The Japs will come, and us H.G.'s will be the silly-buggers-brigade in the frontlines, to get all the Tommy gun bullets and posthumous medals. I really do feel pessimistic about our invasion. I can't see how we can miss one, and for me I don't see much choice but to get in the middle of shit street and take all the pellets. We're better off as guerrillas than the Army, but lack of ammunition will be our real disaster.'

The likelihood of an invasion spurred him to complete his novel which, he told his brother, 'leaps along with all the jerkiness of a cricket, but without its speed'. In the six months since Paul had read the first draft, John had revised it and 'the result is better for the loss of dead wood'. Evenings not spent with the Home Guard were devoted to his novel which he hoped would have an international readership, even if New Zealanders found it objectionable: 'No one is going to like the result,' he prophesied:

> It'll annoy anyone who shirks knowledge of a way of life lived by many New Zealanders with their petty naughtinesses, inveterate blasphemy and obscenity, and peculiar energy. I should think all the NZAC would want to disown me (confirm their previous action), some of the CMC will be disgusted by my document, dear old Canterbury will shudder, the Internal Affairs will say, 'Christ what a viper'; the intelligentsia will say 'how lowbrow', and the lowbrows will accuse 'how highbrow', so whether the great American public will ever get occasion to read it I'm damned if I know. My reason to peg away at it consistently is that I must finish before the Japs come.[28]

But the Japanese did not come – and without this spur John Pascoe's only attempt at fiction was abandoned. He would probably have had to lay it aside anyway, as it was simply not long enough to be a novel. He attempted to rectify this by grafting a new adventure on to the Scimitar story, but after adding only one chapter he could see it was not a viable solution.

Dorothy was also worried by the Japanese. She hoped her baby would be old enough to have a chance of survival if they had to flee into the bush behind Eastbourne: 'It seems logical that the Japs will do more in Australia before collecting us,' she wrote to Paul and Ann Pascoe. 'It will be a few months until I'm capable of putting "Mary Ann" into a pack and running up a hill.'[29] Six weeks later, in May 1942, 'Mary Ann' was born and named Anna. Both parents were delighted and for the next few months John's camera caught her every move.

Anna's arrival altered his relationship with his brother. Before the birth of their first children, the friendship between the twins had been the primary relationship of their lives and this was evident in their regular and candid correspondence, but now that both Paul and John had a wife and child, their twice-weekly exchange of letters diminished to one every few months. Although they continued to correspond for the rest of their lives, their letters were never again as frequent or as revealing.

At this time New Zealand began to feel some relief from the oppressive prospect of a Japanese invasion. In May 1942 American naval forces defeated the Japanese in the Battle of the Coral Sea and a month later were again victorious at Midway Island. Further American victories turned the Japanese tide and the threat to New Zealand receded. As most New Zealand troops were in

John and Anna Pascoe, 1942.
Several months after Anna's birth John wrote the following poem, entitled 'Topicale'.
'Call her savage. Call her mild.
Lay her on an Eastbourne lawn.
Cut her teeth on bush logs, crayfish.
Squeak for Kariol at dawn.
Wiggle in the spray of salt
North-west wind. Tough the tang
Of seaweed rotting in the compost.
Hear Nip's naps swish as they hang.'
DOROTHY PASCOE COLLECTION

Members of the US Marine Corps after a toughening-up route march, Pukekohe, 1943.
WAR EFFORT COLLECTION,
ALEXANDER TURNBULL LIBRARY

Officers of the Second New Zealand Expeditionary Force disembark, with apparent difficulty, on their return to Wellington in July 1943. Other ranks peer through portholes while they await their turn.

WAR EFFORT COLLECTION, ALEXANDER TURNBULL LIBRARY

Europe and North Africa, New Zealand's defence was largely left to the Home Guard and the US Marines who began to arrive in New Zealand in the middle of 1942, either to train for active service in the Pacific or for rest and recreation after a stint in the war zone.[30] The Marines were, however, unfamiliar with New Zealand topography and would need local assistance. In the Wellington region, where there was a concentration of American troops, four specialist platoons were established to train as bush guides, and John Pascoe was pleased to be selected to join them. The activities of the Eastbourne Signal Unit had been fun but often spoilt, in John's view, by 'ceremonial parades and the officiousness of those with more pips than sense. The lack of officer ability to harden men to necessary fitness, and the complacency of the very men who needed training most, browned us off properly.'[31]

The élite Army Bush Guides were more to his liking. Led by mountain veterans and government deerstalkers, many of whom he knew, the platoons thrived on tough training to become efficient, self-reliant units. Pascoe was relieved that all their training was done in the bush, not on the parade ground. He was also tickled by 'the irony that most of us were graded CIII, i.e. unfit for military service, though any regulars we led had to be graded A1'. During the first two months of 1943 the Bush Guides trained intensively while exploring and mapping routes through the Orongorongo Ranges as well as the extensive area of bush country between the Hutt River and the Kapiti Coast. It was in the headwaters of the Whakatikei, a tributary of the Hutt River, that John Pascoe had his first experience of simulated warfare when the Bush Guides ambushed regular troops sent in from Paekakariki. He and Geoff Wilson, a Tararua veteran and friend, were chosen to be scouts. While 'Wilson slid away ahead of them, I took their photographs as they passed me. They did not know that I was there or that I had "shot" them with my camera.' When the regulars eventually managed to sabotage the Bush Guides' signalling system, Pascoe stealthily skirted the 'enemy' to give headquarters an up-to-date report on the situation.[32] It is evident from Pascoe's later account that he thoroughly enjoyed this encounter and that he would have made an excellent army scout had he not had such a strong aversion to killing — or being killed.

Pascoe also enjoyed military exercises in the nearby Tararua Ranges with US Marines sent there to train at Major George Yerex's School of Bush and Mountain Warfare. Yerex's job was to prepare the Americans for jungle warfare. In his capacity as official photographer, Pascoe accompanied them on several exercises and again was in his element. His stoical resilience, the legacy of many adventures in the Southern Alps, was called on during an

American troops training in the Tararua Ranges, January 1943.

PASCOE COLLECTION,
ALEXANDER TURNBULL LIBRARY

Major George Yerex, Commander of the School of Bush and Mountain Warfare, briefs Marines and Bush Guides before an exercise in the headwaters of the Hutt River, January 1943.

PASCOE COLLECTION,
ALEXANDER TURNBULL LIBRARY

overnight sortie on the exposed Marchant Ridge. He later described how 'A strong nor'-west wind howled itself to a gale and when we huddled up on the ridge to sleep, the storm rocked the trees whose roots rose and fell to our discomfort. This was a toughening up trip, and the boss had said "no tents", so when the wind turned to the sou'-west at 2 a.m. and the rain fell in a torrent, there was a deal of shivering and wetness.'[33]

Photographing Marines in the Tararua Ranges was only a part of Pascoe's larger brief to record all aspects of life in wartime New Zealand. As the Americans arrived in considerable numbers in 1942 and 1943, he made several trips around the country to record the American 'invasion'. He photographed the construction of their camps, the growing and delivery of their food supplies, as well as Marines interacting with New Zealanders. At the same time, he documented the local war effort and built up an invaluable record of New Zealanders at work: in factories and laboratories, on farms and in coal mines. He made a point of recording the work of women, such as land girls, who did jobs usually performed by men.

There was a specific purpose for his photographic survey. Joe Heenan found that many of the Marines, especially the officers, were keen to learn about New Zealand and he gave them numerous sets of bound volumes of *Making New Zealand*. But Heenan also realised that, having been designed for New Zealanders, it was not an ideal publication for this purpose, so he decided to produce a book that would explain New Zealand to the US forces.[34] In May 1942, Janet Wilkinson, one of John Beaglehole's brightest history graduates, was employed by the Historical Branch of Internal Affairs to write the text for *Introduction to New Zealand*. John Pascoe's job was to obtain photographs to illustrate it and to lay it out. Beaglehole was responsible for the overall design.[35]

Introduction to New Zealand *bears the unmistakeable imprint of John Pascoe. It opens to reveal a dramatic, double-page photo of Mount Cook on the endpapers and the back cover includes a photo of the east face of Mount Tasman. Within the covers, the many photos are arranged in portrait galleries or adroitly juxtaposed with brief, pithy captions — a technique Pascoe used again in his later books and articles.*

Pascoe was ideal for the job. In addition to his characteristic energy and enthusiasm, he was now an experienced photographer. Most of the photos he had taken for *Making New Zealand* had been of inanimate subjects such as buildings, roads, ships and trains, which had given him a technical understanding of photography; now he had to photograph people. Fortunately, he had that indispensable ability to be unobtrusive when circumstances required it, and the social dexterity to gain the confidence of a wide range of people. This is evident in his photographs from this period

John Beaglehole by Joan Fanning.

John Pascoe met the historian, John Beaglehole, while working on Making New Zealand. *After its completion they worked together on* Introduction to New Zealand, *an illustrated guide for American forces stationed here. Beaglehole, who was interested in book design and typography, was responsible for the innovative design and his ideas influenced both John Pascoe, who contributed the photos, and Janet Wilkinson, who wrote the text and later, as Janet Paul, became an important publisher with her husband, Blackwood.*

Beaglehole and Pascoe had other interests and habits in common: both were keen trampers and pipe smokers. Both were also occasional stutterers.

ALEXANDER TURNBULL LIBRARY

which show a variety of New Zealanders, all looking relaxed. Pascoe's trusty Rolleicord was partly responsible because it was less intrusive than other cameras. As it was operated from his chest, he looked down into it rather than at the subject so people were often unaware of being photographed. (Later, Ans Westra would also use a low-slung camera to candidly record New Zealand's post-war society.)

John Pascoe's wartime photographs are also memorable because they show his clear understanding of what made a strong image. His training as illustrations editor taught him the value of direct, simple images devoid of artifice. He recognised that photography was not so much a technical matter as an exercise in perception, a view he expressed forcefully in a later article. 'As an instrument of social reportage the camera has uses. In the hands of salon competitors or people who are tied to technical apron strings it has affectations that are at best irritating. An interest in people related to their physical environment is more healthy than the ability to fake million dollar

AIR ACE

RED CROSS DRIVER

SEAMAN

These are New

JOURNALIST

PRECISION WORKER

COW COCKY

NAVAL RATING

HOUSEWIFE

BOXER

John Pascoe selected these portraits from his wartime photo collection to illustrate the diversity of his compatriots for Introduction to New Zealand.

MAORI SCHOOLGIRL

GOOD COMPANION

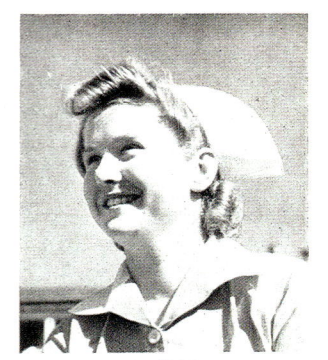

NURSE

Zealanders

SCHOOL TEACHER

LAWYER

MUNITION WORKER

TRAM GIRL

HORTICULTURALIST

GRANDMOTHER

clouds in skies that were grey when the photograph was taken.' Pascoe saw his work as repudiating an earlier, romantic tradition of photography which had presented a false view:

> New Zealand in the past has suckled men who have photographed barrels of lush pastureland dominated by posterish Egmont, trainloads of pseudo-Maori dances, while Mount Cook from the bathroom window of the Hermitage has sadly slunk through lots of lenses. Where are the documentary stories of the gold prospectors, the deer killers, the growth of a dairy factory, the monotony of wharf labour, the discomfort of a miner's calling, the adaptation of the Maori worker to city life and environment?[36]

As official photographer for Internal Affairs, John Pascoe relished the opportunity to record the lives of New Zealanders. Years of yarning with old-timers on the West Coast and station hands in the Canterbury high country had taught him how to get on with all kinds of people. His wartime photographic assignment was little different from photographing, for instance, the cook at Manuka Point Station or a musterer on his horse. He had also con-

John Pascoe's designation as 'official photographer' gave him access beyond barriers and allowed him to record scenes such as this returning soldier's reunion on a Wellington wharf.

WAR EFFORT COLLECTION,
ALEXANDER TURNBULL LIBRARY

Reinforcements from the Maori Battalion leave for overseas service, Rotorua, 11 January 1944.

WAR EFFORT COLLECTION,
ALEXANDER TURNBULL LIBRARY

sidered the relationship between the land and the people who depended on it for a living; this understanding was the theme of his 1938 article about the lives of workers on a high country station and also an important part of his later novel.

The War Effort Collection, as it is now known, also shows that John Pascoe kept up with developments overseas. As the contributor of articles and photos to a variety of magazines and newspapers he was familiar with the popular press at home and abroad, and he realised that the advent of 'documentary photography' was revolutionary. The 'new photography' as

WAR EFFORT COLLECTION, ALEXANDER TURNBULL LIBRARY

John Pascoe photographed these 1100 state houses under construction in Naenae in 1944.

During the Depression house construction in New Zealand dropped dramatically, forcing families, especially in the cities, to rent sub-standard houses. The Labour government embarked on an ambitious house building programme, particularly in the Hutt Valley, where planners and architects relished the opportunity to create ideal urban communities from scratch.

During the war demand for housing increased because industry and manufacturing grew rapidly, particularly in *Auckland* and the *Hutt Valley*. John Pascoe photographed these munition workers in a block of state flats in the *Hutt Valley*.

THE HOME FRONT

WAR EFFORT COLLECTION, ALEXANDER TURNBULL LIBRARY

WAR EFFORT COLLECTION, ALEXANDER TURNBULL LIBRARY

Pascoe's file note for this photo was 'spit and polish for the baby in a state house'.

it was also known, exemplified the impact of modernism. It originated in Russia during the revolution and soon influenced photographers in Europe. Just as progressive architects favoured the clean, uncluttered lines of modern buildings, avant garde photographers emphasised the abstract patterns and hard-edged realism of the modern city. The spread of the 'new photography' was assisted by technical innovations, especially in Germany in the 1920s, which made small, hand-held cameras possible. The first of these was the Leica, which could be used quickly and unobtrusively in a variety of light conditions. Previously a photographer had had to set up a bulky camera on a tripod; now people and events could be recorded spontaneously in a direct and candid way that did not require the subjects' cooperation. These new photographs soon appeared not merely as illustrations but as stories in themselves. The publication of a sequence of photos on a related theme was called 'photo journalism', which in turn spawned a new range of pictorial magazines.[37] Pascoe would have loved a Leica but could not afford one, so he continued to use the Rolleicord Heenan had given him at the start of *Making New Zealand*.

In the 1930s the rise of the Nazis had forced a number of Germany's Jewish photographers to flee, and they took their innovative cameras and ideas to Britain, the United States and further afield, where their influence was soon apparent. Irene Koppel was a typical example. Born in 1911 in Hamburg, she trained with several studios there before escaping to England in 1934. Three years later she emigrated to New Zealand and established a studio in Wellington. Portrait work was the backbone of her business, but she also took her camera outside to record people and events such as Home Guard training exercises, buildings damaged in the 1942 earthquake and women working in factories and on trams.[38]

In the United States the new documentary approach was exemplified by a Farm Security Administration project in which a number of photographers recorded the lives of farmers and agricultural labourers, especially in the mid-western 'dust bowl' where the soil had blown away. Harrowing images of these rural casualties of the Depression were influential in highlighting the plight of migrants, the poor and the dispossessed. On the other side of the Pacific, John Pascoe was aware of this photography and the work of other innovative American photographers such as Robert Capa; *Camera USA* was one of Pascoe's favourite books at the time. He was also an avid reader of such contemporary American writers as Erskine Caldwell, Theodore Dreiser, William Faulkner, John Dos Passos, Clifford Odets, Damon Runyon and John Steinbeck whose novels portrayed the often harsh reality of life.[39] In 1936, when the first issue of *Life* was published, its documentary photography quickly became popular and the hugely successful magazine prompted a number of similar pictorial publications including *Picture Post* in Britain and *Pix* in Australia.[40]

John Pascoe contributed to these magazines. In 1938 his photographic account of the first ascent of Mount Evans was published in *Pix*; later, as he travelled extensively in New Zealand to report with his camera on the lives of ordinary people in wartime, he sent some of his photos to publications in the United States, Australia and England.[41] New Zea-

Japanese prisoners clear debris from the bed of the Tauherenikau River, November 1943.

In February 1943, a Japanese officer's refusal to join a work party led to a riot at their Featherston camp. The guards responded by firing at the prisoners, killing 48 and wounding 74. Nine months later Heenan sent Pascoe to the camp to take photos. He found the prisoners friendly and keen to communicate as he photographed them working in the camp's furniture factory, in nearby fields, tending rows of cabbages and tomatoes destined to feed American troops, and down by the river.

WAR EFFORT COLLECTION,
ALEXANDER TURNBULL LIBRARY

land had its own pictorial magazines such as the *Free Lance* and the *Auckland Weekly News*, but the images selected were usually conventional, in contrast to the dramatic, sometimes disturbing examples of the new photography. In the past Pascoe had been a contributor to the *Free Lance*, which published his photographs of alpine adventures, but he now chose to submit his wartime photos to overseas magazines, presumably because he thought they would be more receptive, and because he and Heenan wanted to show the Allies the effort New Zealanders were making to support the war.

Pascoe's first wartime photo essay was published in *S & D*, an English farming magazine, in September 1943. Three pages of photos depicted life on a South Canterbury hill farm, from shots of musterers driving sheep down from the tops to portraits of 'The Musterer', 'The Farm Gardener' and 'The Boss' – an older man who managed the farm while the owner was overseas on active service. A few weeks later more Pascoe photos were published in the *Argus*, an Australian newspaper, to illustrate 'What New Zealand is doing in this conflict'. During the following 18 months similar Pascoe photo essays were accepted by a variety of overseas magazines; for example, a story about the Marines in New Zealand in New York's *PIC*, and others about a 'New Zealand sheep muster' and life on the high country run at Manuka Point in the English *Sport & Country* and *Picture Post*.[42]

WAR EFFORT COLLECTION, ALEXANDER TURNBULL LIBRARY

HIGH COUNTRY LIFE

Farming in New Zealand was the most frequent subject of Pascoe's photo essays published overseas. They included scenes on a South Canterbury hill country farm such as droving sheep to the yards and a portrait of an old musterer who, according to his caption, 'remembers the great [snow] storm of 1895, when many of the back country farms came near to disaster'.

WAR EFFORT COLLECTION, ALEXANDER TURNBULL LIBRARY

DOROTHY PASCOE COLLECTION

In February 1944, Dorothy and John Pascoe visited his favourite hill country farm, Manuka Point Station, near the headwaters of the Rakaia. Photos of wool being taken across the river, and Dorothy drying their gear on an old cart after a wet and stormy night in camp, later appeared in Picture Post, a pictorial magazine distributed in Australia, South Africa and New Zealand.

WAR EFFORT COLLECTION, ALEXANDER TURNBULL LIBRARY

In October 1943, John Pascoe travelled to Ruatoria to attend the Ngarimu hui. Before the ceremony he spent several days exploring and photographing the East Cape area, including the main street of Te Araroa.

WAR EFFORT COLLECTION, ALEXANDER TURNBULL LIBRARY

Two photographic assignments, in particular, influenced Pascoe. The first was a visit to the Maori township of Ruatoria in October 1943 and the second a three-week sojourn on the West Coast of the South Island in September 1944. For different reasons, both these experiences changed his understanding of his country. John Pascoe saw himself as a New Zealander, not in the self-conscious manner of some of the artists, poets and writers of the time whose work deliberately promoted the concept of cultural independence, but simply because he had no interest in being anything else. He was an intuitive nationalist. Unlike Paul Pascoe, he had never been to England and had no inclination to travel there and much of his reluctance to join the armed forces was due to his lack of identification with Britain as 'Home'.

John Pascoe's contact with Maori made him consider more deeply what it meant to live in New Zealand. As a South Islander, he knew little about Maori life, so the Ngarimu hui at Ruatoria was a revealing experience. The event was organised by the Ngati Porou leader and statesman, Sir Apirana Ngata, to commemorate Te Moananui-a-Kiwa Ngarimu, who was killed defending a Tunisian hilltop position from repeated German attacks. For his bravery he was awarded the highest military decoration, the Victoria Cross – the first time it had been won by a Maori. The award not only recognised the courage of a Ngati Porou warrior fighting with the traditional courage of his tribe, it was also a symbol of the entire Maori contribution to the war.

MOANA NGARIMU V.C.

Maraea and Hamuera Ngarimu (right), parents of Moana Ngarimu, were presented with his posthumous Victoria Cross at a special ceremony at Ruatoria in October 1943. Soon after Ngarimu's death in Tunisia, an account of his courageous leadership was published in the London Gazette:

WAR EFFORT COLLECTION, ALEXANDER TURNBULL LIBRARY

During the action at the Tebaga Gap on the 26th March, 1943, Second-Lieutenant Ngarimu commanded a platoon in an attack upon the vital hill feature, Point 209. He was given the task of attacking and capturing an underfeature forward of Point 209 itself and held in considerable strength by the enemy. He led his men with great determination straight up the face of the hill, undeterred by the intense mortar and machine-gun fire which caused considerable casualties. Displaying courage and leadership of the highest order he was himself first on the hill crest, personally annihilating at least two enemy machine-gun posts. In the face of such a determined attack the remainder of the enemy fled, but further advance was impossible as the reverse slope was swept by machine-gun fire from Point 209 itself.

Under cover of a most intense mortar barrage the enemy counter-attacked, and Second-Lieutenant Ngarimu ordered his men to stand up and engage the enemy man for man. This they did with such good effect that the attackers were literally mown down, Second-Lieutenant Ngarimu personally killing several. He was twice wounded, once by rifle fire in the shoulder and later by shrapnel in the leg, and though urged by both his Company and Battalion Commanders to go out, he refused to do so saying that he would stay a little while with his men.

Darkness found this Officer and his depleted platoon lying on the rocky face of the forward slope of the hill feature, with the enemy in a similar position on the reverse slope about twenty yards distant. Throughout the night the enemy repeatedly launched fierce attacks in an attempt to dislodge Second-Lieutenant Ngarimu and his men, but each counter-attack was beaten off entirely by Second Lieutenant Ngarimu's inspired leadership. During one of these counter-attacks the enemy, by using hand grenades, succeeded in piercing a certain part of the line. Without hesitation this Officer rushed to the threatened area, and those of the enemy he did not kill he drove back with stones and with his tommy-gun.

During another determined counter-attack by the enemy, part of his line broke. Yelling orders and encouragement, he rallied his men and led them in a fierce onslaught back into their old positions. All through the night, between attacks, he and his men were heavily harassed by machine-gun and mortar fire, but Second-Lieutenant Ngarimu watched his line very carefully, cheering his men on and inspiring them by his gallant personal conduct. Morning found him still in possession of the hill feature, but only he and two unwounded other ranks remained. Reinforcements were sent up to him. In the morning the enemy again counter-attacked, and it was during this attack that Second-Lieutenant Ngarimu was killed. He was killed on his feet defiantly facing the enemy with his tommy-gun at his hip. As he fell, he came to rest almost on the top of those of the enemy who had fallen, the number of whom testified to his outstanding courage and fortitude.

Recognising the significance of the occasion, the government helped to transport, accommodate and feed the 7000 Maori who attended. In a splendid and poignant ceremony the Victoria Cross was presented to Ngarimu's parents by the Governor General, Sir Cyril Newall, in the presence of the Prime Minister, members of the Cabinet, leaders of the three armed forces and representatives of Allied governments. Several Pascoe photos of the hui appeared in the *Illustrated London News* and later the Polynesian Society published

KIA KUTIA! AU! AU!

The traditional peruperu or war-dance was one of the many action songs performed at the Ngarimu hui. The words, printed below, were modified to suit the occasion.

WAR EFFORT COLLECTION, ALEXANDER TURNBULL LIBRARY

solo	*Whiti! Whiti!*	*Arise! Arise!*
chorus	*E!*	*E!*
s.	*Ka paahi Itari! Ka poharu Tiamani!*	*Italy is finished, Germany submerged,*
	Ka miere Tiapani!	*And Japan euchred!*
ch.	*Ko to arero tena*	*Was that not your tongue,*
	E whatero i mua ra,	*That protruded aforetime*
	I o rangi koroke whakakapohautia,	*With ghoulish conceit?*
	Kei te poharutanga, pou! pa!	*Now that you taste defeat,*
		What then? Pa!
s.	*Ka tohe au, ka tohe au –*	*I strive! I strive!*
ch.	*Ka tohe au ki a Hitara,*	*I strive after Hitler,*
	Ki taku karaka i whakaura i te waru,	*My karaka-berry boiled in the eighth*
	E tu nei kati kawana!	*month!*
		Here stands the obstacle of the Allies!
s.	*Kia kutia!*	*So close your ranks!*
ch.	*Au! Au!*	*Au! Au!*
s.	*Kia wherahia!*	*Then open, ah open!*
ch.	*Au! Au!*	*Au! Au!*
	E! kia rere atu te kohuru	*So let this murderer fly far*
	Ki tawhiti titiro mai ai	*And regard me with fear and terror!*
	Ae! Ae! Aa!	*Ae! Ae! Aa!*

Sir *Apirana Ngata and his granddaughter watching a poi dance at the opening of the Tamatekapua meeting house, Rotorua, in 1943.*

Among the many wartime events photographed by John Pascoe were the ceremonial openings of a number of meeting houses built to mark New Zealand's centenary.

WAR EFFORT COLLECTION,
ALEXANDER TURNBULL LIBRARY

many more in an elegant booklet. Its author noted that Pascoe's photographs provided 'an admirable and valuable record of an outstanding event in contemporary Maori life'.[43]

The Ngarimu hui, as well as the ceremonial opening of two meeting houses in Rotorua and one in Te Kaha (which he publicised in a photo essay in Australia's Pix magazine), gave Pascoe opportunities to meet Maori people. His colleague at Internal Affairs, Janet Wilkinson, noticed that he was 'particularly delighted by Maori life and customs' and Dorothy Pascoe was also aware of this. According to Dorothy, the hui at Ruatoria made 'a deep impression on him', as did Sir Apirana Ngata, the dominant figure at the ceremony. Pascoe regarded it as a privilege to be present and the friendly attitude of his photographic subjects showed that he was welcome. Above all, his contact with Maori made him ponder the plurality of New Zealand society. He realised that 'we are two quite different people sharing the same land, and need to work out how to do so harmoniously'.[44] Some years later, his memories of the Ngarimu hui prompted Pascoe to write a poem:

ON THE MARAE
Meshed in the velvet of Ngati Porou voices,
Fluidly caught and letting the flow of songs
Lull tremors of hakas down into pakeha quietude,
Spectator of sensuous rhythm, participant passive.
May you rest in the sun. May I rest in the sun.
E noho Ra. Haere ra. Aue! Haere ra.

John Pascoe photographed this mother and child at Te Kaha in 1944, when he attended the opening of a new meeting house called Tutaki. He considered the ornately carved building the finest of the Maori centennial houses.

WAR EFFORT COLLECTION,
ALEXANDER TURNBULL LIBRARY

Knowing that *Tena koe e kuia* means Hail!
Hail to Thee, Old Lady. Once you were *hine*.
Aue! Once *kotiro*. But whether
Maiden, matron, great grandmatriarch, your ear
Was the ear for vowels. Consonants but
Fit for the *potai*, the *kuri*, the *tutae*.

Vocal your hands, and your feet stamped proudly
Whether in planting kumara or rousing
The prelude to passion. Brown your eyes
Deluged with sorrow. For war, like mountains
Takes warriors as yeast for its brew.

Or eyes gleaming an earthly *allegro*.
Incitement to rhythm, incitement.
Participant active – the palm, the frond,
Straight as the punga and supple as song.

Pascoe's visits to various marae taught him a great deal about the diversity of life in New Zealand, an awareness that developed further when he visited the West Coast of the South Island in the spring of 1944. Like most New Zealanders, John Pascoe knew little of the harsh living conditions of the mining communities in Buller. To him, the West Coast was the sparsely populated southern part with its glaciers, gorges and dangerous, sprawling rivers, not the poor settlements of the Buller coalfields where families struggled to survive in a landscape made desolate by mining. Visits to places such as Burnett's Face, Cascade Creek, Denniston and Stockton convinced him that the popular prejudice against the miners (who were widely believed to be the cause of wartime coal shortages) was not justified. Social comment was rarely included in his mountain books, but in *Land Uplifted High* he made his sympathy for the miners clear:

> I went up the 'Burma Road' at 3,000 feet past Stockton to the new open-cast workings, where the alpine solitude looked as bleak as the Aleutians without their glaciers. I met miners who travelled over bush ranges on foot to avoid the risk of pneumonia after working in a warm mine and riding through a gorge in an open truck in which waterfalls spray wet the ones who used it. I liked the miners and found them as self-reliant and as hospitable as West Coasters further south. I noted coal production was limited not by the miners' work but by the bottlenecks in transport in railways and shipping. For all the papers could say against them, the miners of the Buller worked hard.[45]

In his post-war article 'Coal from the Buller', Pascoe described the miners' working conditions to explain their demands which, without an understanding of their circumstances, seemed unwarranted. 'Work in the mine can be done in reasonable surroundings in dry places,' he wrote, 'but sometimes conditions become so wet that water overhead and underfoot entitles the miner to fewer hours. When you learn that a "wet place" by agreement is "a place in which a workman cannot avoid his clothing becoming saturated with water within three hours of his commencing work or where he has to work in more than three inches of water on the floor" you realise that health is relative to bathhouse temperatures and dry clothes at the end of a working day. I had to lend my camera my sou'wester to take photographers of a wet place. Some [miners'] journeys in tubs [coal trucks] up or down an access gorge tramway may include deluges from waterfalls whose spray breaks into the open tubs.'

WAR EFFORT COLLECTION,
ALEXANDER TURNBULL LIBRARY

Stockton, 1944.

The geological process of folding and faulting means that Buller coal is found on top of the ranges where it is extracted by open cast mining. This leaves the countryside stripped bare.

WAR EFFORT COLLECTION, ALEXANDER TURNBULL LIBRARY

Union leaders address a meeting of striking miners on the issue of state control of the Stockton mining field.

WAR EFFORT COLLECTION, ALEXANDER TURNBULL LIBRARY

'Mining is a tough job, and gives an honest thirst and a desire for company,' observed Pascoe who found that 'To drink with miners you must be fit, physically, and energetic. There is none of the hurried pig swilling of the city rush between five and six.
There is no rush about drinking. It is quite normal to find a room full of men drinking, but they can hold their liquor.'

WAR EFFORT COLLECTION,
ALEXANDER TURNBULL LIBRARY

Pascoe's coalfield photos are among his finest work. Soon after the war, the *New Zealand Geographer* published his article 'Coal from the Buller', illustrated with 27 of his photos. Both the captions and text reiterated Pascoe's view that the miners were blamed for shortages really caused by inadequate transport:

> I had this impressed on me as I froze on a rock above the Denniston incline waiting for a truck or series of trucks to go down filled with coal. After an hour I found that though the first shift of miners had hewn coal for some time, no trucks were then available to take the coal. No trucks were available to take the coal because full trucks were piled up on the Westport wharf. Full trucks were piled up on the Westport wharf because the colliers had not left. The colliers had not left because they could not cross the bar. Because they could not cross the bar, the North Island went short of coal, gas, rail transport, and coal by-products. So ran this explanation. But it was not featured in the newspapers.[46]

Miner's daughter, Denniston.

WAR EFFORT COLLECTION,
ALEXANDER TURNBULL LIBRARY

With characteristic energy, Pascoe went to considerable lengths to verify the situation: he climbed Buckland Peak behind Westport and photographed the Buller rivermouth to show how silt built up the bar, and he also went out to the harbour bar 'with three skippers of colliers that were held up and admired their cursing, and sympathised with the monotonous work of dredges in the background'.

WAR EFFORT COLLECTION, ALEXANDER TURNBULL LIBRARY

THE CASCADE RIVER COAL FLUME

When John Pascoe visited the isolated mining town of Burnett's Face high on the hilltops, access was up a 'hair-raising road'. Rather than return the same way, he and his companion tramped down the Cascade River, an experience he later described in his book Land Uplifted High:

The day was fine and we had only some seven miles to walk. But there was no route through the gorge save on a wooden flume down which coal was sluiced from mine mouth to railhead. The flume was waterworn in a slippery concave runnel, and was only eighteen inches wide with walls of eight inches. The first three miles or so were so treacherous in nailed boots that we walked barefoot, which was not so bad for me as my feet were hardened from running round without shoes at Eastbourne in Wellington. But my companion found this awkward and was unhappy till our boots gripped over the last stretch of four miles. Some of the swaying spans of the flume ran across ravines of a hundred feet in depth, and it was tricky balance work, though I got unusual shots of the tops of rimu trees. The magnificent gorge scenery was varied by an odd hut or tent used on week-days by men who patrolled the flumes when coal was running.

Pascoe was conscientious; he took this photo of a ball in Westport after midnight.

WAR EFFORT COLLECTION, ALEXANDER TURNBULL LIBRARY

In his three years as the department's official photographer, John Pascoe took numerous photos of a wide range of subjects, so it is somewhat ironic that he is best known for a series taken on just two days – 8 May 1945 when Germany surrendered and 15 August 1945 when Japan did the same. Throughout New Zealand people of all ages celebrated on the streets, in pubs and homes. Pascoe worked Wellington's streets tirelessly, capturing scenes of the joyful crowd singing, dancing and kissing servicemen. When Japan surrendered Pascoe's exciting job as 'a traveller who reports with a camera' came to an end.[47] In 1947, his wartime archive of 1500 photos was given to the Alexander Turnbull Library, then a part of the Internal Affairs Department. The War Effort Collection, as it has become known, and the illustrations used in *Making New Zealand* (which had also been given to the library), are one of the cornerstones of the Turnbull's photographic collection.[48]

Pascoe's photographic record of New Zealand in wartime undoubtedly justified the freedom Heenan had given him; now his boss had a new job in mind for him as the illustrations editor for a series of official war histories. This would mean a return to a departmental desk in Wellington and the kind of work he had done for *Making New Zealand*. In those days he had been single and constrained only by deadlines; now he had a wife and two small children, for soon after his return from the Buller coalfields Dorothy had given birth to their second child, Sara, now a toddler. When Dorothy had only one child,

WAR EFFORT COLLECTION, ALEXANDER TURNBULL LIBRARY

WAR'S END

John Pascoe was active in *Wellington during the celebrations and events that marked the end of the war. His photographs included a crowd outside the wooden Government Buildings listening to speakers the day after Germany's surrender, sailors celebrating news of the Japanese capitulation and VJ Day in a Wellington pub.*

WAR EFFORT COLLECTION, ALEXANDER TURNBULL LIBRARY

WAR EFFORT COLLECTION, ALEXANDER TURNBULL LIBRARY

Celebrating VE Day on Lambton Quay, 8 May 1945.

WAR EFFORT COLLECTION, ALEXANDER TURNBULL LIBRARY

During the war many New Zealand women cared for children on their own. With her husband often absent on army duty, or away with his camera, Dorothy Pascoe was a typical example. She realised the need for a place where mothers could meet while their children played, and where their babies could be looked after when mothers needed to catch the ferry into the city. She established the Eastern Bays Playcentre and was its first president.

In 1945 John Pascoe took this photo of playcentre supervisor, Lisa Huppert, and children. Anna Pascoe, aged three, is on the top of the slide.

DOROTHY PASCOE COLLECTION

John and Sara Pascoe, c.1945.
John and Dorothy enjoyed family trips into the bush, especially to the Orongorongo Valley. They were among the first trampers to take their children with them.

DOROTHY PASCOE COLLECTION

she had no difficulty with John's lengthy absences on assignments as she simply went to stay with her brother and his wife who also had a small daughter. With two little girls this was not feasible. Even though John loved the life of the roving cameraman he recognised this, and after Sara's birth he took photos only in and around Wellington.

As servicemen returned from overseas the women who had done their jobs while they were away were encouraged (and sometimes forced) to return to more traditional female occupations and the home. After five years of war, men hankered for the security and stability of family life: the love of a wife and children, a bed to sleep in and their own home. In the post-war period, New Zealanders and their government embarked on an unprecedented phase of house building. John Pascoe's life reflected these national aspirations; for the next 10 years much of his energy was focused on home and family – and writing.

CHAPTER SIX

Family Man

Marriage and family life gave John Pascoe emotional security and the confidence to become a writer. After the Second World War he found his role as the author of books and articles about alpine adventures and life in the high country. As unprecedented numbers of New Zealanders rushed to live in the cities, his writing gave them a sense of their pioneer past and the country-side they had left behind.

He and his wife built a house in the bush behind Eastbourne while John continued to work for the Department of Internal Affairs, illustrating official war histories. At first he had little time for writing, as all his spare hours were spent clearing the section and hauling materials up to the building site. Once the house was completed, however, he returned enthusiastically to writing. In the early 1950s he had three books published in quick succession: a collection of his photographs, a route guide to the northern half of the Southern Alps and a second edition of Unclimbed New Zealand. In the public mind, his name became indelibly associated with the mountains.

The demands of family life made his alpine trips less frequent. Yet family life more than compensated. He enjoyed introducing his daughters to the outdoors, especially around Eastbourne or on family holidays in the Marlborough Sounds. Pascoe's photos from this period reflect the national preoccupation — and his own — with building homes and raising families, as New Zealanders put the war behind them and concentrated on creating the ideal society.

From left: Dorothy Pascoe holding Jane, Anna, Sara and John Pascoe holding Martha.

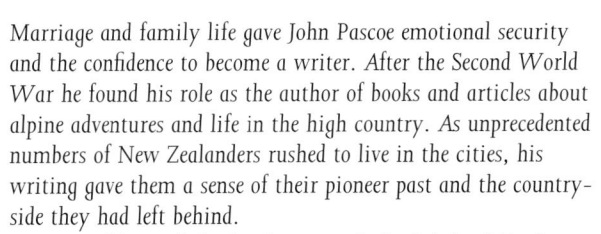

DOROTHY PASCOE COLLECTION

'IDON'T KNOW WHY I've kept paying rates on it all these years,' the solicitor who owned the steep section at Eastbourne had said, when John Pascoe asked if it was for sale. With no road access, the bush-covered land was of little value and the lawyer readily agreed to sell it for a small sum. The solicitor's albatross was the Pascoes' delight. On this one-acre section in Blackey's Gully they could live in the bush, with a stream running through it and the sea close by, and John could continue to commute to the city.[1]

The addition of Anna and Sara had made their cosy little bungalow on the main road too crowded and the prospect of more children required a move to a larger house. But most of the homes in Eastbourne were beyond their means, so the cheap section with a house designed by Paul Pascoe (to be built in stages as more space was needed) was the best solution. It was also an irresistible opportunity for John Pascoe to emulate the early European settlers he had admired for so long. 'The pioneer age, of all our different periods, is to me the most stimulating,' he wrote to Anita Crozier, the daughter of a Fiordland explorer, 'and we are lucky that even today we can still enjoy its flavour.'[2] As John later recalled:

> We had all the excitement of pioneer settlers without their inaccessibility. We cleared space for a house, stumped the clearing and excavated for top storey and basement. This was hard pick and shovel work including both clay and

Dorothy Pascoe in one of the chairs designed by the émigré Austrian architect, Ernst Plischke.

DOROTHY PASCOE COLLECTION

NEW ZEALAND
Design Review

Two-monthly journal of the Architectural Centre, Inc., Wellington
Subscriptions: New Zealand Design Review, Box 16 28, Wellington

No. 2 JULY 1948
3/- a year, 9d. a copy

FAMILY IN A FOREST
by John Pascoe

The Ambition: Wellington is one of the few New Zealand cities where it is possible to live in the bush and to work in a building. My wife and I decided that a bush environment for a home would compensate us for the natural disadvantages of living away from mountains. We also wanted a harbour view, sun compatible with shelter, and privacy. We found a bush section of nearly one acre in Eastbourne, took bearings on the sun in mid-winter and summer, visited the place in a cloudburst, and were satisfied with everything.

The Problems: Patiently we felled trees and scrub, and drew stumps from the immediate site of the house. With the whiskers removed, the architect came and brooded on the site, the builder quoted on drainage, and I was told where to excavate. We built log retaining walls and took all excavation spoil away from the foundations' area. Excavating was slow, as we struck a rock outcrop, which, however, gave metal for bush tracks. A neighbour helped me re-grade a private road. We built a culvert bridge across a small creek, and a bush tramway and trolly. Over a long period, and often at night, we worked a hand winch to transport the forty-five-odd tons of building material for the house.

(Continued on page 7)

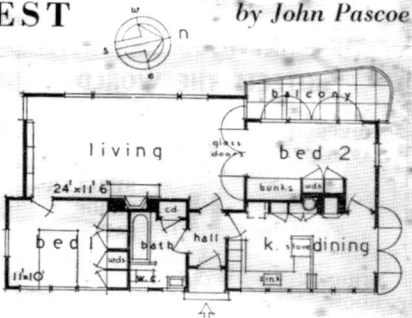

Architects: Pascoe & Hall, Christchurch.

Owners: Mr. and Mrs. John Pascoe, and family of three.

Builder: Mr. G. H. Aitken, Eastbourne.

The argument is unanswerable.

Photo: John Pascoe

DOROTHY PASCOE COLLECTION

rock. We dragged logs down the hill for a retaining wall for a terrace in front of the house, which was designed in the modern style by my brother Paul. We bridged a creek, perfected an access track, built a tramway, trolley and installed a hand winch. Over a period of eight months I carried up forty-five tons of building material for the house which we occupied in November 1947.[3]

The house was a typical example of Paul Pascoe's modernist architecture, though subdued in comparison with his own house in Sumner which

he designed at about the same time. The beech forest softened John and Dorothy's home and almost hid it from view, whereas Paul's house rose starkly above the surrounding suburban bungalows, boldly asserting the arrival of a new architectural style.

Although neither Paul nor John actually built their own houses (work well beyond their limited handyman skills), John did everything he could to help the builder in order to save money. He spent many evenings and weekends hauling building materials up to the site. Sometimes friends gave him a hand, in particular Stan Conway who seemed to find in the Pascoe family's activities an antidote to his experiences during the war. He had a serious shoulder injury but still managed to help John considerably. Pascoe's work diary records that in February 1947, for example, he and Stan winched 14 loads of timber and 22 tons of shingle up the steep hillside, while Dorothy made a track in from the road and carried up bricks.[4] As the adults toiled the children played, finding endless entertainment with the long earthworms they dug up on the site. To Conway, a confirmed bachelor, Anna and Sara were part of the attraction and Dorothy could see that Stan and several other returned servicemen 'enjoyed being part of our family life. We all felt the horrors of war. I guess playing with the kids and the wisecracking that is part of the camaraderie of the mountains, gave these young men a sense of another reality.'[5]

Working together on the winch deepened the friendship between John and Stan which, in the next few years, was to become the most important of

Paul and Ann Pascoe's house at Sumner caused a sensation in 1948. Today it remains in its original condition, an enduring example of Paul Pascoe's uncompromising modernist design.
DOROTHY PASCOE COLLECTION

Sara Pascoe dressed as the white rabbit from Alice in Wonderland, Eastbourne, 1946. Anna Pascoe holds a bottle of 'growth potion'.
DOROTHY PASCOE COLLECTION

all Pascoe's mountain friendships. As CMC members he and Stan had known each other before the war, but it was not until 1940, during the controversy caused by Pascoe's provocative comments in *The Mountains* issue of *Making New Zealand*, that they became firm friends. Stan Conway, who was president of the CMC, defended Pascoe in the Christchurch and Otago newspapers and John never forgot it. Conway returned from the war with a decoration but was depressed because he feared that his damaged deltoid muscle, which prevented him raising his arm above his shoulder, had put an end to his climbing career.[6] How could he haul himself up ropes, clamber over rocks or cut steps in ice? John refused to accept that Stan was finished as a climber and to prove it he organised a trip up the Rakaia to climb Mount Whitcombe. He and Stan were joined by another war veteran, John Clegg, an airman who had been a Japanese prisoner of war.

In comparison with his friends, Pascoe's wartime activity had been free of injury or trauma, but he had his own compelling reasons to climb Mount Whitcombe. It was 15 years since he had been denied his chance to be in the first party to reach the top of Canterbury's most coveted peak (although he had organised the trip), when 'Boney' Chester's impetuous decision to change a reconnoitre into a summit bid was successful. John had tried for Whitcombe again in 1944 with Dorothy, but they were foiled by stormy weather. So the trip in February 1946 with Conway and Clegg was his third attempt. Dorothy and their two daughters travelled with them to Manuka Point Station and although Dorothy brought her climbing gear, she stayed behind at the homestead with the children.

The trip did not begin well. On the first day, while sidling a bluff above the Rakaia, Clegg lost his gear and their climbing rope when his pack fell into the river and was swept away. He returned to Manuka Point, borrowed Dorothy's crampons and storm clothing and other items from the station hands, as well as a 20-metre rope previously used 'to tether an amorous bull and to lash wool bales onto the dray'. Clegg then raced back up the valley to rejoin Conway and Pascoe. Two days later, after waiting out a storm while camped on the Ramsay Glacier, they set off for Mount Whitcombe in clearing weather. With remarkable confidence they chose an unclimbed route, up the aptly named Menace Icefall. At times, as Pascoe later recalled, it was risky: 'One unbridged crevasse was crossed by swinging on the bull rope as though it was the arm of a pendulum. Another unbridged ice-chasm was too high to jump across though it was narrow. Stan cut a big step in the side and let John [Clegg] stand on his shoulder, crampons and all.' The effort was worth it. Once they reached the Main Divide Mount Whitcombe was relatively accessible although 'the last few hundred feet gave us steeper climbing than we had expected'.[7] On top conditions were so calm that 'a

John Clegg and Stan Conway on the summit of Mount Whitcombe, February 1946. John Pascoe's caption for this photo in his article 'Back to the Mountains' described his friends' war experiences: 'John, on the left, had nearly three and a half years as a prisoner of war under the Japs. Stan, on the right, was with the 2 NZEF from Greece to Italy, and got bashed badly at Faenza. In a renewal of their pre-war mountaineering, they find satisfaction that cannot be overcome by any hardship or disability.'

JOHN PASCOE COLLECTION,
ALEXANDER TURNBULL LIBRARY

match burnt down without flickering' and so clear 'that we could see the sea on both coasts of the South Island. The panoramas were magnificent.'[8]

Pascoe had once before enjoyed views of both the Tasman Sea and the Pacific Ocean when he made the first ascent of nearby Mount Evans in 1934. Now his appreciation of the moment was heightened by an awareness of his altered circumstances. He was no longer a carefree young man but married, the father of two children, and living far away in Wellington – in short, his opportunities for climbing were precious. Conway and Clegg also found something special on the summit, for their successful ascent showed that their mountain days were not over. They had recovered their pre-war fitness and could now contemplate more climbing with renewed confidence. It was, wrote Pascoe, 'a day for us to dream about for years'.[9]

This expedition encouraged Conway and Pascoe to look for more opportunities to climb together. Comparing past efforts, they found that before the war each had climbed all the peaks in Arthur's Pass National Park except Mount Russell. As far as they knew, no one else had set foot on all 35 summits in the park, so they determined to be the first to do so. At Easter 1947 they set out for Mount Russell which, at 1850 metres, was much lower than Mount Whitcombe. Ironically, it gave them far more trouble. On their first attempt they ended up in a series of steep gulches which they could see led only into danger, so they abandoned the ascent and returned to camp in the valley below. Next morning, a different route seemed more promising until their progress was slowed by an impenetrable band of sub-alpine scrub. By the time they had forced a way through it, the day was waning and they did not reach the summit until 4 p.m. Most of their gear lay far below in

Mount Whitcombe from the Ramsay Glacier. The Menace Icefall, which Pascoe and his companions climbed to reach the Main Divide, lies on the left below the face of Mount Whitcombe.

JOHN PASCOE PHOTO,
JOAN MACLEAN COLLECTION

John Pascoe on the summit of Mount Russell, Arthur's Pass National Park.

confident anticipation of a descent before nightfall. Instead, darkness found them on the bushline where they spent a cold and thirsty night in the open, their only water drips from a slowly melting block of ice Conway had carried down from the summit.[10]

Pascoe wrote an account of this climb for *Journeys*, the illustrated magazine of the South Islands Travel Association, which had earlier published his story of the war veterans' ascent of Mount Whitcombe. Between 1946 and 1950 Pascoe wrote a total of 11 articles for *Journeys*, most of them recollections of his youthful alpine adventures, as he discovered a useful source of supplementary income. To ensure the interest of the general reader, these stories required a degree of literary inventiveness, which Pascoe had developed while writing assignments for Heenan before the war. Now, for the first time since coming to Wellington in 1937, he found he was not required to do any writing at work. His job as illustrations editor kept him busy selecting images and laying out a series of bulletins about the war, but the accompanying texts were written either by subject specialists or by his friend, David Hall. This left Pascoe with creative energy in reserve.

At home in the evenings he wrote articles for *Journeys* and other publications, but with a day's work behind him, tiredness was often an impediment. Music helped. Towards the end of his life he said, 'I remember music in terms of both writing and endurance. In terms of writing because it is absolutely ideal when you are working against fatigue, you can't really get tired if you are hearing a glorious programme of music.' He also found music invaluable when labouring outside. 'If you are pounding clay with a heavy ramrod, and if you've got [J S Bach's] "Mass in B minor" pouring through the beech forest you just don't get tired at all.'[11]

During 1948 John Pascoe wrote his second book, *Land Uplifted High*, in the evenings. Like *Unclimbed New Zealand*, it consisted mainly of accounts of his own alpine experiences expanded to book length with chapters on specific groups such as 'High Country Sheepmen', 'Deer Killers' and 'The Writers — Mountain Literature of the Southern Alps'. But whereas his first book was confined to the mountains of Canterbury and Westland, *Land Uplifted High* included recollections of trips all over New Zealand. The first three chapters described North Island alpine areas from the Tararua mountains to Auckland's Waitakere Ranges, reflecting the variety of assignments he had done for Heenan. The approach to this book also differed from his earlier writing; *Unclimbed New Zealand* was a young man's first book, hastily written and then sent to England for publication without pause for revision. This time Pascoe was more cautious. After completing a first draft of *Land Uplifted High* he put it aside for eight months, then revised it in light of readers' 'helpful criticism'. A further period of gestation was followed by more revision, which meant that the book was not published until 1952, four years after the first draft was written.[12]

In the interim, Pascoe wrote several articles for a prestigious new periodical, the *New Zealand Geographer*, started by Professor George Jobberns of Canterbury University College. John Pascoe's 'Coal from the Buller' and his 'Canterbury High Country: The Sheep and the Sheepmen of the Mountains' were long, thoughtful essays of which he was particularly proud. The latter he described as 'my most serious piece of writing ever'.[13] His description of high country life and personalities was written in 1938, then lay fallow until the end of the war when he revised it for inclusion in the inaugural issue of Jobberns's journal. As it was based on individuals he had come to know while visiting Manuka Point Station, Pascoe took great care to ensure the portraits were accurate, and also changed names to protect identities, although to those in the know it was obvious who the various people were. The description of the station owner, Laurie Walker, for example, was unmistakeable:

> One man stands out in my mind above others as the city worker who left town life in his early twenties and settled down in the backcountry to rise from musterer to manager and finally owner.

John Pascoe and Laurie Walker, Manuka Point Station, c.1933. In addition to their affection for the Rakaia Valley, Pascoe and Walker also shared an enthusiasm for smoking. After the war when tobacco was still in short supply, Pascoe scoured Wellington shops to amass supplies for Walker. He had to be careful because some shopkeepers became suspicious. 'I sent some tobacco up yesterday,' he told Walker. 'Sorry it isn't better quality but things are chronic now, and we get glared at by strange shops.'

JOHN PASCOE COLLECTION, ALEXANDER TURNBULL LIBRARY

He has never lost his dislike of city rush and those who have experienced his serenely peaceful station can understand everything. His run is one of the most rugged and alpine and one of the most isolated; it has taken his sinewy strength to work, yet has not lost him his vigour or good humour. More than any man he is the friend of those who have worked for him. The station runs perhaps 3000 sheep and even before the war he had only one or two musterers. For at least one war year he did all his own mustering, over tops of six thousand feet, and let his sheep be the first call on his patience and resources. In the depression the run had a mighty tough time and was pulled down because it was worked on the books of the stock firm in conjunction with a down-country place that was not over profitable. He got luxuries when he saw them; and that wasn't often. Sometimes the trustees of the estate who then owned the run would inspect the run and promise things that never quite happened along.

However, sheepman-by-occupation so liked the life and its inherent struggle that he took all that the seasons' floods, snow and sun sent. If a dray wheel bust in midstream, he'd ride to the homestead for repair material and fix it there and then. He saved his wages and bought the place. Like other farmers over the whole Dominion he has his mortgage to worry about. In the land of hospitality, he is the most hospitable of men. He would risk his life to help a party over the river, but would resent effusive thanks and call it sufficient if you just said 'It's been bloody good of you'. So, too, would he appreciate letters, magazines or sets of photographs.

He would be quiet when you first met him, but would never forget you and in other visits would delight in news of men who had climbed or stalked in his country. Rarely does he visit the city, and then he cannot get back to his homestead quick enough. An interesting trait is his hatred of bloodshed. Most farmers get inured to the harshnesses of their calling and will cut an animal's throat, shoot marauders, or belt over the head a bird to be eaten with no qualms. Not so this man who, realizing he cannot avoid routine farm slaughter, will not look to do it if someone else does not mind doing it for him.

Here, then, is an example of a man suited to his environment. It is impossible to imagine him as contented in other surroundings. His lack of any sense of time is in itself an outstanding dignity; no hardship would break him because he has met what the back-country can offer in twenty years of work.[14]

The description of his virtues probably embarrassed Laurie Walker, although his reaction to the article is not known. But John was surprised and saddened to learn that others at Manuka Point took exception to his article. Freddy Ambrose, the idiosyncratic cook, wrote Pascoe 'a really angry letter' accusing him of 'disparaging him and all the people at Manuka Point'. And Charlie Cran, a friend of Laurie Walker's, wrote to him suggesting that 'Johnny will soon have to buy a bull otherwise he will run out of ammunition'.[15] Pascoe's response to these complaints was interesting in light of his earlier obdurate refusal to admit to any fault during The Mountains controversy. Then, he had offended sections of the New Zealand climbing community with his inaccurate and provocative comments, but saw no reason to apologise. Six years later, his favourable portraits of high country characters prompted a critical response which he quickly met with letters of apology. In a letter to Charlie Cran, Pascoe asked:

'FREDDIE AMBROSE'

To some people, *Walter Frederick Ambras was a swagger, to others a religious crank. John Pascoe saw him, however, as 'a -character in his own right and a man of great and compelling personality'.*

In his article on the high country in The New Zealand Geographer, Pascoe included a detailed description of Ambras, whom he called 'Joe' to disguise his identity:

The road and the ranges were his haven. He was also an explorer in a generation when explorers were rare. Added to his topographical instinct was a supreme, fanatical faith in his God. He would pick up details of a mountain pass from a survey or geological report in a reference library and set out for the other side. If the rivers were flooded, if the ice was treacherous, if the rain forest was virtually impenetrable, his motto was 'the Lord will provide'. I first heard of Joe from the musterers: He was a tough old dag, and no mistake. Then I met him. He was cooking. The previous year he had crossed Browning's Pass to Westland and swagged down the Coast and back over the Haast Pass to Otago, thence to harvesting in Canterbury. He was in the kitchen till such time as he had enough chips to set off on another wander for many months. He told me other things. Ten years before he had wanted to learn snowcraft, as a means to an end rather than as a mere sport. He crossed Graham's Saddle, nearly 9000 feet, with good guides who taught him much. He had bought an ice-axe and learnt its use. In the depression it was my sad job to sell for him his ice-axe as he needed the money more and was too proud to borrow.

Joe then was equal to fossicking out for himself a hitherto unexplored saddle from the upper Rakaia to the Rangitata and, not content with that, to a first crossing to the Macaulay valley. He nearly lost his life in a slip on frozen snow. A portable gramophone with hymn records gave him the music appropriate to his musings. He'd stay at a hut for a month or two, then look for another valley in which to venture. For years he covered Canterbury and Westland to secure work to pay for his expeditions to the snow. Always alone he'd leave the most comfortable of huts if other men

'Freddie Ambrose' and his concertina, Manuka Point Station, c.1933.

PASCOE COLLECTION, ALEXANDER TURNBULL LIBRARY

came and blasphemed there. The heavy swagging must have been hard because he was a little man and near sixty. He could confound most mountaineers in topographical arguments.

As a cook, Joe wouldn't allow tobacco in his kitchen because, as he explained, he had eaten food from the taste of which you could tell what brand of cigarettes the men smoked. He was a fine cook and the men tolerated his eccentricities. As long as he was clean, with enough money for food and foot-travel, he wanted nothing more. I once offered him a tent for a high transalpine crossing which he reckoned to make, but he refused the obligation. Some months later a climbing party found him installed at a hut waiting for the weather in which to make the crossing. His boots were rubber-soled and he had no ice-axe. The party, also cobbers of mine, was bound for the same adventurous crossing so they said they'd cut steps and rope him up over the range. They did. After some trouble with scrub they descended to the floor of a rough valley and found a Westland flood to block the way. Joe said he'd swim across. He made this risky ford and pulled the other men through on a rope to the desired bank. They had cause to be grateful to the frail, bearded old patriarch who then set off on a five months' jaunt down the Coast.

Music was his delight. He was clever on a concertina, and would play jigs and hymns for hours. Once I spent a wet afternoon at a homestead in transposing some sheet music for him. 'Home' meant nothing to him. He never mentioned the existence of any relations. In one city he had a hide-out, a small room in a slum for which he paid a few shillings a week when he used it. He took me into his confidence and asked me round, turned on a supper of plum-cake, pineapple and tea (remembering perhaps my back-country appetite). When I last saw him, seven years ago, he was on the inter-island ferry and intended to wander from Auckland to the far north because he wanted to see what the country looked like. The South had become too cold for his old bones. I hope I see him again before he dies, if he is not already dead.

In fact, Ambras lived for a further 25 years. He died in 1970, aged 92.

Is there anything else that you think is wrong about that article? I regard it as the most serious writing I have done, and I should like to think it was more permanent than my own exploits in my own book. For that reason I sweated blood on that article to get it fair and accurate, and I should value your criticism if there is anything that you think that strikes a wrong note, particularly in the sketches of the men, many of whom you yourself will know intimately. I feel very humble about my experiences in the back-country, and, as I wrote to Lawry [sic] last year when I was working on the article, I have done my best sincerely and honestly to give an objective description of a way of life that is commonplace to the men who themselves lead it, but that is of interest to the many people who think of sheep only in terms of fat lambs and Hawkes Bay pastures. Some of the writing I did 6 years ago, I found too personal to include, and so, in my revision, I cut out parts that might have caused others embarrassment.[16]

Arguably, Pascoe was slow to realise that no matter how accurate or admiring his article, it was his unsolicited public exposure of the inhabitants of Manuka Point that offended them. The high country hands did not see themselves as unusual; it was talkers like Pascoe and his climbing friends, pausing only briefly at the station, who were the oddities. The very publication of Pascoe's pen portraits was bound to cause resentment. In spite of this, John Pascoe's friendship with Laurie Walker survived and, paradoxically, strengthened, perhaps because the city-bred Walker understood Pascoe's motives. Born in 1902 in Christchurch, Laurie Walker spent his youth in suburban Bryndwr; on leaving school he worked on the wool counter at Beath's department store. This sparked his interest in sheep farming and he soon left the city to work on high country farms before moving to Manuka Point where he eventually rose from shepherd to manager. During the Depression of the 1930s the owners could not afford to pay his wages, which were credited towards Walker's eventual purchase of the property.[17]

As owner, Walker was able to be more hospitable than he had been as manager, and he was especially welcoming to John Pascoe. In 1944, when John and Dorothy visited the Rakaia to climb Mount Whitcombe, Laurie crossed the flooded river to collect them and put them up for three nights while they waited for the rain to stop. John had not seen Walker since his last year as a law student in Christchurch eight years earlier, but their rapport survived. 'We did not say much on our first meeting, we never did. But as I walked into his homestead I felt as though I was coming home again,' Pascoe wrote in *Land Uplifted High*. When John and Dorothy returned from their unsuccessful attempt on Whitcombe, after enduring what John described as 'the worst storm I have ever experienced in the mountains', his reports of Dorothy's cheerful stoicism promoted her from 'Mrs Pascoe' to 'Dorothy' at the homestead. When they had recovered from their ordeal, Laurie took them back across the Rakaia and drove them to Christchurch.[18]

Two years later, Walker was again host to the Pascoes, Stan Conway and John Clegg. While the men were away climbing Whitcombe, Ted Porter, another city man turned shepherd, taught the 15-month-old Sara Pascoe to walk using 'leading strings and bits of biscuit scattered around the kitchen – much as he trained sheepdogs with care and kindness'. Soon afterwards, when Sara was christened, Laurie Walker agreed to be her godfather, a relationship he diligently maintained for the rest of his life.[19]

Eric McCormick (left), Joe Heenan (centre) and Howard Kippenberger (right) at the 2 NZEF unit histories conference, 5 July 1946.

JOHN PASCOE COLLECTION, ALEXANDER TURNBULL LIBRARY

Plans for recording New Zealand's war effort overseas began as early as 1943 when a far-sighted Eric McCormick suggested a series of official war histories. After his appointment as editor of the series in July 1946, Major-General Kippenberger planned a number of volumes to record the various campaigns in detail. Of the 41 titles, the last was Nancy Taylor's The Home Front, which did not appear until 1986.

In the meantime Kippenberger (who died in 1957) realised that in the immediate aftermath of the war public interest required something simpler. He oversaw the production of a series of booklets describing various aspects of the war, to be published as soon as possible. New Zealand in the Second World War: Episodes and Studies (Popular Series), as it was called, kept Pascoe busy in the late 1940s and early 1950s. Of the 44 titles planned, 24 were actually produced. Each dealt with some specific aspect of New Zealand's part in the war, outside the scope of the official histories yet considered worthy of record. Among them were issues on the experiences of prisoners of war in Germany, Italy and the jungles of Burma, and one devoted entirely to escapes.

The popular series owed much to its predecessor, Making New Zealand, in repeating the successful formula of regular individual issues that could then be bound into volumes. Authors usually had specific knowledge of subjects as diverse as Special Services in Greece or RNZAF Assault on Rabaul; others of a more general nature such as Wounded in Battle and Escapes were written by David Hall. All were illustrated by John Pascoe with characteristic flair. The prisoner of war issues, in particular, showed that he had thrown his net wide to collect sketches and photos that prisoners had made or taken surreptitiously, then hidden away.

Prisoners at Campo 57, Gruppignano, Italy, search for lice.
LEE HILL PHOTO, WAR HISTORY COLLECTION, ALEXANDER TURNBULL LIBRARY

John Pascoe's enduring affection for Laurie Walker and Manuka Point owed a great deal, of course, to the nearby Rakaia mountains where he had cut his teeth as a climber, but the man and his run also appealed to Pascoe on a deeper level as a kind of counterpoint to his work at the War History Branch of Internal Affairs. For ten years, as illustrations editor, Pascoe spent each working day sorting and selecting drawings, photos and maps for the official unit histories. Yet, to him, war was anathema. Furthermore, his post-war work lacked the variety and the opportunities for travel that had made the first few years with the department so exciting. Nevertheless, his job was secure and even if he had little enthusiasm for it, security was important now that he was a family man. Nor did Pascoe's lack of enthusiasm for his subject seem to affect the quality of his work. His boss, Joe Heenan, was happy with the popular series the department produced after the war, and told Oliver Duff that 'Kip and his outfit are still working along smoothly, producing a little booklet now and again. Johnnie Pascoe is doing a great job on the illustrations side and on the printing layout.'[20] Uncharacteristically, however, Pascoe rarely mentioned this work either at home or in his letters, articles or books. The only account of his work at this time, an unpublished article entitled 'Illustrate the Text', which he submitted to the *Arts Year Book*, refers to *Making New Zealand* but not to his war history work.[21]

His lack of comment may also have reflected his preoccupation with his own writing projects, of which he had several, and the demands of a young family. In April 1948 Dorothy and John's third child, Martha, was born. John wrote to Laurie Walker with the news and a warning to his shepherd, Ted Porter, 'that if he commiserates with me because I have another daughter I shall wring his neck. I like my females.'[22] Even so, the strain of coping with three small children soon began to tell on Dorothy and John. He, of course, bore less of the burden and was able to use most of his spare time for writing, but he was also aware that Dorothy did not have the same opportunities. In a letter to her father, Guy Harding, John described his routine: 'My writing is done between 8 pm (when at heavenly last the kids go down) and 10.30 pm and I average at least 12 hours a week BUT I do all my planning and brooding in the bus [to and from Wellington] which is another 5 hours a week, so I get far more time than she does'.[23]

Dorothy was an enthusiastic mother and homemaker; John was the breadwinner who left home early in the morning and returned in the evening. In the little spare time she had, Dorothy was an active participant in the developing Playcentre movement, often travelling to Wellington for meetings. In addition to her children, Dorothy also cared for her aging father, whose health was failing. He spent periods in hospital which he did not enjoy, particularly since alcohol was prohibited. He usually had a bottle of whisky secreted away, but its discovery would lead to reprimands from the nursing staff. It was a relief for him to visit his daughter at Eastbourne. Dorothy appreciated John's support. 'When John saw I had a responsibility towards my father he helped in many ways. He would assist in running his affairs and was surprisingly patient. I think we were both aware that this taciturn, lonely old man coping with physical disability was finding it hard to deal with the limitations and disappointment that old age had brought.'[24] But even

In addition to his work on war histories, John Pascoe did other design work for the department including arranging the reproduction of drawings and maps for G. L. Adkin's book, Horowhenua, which was published by Internal Affairs in 1948.

Adkin and Pascoe were both mountain men who might have been expected to get on well. But when Adkin met Pascoe in June 1947 to discuss the layout of Horowhenua, he was not impressed. 'Found Pascoe a surprise,' he wrote in his diary, 'instead of a he-man mountaineer type he is an undersized, diseased-looking, stammering, swearing, rather ill-mannered grouser.'

at Eastbourne life was difficult for Guy Harding when Anna and Sara played pranks on him. In a letter to his longtime friend, the Christchurch political activitist, Elsie Locke, Harding described one incident: 'While sitting in a deckchair taking the sun at Dido's [Dorothy's] the two young demons put a bumble bee on my sock and it headed north, interior route, up my trouser leg. Their giggling warned me that something was afoot. Later on, while taking them for a walk, I felt a strange tickling on my neck – that damn bumble bee still trekking north!'[25]

Harding may have been taciturn but he was an energetic letter writer and his regular correspondence with Elsie Locke included vignettes of Pascoe family life. When measles affected all three children, one after another, Harding described the effect on John. 'When I met him during the week he was looking played out, unshaven and his voice husky-tired. John said there had been little sleep for three nights but he doesn't stand up to domestic stresses and strains. If it were a blizzard now, on a mountain top or a dangerous traverse, he'd be 100%.'[26]

John and Dorothy's response to 'domestic stresses and strains' was to take a holiday. In October 1948 they spent a week at Nelson Lakes National Park, staying in a hut on top of Mount Robert, without their children. Anna and Sara stayed with friends and Martha was left with a Karitane nurse. For the first and only time in his life John Pascoe tried skiing at which he showed little promise; Dorothy did better. The view from Mount Robert was extensive, as Pascoe wrote in *Land Uplifted High*: 'We could trace the line of the Wairau Valley towards Blenheim, see a spur that hid Nelson, recognise the Astrolabe Roadstead and Tasman National Park, and follow the valley of the Buller river from its outlet at the lake down pastoral country towards Murchison. I could

Dorothy Pascoe on holiday without her children at Mount Robert, Lake Rotoiti, October 1948. It was so reviving that she and John planned another break the following winter but it did not eventuate because, as John later told a climbing friend, 'she was preg and I was busy being nurse to kids who variously had measles, scarlet fever and chicken pox'.

DOROTHY PASCOE COLLECTION

explain in which direction lay Westport and the ranges of the Mohikinui which hid the coalfields.' They considered further holidays, with their children, in the northern part of the South Island which they realised was relatively accessible from Wellington.[27]

Three years earlier, when they had only Anna and Sara, the Pascoes had enjoyed a holiday in the Marlborough Sounds. Two weeks at the Bay of Many Coves on Queen Charlotte Sound convinced John of its benefits. 'A Sounds fortnight usually includes bush wandering, or scrub pushing on the ridges, with fishing and sunbathing in the bays below,' he told readers of The Mirror, an illustrated magazine. 'Perhaps it is because even mountaineers raise families, and must give them holidays with free life in good climate, that they may take an occasional visit to the Sounds where the attractions are shorn of the perils of glacier or river, but where camping in the open is a health giving delight.'[28] For John, the highlight of their holiday was his solo ascent of Mount Stokes, the highest point in the Sounds. He camped overnight on the summit and at dusk and dawn contemplated the view of Pelorus Sound, Cook Strait and, in the distance, the North Island. If Queen Charlotte Sound was so enticing, surely the complexity and isolation of Pelorus Sound would offer even more opportunities? He and Dorothy resolved to return and explore.

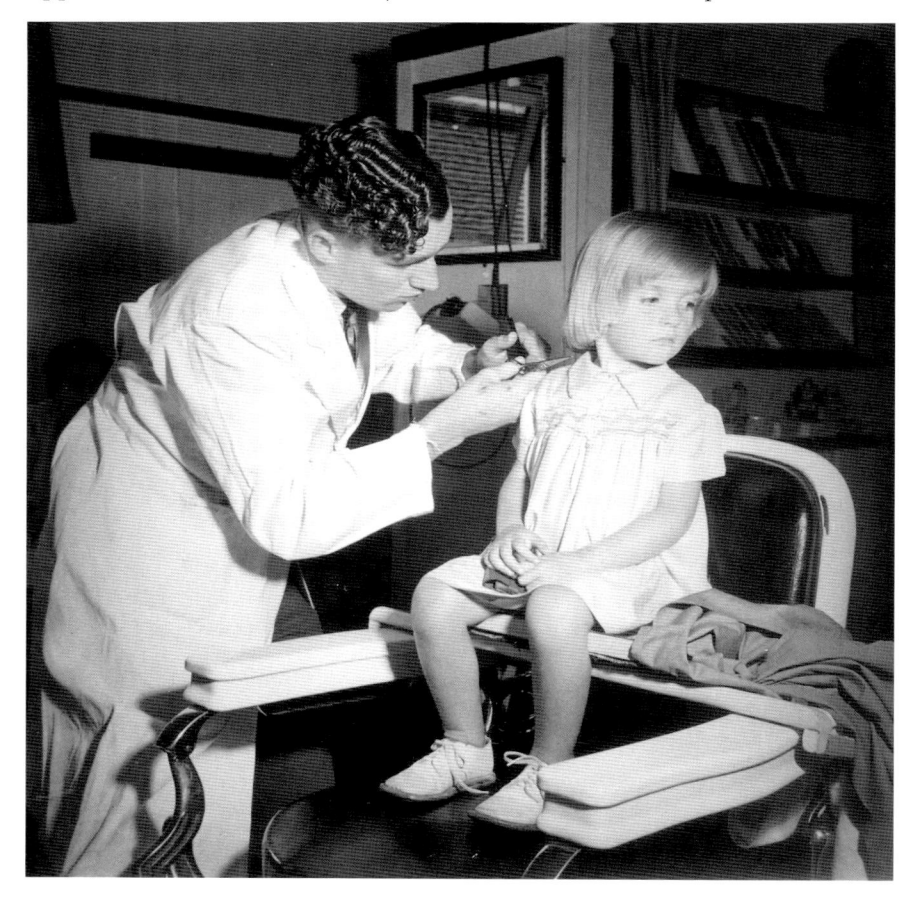

Anna Pascoe endures a haircut in Picton, en route to the Bay of Many Coves where the Pascoes enjoyed their first Sounds holiday in 1945. John Pascoe's skill as a documentary photographer is as evident in his record of family activities as it is in his photos of public events.

DOROTHY PASCOE COLLECTION

The view from the summit of
Mount Stokes at dawn, with the
North Island in the distance.

DOROTHY PASCOE COLLECTION

The Pascoes planned a visit to Pelorus Sound in January 1949. John searched maps for a sunny, sheltered place, accessible only by sea. If cars could not reach it, they could escape the visitor trade evident in Queen Charlotte Sound. Whakatahuri, a small fishing settlement near the entrance to the sound, seemed ideal. John searched titles to find the owners of the land and wrote to the Wells family asking if the Pascoes might come and camp. The reply, with the offer of a cottage by the sea, rewarded his initiative. Once again, Martha was left with a Karitane nurse while Anna and Sara, six and four respectively, accompanied their parents on the ferry to Picton, then a bus to Havelock. A long launch trip the next day took them to Whakatahuri.

It was raining with a cold southerly wind when they reached the settlement, which the Pascoes soon discovered was quite different from their expectations. John's account of the holiday records that they were 'dismayed by the dark two rooms and the dogs' breakfast backyard with its litter of bottles, pilchard barrels and debris'. To make matters worse 'the inhabitants of the bay were reserved and scary. Faces would peep at us from behind drawn curtains and scuttle away as we approached.' For the next few days the weather stayed cold and the locals unfriendly, although 'Grandfather Wells told us we could use a dinghy, and brightened when he saw me tie the anchor rope with a bowline'. John used the boat to bring firewood from nearby beaches as there was none to be had at Whakatahuri. As soon as the sun appeared, the family hiked over the hills to Anakoha Bay where they were welcomed by a friendly farming family who let them camp on their land.

Back at Whakatahuri, it was Anna and Sara who eventually broke the locals' reserve by 'cobbering up with the kids in a fishing family'. Soon

the residents were coming by the cottage to talk and inspect the Pascoes at close quarters. Whenever conditions permitted, the family slept out in the open on nearby beaches and spent the day fishing from the dinghy. One of the local fishermen took them in his launch to fish in Cook Strait. The exposed cliffs of Alligator Head and Waitui Bay reminded John of 'glacier fastness in Westland'. If the receding land was forbidding, the casual attitude of their skipper, Morris Wells, was frightening. John Pascoe had written in the *Mirror* that the Sounds were 'shorn of the perils of glacier or river', but he had overlooked danger at sea. 'At one stage the sea roughened and swamped the dinghy we towed,' he noted in his diary. 'Morris in his long rubber thigh boots leapt into it and baled with a bucket. An uphill struggle but he made it. If the dinghy had sunk the chances were that his boots would have drowned him. There was nothing I could do to help, so I just clung to the mast and photographed the doings while his wife stayed grimly silent.'

Beyond Cape Lambert, they anchored in the open sea to fish for groper. The Pascoe parents' anxiety quickened again when Morris Wells's wife, Jean, 'took over the dinghy with six kids (including our two preciouses) and rowed away in a heavy swell to look for a landing place on the rugged headland'. None of them wore lifejackets. 'Talk about having too many eggs in one basket. At times the rise of the swell hid the dinghy from view. We fished for an hour and a half, and were mighty glad when we saw Jean rowing back

Whakatahuri, January 1949.
As the Pascoes quickly discovered,
isolation was no guarantee
of a pristine environment or
a friendly welcome.
DOROTHY PASCOE COLLECTION

At the time of their Whakatahuri holiday, John Pascoe favoured a cryptic style of caption in both his books and private photo albums which he made for each holiday in the Sounds. Thus this image of a fisherman and his son is succinctly entitled 'Fuel' and Pascoe's photo of six children departing in a dinghy is simply described as 'frail eggs in small basket'.

DOROTHY PASCOE COLLECTION

towards us with all the kids intact.' John and Dorothy were so relieved to have the children back on board that they 'ceased to worry if they hurt themselves on the welter of fish-hooks, keen knifes, fish, barracuta (alive) kingfish, and groper that littered the deck of the launch'. When the Pascoes returned to Whakatahuri late that night they found, as they had after other excursions, gifts from the Wells family on their table: 'date scones, a pot of cream, fresh eggs, jam, fruit or tomatoes'.

John concluded his diary of their fortnight at Whakatahuri with a description of the community:

'Loin cloth and snapper', John's description of himself at Whakatahuri.

DOROTHY PASCOE COLLECTION

> The bay has a regular mail service twice a week, and the house is a post office. When the kids' parents cannot cope with correspondence school, they get packed off to a convent or other school. Dress is fish scales on wool. The bay gets no frost in winter, and the gardens could be very good indeed. The fishermen live in crowded houses of sub-normal standard. Water comes from a spring. All firewood is collected from other beaches by launch or dinghy. The main house is large, clean, and roomy but the grounds and foreshore are a litter of fish and tins, glass, and mess; no one cares.[29]

To the readers of *Journeys*, however, he offered a more hopeful conclusion to his article 'Family Holiday':

> We look forward to more such holidays, tramping, fishing and idling to give parents and children sights of new and attractive coastal scenery, and friendship with men, women and children who make isolation a virtue and a key to happiness.[30]

John Pascoe's holiday plans also usually included a climbing trip for himself in the Southern Alps. Three months after returning from Whakatahuri he spent Easter 1949 in the Arrowsmith Range, adjacent to the Rakaia, with

Stan Conway and two other climbers. Their attempt on an unclimbed peak was frustrated by dangerous, ice-glazed rocks near the summit. When the others returned to work, John crossed the Rakaia and spent several days roaming the heights of Manuka Point Station to photograph the annual muster.[31] Such trips were possible only because of Dorothy's support, which John was always quick to acknowledge. She intuitively understood 'his need of the mountains'. From the days of their courtship she had recognised that 'mountains were his choice' and that his feeling for them was close to an obsession:

> In the alps he found an environment that tested him in many ways. Perhaps one of the most important was self-discovery, with that came tenacity, courage and a sense of humour to ease the burden of heavy packs, uncooperative weather and the discomfits [sic] that beset mountain travellers. This, for him, was a spiritual as well as a physical experience and seemed to give him renewed energy to cope with life in the wider sense. With this awareness and understanding I could accept the call of the high country and his need to take off periodically.[32]

Fortunately for John, Dorothy's own experiences helped her to understand the man she had married. 'It was lucky that I liked the hills. As a kid, I had wandered around the hills behind Khandallah. That was very important. If I hadn't done that, if I'd come from a different sort of background I wouldn't have understood.'[33]

Even so, Dorothy was aware that her 'non-climbing friends were somewhat bothered at my being left on my own with my small ones in our rather isolated home'. Several episodes underlined their concern. The first occurred in June 1949 when the English publisher, Sir Stanley Unwin, visited New Zealand. In addition to his official itinerary he came to Eastbourne to have morning tea with John Pascoe and his family. Dorothy, five months pregnant with their fourth child, had made scones and over the teacups John and Sir Stanley discussed plans for a second edition of *Unclimbed New Zealand*. Not long after the men had departed, Dorothy began to haemorrhage and was rushed to Hutt Hospital where she was diagnosed with a ruptured placenta. Quick treatment saved both mother and child, but when Jane was born four months later she was malnourished and required additional attention.[34] John took over as much of the running of the household as he could, a situation that prompted a rare letter from the bachelor, Laurie Walker, who observed 'Thank goodness you were home and not up here when Dorothy took ill', and an offer of domestic assistance: 'I wish I had been there to help you handle "the nippers". I could have amused Anna and Sara while you did the dirty work.'[35]

Six months after Jane's birth, John was back in the Southern Alps, again with Stan Conway and others, to experiment with building a snow cave, John's latest alpine interest. As he was packing at home, Dorothy felt 'a bit unwell but covered it up not wanting to give him anxiety when he was away from contact with us'. She later recalled that a visiting neighbour suggested Codeine tablets. 'She gave me 3 or 4. At the time I was unaware that I was sensitive to Codeine. My headache eased but I had this weird out of body feeling. With four-month-old Jane in my arms I stood, as I often did, on the upstairs balcony looking across the harbour. It was then that I had this

Chatting over the teacups during Sir Stanley Unwin's visit to New Zealand in 1949 are, from left: John Beaglehole, Walter Nash, Sir Stanley Unwin and John Pascoe.

As the principal of the English firm, Allen & Unwin, Sir Stanley was one of the leading publishers of the time. Before the war, Nash had been the company's agent in New Zealand. During his visit, Unwin and Nash, now a Cabinet minister, took part in a panel discussion about the book trade which was later published in the Listener. In it, Unwin emphasised his opinion that books were far more than merchandise; they were the intellectual food that sustained a nation and therefore should not be subject to import restrictions, then prevalent in New Zealand. 'If you treat them as if they're just any other commodity — whether it be nylon stockings or pianos, or cement, or anything else you like — you are actually condemning the nation to a form of malnutrition. And I think that no nation, especially one that's geographically isolated, can possibly afford to impose any limitation on the nutrition of its population.'

DOROTHY PASCOE COLLECTION

frightening feeling that I could drop her. Appalled, I stepped back into the room feeling giddy and nauseated.' One of the other children realised something was wrong and called the neighbour, who returned to find Dorothy lying on the floor clutching the baby. By the time John returned from the alps Dorothy had recovered, and when told what had happened he was concerned 'but at the same time relieved his expedition was not curtailed!'[36] Nor was he deterred from making similar trips: nine months later he was back at the head of the Rangitata, intent on climbing Mount D'Archaic.[37]

When he was home, however, John was an exemplary parent whose talents complemented Dorothy's. He was not the primary caregiver, but if the children were sick he wrote special stories for them. In 1950, when seven-year-old Anna had scarlet fever and was in hospital, unable to have visitors, John wrote a page of a serial story each day and slipped it under her door. 'Was Wicky Lazy?' delighted Anna. After she recovered, she mentioned the story to an adult who happened to be the editor of the *School Journal*. Soon after, it appeared in that publication with evocative illustrations by Juliet Peter.[38] Two years later, when Sara broke her arm and spent a few days in hospital, John repeated his literary medicine, writing 'The Wicked Witch of Ruapehu' in sections.[39] His daughters invariably called him 'John' but Dorothy was always 'Mum'.

In November 1950, the second edition of *Unclimbed New Zealand* was published. It was widely acclaimed, although reviewers familiar with the first edition regretted the removal of more than half the photos and several important maps. These changes, however, as well as the use of thinner paper, kept the price down and put the book within reach of many younger readers — a new generation unfamiliar with Pascoe and the CMC's youthful exploits. Pascoe did not alter the text, not even the chapter describing his attempts on Mount Tasman, which he might have considered modifying in

20

The field was hard, and every time the plough hit a stone Wicky stopped the horses, threw the stone away to the side of the hedge nearby, and lit another match for his pipe. As there were many stones, he stopped often. The farmer, whose name was Scrumshaw, came over to watch Wicky. When he saw Dapple and Gray resting, and Wicky lighting his pipe, he growled away into his beard, " That Wicky is a lazy young rascal! " or " Hard work never hurt horses " or " I'll get rid of them all one day."

After lunch Wicky and his horses had ploughed all the stony part of the field. The earth was softer where

21

they were working now. But Wicky thought to himself, " Why do Dapple and Gray and I have to work at all? How much nicer it would be to climb that mountain." So he called " *Whoa!* " to his horses, and stopped them. He sat down on a thistle, got up after saying " *Ouch!* " and picked the prickles from the seat of his long pants where they hurt him. Then he found another place which had no thistles and sat down again and lit his pipe.

It happened that the farmer Scrumshaw passed the hedge and yelled to Wicky, " Get on with your work." Wicky did not hear him. He was looking at the snow on the top of the mountain, whose name was Torlesse. The snow was clean and white, and Wicky thought that he would like to suck an orange with a wee piece of snow in it.

Illustrations of the grouchy farmer and Wicky by Juliet Peter from John Pascoe's children's story Was Wicky Lazy? *It describes how a bored young ploughman leaves a farm to become a mountain guide, builds a hut and rescues a tourist from a crevasse.*

THE SCHOOL JOURNAL

light of the severe criticism it had attracted. He realised that if he revised one section, he should also make other changes and that would destroy the unique, youthful flavour of the book which he later described as 'an agreeable sort of naivete and impulsive enthusiasm. ("Say, could that lad be I?")' 'Parts of it are crook,' he told an acquaintance, 'but as a period piece of the depression and as a staccato expression I find it interests me even tho' I wrote it.'[40]

As it was, revision was a luxury for which he did not have time; he had too many other books in preparation. Only a month after *Unclimbed New Zealand* appeared, his first book of photographs, *The Mountains The Bush & The Sea*, was published in time to catch the Christmas market. It was an ideal gift which belonged to, yet transcended, the 'scenic New Zealand' genre – that staple of the bookseller. The title was something of a misnomer, as most of the photos were of the mountains, especially the Canterbury alps, with only a few bush scenes and seascapes from the Marlborough Sounds at the end, but this drew no adverse comment because the strength and sincerity of the photographs immediately captivated most reviewers. Above all, Pascoe's

The cover of John Pascoe's first book of photographs, The Mountains The Bush & The Sea, *shows the Rakaia River and the Matthias mountains where he discovered the rewards of climbing.*

familiarity with his subject was apparent. As the *Southland Times* noted, 'There is something about the commercially-produced "Book of New Zealand Views" that proclaims its origin. The professional photographer rarely belongs to the scene in front of him; he has his eye on the public as he releases the shutter. Mr Pascoe's photographs convey the mountaineer's interest in the landscape, the feeling that he has made himself part of it by his desire to share with others the pleasure of being there.'[41]

Pascoe himself made this point in the 'Photographic Notes' that concluded the book. After a discussion of technical matters and photographic equipment, he suggested that:

> Experience will teach you more than text-books. I intend these notes merely as a guide to my own practice, and stress once again that the most perfect

technique will not help your results unless you temper your judgement with a feeling for people and for the land and the sea. Select your subjects as you would your friends and do not admit a crowd when a handful is better company; that is, take a few good photographs rather than waste film on scenes and attitudes whose interest is mundane and whose indifference is clear to the eyes that must decide when to release the shutter.[42]

The conviction evident in Pascoe's book owed much to his wartime documentary work. He developed such ideas as the juxtaposition of succinct captions, which he had first used in the wartime volume *Introduction to New Zealand*. But neither that book, which was intended for American troops, nor his wartime photographs had been seen by the New Zealand public, except for a limited number of photos that had appeared in local magazines and newspapers. With the publication of *The Mountains The Bush & The Sea* New Zealanders had their first opportunity to see a large body of work by an accomplished photographer, depicting countryside he knew and loved. This was recognised by most commentators. *Newsview*'s reviewer, for example, noted that 'Pascoe's enterprise and purpose are epitomized on every page of this very beautifully produced work. I've seen nothing like it in a quarter of a century. This is the enterprise of youth, allied to the imaginative eye of the poet, the perception of the artist and the deep love of a man for the mountains.'[43]

The *Mountains The Bush & The Sea* had an impact well beyond its first flurry of reviews and it impressed not only the general public but other photographers as well. Writing in the *NZ Journal of Photography* 50 years later, the Dunedin photographer, Gary Blackman, named *The Mountains The Bush & The Sea* as the book that had most influenced his own work. 'It was,' he wrote, 'the first New Zealand book of photographs to capture the feel of the country I knew from family holidays, tramping trips and back country holiday jobs. Here were the unpretentious images that captured the unique qualities of New Zealand mountain country without resort to pictorialist artifice.'[44]

At the time, the cumulative effect of the re-release of *Unclimbed New Zealand* and the publication of *The Mountains The Bush & The Sea* established John Pascoe as a leading photographer and alpine authority. A reviewer in *Freedom* magazine made a comparison that must have pleased Pascoe:

RIVER OF SHEEP  *Manuka Point, Rakaia Valley* SHEEP AND SHINGLE *Mathias Valley*

For most of the 20th century, tobacco was an essential part of social life in New Zealand, especially for men. John Pascoe was no exception. He was renowned as a pipe smoker but also enjoyed cigarettes on occasions such as his reunion with National Geographic reporter, Howell Walker, in 1950. Nine years earlier they had spent three weeks touring the South Island together, a test of any friendship. Pascoe was pleased to find Walker as agreeable as ever. He wrote to a mutual friend, 'He is very nice and is very modest (a surprising quality in a Yank)'.
DOROTHY PASCOE COLLECTION

Few mountaineers become legends in their own lifetime. The legend grows from a locality, so it is Frank Smythe of the Himalayas and Everest; it is John Pascoe of Mt Evans and the headwaters of the Waimakariri and Rakaia. For John Pascoe has made these areas peculiarly his own in mountaineering, exploring, writing, photography and a vast knowledge of their history. Pascoe has done for this region what Smythe had done for his beloved Himalayas — put it on paper, illustrated it with magnificent photography, so that it stirs the imagination of the common man, bringing the mountains to us, who prefer the easy chair and fireside, to the windswept tent on rough scree.

The promise of Pascoe's camera in *Unclimbed New Zealand* has been fulfilled in *The Mountains, The Bush & The Sea*.'[45]

At the age of 42, with bittersweet experience of the capricious judgements of reviewers, Pascoe was wise enough not to take his press too literally. He also found it hard to make an assessment of *The Mountains The Bush & The Sea*. In reply to a friend's admiring letter, he wrote, 'I have been too close to the photos to be able to consider them objectively now, though I may be able to be detached about them in 5 years. Consequently I don't really know whether they are any good. But I supervised the block-making, which was done in Wellington, and am well satisfied both with the process-engraving and the printing, the paper and binding. So I find my pleasure in the book on technical considerations of book production.'[46] The response Pascoe valued above all others came from readers who knew the mountains well, for they were the people he most respected. 'I had a ring from a musterer the other day who had got a copy. He said he was a stranger but wanted to meet me and was shy about it,' Pascoe told Robin Muir, the editor of *Journeys*. 'I persuaded him to come over home one afternoon and had a good yarn. He was a young joker who had mustered in the Rangitata and Arrowsmiths.'[47]

Pascoe was pleased by a reported rush on stock of *The Mountains The Bush & The Sea* at Whitcombe & Tombs bookshops. As the publishers, Whitcombes displayed it prominently in its chain of bookshops in New Zealand, which led to good initial sales. 'I hear the book is very popular in Wellington with the general public as well as with mountaineering people,' he wrote to Muir. Undoubtedly much of the book's appeal lay in the adroit juxtaposition of the photographs as well as the elegance and restraint of the design, which was done by Pascoe. Seldom had a New Zealand author been given such complete control over a book. That a leading publisher was prepared to countenance such freedom showed the confidence Bertie Whitcombe and his editor, Carl Straubel, had in Pascoe's ability as a designer and illustrator. They were repaid with a volume that set a new benchmark for photographic publications.

During 1951 John Pascoe spent his spare time preparing another book for publication that was, in every way, the antithesis of *The Mountains The Bush & The Sea*. His route guide to the northern half of the Southern Alps was commissioned by the Pegasus Press, one of New Zealand's smallest publishers. The pocket-sized book was mostly text with a limited number of photos intended to show alpine routes. Since the guidebook contained specific material on which the safety of climbers, hunters and trampers might depend, Pascoe circulated it widely before publication, sending it to 30 people and clubs for their comment.[48] *The Southern Alps — From the Kaikouras to the Rangitata* appeared late in 1951, without the fanfare that had accompanied his photographic book the previous Christmas. Nevertheless, it was well received by the New Zealand outdoor community not only because Pascoe clearly knew what he was describing, but also because the guidebook was written in suitably simple prose, free of embellishment and provocative opinion.

The publication of three Pascoe books in two years, established him in the minds of the general public as one of the country's alpine experts. Yet, as John Pascoe was aware, he could not convincingly fulfil this role while he remained estranged from the New Zealand Alpine Club. Eleven years earlier he had resigned in response to A. P. Harper's criticism of his comments in *The Mountains* issue of *Making New Zealand*, but by now Harper had mellowed and Pascoe had matured. The time was ripe for reconciliation. In September 1951 Pascoe applied for membership of the NZAC, enclosing, as required, a list of his climbs.[49] The response was an immediate welcome from the Canterbury branch, of which he had once been so critical. A member wrote to him 'that when the subject of your re-joining the club was brought up it was unanimously agreed that we would be very pleased

The woodcut scene on the cover of John Pascoe's guide to the northern half of the Southern Alps is the work of E. Mervyn Taylor. It shows Carrington Peak at the head of the Waimakariri, from Carrington Hut, the CMC's first mountain shelter.

Wellington Public Libraries Association

Mountaineering and
Tramping in New Zealand

Lecture Hall, Central Library,
Tuesday, 28th August, 1951,
at 8 p.m.

Chairman: Lieut.-Col. J. B. Harrison

Speaker: Mr. John Pascoe

Author of "Unclimbed New Zealand," also Photographer and Author
of "The Mountains, the Bush and the Sea."

**This Address will be illustrated with Photographs
and Lantern Slides.**

The Films "Prelude to Aspiring" and
"Winter in the Swiss Alps" will be shown.

SEATS WILL BE RESERVED FOR MEMBERS OF THE WELLINGTON PUBLIC LIBRARIES
ASSOCIATION.

Anyone may join: Enrolment forms are available at all Library Desks or on application
to the Hon. Sec., P.O. Box 1529, Wellington.

Associate Membership costs 5/- per year.

Funds are devoted to improving the facilities of the Libraries.

No Admission Charge — A Voluntary Collection.

DOROTHY PASCOE COLLECTION

to have you back with us'.[50] And when the club's national secretary, Doug Hanning, formally advised that the application had been approved, he told John, 'There is little doubt that your extensive knowledge, imparted to younger climbers, both personally and through your various books, has done much to elevate the standard of climbing in the Dominion, while your excursions into little known valleys keep alive the spirit of adventure.'[51]

Pascoe's willingness to rejoin the NZAC may also have been motivated by disillusionment with the CMC. At the time the CMC was wrestling with the question of whether to include women in the club (something the NZAC had always done). Despite the important contribution of women during the war in New Zealand and overseas, a number of CMC members resisted allowing them to join. Bill Hannah, one of the self-confessed 'diehards' who 'vigorously objected to what we consider to be contrary to the accepted traditions and principles of the club', wrote to John for his opinion,[52] although he should have known what Pascoe's position would be. John was astounded that his view was not discernible – even from a distance. He often climbed with Dorothy, had four daughters and was the author of a recent article in *Journeys* entitled 'Women in the Mountains', as well as a series of radio talks on the same subject. In *Journeys* he had written: 'There is a changed attitude to women in the mountains. Once they were exceptional people whose clothes hampered every movement. Today they are comrades of the snow whose equipment differs little from that of men.'[53]

In his reply to Hannah, John Pascoe argued that

> In an age that strives for equal pay and equal opportunity for women it would surely be an anachronism to bar women from the right to share mountaineering trials and difficulties as club members. The growth of proficiency of women as climbers is assured and is documented by the achievements every year of mountaineers of the calibre of Tararua, NZAC, and other club members who have made a stamping ground of Tutoko, Evans, Arrowsmith and other peaks dear to the ambition of all climbers. Nor have they been less effective in difficult transalpine crossings involving patience and persistence in Westland travel.

Not only should the club admit women, it should also train them 'with the same enterprise and effect that it has shown in the past for young men'.[54] Despite Pascoe's advocacy the status quo prevailed and the CMC did not admit women until 1977.

Pascoe's position in this controversy showed how much his views had broadened since he had left Christchurch. Although he was always mindful of his Canterbury roots, distance allowed him to see that the CMC was not the exclusive vanguard of New Zealand climbing, as he had once supposed. Nor were some of the club's attitudes, which he had previous espoused with an almost religious fervour, either convincing or appealing when viewed from afar. Just as Pascoe's attitude to women was influenced by his wife and family, so his inflated ideas of the importance of Canterbury climbing gradually diminished as he learnt of achievements elsewhere in New Zealand and overseas. By the early 1950s, the attention of a new generation of keen, young climbers was focused on the Himalaya, especially Mount Everest. Before the war Pascoe had hopes for an ascent of Kachenjunga but in 1951, at the age of 43 and with family responsibilities, he could not seriously consider a Himalayan expedition. Nevertheless, he was able to assist by contributing vital information.

In 1951 a team of four NZAC members – Edmund Cotter, Edmund Hillary, George Lowe and Earle Riddiford – were climbing in the Garwhal Himalaya when the president of the NZAC sent a telegram to Eric Shipton, the leader of the British Everest Reconnaissance, asking if two of the New Zealanders could join their team. Shipton agreed, so the leader of the New Zealand party, Earle Riddiford, and Ed Hillary accompanied the British climbers as they probed the flanks of Everest looking for a likely route to the top.[55] On their return to base camp, Riddiford received aerial photos of the summits of Everest and its neighbour, Makalu, sent from New Zealand by John

An aerial view of the south ridge of Mount Everest. In 1945 Squadron Leader C. G. Andrews took a series of photos of the summits of Everest and neighbouring Makalu. After the war, Andrews worked with the Air Department in Wellington and it is probable that Pascoe came to know of these photos then. He immediately recognised their value to New Zealand climbers who were in the Himalaya at the time, searching for the best route to climb Everest. Hillary and Lowe were delighted with the photos, which gave them a new view of the likely route up Everest. In 1953 Hillary and Tenzing Norgay made the first ascent of Everest via the south ridge.

DOROTHY PASCOE COLLECTION

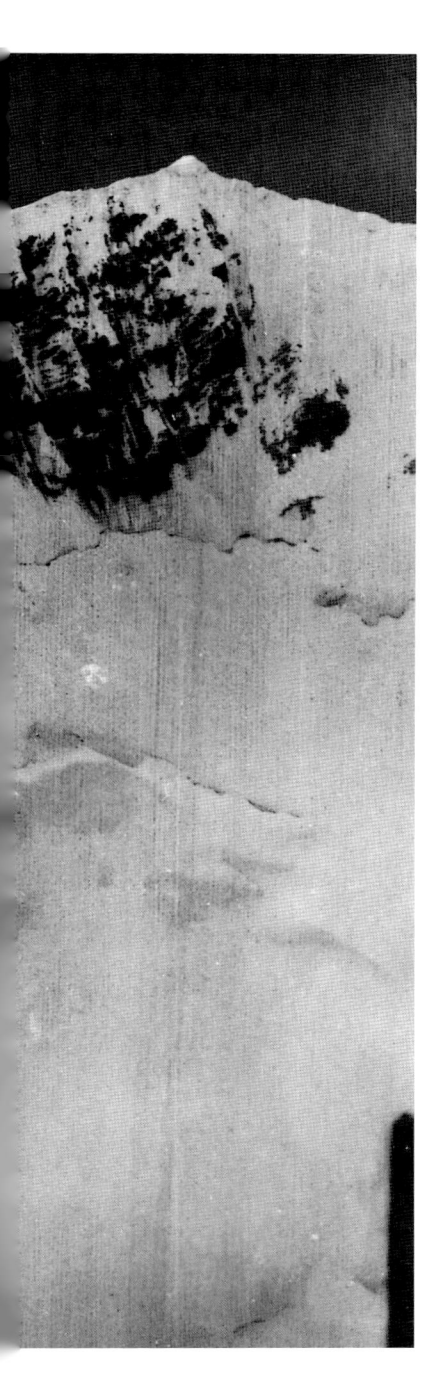

Pascoe. Riddiford passed them on to Shipton. In a letter to Pascoe, Riddiford thanked him for 'the most revealing aerial photos we have seen' and acknowledged their value in discerning the true nature of the final approach to Everest: 'That section of summit ridge above the slopes above the South Col – from below it doesn't appear to amount to much at all but the photos show that there is a long technical bit of ridge leading to the summit which would need good windless conditions and fitness for that altitude. Naturally, everyone was interested in them.'[56] Pascoe also received letters from Ed Hillary and George Lowe, who had both been invited to join a planned British attempt on Everest. 'Many, many thanks for the full plate prints of the summits of Everest and Makalu,' wrote Lowe. 'Both sets are of very special interest to Ed and I. Firstly, because we've been around the skirts of both. Secondly, because we expect to get a crack at Everest next year.'[57] Hillary echoed Lowe's and Riddiford's comments and added that he was looking forward to several forthcoming Pascoe publications. 'I'll be interested to see the new books when they are published. An original edition of your *Unclimbed New Zealand* has always been one of my prized possessions. I hope to be in Wellington some time before Christmas and hope to have the pleasure of a yarn with you then.'[58]

Pascoe was not as accomplished a mountaineer as either Hillary or Lowe; his role on any Himalayan expedition would have been as the recorder, intelligence officer and photographer, rather than as an assault climber. For a family man in Eastbourne, however, a world away from the action, these letters were the next best thing to being there. In retrospect, Pascoe's association with the élite of New Zealand Himalayan climbers crowned his rapid rehabilitation in the New Zealand Alpine Club. By 1952 his reputation as an intemperate critic of the NZAC was in the past: the prodigal son was back and in contact with the most dynamic climbers of the day. His return to the fold was complemented by the popularity of his books, which fed a national audience eager to be reminded of its links with the land, and established John Pascoe as New Zealand's foremost mountaineering photographer and writer.

CHAPTER SEVEN

The Re-Explorer

Since he was a young man, John Pascoe had been fascinated by early European explorers including the surveyor, Thomas Brunner, who made three journeys from Nelson to the West Coast in 1846. On the first he was accompanied by another New Zealand Company surveyor, Charles Heaphy, and the company's Nelson agent, William Fox. At the mouth of the Taramakau River, Heaphy painted the view to the south with the highest peaks of the Southern Alps in the distance. On the second journey, Brunner was also accompanied by Europeans eager to find new land for settlement. But on the last journey, which lasted 18 months, he was the only Pakeha and depended on his Maori guides for survival. His final extraordinary exploration of the West Coast was recorded in his journal, which was edited by John Pascoe and published in 1952 as The Great Journey.

Working on The Great Journey prompted Pascoe to start writing about another explorer, Charlie Douglas, who spent 30 years probing the valleys of South Westland. To understand Douglas's 'state of mind and to evaluate his months of solitude', Pascoe and three companions made a major transalpine journey from Lake Wanaka to Jackson Bay. In doing so, he found the life of a 're-explorer' (as he called himself) even more demanding than mountaineering. Ultimately he realised, as perhaps all explorers do, that the essence of exploration is self-discovery.

Mount Cook, Greenstone Country, Middle Island
by Charles Heaphy, 1846.

ALEXANDER TURNBULL LIBRARY

'I FELT AS THOUGH I WAS PAPA TO TWINS,' said John Pascoe when *The Great Journey* and *Land Uplifted High* appeared at the same time. Authors and publishers usually try to avoid such coincidences, which complicate book promotion and confuse the public, but in this case simultaneous publication was the unforeseen result of their different gestation. Brunner's journal had a quick and uncomplicated birth. It was commissioned in February 1952 and by the end of March Pascoe had written an introduction and annotated the text with an alacrity that astonished the publisher, Robin Muir of the Pegasus Press (who also edited *Journeys* magazine). 'Being ahead of schedule is part of my writing vitality,' he told Muir. 'The truth is that I find my official work progresses well if I keep pushing ahead. Delays breed delay. So with my spare writing I also keep my nose down and bottom up.'[1]

The most time-consuming part of *The Great Journey*'s production was Denis Glover's meticulous typesetting. Muir and Pascoe were rewarded with some of Glover's best work, the result of his renewed enthusiasm after an especially difficult period in his life, when his marriage had broken up and he had been forced out of the Caxton Press (which he had founded with others) because of persistent drunkenness.[2] The offer of a job with Caxton's rival, the Pegasus Press, gave him a fresh start. He told his English lover, Dorée Elkind, 'Am really enjoying myself immensely, now all the turmoil has subsided, and there's lots of beautiful printing and publishing to be done here.'[3] When Pascoe saw his first copy of *The Great Journey* he was delighted. 'I must say that I am very happy to have been associated with the fine Brunner job,' he told Muir. 'Please shake Denis by the hand for me and tell him how much I admire his typo. work.'[4]

By contrast, *Land Uplifted High* had a long and frustrating pathway to publication. When Sir Stanley Unwin visited New Zealand in 1949 he told Pascoe that it 'looked more interesting than *Unclimbed New Zealand*' and he encouraged him to send it to Allen & Unwin in London. Nevertheless, it was rejected on the advice of a professional reader who considered it a New Zealand book that would be of little interest in Britain. When he wrote to Pascoe, Sir Stanley was apologetic. To soften the blow he suggested that if John could get A. H. & A. W. Reed in Wellington to publish it, Allen & Unwin would take 500 copies to sell in Britain.[5] 'Unwins have turned down *Land Uplifted High*,' John lamented in a letter to his brother. 'This is of course a blow. But I have to take the rough with the smooth. No work is wasted. I won't broadcast my disappointment. You have the parallel experience of some of your best competition work getting set aside, and I know you bow to the wind but do not bend low. As with climbing the game is worth the struggle, and the fortuitous fruit is work for work's sake.'[6]

John was confident a New Zealand publisher would accept his book. In October 1950 he sent it to Whitcombe & Tombs rather than A. H. & A. W. Reed because, as he told Whitcombe's editor, Reeds' work 'is shoddy, their treatment of authors niggardly, and their standards low'.[7] It was six months, however, before Whitcombe & Tombs confirmed publication and even then the book would not appear until 1952.[8] Pascoe had no choice but to accept the delay. In the meantime he returned 'to a novel I half did some seven

Thomas Brunner's journal gives great insight into the sufferings of an early explorer, summarised in his entry for 21 March 1847: 'Rain continuing, dietary shorter, strength decreasing, spirits failing, prospects fearful'.

His account also shows the impact of Christianity on the small Maori population of the West Coast. Six months earlier, when he stayed briefly in Okaritu (Okarito) he wrote: 'I am astonished to find amongst the natives in these distant parts so much attention paid to their forms of religion, which is the Church and Wesleyan. Much animosity appears to exist between them: and although in some places there are only six or seven natives, yet they have separate places of worship, two schools, and are always quarrelling about religion, each party asserting its own to be the proper service to God.'

The title of John Pascoe's book was taken from an entry in *Abel Tasman's* journal describing his first view of *Te Wai Pounamu*, near Punakaiki, on 13 December 1642: 'Towards noon saw a large land, uplifted high, bearing southeast of us'.

Jane and Martha Pascoe abandon dress conventions at Te Towaka.

DOROTHY PASCOE COLLECTION

years ago. Since it has been locked away under tapu in a drawer, I can now return to it as a stranger's work and decide whether I have any skeleton to put flesh on or whether cremation is the only decent fate for it.'[9]

So once again John Pascoe took up his story of Scimitar (Mount Evans) and expanded it to novel length by adding three new chapters. Pete, Mac and Snowy's first ascent of Scimitar in the 1930s was now preceded by a lone prospector's fatal attempt on the peak 60 years earlier. The prospector known as 'Man' and his 'Dog' owed their appearance to Pascoe's quickening interest in the explorer Charlie Douglas who had a dog called Betsey Jane. Man and Dog climb a glacier on Scimitar but Dog falls into a crevasse. Man retreats to his cave beside the river below the glacier where he falls into an exhausted sleep. During the night there is a rockfall which traps Man, 'his feet pinned with imprisoned numbness', the river floods and he is drowned.[10] Even with this new flesh, Pascoe seems to have recognised that cremation would be the likely fate of his novel for he did not continue it. Instead he put it aside in favour of a family holiday in the Marlborough Sounds.

In January 1952 the Pascoes went to Te Towaka in outer Pelorus Sound where they were hospitably received by the Leov family, who let them camp in a grove of trees near the homestead and immediately made the Pascoes part of their lives. Each day various combinations of the two families would go swimming, fishing or exploring together and in the evenings, once the children were asleep, John and Dorothy would talk with Harold and Ida Leov in the farmhouse. The Pascoes' company was particularly welcome because Te Towaka was so isolated: apart from the radio, the Leovs' only contact with the outside world was the weekly mailboat. Despite this rapport, the dress and behaviour of the Leovs, living far from the nearest town, showed that they liked to observe the conventions. The urban Pascoes, on the other hand, were unconventional; they loved to shed their clothes to feel sun on skin, but quickly realised that their habits would be regarded as offensive. Dorothy thought their stay at Te Towaka was 'like stepping back in time' because the Leov children were always formally dressed. She and John recognised, however, that their hosts had a compelling reason to maintain such standards:

> They never ceased to wonder at our dressing the kids in shirts and shorts or longs when cold and sunsuits when very hot. The Leov girls, young ones too, all wore frocks, probably handed down from elder sisters, and though they were freshly ironed at breakfast by the evening they were somewhat dishevelled, and the odd bit of lace would hang limply like a piece from a remnant counter after a shop sale. We realised they were not allowed to bathe without clothes, so made our kids wear bathing suits, except for Jane and Martha who would sometimes shed them. Our explanation of this dressing up was that many of the Sounds people living in a primitive environment are so scared of an easy reversion, if not to savagery in the gentler sense of the word (beachcomberism of the city man on holiday who welcomes a break from collar, tie and convention), then a reversion to semi-nudity. The Sounds people must keep even young females looking fully clothed as females all the time, so that their menfolk treat them with the respect that convention demands. This was one flaw in our holiday when we would have preferred an occasional naked sun-bath.[11]

Even with their clothes on, the Pascoes were unusual. The Leovs' son, Harold, was then five years old; 50 years later he still remembers their insistence on camping and John's yodelling which, on a calm evening, could be clearly heard in the farmhouse.[12] Despite their differences it was a very happy fortnight, 'the best holiday I have had with the family', wrote John. Undoubtedly, the highlight for him was a trip to remote D'Urville Island with the Leovs who owned a farm at Patuki, near the island's northern tip. From the farm manager's house John climbed a ridge to see Port Hardy, the harbour where New Zealand Company emigrants of 1839 and 1840 made their first landfall after months at sea. Although John had never been to Cornwall, Port Hardy reminded him of the land of his forebears:

> What a scene. Rolling sheep and cattle country, undulating with rounded spurs falling steeply to rugged headlines and coves reminiscent of Channel Island cliffs. My Cornish blood must have been stirred magically because I was as moved as though I was looking at new mountain cliffs and glaciers. So indescribable was the contour of the inner port that I leapt round the main spur and was bound by the spell of waving kelp, shattered reefs, bold precipices and the distant upheaval of Stephen's Island.[13]

When he returned to Eastbourne at the end of January, feeling 'brown, fit and sassy', he found a letter from Whitcombe & Tombs advising him work had finally started on *Land Uplifted High*. By May he had seen the galley proofs and was pleased with the look of the book. In the meantime, he had edited *The Great Journey* which, in turn, inspired him to plan an ambitious trip with Stan Conway across the Southern Alps to South Westland.

Transalpine trips of exploration were not new: David Hall had made several from the Godley to Whataroa with Stan Conway, George Lowe and others in the late 1940s, and John was aware of their adventures. At the time, however, he had been preoccupied with making snow caves and building igloos on the Canterbury side of the Main Divide, and apart from his two

Te Towaka lies at the foot of Mount Shewell, which John Pascoe and his 10-year-old daughter, Anna, climbed when they were on holiday there in 1952. The climb was straightforward. John was pleased to find that Anna, on her first significant ascent, had 'a steady head for heights'. Their descent, however, was more difficult. 'We ran into deep pig fern,' John wrote in his diary. 'In one place I nearly overturned a huge boulder on myself, which would have broken a leg, but pushed it clear in time and told Anna how careful we had to be of footing when we could not see the going. She was very philosophic about difficulties, and did not growl at thick scrub. We sidled round the hill to try to maintain contour, but ran out into bluff country so steep that it would only have been safe with a rope.' Eventually John found an alternative route that enabled them to return safely to Te Towaka.

Anna Pascoe looks out over Admiralty Bay after traversing the summit ridge of Mount Shewell.

DOROTHY PASCOE COLLECTION

Most of John Pascoe's photos of his family's holiday at Te Towaka are of his children but he also photographed farm workers, including these musterers waiting for the mail launch.

DOROTHY PASCOE COLLECTION

trips to the Garden of Eden in the 1930s, he had little experience of transalpine travel. But after studying Brunner's epic journey, Pascoe was suddenly keen to experience the life of an explorer and when Stan Conway suggested a journey across the alps to the remote Olivine Ice Plateau in South Westland he eagerly accepted.[14]

Working on Brunner's journal also stimulated Pascoe's interest in another early explorer, Charlie Douglas. Although he had known of Douglas since the early 1930s, he had been unable to write about him because Douglas's papers had been jealously guarded by an old West Coast surveyor, William Wilson, who had acquired most of them after Douglas died in 1916. How his field reports and letters to the Lands Department came to be in Wilson's possession has never been clear, nor his reason for denying others access to them. Fortunately, Wilson did allow a friend in Christchurch to borrow them and he, in turn, passed them on to Pascoe. 'I get a lend of one book per year through Aitken and copy it,' Pascoe confided to a fellow climber, 'but if old Wilson found out, or saw extracts or references to the notes in the NZAJ [*New Zealand Alpine Journal*] articles, the "goose would stop laying golden eggs" and I would see no more diaries.'[15]

In 1938 Wilson died. Pascoe immediately told his boss, Joe Heenan, of the situation and Heenan quickly arranged for Pascoe to travel to Hokitika to try to persuade Wilson's widow to donate Douglas's papers to the Alexander Turnbull Library. Mrs Wilson agreed and also gave her approval to John

Pascoe and Monty McClymont, then the country's leading historian of exploration, to edit and publish the papers. This was a coup for Pascoe, but neither he nor McClymont had time to begin the work. After the war, Pascoe was kept busy illustrating war histories and McClymont was fully committed to writing the official history of the NZEF campaign in Greece.[16] Editing Brunner's journal in 1952, Pascoe was reminded that Douglas was still waiting in the wings. He first mentioned it to Robin Muir at the Pegasus Press. 'I think your Brunner book will be a real event in the New Zealand publishing world,' said Pascoe. 'If it is a success I may be able to work out a scheme for you to publish the Charles Douglas exploration papers, for which the government has copyright and which is a real scoop. Douglas is the only other New Zealand explorer who measures up to Brunner's standards. If McClymont was too busy to do a collaborated effort, I'd take it on myself.' When McClymont confirmed that he was unable to work on Douglas's biography, Pascoe realised it was time to seize the opportunity.

Pascoe saw his forthcoming expedition with Conway as a chance to become familiar with Douglas country. 'I hope to do a full three week trip this Xmas up the Matukituki, over Arawata Saddle, across the Olivine Ice Plateau, down Pyke to Hollyford, caving, igloo-ing, and climbing on the way,' he told Muir. 'A tough trip of real New Zealand flavour with inevitable delays of river and storm. Am going with a good Christchurch party. This glimpse of Arawata will help me interpret Douglas.'[17]

By November, Conway and Pascoe were absorbed in detailed planning for the journey on which they were to be accompanied by two CMC stalwarts, the club secretary, Bill Hannah, and the editor of the club's journal, Ray Chapman. Both had done a number of trips with Conway and although Pascoe knew neither Chapman nor Hannah, if Conway thought them suitable company for three weeks in the wilderness that was sufficient. Conway had written an appendix on 'Equipment and Food' for climbers and trampers in *Land Uplifted High* and he now took charge of those matters while Pascoe, as always, was the intelligence officer. 'I have spent many nights on the intelligence summaries for the trip,' he told Conway. 'I have aimed to become so saturated with knowledge of the country that if I was dropped at night by plane I would in the morning know where I was and what the escape routes were. I shall take the originals of these notes on the trip to beguile wet days and give on the spot information. They are on rice paper and light to carry.'[18] So thorough were Pascoe's preparations that he also typed brief details of the party on strips of rice paper. He proposed to leave them at campsites and under the occasional dry rock so that their route could be followed by search parties should an emergency arise.[19]

While John was away, Dorothy planned to take Anna and Sara to Sydney to stay with her brother, Peter, and his family. Martha and Jane were to be left with relatives and friends in New Zealand. In the midst of preparations for departure both *The Great Journey* and *Land Uplifted High* were published. *The Great Journey*, as Pascoe had predicted, provoked widespread interest and *Land Uplifted High* was also well received; most reviewers made particular mention of its descriptions of Manuka Point sheepmen. The *Evening Post* regarded it as 'the outstanding chapter' and the sheepmen as 'surely some of New

Ray Chapman (left), Stan Conway and John Pascoe in the Matukituki Valley at the start of their three-week transalpine trip. All wear red and white bandanas, Pascoe's habitual accessory in the hills.

BILL HANNAH PHOTO, RAY CHAPMAN COLLECTION

Zealand's sturdiest and most rewarding characters'.[20] The English Alpine Club's reviewer also thought it the best chapter and considered the book to be 'a work of high merit and evocative writing. Mr Pascoe serves the mountain scene in New Zealand well.'[21]

In the days before Christmas he had little time to enjoy accolades, however, as he was preoccupied with last-minute preparations for his own mountain trip. As twilight fell on 20 December 1952, he and his companions farewelled their taxi from Wanaka at the road end in the Matukituki Valley. At the age of 44 John Pascoe was the oldest of the party, Stan Conway a year younger, while Bill Hannah, 29, and Ray Chapman, 24, represented a younger generation. Chapman was only a boy when *Unclimbed New Zealand* was first published; it was one of the first books he bought when he became a mountaineer, never thinking that one day he would climb with the author.[22]

With food for three weeks, carefully calculated by Conway, each carried a pack weighing 30 kilograms. This load made the climb up to the Arawata Saddle and the Snow White Glacier hard work. For the first four nights Pascoe slept under the stars, but on Christmas Eve it was so cold in their camp above the glacier that he joined the others in the small tent – so cramped, Chapman recalled, that 'if one person rolled over we all had to move'. Outside 'the spot was wild and grand. In full view were huge ice towers of the Snow White, and blue crevasses between them.' Their only company was eight keas – very different, John reflected, from 'Dorothy's half a million shoppers in Sydney'. Christmas Day was their first rest day, an opportunity to wash clothes, sunbathe and sleep. 'By now we were fit, used to the swags and each other, and felt ready for mischief,' Pascoe noted in his diary.[23]

Their first week in the wilderness was marked by an ascent of Mount Maoriri then a long, tiring descent to the headwaters of the Arawata River.

Pascoe's party began their transalpine journey in the Matukituki Valley (beyond edge of map, lower right) near Lake Wanaka. They crossed the Arawata Saddle to the Snow White Glacier, climbed Mount Maoriri (not marked on this map) then descended to the headwaters of the Arawata. After crossing the Arawata near its junction with the Williamson River, they forged a new route to Trinity Col via the Tornado Glacier.

A first ascent of Mount Holloway was made from Trinity Col before they descended to the Pyke River which, in turn, gave access to the Cascade Valley via Simonin Pass. A long walk down the Cascade Valley took them to the West Coast at Jackson Bay.

(Scale 1 cm: 3.5 km approx.)

DEPARTMENT OF SURVEY AND LAND INFORMATION

On John Pascoe's initiative, Charlie Douglas's letters and field reports were donated to the Alexander Turnbull Library in 1938. The following year he also secured Douglas's sketchbooks for the library. They include this view of the Harper Glacier (now known as the Andy Glacier) and Olivine Ice Plateau with the serrated peaks of The Ark in the distance, which Douglas had sketched while exploring in the 1880s. When Pascoe's party visited the area 70 years later, they camped on Trinity Col on the far right of Douglas's sketch.

Charlie Douglas was not as technically accomplished a painter as his brother, Sir William Fettes Douglas, who was president of the Royal Scottish Academy. Charlie's sketches were intended only as a topographical record to be coloured later. He often gave them to friends with whom he stayed between bouts of exploration.

ALEXANDER TURNBULL LIBRARY

The Ark & Harper Glacier Williamson River

'As the forest grew taller and the birdlife more abundant' snatches of choral music repeated in Pascoe's mind, helping to keep tiredness at bay, and he thought how appropriate Bach's *Mass in B Minor* would sound in such a setting.[24] On reaching Williamson Flat, seldom visited except by explorers such as Douglas and gold prospectors like Arawata Bill, they were pleased with their progress and their luck in having an unbroken run of fine weather in a region notorious for rain.

Their objective was a group of peaks on the western edge of the Olivine Ice Plateau. To reach them they decided to cross the Arawata River at McArthur Flat, below its junction with the Williamson, an icy torrent that drains the huge icefield. By now the Arawata was 'a full-throated monster; milky, ice-cold, swift and deep'. In Pascoe's diary the entry was headed 'THE EIGHTH DAY AND NEARLY THE LAST'. Conway attempted to cross but was swept into a hole and rescued only because he was tied to a rope. To the watching Pascoe this was ominous. Since he weighed only 57 kilograms, river crossings were more difficult for him than the others, and although courage and determination were invaluable qualities, they made little difference in a strong current. He also had the traumatic memory of being swept away by the Rakaia. When crossing Canterbury rivers, he usually had the security of a rope with which stronger companions would pull him across; here the Arawata was simply too wide, even for their two climbing ropes joined together. So they had to devise a new technique: crossing in pairs, with one person in each pair linked by the joined ropes.

> Stan tied on the rope and with Bill stayed in dead water as anchors, to payout me (on rope) linked with Ray. Thus two pairs moved as two men. When Ray and I were paid out on two ropes tied together, total 170 feet, we had to steady

ourselves as best we could in the swift current, wait for our cobbers and take in the slack as they came down to us.

They crossed at a place where a shallow spit running diagonally down the river offered a longer but perhaps safer route. A kilometre downstream the Arawata narrowed and deepened at the entrance to the Ten Hour Gorge: not an ideal run out. They expected that being linked by the rope would give some security, but as the first pair, Ray and John, approached the centre of the river it became clear that the rope was, in fact, an unforeseen danger. 'The second section was fearful,' Pascoe wrote in his diary:

> Current grew swifter and deeper, and as the full weight of the river bellied out the 170 foot rope the tug at my waist <u>backwards</u> was as tho a tug of war team was trying to wrest me from every foothold that the combined strength of Ray and me made. I did not panic but resolved that if I tumbled it was possible that the anchor men could not hold my weight in which case I would gladly lose my pack to stay alive.
>   I used every latent reserve and strength I ever had. Numb from the knees down my feet had little power. Ray was steady and helped me fight the rope tug. If I was going to go down, it was to be a fighting finish. The slowness of the struggle was the worst, and I was panting as tho pushing a car uphill. As the river surged we found a pothole to balance in, and again waited for our cobbers to rejoin us, with that awful rope slack to complicate things. Then at last we were on the third and last leg of our endurance. Finally on a safe bank we lurched as tho drunk, and for some minutes the nervous reaction was so great that I had to fight back a compulsion to break down and howl in tears.[25]

A brew and a smoke on the riverbank restored their nerves before they set off up the Williamson Valley towards the Olivine Range.

The view from the top of Holloway of the Olivine Ice Plateau and surrounding peaks.

JOHN PASCOE COLLECTION, ALEXANDER TURNBULL LIBRARY

The river crossing affected Pascoe more than the others, who had been concerned but had not felt as vulnerable. Chapman had been linked arm in arm with Pascoe, so he knew how frightened he had been and he admired John's honesty in admitting it. Later, when Pascoe wrote accounts of their journey for alpine journals and magazines, as well as the prestigious international annual *The Mountain World*, he described in detail his fearful reaction. This also impressed Chapman. 'The 1950s was not a time when you wrote about your feelings if you were a mountaineer,' he later recalled. 'It just wasn't done.'[26]

With the Arawata behind them, the journey took on a different ambience as they encountered tougher terrain. 'Huge boulders, greasy logs, steep faces and much scrub in tall bush made it slow,' noted Pascoe, 'or was it that our river fight had tired us more than could be admitted?' From then on, tiredness was a constant problem which John dealt with by catnapping, snatching half an hour's sleep, for example, while the billy boiled for morning tea. Exhaustion affected Conway and Pascoe more than the younger men. John recalled one occasion when Ray and Bill went ahead to reconnoitre while he and Stan rested: 'I waited packsore and glum. Stan smoked a pipe, then dozed off as it slipped from his lips.' A rest day in a high-level campsite on Trinity Col was a welcome respite and a prelude to their ascent the following day of the virgin Mount Holloway. Others had tried for this peak only to be rebuffed time and again by bad weather.[27] Pascoe's party had unusually fine conditions, but even so he found that the climb, like the Arawata, was almost beyond his capability. To reach Holloway they had to traverse the steep slopes of Mount Temple, which were dissected by crevasses, and as they slowly worked their way across, Pascoe worried about avalanches. He had plenty of time to contemplate this prospect, as 'most of it was only safe for one man to move at a time'. So drained was he, that he did not display

The adjacent summits of Temple and Holloway(centre), photographed from Trinity Col.

Jack Holloway was an Otago mountaineer who explored the Olivine area in much the same way as Canterbury climbers explored the Rakaia mountains.

GEOFF SPEARPOINT

his usual curiosity on the summit of Holloway. 'I could not have cared less about mapping, all I wanted to do was to flop till it was time to concentrate on problems of re-traverse of Temple.' Safely back in camp, he reflected on what had been 'a wonderful day', but also admitted that 'in parts I was climbing beyond my powers because of the virtuosity of my party'.

The ascent of Holloway crowned a fortnight in the mountains, longer than any of Pascoe's previous trips, and it began to show in his insatiable need for sleep. Undoubtedly this was exacerbated by his habit of rising earlier than his companions to get the fire going and make a cup of tea. He could do this without disturbing them as he usually slept outside while they slept in the tent. On the sixteenth day, for instance, his diary records that he got up at 3.30 a.m. and by lunchtime was exhausted, so while his friends cooked porridge beside the Pyke River, he catnapped. 'Sleep was better than food for me.'

That afternoon, as they climbed up to Simonin Pass, which led them into the Cascade Valley, Ray Chapman discovered a trail of distinctive rock cairns. These, they realised, had been made by the legendary gold prospector, William O'Leary, better known as Arawata Bill. Next day more traces were found: 'a rusty shovel and a hut rotted into a heap of fragments'.

By the nineteenth day, hunger – that persistent feeling so familiar to the early explorers and prospectors – was palpable. 'It was interesting to find

It took the 're-explorers' a day to negotiate the Cascade Gorge in January 1953 and by the end John Pascoe was so tired he 'could have fallen asleep standing up'. Despite continual exhaustion, Pascoe still managed to take more than 120 photos on the trip, 'the best photos I have ever taken'. Although some were published in newspapers and magazines, as well as several in Mr Explorer Douglas, the rest remained unseen until the 1970 publication of Pascoe's Of Unknown New Zealand, which included 30 Arawata photos.

JOHN PASCOE COLLECTION,
ALEXANDER TURNBULL LIBRARY

PETER COATES, 1970

ARAWATA BILL

William O'Leary, better known as *Arawata Bill*, was born to wander. His father, a Canadian gold miner, arrived in Otago in the early 1860s from Australia. In Dunedin he met Mary O'Connor who had emigrated from Ireland. They married in 1863 and had eight children before Timothy O'Leary abandoned wife and family to seek his fortune on the West Coast.

William, their second child, was often absent from school, preferring to roam the countryside. After his father's departure, he left home for an itinerant life as a casual labourer, shooting rabbits and droving cattle throughout Otago and Southland. Like his father, he was a keen prospector who fossicked in remote areas, particularly the head of the Arawata River, first explored by Charlie Douglas in the 1880s.

William O'Leary was known as *Arawata Bill* because he spent so much time in that valley. Usually he had only his horse, Dolly, for company; their partnership lasted more than 20 years. *Arawata Bill* was a distinctive figure, invariably clad in a three-piece suit with gumboots up to his thighs. He never drank or smoked and existed on porridge, damper and black tea, supplementing this limited diet with native birds such as kaka, kereru, kea and weka. Kiwi, he considered, were 'beautiful to eat'.

In middle age he moved to the West Coast where he worked for the Westland County Council on track maintenance and as the ferryman at the mouths of the Arawata and Waiatoto Rivers. But a settled life was not for him. He was often absent, exploring and prospecting in the upper Arawata where he had a permanent camp under a massive overhanging rock. At times he was away for so long that search parties were organised.

During the 1930s, as climbing became popular, young mountaineers sometimes came across *Arawata Bill*, now in his 60s, high on the slopes of snowy passes in his big gumboots which, according to Jack Holloway, 'slipped horribly on the snow', cutting steps with a long-handled shovel. But as they negotiated steep and difficult gorges, climbers found his tracks and cairns invaluable.

As he grew older, *Arawata Bill* spent most of his time at the head of Lake Wakatipu, staying with friends and prospecting in the nearby mountains. Returning from the hills, he and Dolly fell over a cliff, she broke a leg and he had to shoot her — 'the hardest thing I ever had to do'. He was also injured, but managed to reach Glenorchy. When he recovered, *Arawata Bill* surprised a sister in Wellington, who had thought him long dead, by turning up on her doorstep. He particularly enjoyed the Centennial Exhibition at Rongotai and even rode the roller-coaster. After his return to Otago, his health deteriorated and he went to live in a home for the elderly.

Although he enjoyed life with the Little Sisters of the Poor in Dunedin and wished he had moved there earlier, he still had an urge to wander and 'absconded' more than once. In 1947 he made another surprise visit to Wellington; a few months later he went to Glenorchy intent on prospecting again but, after a night out in a snowstorm, he was returned to Dunedin. He died the same year, aged 82.

that Stan and I were least affected by the hard diet and the rationed food,' observed Pascoe. 'The young jokers talked lovingly of food, but I was not as worried and was content to let them have much of my second helpings on the grounds that they needed it.' He also found diversion from hunger in his pipe, which dampened his appetite and also gave him solace. All four found tobacco essential: it was, said Chapman, a choice of either smoking or 'sucking a stone'.[28]

The sense of being 're-explorers' following in the footsteps of 19th-century pioneers such as Brunner and Douglas, or prospectors such as O'Leary, was accentuated by their slow passage through the Cascade Gorge. 'Sometimes a hundred yards would take an hour. Under logs, hand over hand up mossy cliffs, into lawyer tangles, across slimy boulders: usual Westland story,' wrote Pascoe, who remembered similar misery while descending gorges below the Garden of Eden on the West Coast in the 1930s Then he was a young man irked by any impediment; now he found age and experience gave him a patience not possessed by all the party. While John 'conserved nervous energy by thinking of worse places I have been in', Bill Hannah 'got in a temper and scraped the bark with his boots and crampons, fought the branches and got so mad we had to let him take us to the river (often the worst going)'.

Three weeks after leaving Wanaka they crossed Martyr Saddle above the Jackson River and saw the Tasman Sea less than 20 kilometres away. With swags reduced to 16 kilograms and a horse track to follow, the travelling was easier and 'tho bitchy because light on tucker' they enjoyed 'good sun and easy flats and stream wading'. On the 22nd day the party reached the coast. Two penguins plodded up the beach as if to greet them and the view out across the Tasman reminded John of his family in Sydney: 'the surge of the sea — did it bring me news of my darlings in Australia?'[29]

Pascoe later told Conway that the transalpine journey was 'perhaps the finest trip I will ever do'.[30] On his way back to Wellington, he called in to see Robin Muir at the Pegasus Press in Christchurch. Muir was absent but Denis Glover was there and very interested in Pascoe's account of the trip. Pascoe had gone to South Westland because he was interested in the experiences of the early explorers such as Brunner and Douglas, but it was Arawata Bill who made the strongest impression on him. The nickname appealed to Glover who had recently published a series of poems, *Sings Harry*, about the experiences and thoughts of a back country loner, and Arawata Bill sounded like a similar, archetypal figure. Glover was also taken by Pascoe's sunburnt and bearded appearance. A few days later another mountaineer, Rod Hewitt, visited Glover at the Pegasus Press. He, too, had been in the mountains but unlike Pascoe, was clean-shaven for, as he told Glover, he always took a razor with him. Hewitt's habit and Pascoe's tales of finding traces of Bill O'Leary prompted Glover to write a poem he called 'Arawata Bill' and dedicated to 'JDP'.[31]

In the meantime John Pascoe had returned to Wellington, but was finding it hard to settle back into his old life. Except for Martha, his family were still away and on lonely evenings at Eastbourne memories of South Westland filled his mind. As usual, he wrote accounts of the trip for newspapers and

John Pascoe at the end of the Arawata trip.

JOHN PASCOE COLLECTION, ALEXANDER TURNBULL LIBRARY

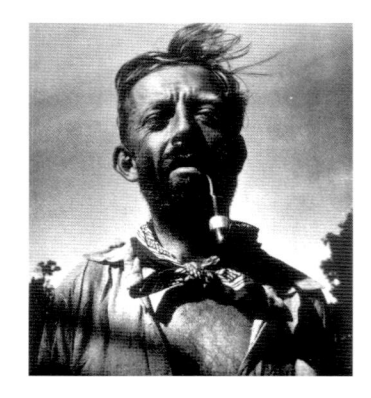

magazines such as the *Weekly News*, which published a double-page spread of his photos. But without Dorothy to talk to, he looked for other ways to record his experiences. He wrote a candid, confessional diary 'Beyond the Arawata – Personal Notes on an Overland Journey', marked it 'Personal – not for publication' and sent copies to Dorothy in Sydney, his mother and brother and to A. P. Harper, because Harper had spent two summers exploring with Charlie Douglas. Late one evening, soon after his return, he also wrote a poem he called 'Arawata Bill':

ARAWATA BILL

William O'Leary made his trails and cooled gold fever
in rivers and gorge.
He scratched the outcrops of basic rock intrusions,
dug alluvial gravel, sifted it and found a pass
over the land to the sea.

The Tasman Sea flowed full to ragged cliffs and its tradition
gave granite hardness to resolution shrunk by hardship.
He smelt the sea and headed far up valleys
for solitude. Rare metal his aim on the rocks
over the land to the sea.

Before Bill came to traverse the Dart, the Pyke, the Cascade,
the Joe, the Barrier, the Jerry, the Woodhen, the silt of
the Williamson, the lush flats, the barren bluffs and
turning course of torrents, great peaks primeval raised up in lofty quietness
over the land to the sea.

Before his boots had scraped the moss from the boulders,
explorer Douglas and the prospector Barrington
had fused their sweat in the sweetness of mist. The terror of time
and the anger of stonefall had marked the passage of all men
over the land to the sea.

Yet the terror of time had been chafed by the patience of reason,
the anger of stonefall had melted before the agility
of men who found no bush hostile. Camp oven, crowbar,
flour, bird flesh, sleep made travel possible
over the land to the sea.

What did Bill think of Christ? Was he Saviour or used in epithet hot
to exorcise the scrub of animate devilment?
Bill died in Catholic sheets. Were memories strong of flight
from storms, fights with floods and snow that fell
over the land to the sea?

The shovels have rusted, the improvised huts have rotted.
Men go the way of all men and perish their tea leaves
on mica schist flung. Their names a legend in hills of no legend
their footmarks buried by leaf mould and the mating of deer trails
over the land to the sea.

Next day John Pascoe returned from work to find a letter from Denis Glover.[32]

Dear John,

It just shows you what a chance word will do. I have been brooding over Bill and now Rod Hewitt has just been in, and I learn he always shaves when climbing!

Anyway, here's a redhot first draft, because I know you'll be interested. I am sending it to the *Press*, but if it doesn't come up to their standards I'm sure Monty [Holcroft, editor of the *Listener*] will tuck it in somewhere.

Thanks for the idea.

Cheers

Denis

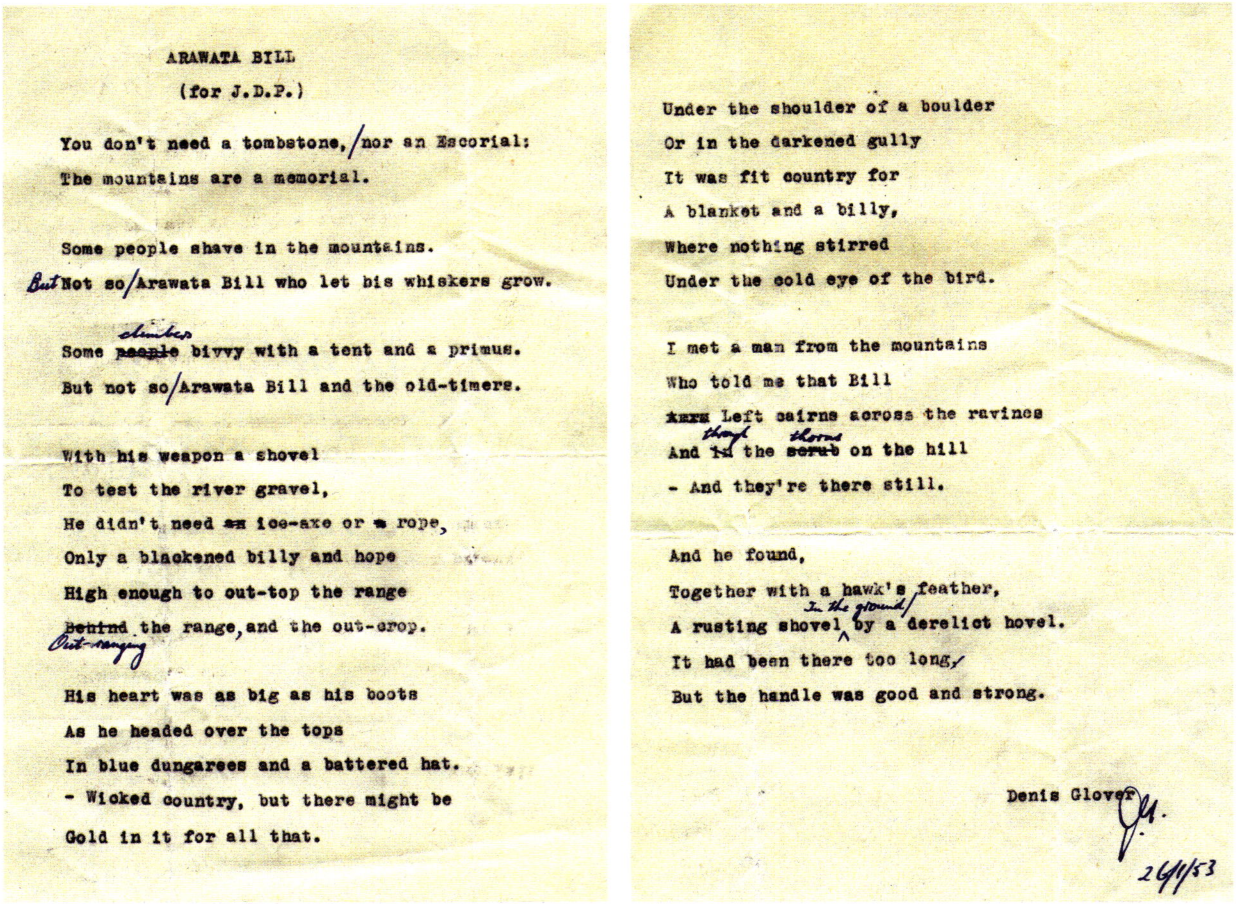

```
                ARAWATA BILL
                  (for J.D.P.)

      You don't need a tombstone, /nor an Escorial;
      The mountains are a memorial.


      Some people shave in the mountains.
 But  Not so/Arawata Bill who let his whiskers grow.

                  climbes
      Some people bivvy with a tent and a primus.
      But not so/Arawata Bill and the old-timers.


      With his weapon a shovel
      To test the river gravel,
      He didn't need an ice-axe or a rope,
      Only a blackened billy and hope
      High enough to out-top the range
      Behind the range, and the out-crop.
      Out-ranging

      His heart was as big as his boots
      As he headed over the tops
      In blue dungarees and a battered hat.
      - Wicked country, but there might be
      Gold in it for all that.
```

```
      Under the shoulder of a boulder
      Or in the darkened gully
      It was fit country for
      A blanket and a billy,
      Where nothing stirred
      Under the cold eye of the bird.


      I met a man from the mountains
      Who told me that Bill
      xxxx Left cairns across the ravines
                   though    thorns
      And in the scrub on the hill
      - And they're there still.


      And he found,
      Together with a hawk's feather,
                        In the ground/
      A rusting shovel, by a derelict hovel.
                       ^
      It had been there too long,
      But the handle was good and strong.

                              Denis Glover
                                        26/1/53
```

DOROTHY PASCOE COLLECTION

By return post, Pascoe sent Glover his 'Arawata Bill' with a note saying: 'What will rock you is that I stimulated myself and not only you by my chance word. And made my first fumble at poetry. What do you think? Criticism welcome.'[33] He also invited comment from David Hall – having first

DENIS GLOVER AND THE CAXTON PRESS

In 1935 Denis Glover and John Drew established the Caxton Press. 'It was a time to impart new vitality to New Zealand verse. No more leisurely-whimsy, feminine-mimsy stuff,' Glover later wrote in his autobiography Hot Water Sailor. At a time when Christchurch was the centre of cultural life in the country, Caxton quickly became the leading publisher of poetry. In 1937 Glover and Drew were joined by Leo Bensemann, an artist and typographer, who soon became, in Drew's words, 'the backbone of the whole show'.

While Glover was overseas during the war, Bensemann kept Caxton going, but when Glover returned with a drinking problem exacerbated by navy service, Caxton was soon in crisis. Despite his personal difficulties, however, Glover continued to publish much of the progressive poetry produced in New Zealand at the time. After Glover's marriage ended, problems increased and Bensemann suffered from stomach ulcers caused by the stressful situation. In 1951, Glover was fired from Caxton and was lucky to be given a job by the rival Pegasus Press.

John Pascoe and Denis Glover had known each other as students, as well as during Glover's brief period as a mountaineer, but because Pascoe was in Wellington, he was removed from the ructions caused by Glover's conduct. From a distance Pascoe could appreciate Glover's considerable cultural contribution, something not always apparent to those living in Christchurch. Nevertheless, Pascoe knew about Glover's behaviour. 'He was a character and I always

Denis Glover by Leo Bensemann, c.1950.
ALEXANDER TURNBULL LIBRARY

stuck up for him in Christchurch society where his booziness and lack of domestic happiness was held against him,' Pascoe later told the poet Louis Johnson.

outlined the curious coincidence that led them both to write the poems at the same time – and conceded that 'Denis has made a simpler poem than mine, and of course more skilled, and with the witty resonance that he alone possesses'.[34] At this stage a less determined person might have withdrawn and simply accepted Glover's dedication and mention of Pascoe in the poem as the 'man from the mountains / Who told me that Bill / left cairns across the ravines', as adequate acknowledgement. But Pascoe could not let Arawata Bill go. He thought his own poem good, but anticipated that he would be seen as simply imitating Glover.[35] To counteract this perception he determined to become a poet and battle it out with Glover.

David Hall was both critical and encouraging, suggesting that Pascoe revise 'Arawata Bill' then try to get it published. 'Why don't you try the Listener? Better be in first. If the Listener won't have it, why not see if Louis Johnson's [Poetry] Yearbook has a place for it?'[36] Although Pascoe did not revise it, he did send it to both publications, then quickly wrote three new poems: 'Bushman', about Thomas Brunner, 'The Rope', describing the Arawata River crossing and 'A Welcome', an erotic view of marriage and mountains which he sent to Dorothy in Sydney.[37] Again he sent his verse to David Hall with an explanation of his sudden interest in poetry:

> One of the reasons that put me off trying verse till my 44th year was that in the effort to chase rhyme and rhythm I felt I would be constrained by form and would find fluency stuttering over such limitations. But with Arawata Bill I felt the subject was not right for prose and that new disciplines of economy and thought would have to emerge. Hence attempt at a poem. And hence the faults of broken rhythm. I wrote it all in one hit and did not dare look backwards as I wrote it for fear that I should lose the continuity of what I had been brooding over.

Although Pascoe was pleased with 'Arawata Bill' he was not so sure about his other efforts. For instance, he wrote three versions of the river crossing poem and 'purred over them when I did them, put them away for three nights, and tore all copies up with snarls of rage when I re-read them in the cold light of afterthought. It is bloody hard not to be corny.' And when he looked back at 'A Welcome' he also had misgivings which he confided to Hall:

> I also did a sentimental poem for Dorothy which I sent her. It is all right as between man and wife, where sentiment is fair enough as are more strenuous vices. But publication? No, sir! I would be qualifying for the *Woman's Weekly* before I knew where I was. Yet strangely enough I find less technical faults in my crumby sentiments; the trouble is that my ideas and theme are trite.[38]

Meanwhile, Glover had replied with his thoughts on Pascoe's 'Arawata Bill'. 'You ask for my comments, but I can only say that you may perhaps underestimate the difficulties of verse, and that I find you too factual, not purely imaginative enough, to have written, or rather achieved, a real poem. But would to God most of us could fall as little short.'

Glover, too, had been busy writing verse. 'For better or for worse, this theme has taken hold of me,' he told Pascoe.

> Bill is now up to twenty poems of greater or lesser length, and, I think, as good as anything I have ever done on a single theme. Libraries and interloan files have been a great help; but I have chosen to treat O'Leary as the symbol of all the great unknown explorers, prospectors, even mountaineers, who have been looking for something intangible round the next bend.

Glover was on a roll. But before the public could read his poems, Pascoe would have a chance to publicly stake his claim to have been the one who first thought of Arawata Bill, because Glover had written to the New Zealand Broadcasting Service to suggest that both his original 'Arawata Bill' and Pascoe's poem be read together on radio, as part of a new poetry programme scheduled to begin shortly.[39] In May 1953, 3YC's *First Hearing*, with Denis Glover as compere, broadcast previously unpublished poems by Elsie Locke, Louis Johnson, Anton Vogt, Ruth Dallas and Nancy Bruce as well as Pascoe's and Glover's versions of 'Arawata Bill'. Before they were read, Glover made it clear that until he talked to John Pascoe he had no knowledge of Arawata Bill. Pascoe was relieved. 'That removes any suspicion of imitation from my work,' he told Louis Johnson.[40] When the *Listener* reviewed the programme it made no reference to Glover's verse but noted that 'John Pascoe leapt out

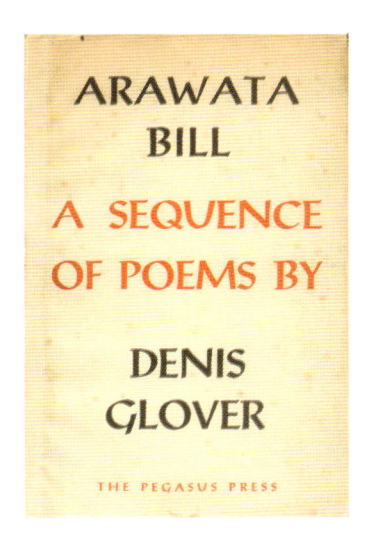

ARAWATA BILL

A SEQUENCE OF POEMS BY

DENIS GLOVER

THE PEGASUS PRESS

John Pascoe always acknowledged Glover's skill as a poet and readily conceded that Glover's 'Arawata Bill' was better verse than his, but he declined a request to help publicise Glover's Arawata Bill poems.

'The Listener gave Denis a poster, a cover photo, a story and a leader. Good work for "Arawata Bill"', Pascoe told Robin Muir, Glover's employer at the Pegasus Press. 'But I must say when the Listener sub-editor asked me for my Xmas photos to illustrate the story I thought that was a bit on the nose and said so. After all I don't just take photos to illustrate other people's articles, and I have definite plans myself for their ultimate publication. But I was glad Denis got the publicity.'

A year later, Pascoe's attitude had hardened. When he sent some of his verse to the editor of the Canterbury Mountaineer he suggested a second opinion to see 'if it is worth publishing', but warned against showing it to Denis Glover 'as he is apt to pinch my ideas'.

of a prose blue with considerable force in his poem on Arawata Bill. The words and images showed a sure grasp of local idiom and of the kind of country in which the old prospector worked.'[41]

Both poems were also published in the *Poetry Yearbook*. Its editor, Louis Johnson, told John Pascoe that he preferred his version. 'Glover's book [*Arawata Bill*] is quite the worst thing he has done – and probably your poem invokes more atmosphere than his – but this is a private and personal view.'[42] Pascoe did not agree. 'I think they are very fine,' he had written to Glover earlier. 'I find them more even in quality than *Sings Harry* and I expect them to be among your most lasting work.'[43] Time has shown this to be so. The first edition of Glover's *Arawata Bill* sold out in two weeks; it has since been reprinted twice and remains a landmark of New Zealand verse. Pascoe's poem did not fare as well. As he feared, he has come to be seen as an imitator, as Glover's biographer implies:

> On his return to Wellington after visiting Christchurch, John Pascoe received in the mail Glover's initial shaving verse, and then attempted something himself. Pascoe, an industrious and frequently eloquent non-fiction writer, was very much a novice poet. The result was an appalling poem, thoughtful and observant perhaps, but full of sweat, resolution, basic rock intrusions and self-conscious poeticising.[44]

Meanwhile Dorothy had returned from Sydney in February to find that the very different experiences she and John had enjoyed during their time apart now, unexpectedly, created a distance between them. 'This was my first overseas experience. It was a far cry from my quiet life in Eastbourne,' Dorothy later recalled. 'Sydney offered so much to excite me with theatre and art galleries – and ideas to explore with my brother and his wife. I arrived home thoroughly stimulated and John was back from the mountains equally excited and wanting to share his experiences. For a time we talked across each other – neither listening – until finally we reached some sort of balance.' When she read John's poems she found the ideas and images laboured, but with little experience of poetry she felt unable to offer either encouragement or criticism. Besides, she had a more immediate problem to deal with: she was not finding her return to Eastbourne as easy as she had anticipated. 'The children seemed to pick up their old life on our forested hillside happily but I took longer to settle back into domesticity. John's life always seemed so organised and full of activity and always the clackerty-clack of his well-used typewriter in the background. I was busy with Playcentre and school fundraising activities but after Sydney my appetite was whetted for something more.'[45]

Reunited with wife and family, John continued to write poems. Ironically, John's most accessible verse was his slightest, a series of treasure hunt clues, written without effort in language free of portentous purpose:[46]

Hunt your hardest, do your best,
There is one clue behind the chest.

Are you a frog? Are you a monk?
Look beneath the bottom bunk?

Down the stairs, along the floor,
Against the wall behind the door.

Call me silly, eat my bread,
The clue is near old Anna's bed.

Blow me down and shine a torch,
but try the mat by the back porch.

Get out children! Hop it! Scram!
The answer's in the big doll's pram.

Sweets are sweet but all the sweeter,
When the clue is on the heater.

Read a book or read a fable,
Also search the kitchen table

Kiss a rabbit, hug a weasel,
Find the answer on the easel.

Red is not blue,
Mum's bed is a clue.

Final clue is hot as hot,
Under pillow of Jane's cot.

Pretty heads like lovely fans,
But hunters try the pots and pans.

Paul and Ann Pascoe and their sons Luke, Jonathan and Simon, Christchurch, 1953.
After the war both John and Paul Pascoe were preoccupied with work and family, but kept in touch with letters and occasional visits. When John travelled to Christchurch, Paul would meet the ferry at Lyttelton and take John back to Sumner for breakfast. Paul's boys enjoyed John's visits, especially his yodelling, and he was always happy to perform for his nephews.
DOROTHY PASCOE COLLECTION

For his more serious verse, John received encouragement from Jean Johnson, the widow of an old friend. Only days after John had returned from South Westland, he and the New Zealand climbing community were shocked by the death of Christopher Johnson, editor of the Alpine Club *Journal*, who was killed in a plane crash in the upper Matukituki Valley while searching for two missing trampers.[47] John had known Christopher for many years and, with David Hall, regarded him as 'one of my best critics'. John wrote to Jean, whom he had known as a student, to offer sympathy and support. Jean responded by sending him two poems written by her husband: 'The Mind, Mind Has Mountains' and a paraphrased climbers' version of the 23rd Psalm.[48] John, in turn, sent her a copy of his 'Arawata Bill' because, as he explained, it was Otago climbers like her husband who had 'inspired me to make the effort to cross some Otago ranges and the experience was so rewarding that I had much to discuss with him'. Death denied John that opportunity, but at least he could share his poem and his observation that: 'To distil the essence of thought is the hardest discipline of literary expression, and it seems that only in poetry can ultimate perfection be gained'.[49] 'Thank you for your letter and "Arawata Bill",' Jean wrote. 'I like it. I do like it, truly.' And she added: 'write to me occasionally if you can find the time'.[50] Their correspondence quickly became primarily a discussion of poetry. Jean, like her husband, was erudite; he had edited the Alpine Club *Journal*, while she was an occasional reviewer and literary critic. John wrote regularly, Jean less often: as a solo parent raising three children she did not have the time.

The interdenominational chapel at Arthur's Pass, built in 1955, was designed by Paul Pascoe. The window behind the altar frames the view of a waterfall and beech forest on the slopes of Avalanche Peak.

Throughout 1953 and 1954 John Pascoe continued to write verse, encouraged no doubt by his radio exposure, but also for more personal reasons. 'It is some consolation to write stuff like poetry that has no commercial value,' he told Jean Johnson, 'a healthy corrective to my dreadful facility to write a pot-boiling article for a magazine when one of us needs a new raincoat or something.'[51] But the real benefit of Pascoe's interest in Arawata Bill was that it prompted him to begin his book on Charles Douglas. Writing poetry, he knew, would always be difficult, unlike prose, which he wrote with ease.

In April, Pascoe had sent an article describing his trip to the editor of the *School Journal* with the comment that the experience 'has spurred me to start work on the Lifetimes and Diaries of Explorer Charles Douglas which will be spare time work for me for four years. Going over the country Douglas covered has been a great help to me.'[52]

In the meantime, Pascoe's two recently published books continued to receive the sort of positive comment his poetry did not. Glover for one was generous in his praise of *Land Uplifted High*:

> Curiously enough, I like your new book for the reason that most reviewers quarrel with; its scrappiness at the end is implicit in the enormous task you set yourself. How much more difficult it is to write about the bend in the Wilberforce, known but always respected, than to pour out panygyrics about a first attempt at the high Himalayas. For the local scene every detail may be of vital importance: what strikes some as embroidery may, by chance, be the means of getting somebody else out of a dirty jam.[53]

The letter John most enjoyed, however, came from George Lowe, written on a steamer in the Indian Ocean en route to Mount Everest. 'I have your latest book with me. I've just enjoyed an hour on the bunk reading the first two chapters. I think the English boys will enjoy reading this when we're in the [western] cwm. It gives a great idea of the New Zealand hills. It's a good book.'[54] Three months later, on 29 May 1953, Hillary and Tenzing made the first ascent of Everest, with Lowe in support not far below, waiting to have a go should the pair fail. The successful climb coincided with

George Lowe, John Pascoe and Ed Hillary at the Pascoe home, August 1953.

DOROTHY PASCOE COLLECTION

the coronation of the young Queen Elizabeth. For New Zealand it was a double celebration with unprecedented scenes of jubilation. In August, Hillary and Lowe returned to New Zealand and travelled the country giving public lectures. Everywhere they went the press besieged them. In Wellington they stayed with the Pascoes, which gave them a welcome respite from the media attention. 'They were amusing and considerate guests and we tried to give them a restful time,' John reported to Jean Johnson. 'We let them sleep till 9 a.m. and lie in till 11 a.m. and another sleep after lunch, to recuperate on a strenuous trip through New Zealand.'[55]

Mountaineering was a prominent topic in New Zealand newspapers during the winter of 1953, and not only because of Everest. On 27 July an *Evening Post* headline announced 'Five Die on Mount Egmont' and described how, the previous day, a Nurses' Tramping Club ascent had ended in tragedy when seven members of the group, who were roped together, slid over an icy bluff. Two were killed instantly, three more died while being carried down the mountain and two others died a week later in hospital. There was considerable criticism of the 29 strong climbing party because, although snow and ice could be clearly seen on the upper slopes, only one of the group carried an ice axe, there was only one rope and no one had crampons. Because of the conditions, the group did not reach the top until mid-afternoon and by the time they began to descend the snow had frozen. When one person on the rope slipped, all seven slid down the slope and over a bluff.[56]

The deaths were the latest of a series of misadventures on the mountain that led the public to question the safety of climbing and skiing on Egmont, particularly after the Federated Mountain Clubs' report on the accident and a coroner's inquiry revealed that the nurses had asked the Taranaki Alpine Club to assist them, but only one guide had been supplied. As a result of this adverse publicity, and acrimony within the wider climbing community about the accident, John Pascoe and Rod Syme (Taranaki's most experienced climber) decided to show the public that, with proper equipment and leadership, Mount Egmont could be safely climbed by anyone – including children.

At the end of August, Anna and Sara Pascoe and their father, with Rod Syme and others, set out to climb the mountain. Following a night at a hut on the southern side they began the ascent, but after cutting thousands of steps in the icy snow John Pascoe realised that they would not reach the summit until 3 p.m., too late to make a safe descent, so they retreated to the hut. Next morning they set out again, except nine-year-old Sara who stayed at the hut with another party. All carried ice axes and wore crampons, apart from Anna who wore a pair of her father's 'well clinkered boots', and they were all tied to a rope. Using steps they had cut the previous day they made good progress until the steps ended on steeper icy slopes beneath the summit. John explained to Anna 'we were now in places where a slip would be fatal if we were at all careless. She understood this,' he later wrote to his mother, 'and while it did not make her nervous it made her respect the need for attention to placing of feet, use of ice pick and tautness of rope. At 12.15 p.m. we topped the crater lip, and once inside had an easy route to the actual summit where I photographed and kissed her.' After lunch and a rest in

John and Anna Pascoe on the summit of Mount Egmont, August 1953. Later John chose this as the author photograph on the dustjacket of Great Days in New Zealand Mountaineering.

DOROTHY PASCOE COLLECTION

a 'snug possy' they returned to the 'very steep upper slopes where care was essential. Coming down is always more difficult than going up for a novice, so it was a delight to find that Anna was careful and extremely steady in her steps, did not falter or waver, and even gave a shimmer of delight and said "isn't this super". Then we ran into one of those sudden snow flurries for which Egmont is famous in winter,' Pascoe's letter continued. 'It was just steady snow falling and no visibility, but as we had our tracks and steps to show us the way we were not worried.'[57]

A photo of Anna with her father and the other climbers on the snowy summit of Egmont appeared on the front page of the *Evening Post*. This exercise in publicity was an example of John Pascoe's developing role in the mountain world. In the past, he had been a climber who also wrote about the mountains, but took little part in the administration of alpine affairs. For a brief period as a young man he had been a member of the executive of the CMC, but later took little interest. But in 1953, he accepted nomination from the New Zealand Alpine Club to be its representative on the executive of the Federated Mountain Clubs (FMC), an honour that indicated his complete rehabilitation within the organisation he had once spurned.[58] He soon found, however, that it was time-consuming and tricky, particularly as far as his old club, the CMC, was concerned. The CMC had planned an expedition to the Himalayas, which was deferred because of the war. Later, the ascent of Everest rekindled the club's plans. John Pascoe was delighted that Stan Conway was likely to lead the expedition: 'Your organising ability, reserves of energy, unselfishness, and experience, together with your calm appraisal of Himalayan tactics would make you a "must" for leader of a CMC party'.

He was less certain about a CMC proposal to change its name to the New Zealand Mountaineering Club to improve its chances of gaining the approval of the Department of External Affairs, which arranged permits to climb in India, Nepal and Pakistan. At the time, a Tararua Tramping Club party was already climbing in the western Himalaya and other New Zealand groups, sponsored by the New Zealand Alpine Club, were keen to follow its lead.

In February 1955 the Pascoe family farewelled the CMC's Masherbrum expedition from Wellington's wharves. From left: Martha, Sara, John, Jane and Dorothy. Although John Pascoe could not go to the Himalaya, he helped his climbing friends by lobbying the Education Department to grant leave of absence to three of the team who were teachers and he also wrote an article describing their proposed trip, 'From the Arawata to the Karakoram', for the Listener. As a result, John was invited to write a book about the expedition by the English publisher, Robert Hale Limited. John had to decline. 'Unfortunately, although one of my greatest ambitions is to see the Himalayas, I am a married man with four young children, so it is quite impossible to consider joining any party or to get leave without pay for such a long period.'

DOROTHY PASCOE COLLECTION

Best wishes for this Christmas and a mountainous Christmas next season.

May you climb until the end
Up every peak and snowy bend.
May your successes come one by one
With climbing friends and maybe mum.

To John.
From Anna.

Anna Pascoe, like her mother, understood the importance of mountains to John Pascoe.

Pascoe could see that some kind of independent Himalayan Committee was needed to evaluate these plans and that the committee should be an initiative of the FMC or NZAC. As a representative of both organisations he could not, therefore, endorse the CMC's ploy to increase the likelihood of it gaining government approval. On the other hand, the CMC party included his Arawata companions, Ray Chapman, Stan Conway and Bill Hannah. If he failed to support them, would he ever be asked to join a transalpine trip again? 'I don't think the change of name to NZMC a good one,' he told Conway. 'I would not be dogmatic, as I would not wish to stand in the way of any move that the majority of members wanted as progress, and I think the most honest course would be for me not to record any preference either way. After all I have had my day and tho' I hope for many future hard trips I cannot consider myself as an active member [of the CMC].'[59]

FROM CANTERBURY TO THE KARAKORAM

The CMC expedition was the first to climb in this area since a British team in 1938. A Pakistani army contingent consisting of a doctor, a liaison officer and several soldiers accompanied the New Zealanders. In return for their assistance the Pakistanis were given experience in living and climbing at high altitudes.

Problems arose as the large party of 11 climbers, four army scouts and 14 porters ferried supplies to a series of high camps on Masherbrum (7821 metres). In May a soldier died from pneumonia and two others were evacuated because of illness and injury. Several New Zealanders also had health problems. At the same time the CMC climbers were unlucky to be delayed by a series of unseasonal storms, fierce blizzards and avalanches, one of which buried a high-level food dump. By mid-June they had reached 7500 metres, close to the summit, but realised they could not climb higher as the arrival of the

The CMC's camp on the upper slopes of Masherbrum, Karakoram Mountains, May 1955.

RAY CHAPMAN COLLECTION

monsoon season was imminent. Reluctantly their leader, Stan Conway, was forced to abandon the attempt on the unclimbed peak.

Betsey Jane and Charlie Douglas. In Mr Explorer Douglas Pascoe wrote: 'His dogs filled the need in his life to express fondness for animals. Topsy, Betsey Jane and their successors could gather birds, help with the route finding, provide relief for lonely days and never be critical.'

In 1894 Douglas lost Betsey Jane, as he explained in a letter to A. P. Harper: 'Betsey Jane is now gathered to her fathers, when on Ryan's peak I sent her back to camp as there was some rock climbing to do and I have never seen her since. She must have tried to follow me and gone down a crevasse or over a precipice — peace to her ashes.'

A. P. HARPER PHOTO,
DOROTHY PASCOE COLLECTION

Of even greater concern was the inroads Pascoe's work for the FMC made into his time for writing, particularly on Charlie Douglas. 'I find the FMC work has slowed down my work on this book. I am on committees for national parks, safety in the mountains, dehydrated food, general executive. I regard my capacity for continuous work on writing books as more important than club or FMC administration which can be left to other people. But how many people would give four years of their life in spare time to write a book? *Land Uplifted High* was virtually three years work, *Brunner* six months, *The Mountains The Bush & The Sea* one year, the guidebook [to the Southern Alps] one year, so it is not as though I was idle.'[60]

Pascoe could have added another title to this list. In 1953 he briefly put aside Charlie Douglas's papers to edit the journal of Jakob Lauper who accompanied Henry Whitcombe on his trip across the Southern Alps in 1863. Pascoe began by making spot checks of the translation of the original German script, then wrote an introduction, added footnotes and found illustrations — all done in a hurry as Whitcombe & Tombs planned to publish it later that year. As it happened, there was no need to rush. *Over the Whitcombe Pass* was not finally published until 1960, seven years after he put all else aside to edit it.[61]

Frustration at these distractions from his essential work on Douglas was increased by concern about the health of several key informants, in particular A. P. Harper, now aged 87, and Colin Macfarlane who had known Douglas when the Macfarlanes ran cattle in the lower Cascade Valley in the 1880s and 1890s. Harper's involvement was crucial as he had letters from Douglas as well as valuable photographs and also 'his own essential recollections from a virile memory'. Even more important, he had moral authority over the exercise, maintaining that Douglas had entrusted him with the job of edit-

OVER THE WHITCOMBE PASS

Jakob Lauper
1863

edited by
JOHN PASCOE

Charlie Douglas dries his socks in front of the campfire beside a tributary of the Cook River, March 1894.

Douglas sometimes suffered from rheumatism, the consequence of years of wearing wet clothes and sleeping on the ground.

A. P. HARPER PHOTO, JOHN PASCOE COLLECTION, ALEXANDER TURNBULL LIBRARY

ing his papers. Harper was too old and knew he would never do it, so he put aside his antipathy to Pascoe and gave him all the help he could.[62]

Pascoe soon realised that Harper's scrutiny of the completed typescript would be invaluable, but he would have to work fast to complete it in Harper's lifetime, so four years planned work was telescoped into two. In 1953 and 1954 Pascoe ordered and edited the letters and reports and, in places, restored details deleted by the Lands Department. 'This Douglas book is going to be a corker,' he told Ray Chapman. 'I find that the Parliamentary Papers which use Douglas reports have ironed out some of his most inimitable stuff and that his borax at tourists etc gets wiped. So I can not only print his original document, written in pencil under a rock in the rain, but can say how, when it became a Lands and Survey Dept Annual Report, it was tampered with in such a fashion.'[63]

In 1954 Pascoe resigned from the FMC executive to regain the time to write the Douglas book. It was undoubtedly the most scholarly work he had undertaken. Respect for his subject, the need for accuracy and an uncharacteristic lack of detailed descriptions of Pascoe's own adventures combined to produce his best writing. But the task demanded discipline and sacrifices. 'If I was a man of letters and leisure it would be a satisfying whole time job,' he wrote to an English friend. But the reality was quite different:

> As it is I spend an average of 50 hours a month spare time (so-called) on this work, trying to average 2½ hours from 8–10.30 pm, 5 nights a week, four weeks a month. Regular work like that eats up the problems. When I do work it is concentrated not doodling. But something has to be given up. I have shortened my reading hours (a hardship because I like to read modern fiction and translations of French, Italian and other novels) and have tried to cut out club administration jobs and shy off giving lectures or other time

A. P. Harper, his son Tristram and Charlie Douglas at Lake Kaniere, January 1908.

Douglas had suffered a stroke in 1906 while working at Paringa and was carried out of the bush by friends. He recovered but his speech was affected and he never roamed again. Nevertheless he continued to live an independent life as A. P. Harper and his family found when they stayed at Lake Kaniere. Douglas camped nearby and often visited them. Soon afterwards Douglas wrote to Harper, 'What I am going to do next or where I am to go I haven't settled yet. At any rate I must leave the Survey [Lands Department] for good and all. I think I'll clear away south with a Batwing [tent fly] and turn Hermit.' Before Douglas could do so, however, a second stroke left him permanently incapacitated. Like Arawata Bill, Douglas was a bachelor, but friends in Hokitika looked after him. When his condition worsened in 1914 he was admitted to Westland Hospital where he was cared for until his death in 1916 at the age of 75.

JOHN PASCOE COLLECTION, ALEXANDER TURNBULL LIBRARY

consuming things. My wife is patient and helpful and does not resent my pre-occupation with Douglas. When I have finished Douglas in 2–3 years I may become more sociable to live with.[64]

For Dorothy, who maintained the family while John typed away in their midst, the difficulty was not so much her husband's absorption in his writing as the incapacitating headaches that were increasingly blighting her life. As John reported to Jean Johnson, 'Dorothy has had a fair few migraines lately – a rotten business for her as they entail inability to hold food and the pain is v. bad. She has been to quacks and tried injections, diets, drugs, allergy tests. However as the kids get older these situations are easier to cope with and she recovers well when they are over.'[65] When Dorothy was laid low he stepped into the breach and organised the household, but as soon as she revived he returned to Douglas. When the first draft of Mr Explorer Douglas was completed he sent copies to Harper and others, then rewrote it in light of their comments. 'To revise and to polish, to correct and to weigh evidence with all the objectivity of which one is capable, is one of the most fascinating experiences for a writer groping for a biographical perspective.' At the same time Harper wrote a foreword for the book. Less than three months later he died, and Colin Macfarlane soon after.[66]

'I helped to carry APH to his last bivy today,' John told Jean. 'I rejoice that the Douglas book brought me closer to APH in his last years. How glad I am that APH wrote his foreword – thus his last written word may be more permanent than ever he realised.'[67] The day after Harper's death a lengthy tribute by Pascoe appeared in the Evening Post. It was a far cry from the sustained criticism he had made of 'the great I AM' of New Zealand mountaineering 20 years before.

A. P. H. was a man who loved the mountains, who delighted in charting their secrets, and who shared his enthusiasm. He was never a peak conqueror. His wide culture and interest in the humanities made life long friendships among younger men, and his ability as lecturer and raconteur was given generously to any tramping or climbing club which asked for his services.[68]

Apart from the remark 'he was never a peak conqueror', Pascoe might have been describing himself. In a sense he was, for both he and Harper were remarkably alike, which may have been a reason for their earlier enmity. Both grew up in Christchurch, attended Christ's College, studied law and shunned conventional society for adventure in the mountains. Each made a name for himself as a climber and explorer before redirecting his energy, in middle age, to helping others. Later still, both assumed the mantle of mountain expert. By the time John Pascoe joined the executive of the FMC, which Harper had been instrumental in establishing, he had begun to sound a little like the pontifical Harper he had railed against.

When Harper died, his position on the National Geographic Board (whose responsibilities included deciding on names for landscape features) fell vacant, and John Pascoe was appointed to take his place. Usually he avoided committee work, but he was delighted to join this one because he had definite ideas about the sort of names that should – and should not – be bestowed. His appointment had significance beyond this, however, for it also symbolised his succession to Harper as New Zealand's 'man of the mountains,' a role Pascoe was happy to accept and would build on in the years to come.

CHAPTER EIGHT

The Historian

'Some blokes like geology and others botany, but my "bug" is history and plenty of it,' John Pascoe told a fellow climber in 1933. He was then 25 and his life might have been different had he been free to study history but, as the elder son (if only by three hours), he was expected to follow his father's example and become a lawyer in the family firm.

It was not until he was 47 that John Pascoe found work that allowed him to develop this interest fully. In 1955 he became the inaugural secretary of the newly created National Historic Places Trust. He was immediately faced with the problem of preserving numerous historic buildings and sites, including the crumbling remains of the old military barracks at Paremata, built in 1846 to protect the small settlement of Wellington from possible Ngati Toa attack. The poorly constructed barracks were abandoned after earthquakes in 1848 and 1855 caused serious damage. A century later, members of the New Zealand Archaeological Association cleared the overgrown remains under the supervision of Susan Davis, seen here inspecting the site with John Pascoe.

At home in the evenings, he continued to write on the history of mountaineering and exploration. He also wrote numerous scripts for radio which, in the days before television, attracted large evening audiences across the country. Buoyed by the success of *Mr Explorer Douglas*, he found writing a stimulating antidote to his daytime work.

DOROTHY PASCOE COLLECTION

IN 1937, WHEN JOHN PASCOE became a civil servant, he was one of a small group of enthusiasts working on the forthcoming centennial celebrations, an exciting and unusual introduction to departmental life. By the mid-1950s, however, he was employed by the War History Branch of Internal Affairs which had more than 40 staff. It was a typical government department whose bureaucratic procedures and social conventions did not appeal to Pascoe. Nor did he like his work as illustrations editor: he had an antipathy to war, and no longer found the job challenging. 'The interminable morning teas on nags, cricket and shop, the occasional duties on washing up, the regurgitation of damned photos through all the days, the tedious captions, and the lack of change or responsibility made the job one that had to be confined between 8.30 a.m. and 5 p.m.,' John wrote in a private reflection on the War History Branch. 'On the credit side, I can say that Kipp [General Kippenberger, head of the branch] did not interfere with the work, and that we were free agents unhampered by red tape. But it was often a relief to turn to the joys of re-creating Charlie Douglas or writing for radio.'[1]

In 1953 Pascoe applied for the position of editor of the *School Journal* to which he was an occasional contributor but, 'as I have no school teaching qualification I imagine I have no chance of success,' he told Lance Davison, of Whitcombe & Tombs, and added, 'I would have preferred to get an opening in editorial work with your firm.'[2] Neither possibility eventuated, and he remained at the War History Branch for another two years until he left to become secretary of the National Historic Places Trust.

His appointment was a logical transfer from one part of Internal Affairs to another. Since the early 1900s the department had been responsible for dealing with historic buildings and sites, usually in response to requests from the public. From 1913, for example, it was responsible for the upkeep of graves from the New Zealand wars of the 1860s and later it helped to preserve old churches and battle sites. When the 1940 centennial celebrations increased public interest in the past, particularly old buildings, it was Internal Affairs that responded to calls for the preservation of specific buildings of national significance, such as Bishop Pompallier's printery at Russell. In 1949 the department's under-secretary, Joe Heenan, advised the Cabinet that he had first option to buy 'the old stone store at Kerikeri and the old Kemp homestead next door'. Until then the department had simply responded to individual cases as they arose, but Heenan saw the need for a policy to determine criteria for purchasing and maintaining these and other buildings of historic importance. He suggested a National Trust, like the body 'which has functioned so admirably in England for some years'.[3] It was not until 1954, however, that the National Historic Places Trust Act was passed. Heenan had retired in 1951 and died in 1953 so he did not live to see his protégé, John Pascoe, become the trust's first secretary. Had he lived, Heenan would most likely have approved of the appointment as he had long admired Pascoe's energy, enthusiasm and organisational skills – characteristics that now made him ideal for the job.

It was exactly the sort of challenge Pascoe had been hoping for. In a letter to the illustrations editor of the *Weekly News* he wrote, 'It was quite a break to have to leave layout and typographical work but I felt it had become

The Wilberforce from Browning's Pass.

John Pascoe marked his appointment to the Historic Places Trust by writing two articles for the magazine *Te Ao Hou*. The first described Maori equipment for alpine travel. The second described South Island transalpine routes from the east to the greenstone rivers on the West Coast; in particular, the trail that followed the Wilberforce River to the low point on the Main Divide now known as Browning's Pass, before descending to the head of the Arahura River, where much pounamu (greenstone) was found.

routine to me, was too easy, and therefore I sought a new job with a heap of new responsibilities, new problems and plenty of headaches.'[4] He was not disappointed. Soon after taking up his new position on 1 September 1955, Pascoe reported to Ray Chapman, with whom he was planning a transalpine trip in the summer, his initial impressions of the trust:

> This new job is very perplexing, has great troubles and responsibilities but I lap them up and am glad I am away from the easier routines of War History. I guess I am old enough to carry some good burdens now and will find the new problems fascinating. I got through my first meeting without losing any tail feathers. I had to make my own shorthand notes and take the minutes and write them up fully as no typist was available. I have been busy drafting rules that follow on from the Historic Places Act and have found the return to legal work both salutary and refreshing.

He also hoped that their proposed trip, from Lake Ohau to the West Coast with Stan Conway and Bill Hannah, would be an opportunity to mull over these challenges: 'Like the prophets of the Old Testament I want to get my three weeks in the mountain wilderness to think out some of the stickier problems I will have next year, forming regional committees, standing up to politicians and so on'.[5]

Pascoe also wanted to know whether Chapman and his other Christchurch climbing friends had been listening to his series of radio talks entitled *Men of the Mountains*. 'Did you ever hear any of the "I'm a hairy dag"

Martha and Jane Pascoe,
Te Towaka, January 1955.
John Pascoe enjoyed children
and often photographed his own
daughters, as well as other
children.

DOROTHY PASCOE COLLECTION

series I did for ZB stations, 13 talks, started five weeks ago, Sundays 7.15 p.m.?' he asked. 'R. H. Thomson does them in a "Dad and Dave" accent.' The programmes were hill country stories, mostly drawn from Pascoe's alpine adventures with titles such as 'Dangers of the Ford' (with recollections of narrow escapes in the Rakaia and the Arawata), 'The Hunters' (including one who slept inside a deer carcase), 'Hard Cases' and 'Practical Jokers.' Pascoe's purpose was to recreate on radio the camaraderie and humour of a back-country raconteur. 'Told in the first person, the talks would be as though a group was yarning round a campfire, sitting on the bunks of a smoky hut, resting on a grassline, or in a crowded truck, with one man holding the centre of attention and regaling his listeners with stories of men and mountains. Intimate and colloquial, they would aim to bring to life some of the varied incidents and characters of mountain travel, and would create something of the atmosphere and camaraderie of high country days and nights.'[6]

Pascoe's radio yarns were popular. He was writing in the same vein as Barry Crump, a young Wildlife Service deer hunter who was then collecting the back-country stories that, a few years later, would evoke even greater interest in his first novel, *A Good Keen Man*. Both Pascoe and Crump played on New Zealanders' identification with the pioneers. Although most people now lived in the cities, they nevertheless felt an affinity with the laconic and enterprising back-country 'jokers' who featured in Pascoe's radio stories and Crump's books. Both writers appealed shamelessly to this popular sentiment which, as Pascoe admitted to an old Christchurch friend, pleased some but irritated others:

> The ZB radio series is getting wide support from the general public who never
> listen to my YA or YC programmes. My more intellectual cobbers quite frankly

hate Thomson's uncouthness and moan about the 'I'm a hairy dag' act. But nine people out of ten I discuss it with on trams, the bus, in butcher's shops, etc are tickled pink. Personally I find him almost suitable (tho not ideal) for what I planned as a highly colloquial and discursive series; it was to let my hair down. I find it rather agreeable to hear my stuff plugged by a man who has not that manicured elegance of the YA etc stations. But whether my vulgarities are really permissible because they are popular with the public is debateable.[7]

The Broadcasting Service evidently approved, for after the series finished the NZBS arranged for it to be re-recorded by a different narrator whose voice was better suited to the YA stations' audience. This was an unexpected bonus for Pascoe, who had already been paid a guinea for each episode and now received another cheque for £13 13s – a real windfall.[8]

The series ended on the ZB network in December 1955. A few weeks later Pascoe was again among 'men of the mountains' when he joined Chapman, Conway and Hannah to make a second major transalpine trip. This time they planned to cross from Lake Ohau to the West Coast via Broderick's Pass and the Landsborough River, following in the footsteps of Charlie Douglas and Gerhard Mueller who had explored the Landsborough in the 1880s, and A. P. Harper who did further exploration in 1894–95. As usual, Pascoe had done a lot of research beforehand. 'I have typed summaries on rice paper of articles in the *Alpine Journal* so have got the hang of quite a lot of country,' he told Stan Conway. He also obtained useful information from deer cullers and members of the Wildlife Service familiar with the terrain.[9]

Pascoe's reunion with his Arawata companions exceeded his expectations. Since their first transalpine trip three years earlier, the others had been to the Himalaya with the CMC Masherbrum expedition, an experience that Pascoe could see had changed Bill Hannah, the one member of the group he had sometimes found difficult. While sheltering in a rock bivouac at Marks Flat during a storm, John wrote in a letter to Dorothy: 'We slipped back to the Arawata pattern as tho it was last week, with this very importance difference. Perhaps as a result of the Himalayas Bill is gentle, considerate, good-tempered and in all ways an equable and fine cobber.' Their equanimity and shared sense of purpose enabled the party to achieve its major objective, an ascent of Mount Hooker. Despite this success, however, John Pascoe found carrying a heavy pack across rough country very tough. 'Altho after eight days I have good steady nerve and can stand the bulk, bulk and the weight, weight of heavy packs it is only by devotion to the end ie an "over the land to the sea" attitude, that makes this possible,' he confided to Dorothy. 'This country here is so vast and big.'[10]

The Landsborough was not as isolated as the Arawata. They met several other parties, one of whom took John's letter to post, and they also saw a plane drop food supplies for a deer culler working in the valley. As a rule Pascoe disapproved of airdrops, particularly for transalpine travel. He regarded himself as 'a mountain Puritan, inwardly scornful of tourists and their necessities of chair-lifts, natty ski-pants, air drops, cocktail parties in lace-curtained huts, ski-tows, Harry Wigley ski-planes (which I would not scorn in accidents or rescues),' he wrote afterwards to the Canterbury geographer,

At the start of transalpine journeys such as the Landsborough trip of December 1955 – January 1956, John Pascoe and his companions each carried packs weighing 30 kgs, containing food and equipment for three weeks. For Pascoe, carrying heavy loads across difficult terrain made these expeditions 'a constant struggle against the weakness of the flesh'.

RAY CHAPMAN COLLECTION

Bill Packard, who had noted Pascoe's nostalgia in a newspaper account of their Arawata expedition. 'Now being a mountain Puritan isn't just being prudish; it is an ascetic way, self-chosen and rewarding because of communion with the Douglases and Harpers of the past.' This second journey of 're-exploration' clarified Pascoe's thoughts: 'The Puritan transalpine trip for me involves a total war with the weakness of the flesh, and I must not boast about that, but rather relate it to a satisfaction that cannot be felt in easier country,' he told Packard. 'We conquer ourselves, not the mountains. In acclimatising to fatigue, overcoming fear, strengthening links of comradeship, one can seem linked closer to mother country, even if that mother is a barren tuft of scrub above a horrible rock slab. And to be close to ones friends or to ones country is a good destiny.'[11]

Was it this that reminded Pascoe he was not spending his three weeks of annual leave with his family? In his letter to Dorothy he had written, 'I find myself brooding and deciding that altho' the company is marvellous and the mountain experience unrivalled within NZ, I must, if you agree, make every effort to get you and at least the older kids into good boots, accessible snow-rock-ranges and, as a family unit, experience the thrill of alpine places.' Mountain Puritan rested uneasily with family man. 'So with all the beauty of this gigantic arena of cliffs, rainbow-hued waterfalls, noise of rivers and avalanches and a mountain climbed that towers far above us [Mount Hooker], I feel the need to say goodbye to it, to get you and the family with me in less fierce mountains.'[12]

True to his word, John and his family had a holiday the following winter on Mount Egmont where he taught his daughters basic alpine techniques.[13] In 1956 and 1957 he also spent much of his spare time writing for children, including a four-part series on New Zealand explorers for the

'Lessons which may later stand in good stead, can be taught early. Here children aged from six to ten years (led by Martha Pascoe) receive lessons on an alpine rope in a snow gully on Mount Egmont', ran the caption for one of John Pascoe's photos of his family holiday, which were published as a double-page spread in the Free Lance in August 1956.
DOROTHY PASCOE COLLECTION

In 1956 John Pascoe revised his guidebook to the northern half of the Southern Alps before the publication of a second edition. He vowed never to write another guidebook because the work was 'too exacting'. Nevertheless he was pleased the first edition was so popular. 'If nearly 3000 people bought a copy it must be of some use, and it is a good way of encouraging young jokers', he told Bill Hannah. 'Some 18-year-olds who traversed the NE and E ridges of Evans and also the Spires [in the Arrowsmith Range] wrote me a corker letter and finished up by saying they called the booklet the "Gospel according to St Pascoe" — how irreverent!'

School Journal. Thomas Brunner and Pascoe's favourite, Samuel Butler, were followed by accounts of John Bidwill's 1839 ascent of Ngauruhoe and A. P. Harper's Landsborough exploration.[14] Pascoe's transalpine trip had reminded him of Harper's achievements and he had written to Harper's son, John, to tell him that 'I felt very close to your father for three weeks because I was camping in his trails, meeting the same obstacles of rivers and gorges and perhaps slipping on the same boulders. We talked of him, Douglas and Mueller a lot.'[15]

Douglas, in particular, remained on Pascoe's mind. It was now some months since he had sent *Mr Explorer Douglas* to Whitcombe & Tombs for publication, but little progress had been made. Eventually Whitcombe's editor, Carl Straubel, decided that at 410 pages it would be too expensive to produce. Fortunately, A. H. & A. W. Reed were prepared to take the risk, providing the Literary Fund contributed £350, which it agreed to do. Even then, Reeds were uncertain of its market and decided to print only 1000 copies.[16]

During the 1950s New Zealand enjoyed unprecedented prosperity, but this did not improve the prospects of publishers in such a small local market. John Pascoe's books always sold well so he was dismayed that it was such a struggle to get *Mr Explorer Douglas* published. In a letter to Peter Maling (who was having difficulty finding a publisher for the letters and journals of the Canterbury explorer Charles Torlesse) John Pascoe reflected on the lot of local writers:

> Authorship in this country is dicey and difficult; one has to persist in spite of every discouragement. I think the climate for young writers today is particularly bad, so far as their chances of publication are concerned. After all, when jokers like Randall Burdon [biographer of Seddon, Vogel and other notables] and me are forced to fight to secure publication how much harder it is for newcomers. I am not being conceited in this. *Unclimbed New Zealand* has sold c.4,000; *Land Uplifted High* 2,000; *The Mountains The Bush and The Sea* 2,400; guide booklet [to the Southern Alps] 3,000 and yet Whitcombes would not support *Mr Explorer Douglas* – the best of them all. If I had the dough I would publish my work myself but I haven't and am dependent on a commercial publisher.[17]

By April 1956 Pascoe was much happier. *Mr Explorer Douglas* was scheduled to appear early the following year and the protracted process of publication would, he realised, ultimately result in a better book. To cut costs, Reeds had redesigned the book, reduced it by 80 pages and sent it overseas to be printed. 'I have just finished my 20 years work on *Mr Explorer Douglas* which is being printed by Halstead Press in Sydney, impeccable work and I think they are among the good printers of the world – as good as London,' Pascoe wrote to an Australian friend, adding that *Mr Explorer Douglas* had been 'a fascinating job and my main life work. I might write other books but never so much time will I spend on any other publication.'[18]

With the Douglas biography back on track, Pascoe was free to devote his entire attention to the National Historic Places Trust. A priority was to establish committees of volunteers throughout the country, a daunting task involving constant travel. When he was in Wellington there was always copious correspondence from enthusiasts to answer. They expected that the trust would at once be able to save all historic buildings and sites. Pascoe struggled to convince them that because of a lack of resources the reality was quite different. As he explained to an expatriate:

> I am now the humble Secretary of the National Historic Places Trust; its only full-time officer and therefore grossly overworked, without proper accommodation and hoping to do miracles from skeletons of fishes and very crumbly loaves. However I am progressing and am trying to develop a vast organisation of 17 Regional Committees throughout New Zealand to 'mark, preserve and record' historic places which includes pre-pakeha stuff, early settlement, Maori wars, and Uncle Dick Seddon and all, with a diddly-umpty-dee. It is not unlike trying to start a bank, a new church, a newspaper or a racing stable on a shoestring.[19]

The job was so demanding that Pascoe was spending three nights each week working overtime, which was a considerable sacrifice as it was at the expense of his own writing. Consequently, he looked forward to a family holiday on D'Urville Island at the end of 1956: three weeks of family fun in the sun far away from files and telephones. Food supplies had been ordered, and a boat arranged to take the Pascoes to isolated Greville Harbour on the island's west coast where they were to camp on land owned by Len Leov, brother of Harold Leov of Te Towaka.

In mid-December John Pascoe flew to Nelson on trust business. The return flight delighted him: 'we flew all around D'Urville and had a good look at Port Hardy and Greville Harbour from about 2500 feet,' he wrote to Len Leov.[20] But he arrived home to find Dorothy ill and the holiday had to be cancelled. In a letter to Dorothy's sister, Judy, he explained that:

> Dorothy has been ill from nervous exhaustion for a week. It has been a combination of many things, perhaps. The pills she took to combat her migraines had been successful. But they may have had a bad effect in another way, and a time lag in having such an effect. Then Dorothy has worked very hard for her family (as you do too) and for Home and School Association activities, and then Pop's visit added a great burden. The accumulation of these things meant in effect that she felt unable to cope any longer, was weak, and at times under very unexpected nervous strain. Her heart would go fluttery and she was very tired.
>
> Dorothy sleeps well many but not all nights. She eats after a fashion, with a lot of indigestion. She gets jittery once in a while and than needs calming. She has no strength for any continuous or substantial tasks but when she is feeling perky she can do some quite effective works, and is better for having done so.[21]

The family doctor stopped the anti-migraine medication (ruawolfin) and recommended three weeks complete rest. In hindsight, this may not have been the best treatment, for she had little to do except dwell on the situation. 'I lay in my bed without distraction,' Dorothy recalled later, 'feeling all the more distressed and guilty at the stress I was giving my family.'[22]

Although her illness was a surprise to John, it had come upon Dorothy gradually. She had been relieved to be free of crippling migraines, but they had been replaced by a deep depression that brought back memories of her mother's suicide. 'I was invaded by a paralysing fear, leaving me perplexed as I could not understand just what was happening. After all I had a husband and family that I loved deeply. I lived in a beautiful environment and valued my friends but still these crippling feelings increased.' John, too, was bewildered. He arranged for the children to stay with friends and relatives, and took his annual leave to look after Dorothy. When she suffered what he described as 'attacks of terror' she was 'like a poor frightened little child, heart fluttery as hell, body temp low, panting for breath and quivering all over', he told her brother, Peter Harding. 'I would leap into bed, hold her reassuringly tight and soothe her till she was calmer.' Dorothy coped with these incidents by trying to concentrate her thoughts on 'lying on the snowgrass on Mount Robert above Lake Rotoiti in beautiful spring sunshine and serene mountain atmosphere'.[23] She told John of her fears, which went back to her childhood and the tension between her parents. Their marriage began badly when her mother invited her sister, Muriel, to accompany them on their honeymoon and because of her parents' incompatibility it never improved; she was musical and mystical, he was physical and political. Dorothy's fear that her depression might lead to insanity began to recede as she discussed it with John. 'Thank God she turned to me for comfort and found it,' he told Peter Harding. 'Giving comfort is as exhausting for the giver as more violent kinds of physical effort, such as facing mountain troubles, and it was rewarding to know that the comfort helped.'[24] Later Dorothy had a series of electric shock treatments, under anaesthetic. 'The treatment is a tough affair, there's no hiding that,' John told her sister, but he was hopeful that it would help. By March 1957, three months after she had first shown signs of distress, Dorothy was able to resume her usual life, although she had to forsake some community activities.[25]

Afterwards she was relieved to find that her breakdown was probably triggered by her migraine medication. Reports from Australia suggested that it led to an increase in cases of depression and suicide. But a number of underlying factors also contributed to her vulnerability including the demands of family life, lack of opportunity to pursue her own interests and John's preoccupation with writing as well as his many, long trips in the

One of the factors that precipitated Dorothy Pascoe's nervous breakdown was undoubtedly the stress of having her father to stay for a month. He was critical of both her husband and her children and she struggled to keep the peace.

In the 1930s Guy Harding and John Pascoe had been friends; by the 1950s, however, John had become well known and Guy was jealous. He took every opportunity to belittle his son-in-law. While staying with the Pascoes, Harding wrote to his old friend, Elsie Locke: 'A letter started days ago had to be scrapped because under the influence of vino. I like good wine and once when John, as host, poured me a glass I protested "Oh, top it up John — top it up". John refused. It isn't that John is mean, perhaps, but is very, very careful. For that reason he could never be much of a mountaineer — playing safe and never risking it. There was an expressed wish to go to Nepal, Hillary's country — a small dog following after a big dog, piddling on the same posts.'

DOROTHY PASCOE COLLECTION

THE PLUS FACTOR

At the time of Dorothy's illness, Paul Pascoe had recently returned from a study tour of overseas airports,
before designing the new international airport at Harewood, Christchurch. When John wrote
to him about Dorothy he sent the following reply by return post:

Dear John

I was sad to get your letter and I hasten to drop tools to answer it.

Now I must unburden myself and tell you of myself, your letter has brought this out in white heat as it were because I have proved what I am talking of. I have helped cure a migraine subject and I would never have written to you as I write now had I not received your letter saying Dorothy is not well.

In the first place I fully believe in medical science and when ill do all that I am told but also go for the 'plus' factor, more of that later.

Psychology I believe in also but not all the road. I know that I for instance have certain odd features that could be attributed psychologically to episodes in early life. OK. that is a cause. But I say too there is a cause beyond, and that is where the 'plus' factor comes in. And that deeper cause

we cannot always know because to know it we would have to know the meaning of life itself. I think psychological treatment very good but even better if assisted by the 'plus' factor.

I could not have done this world trip without the 'plus' factor because you have no idea what a strain it was to a body as lousy as mine, and mine has always been and is lousy and is only saved by the 'plus' factor.

Now about the 'plus' factor. It is very personal which I cannot help.

When I was at the bach [at Arthur's Pass, right] this week, the second day I was there the fog was low, ceiling low, so you could see tussock and shingle at 200 feet and no more, though with the sound of avalanches. A person using only his eyes could say there are no 12,000 ft. mountains here, except if he heard the avalanches and then he might say they were from some other cause (like David Hall who said ghosts were phantoms or hallucinations of the mind). Yet a person with faith and inner vision knows that life is not all it seems and we have a higher power to draw on. The chap I helped with migraines was an ultra bad case. I used to tell him the secret would be to relax completely, hold the mind on a higher level such as the Lord's prayer or an alpine scene (but not mundane jobs — should I peel the spuds or not?) and then the sack of clothes, the body can rest and the soul or higher self takes over, refreshes itself and back you come revitalised. *As you know I passed through bad years. A doctor in Wales told me I had had it, I was 'burnt out' (his words). I count it a blessing it happened to me as it made me in the end powerful as no otherwise because of my beliefs. This chap who had migraines relaxes at odd times and has had far less attacks because he releases his inmost tensions on a higher plane and they being dissolved he can return free.*

I don't think I told you but when *Ann* was in England *Simon* was very ill (measles or one of those things) so much so that the doctor came twice that day. That night I went up to his room (quietly, I can only work in quietness) and held up my hands after he was tucked up and prayed a healing prayer. Some thing passed through me (it was not me) and he slept 12 hours in peace and was much better.

Liken the mind to a mirror. It can reflect the higher unseen, it can focus to a point (such as a prayer for a person) and charge that person with the higher unseen healing force. I do not tell people but I pray daily for a number of people and have always kept you and D. on the beam.

You see this plus quality is there if people will but use it. You cannot tune into 3YA unless you turn the knob. You cannot achieve the higher plus unless you relax, be still and direct the mind to that end.

The office responsibilities get more and more staggering, including adolescent problems and boys growing up at home and all, and the more awkward things become for me the more calm and collected I need to be, and the more I seek that ½ hour midday rest (sometimes office, sometimes Cranmer Square or elsewhere) where I can relax and contact the higher plus.

Please write and give me news and if you would rather that I did not write such letters tell me with no offence taken because each has to seek his own way and I only speak if it seems urgent or if a person asks for it.
Love to D.
Paul

mountains. At the time, however, his behaviour was not unusual. The rigidly separate roles of men and women in the post-war era meant that men went out to work, while women ran the home, cared for children and had little expectation of time on their own. Dorothy did not question this. She saw her role as 'providing John with an environment which would allow him to write'. As she recovered, Dorothy and John recognised that 'the toughest of times can bring new depths of love and understanding to a relationship', and it also gave them an explicit philosophy. 'It was during these trying weeks that John would talk of "Mountain Philosophy", of how one met each difficulty the terrain presented and confronted it with courage and determination.'[26]

Dorothy's return to health gave John cause for a double celebration with the publication early in 1957 of *Mr Explorer Douglas* to widespread acclaim. By August the first edition had sold out and it was quickly reprinted.[27] Buoyed by its success and with Dorothy once again in charge of the family, John returned to his typewriter and began a series of radio scripts about notable New Zealanders 'with whom I have had close contact at some time in my life'. Much to his disappointment, however, the NZBS was interested in broadcasting only five of the 12 he had written. Sketches of John Beaglehole, Syd Brookes (a former Canterbury climber now a Reuters journalist in Tokyo), David Hall, Ed Hillary and Sir Howard Kippenberger were accepted but the remainder (which included Paul Pascoe) were rejected because, in the words of the Supervisor of Talks, 'the cumulative opinion here is that in too many of these sketches, the men sound exactly the same. The biographical facts of their lives differ, but the men themselves don't come to life as individuals.' Pascoe disagreed. 'I do really regret the fizzling of my ideas, I thought they were good,' he replied the same day. 'It is not unlike an art show. The unhappy artist finds his best work in his view gets a raspberry, while lesser things please the palate of others.'[28]

This rejection was discouraging. So was the failure of a series on Douglas's observations of native birds which was written for the children's session, but apparently never broadcast.[29] By the mid-1950s he had tried poetry with very limited success; now his radio scripts had a lukewarm response. It is not surprising that he returned to writing about men and mountains – the genre he handled so well and others appreciated. In 1957, at Reeds' request, he began work on a new book to be called *Great Days in New Zealand Mountaineering*. The title did not please him but, as he wrote in the preface, 'It was chosen by the publisher as a series title and therefore must be used. Though inhibiting, it has not prevented me from including a few of my own experiences.' His preferred title *The Rock and the Snow* at least appeared on the title page and he also had the satisfaction of seeing a book about mountaineering included in the series alongside the two titles already published, *Great Days in New Zealand Rugby* by Terry McLean, and a similar book on cricket by Dick Brittenden. That climbing should be ranked by Reeds among the most popular sports in the country no doubt owed much to Hillary and Lowe's success on Everest, and this was underscored when Hillary wrote the foreword. Pascoe knew exactly what he was doing. 'I wrote it firstly for the layman, secondly for the layman, thirdly for the layman, and only incidentally for the mountaineer.'[30]

Pascoe completed the text remarkably quickly: its 75,000 words were typed between May and November. 'I find writing books in my evening spare time very relaxing and even creating surplus vitality when otherwise I would be wan from an exacting day's work,' he explained to a climber in a letter asking about the best route to climb Mount Fettes, a West Coast peak named by Charlie Douglas in honour of a Scottish forebear.[31] Pascoe's interest in Mount Fettes was part of his research for another major alpine expedition in the coming summer. Now that Dorothy was well again, his rationale for spending his annual leave in the Southern Alps was based on his convenient perception that she needed a flow of life and chatter around her. 'Myself, I need solitude in distant places, and brooding rather than talk. Dorothy needs the opposite,' he told her brother, 'to be in a compact group that never broods but talks a lot.' So she went with the children to her sister in Hawke's Bay while he headed for the hills. Once again he planned to 're-explore' with Chapman, Conway and Hannah: 'No air drops. Just an old-fashioned sort of trip like Douglas may have made, except for our wish to climb tops as tops.' Their intended route was 'up the Copland, over the Sierra Range, ascent of Sefton (we hope), descent to the head of the Douglas (Twain) River, crossing of Douglas Pass to McKerrow Glacier, down Landsbro River, over top of Mount Fettes (we hope), down Maitahi and so out to Bruce Bay. 25 Dec – 15 January'.[32]

In fact they set out to do it in the reverse order, beginning at the Mahitahi (or Maitahi) River on the West Coast. It was an ambitious schedule, but achievable given their previous efforts. The Arawata and Landsborough expeditions had, however, been largely free of bad weather. This time their luck was out. As John sweltered in a hot nor'wester in Christchurch en route to Hokitika, he wrote to Dorothy of his longing for cooler Westland: 'It won't be long now before I am seeing the rain and clouds battle the lone trees on the fields and

Stan Conway, Ray Chapman, John Pascoe and Bill Hannah at Fox Glacier at the start of their Mahitahi trip.

DOROTHY PASCOE COLLECTION

blacken the entrance to valleys.' But when he and his companions arrived on the Coast there was no romance in the torrential rain: the rivers were up and the usually sanguine locals were full of foreboding. It had been the worst season ever for rain, they said, and it seemed set to continue. John Pascoe was far from subdued, however, even though they could not start tramping immediately, because 'I can barely move without being hailed "Mr Explorer Douglas". The local Mayor was the first to do so,' he wrote to Dorothy. 'In the hotel lounge a pair of young chaps told me they had read it. One of them travels down to Haast for his firm and he said it is being widely read by the settlers. It is in the local bookshop in the window.'[33] Further downpours washed away a bridge north of Hokitika and a slip blocked the road to the south. When they finally put on their packs and started up the Mahitahi Valley, it was clear that their plans would have to be revised. In an uncharacteristically brief report on the trip Pascoe recalled that:

> The unseasonal floods and heavy snowfall of December accounted for many changes of plans in the mountains. Our hopes of making a long series of hops from the Maitahi to the Copland were dashed or rather washed away. In light of the season we travelled up the Maitahi, unfordable as it was for its whole course; normally a blue and beautiful stream, it was throaty with thaw and rain. We stuck at the head of the valley, gladly accepting the shelter of a large rock, and scratched three climbs out of the prevailing murk.[34]

A detailed description of the Maori rock drawings at Waipapa on the Waikato River was attached to the Historic Places Trust Annual Report for 1957. According to its authors, W. Ambrose and F. Davis, 'The meaning of the paintings can only be surmised, although some individual drawings can be quite easily interpreted. However, it is likely that their intention was magical, and that they had been used in ceremonies of a ritualistic nature.' Locals in nearby Mangakino called the figure on the lower left Mickey Mouse.

HISTORIC PLACES TRUST

Left: During their Mahitahi trip Pascoe and his companions made several climbs in the few breaks in the bad weather. One was a second ascent of Crystal Peak, first climbed in 1935.

As they approached the summit ridge they saw it had a heavy cornice (overhanging edge of ice and snow). Pascoe was asked to lead, a role he was not accustomed to: 'I felt as nervous as a chicken to begin with, but gained more confidence as time went on,' he noted in his diary. On the summit itself 'the others got photos but I did not feel secure enough to take out my camera'. After their descent, however, he relaxed and took out his Rolleicord. 'At least we have climbed a peak, if a minor one. The major peaks would be very dicey this awful season.'

RAY CHAPMAN COLLECTION

It was perhaps appropriate that John Pascoe spent most of his annual leave sheltering under an overhanging rock, for he had spent much of the previous year trying to protect Maori rock drawings, done centuries earlier on similar rocks and cave walls elsewhere. His interest was prompted by Ministry of Works plans to build a dam on the Waikato River, which would destroy rock drawings at Waipapa. The trust learnt of their existence only two months before they were due to be blown up to make way for a diversion tunnel. While archaeologists recorded the drawings, Pascoe succeeded in convincing the engineers that at least some of the rock art should be saved. As a result, a selection was carefully cut away from the surrounding rock and transported to the Auckland Museum. At the time, hydro-electric dams were being built throughout the country and the trust was kept busy recording and trying to protect Maori rock art. Valuable examples had already been destroyed and Pascoe was determined there would be no more losses. He soon became a well-known figure in the head office of the Ministry of Works. 'The jokers in State hydro design think I am a bit of a dag the way I am always romping in and saying "Power man, spare that cave". I have told them that the Trust think the easiest way to find rock shelter art is to wait for a power scheme to develop and then to accuse Works of bashing moa hunters pix,' he wrote to the trust's chairman, Ormond Wilson.[35]

In fact, the trust was far more proactive than Pascoe's jest might suggest, but its lack of resources meant it had to rely on volunteers, such as members of the New Zealand Archaeological Association, to locate and record examples of rock drawings. Fortunately the trust had a number of dedicated members who, together with Pascoe and Wilson, worked tirelessly to protect not only rock art but all manner of historic sites and buildings. The jocular tone of Pascoe's letter to Wilson reflected their easy relationship, which began at Christ's College. In many ways, however, their characters were as different as their respective roles at the trust. As chairman, Wilson would either discuss or dictate what should be done (often by letter from his home in the Rangitikei) while Pascoe ran the office and arranged all manner of things. Wilson was a rather feudal figure with a booming voice and an English accent, who would come to Wellington for a day or two then return to his property near Bulls, leaving Pascoe to carry out the work. In some respects Ormond Wilson was unconventional: he had, for example, an enthusiasm for nude tramping. Given his family background, it is perhaps surprising that he was a staunch Labour supporter. After leaving Christ's, he had gone to Oxford University where he became a socialist and on his return to New Zealand was elected to Parliament as a member of the first Labour government. When the second Labour government was elected in 1957 Wilson hoped to be appointed New Zealand High Commissioner in London, but instead was offered the chairmanship of the National Historic Places Trust, to replace the inaugural chairman, Charles Bowden, a National Party appointee.

Ormond Wilson was enthusiastic about the trust and, like Pascoe, enjoyed being part of a small team. 'The early stages of any organisation are invariably more rewarding than later ones when disappointments have blunted high hopes,' Wilson wrote in his autobiography, *An Outsider Looks Back*. Pascoe also found the trust stimulating. Both he and Wilson particularly enjoyed working with John Beaglehole who represented Victoria University on the board. Wilson appreciated Beaglehole's concern for accuracy. 'As a meticulous scholar he left an indelible impression on the Trust's approach to its tasks. He and like-minded members ensured that authenticity would be its hallmark and that whether in the wording of its plaques and noticeboards or in the restoration of historic buildings and sites, care would always be taken to get the details, within the bounds of the attainable, exactly right,' Wilson recalled. 'I presided over the Trust but he guided it.'[36]

Beaglehole was in the forefront of what was to become the trust's longest campaign, the struggle to save the church in Mulgrave Street, Wellington, since known as Old St Paul's. Built in 1865, the church had been the centre of Anglican worship in the capital but it was due to be demolished once the new cathedral in nearby Molesworth Street was completed. Discussions about the new cathedral began in 1937 and Cecil Wood had drawn plans in 1942, but building was deferred until after the war. The foundation stone was laid by the Queen during her visit in 1954 and within a few years the large concrete structure was taking shape. The idea of including sections of Old St Paul's

The campaign to save Old St Paul's from demolition lasted for more than a decade and it was not until 1966 that the government finally agreed to purchase and restore the old church. The long struggle publicised the need to protect historic buildings in general, in much the same way that the equally long campaign to preserve Lake Manapouri raised public awareness of environmental issues.

within the new cathedral was acceptable to some parishioners, but others were unhappy at the prospect and mounted a vigorous campaign to have it preserved intact.[37] They were supported by the Historic Places Trust. Understandably, the Anglican authorities did not want the expense of maintaining two large churches within a few hundred metres of each other, but the underlying reason for demolishing the historic church was the equity that could be realised from the sale of the land on which it stood. Aided by an acquiescent city council and a government that seemed not to care, the Anglican hierarchy was deaf to the preservationists' pleas.

John Beaglehole wrote and spoke eloquently for the church's preservation and restoration. In 1958 his advocacy was strengthened by the comments of the influential architectural historian, Nikolaus Pevsner, during a visit to Wellington. In keeping with the New Zealand tradition of according great respect to the views of experts from overseas, Pevsner's opinions gave the campaign to save Old St Paul's a much needed boost. Pascoe had made sure Pevsner was well briefed before he spoke to reporters and his remark that 'even in England its interior woodwork would be regarded as outstanding' gave the campaign greater credibility, but was not enough to sway the Anglican church.

Some observers, including Charles Brasch, thought the trust was not doing enough to save Old St Paul's. Pascoe's reply to Brasch's letter was polite and restrained, but he was clearly peeved. Had it been a mountain matter he

Members of the Historic Places Trust board at Old St Paul's in 1960. From left: Ormond Wilson (chairman), Vic Fisher, John Pascoe (secretary), Jim Gardner, Fergus Sheppard and Roger Duff.

HISTORIC PLACES TRUST COLLECTION

would have been free to be forthright, but as the trust's secretary he was not. 'I fear you think those things have not been done which ought to have been done,' he responded to Brasch. 'May I say that I spend much time on the St Paul's ramifications not necessarily each and every day, but regularly. Most of the struggle against the church cannot be conducted in the glare of publicity.' 'Much time' already included organising a deputation to the Prime Minister to press for the Crown's purchase of Old St Paul's, and there was little more the trust could do. 'I hope I have written enough to affirm that St Paul's is by no means a dead duck,' he concluded. 'I can emphasize that I am more than fully occupied with fights against the materialists from North to South on matters so numerous it takes a card index to keep track of them.'[38] Old St Paul's was eventually saved in 1966, well after Pascoe had left the trust, when the government finally agreed to purchase and renovate it.

As usual, Pascoe found relief from the pressures of work in his own writing. During the winter of 1958, for instance, he wrote a sequel to his general history of mountaineering. 'My new book is about exploration,' he wrote to Ormond Wilson. 'I enjoy writing it more than I can say. Seems to give characters like Colenso a new dimension to have to study their biographies and summarise their travels. I'm more at home with the South Island jokers knowing their country better, but even the Ruahines make me itchy booted when I pore over their maps.'[39] In October, Pascoe spent a weekend as an alpine instructor on Ruapehu with the Tararua Tramping Club. Returning to Wellington in the back of a crowded truck with high-spirited companions horsing around, he was accidentally flattened, damaging a ligament in his knee.[40] Fortunately the injury improved sufficiently to avoid postponing a summer family holiday in the Marlborough Sounds. He had not forgotten their earlier plans to visit D'Urville Island which had been abruptly cancelled when Dorothy became ill, and John was keen to return to Te Towaka and, perhaps, to get to the island. But it would be without Dorothy because her psychiatrist, John Hardwick-Smith, did not think she was robust enough. He was concerned that 'if she went with us to the Sounds and got in a tizzy patch in a remote place with little contact with the outside world' she might become 'shut in on herself', John wrote to his mother; so when John took Anna and Martha to Te Towaka, Dorothy, Sara and Jane went to Hawke's Bay.[41] On their return, John resumed writing and work with characteristic energy and enthusiasm. Early in 1959 he completed *Great Days in New Zealand Exploration* and, as if to celebrate, immediately took on a new project, signing a contract with Oxford University Press to edit and produce an encyclopaedia of New Zealand – a huge task for which he would be well paid.[42]

Meanwhile, his National Historic Places Trust job was as demanding as ever and he found the frequent travel increasingly irksome. When he was able to stay with friends it gave him the chance to forget his work and to get away from 'the boredom of pubs and booze', he told Monty McClymont with whom he hoped to stay in Dunedin. 'If I stay privately I will not be at the mercy of people who want to talk historic places to me all night,' he explained. 'I do have to live with my job a lot on my travelling – and there are other topics, such as exploration.'[43]

Travelling could also spring nasty surprises. When John Pascoe and Pirimi Tahiwi, a Wellington regional committee member, visited New Plymouth, Pascoe had made reservations at a city hotel. When they arrived he was told he was welcome, but Tahiwi was not. 'If he can't stay, I won't either,' replied Pascoe and they went elsewhere.[44]

At the time, racism was a hot topic as New Zealanders debated the Rugby Union's unquestioning acceptance of South Africa's demand that no Maori be included in the All Black team to tour South Africa in 1960. The Prime Minister, Walter Nash, 'has been doing his "neither for or against" line', John Pascoe wrote to Ormond Wilson who was on holiday in England. 'There is talk of a petition signed by 100,000 Kiwis against racial discrimination, and Maori mothers may forbid their sons the game. *Truth* is running a Gallup poll. So you see we can still get excited about something.' John and Dorothy had been to a protest meeting in the Wellington Town Hall where 2000 people listened to a number of speakers:

> The fiercest speech was by a Trade Union Secretary, a cross between J. A. Lee and Hitler. The most eloquent speech was by Col. Peter Awatere and his lack of sophistication and his vigour were admirable. The most powerful speeches because they were so short were by Dr Paewai and by George Nepia who also sang "Under the Maori Moon". Of 2½ hours of meeting only Shirley Smith was boring. The congregation included all walks of life, ages from 14 to 84 and colours from ebony to ivory.[45]

Pascoe also mentioned the 'No Maoris – No Tour' controversy in correspondence with Ruth Ross, a Northland member of the trust. 'Dorothy and I and the older girls are united in supporting protests against race discrimination. What are your views?' he asked Ruth, who was teaching at Motukiore Maori School on the Hokianga Harbour. She replied 'our views on the South African tour are pretty definite. As we see it there is no question of whether Maoris could go – they couldn't. The only question is whether any team should go.' Despite public meetings and protests against the tour throughout the country (the first rumblings of the explosion that was to come in 1981), the New Zealand Rugby Football Union remained unmoved, as did the government, which refused to intervene – even after South African police shot 69 blacks and wounded hundreds more in a massacre at Sharpeville on the eve of the tour. 'If a team does finally go,' Ruth Ross wrote, 'they are not going to have a happy time, on or off the football field. Serves them damn well right.'[46]

The tour was, however, only incidental to John Pascoe's correspondence with Ruth Ross (*née* Guscott), which began when the trust asked her to join its Northland committee. Her impressive credentials made Ross an obvious choice. After graduating from Victoria University College, she was one of a number of bright young historians who worked in the Department of Internal Affairs on a variety of historical projects under the supervision of John Beaglehole. Known as 'Beaglehole's babies', they might well have been called 'Beaglehole's babes', for they were all young women and his interest in some was more than intellectual.[47] Janet Paul, for instance, had an affair with Beaglehole and remained a lifelong friend. Ruth Ross, on the other hand, seems to have fallen out with Beaglehole, for he was noticeably unresponsive: 'That blasted man will do everything but answer a letter of mine I sent him two and a half years ago,' she complained to John Pascoe.[48]

The ill feeling between Beaglehole and Ross had unfortunate ramifications for the trust, because it was Beaglehole who usually chose the wording for the plaques marking historic sites, including a number of important battles and pa in Northland. Ruth Ross was very knowledgeable about Maori history, especially in Northland, and was concerned about a lack of accuracy in the wording of the trust's plaques. 'In some respects I'm sorry I can't allow myself to be nominated for the Northland Regional Committee, in other respects I'm relieved to have a watertight excuse. You realise of course there is nothing personal about this,' she told Pascoe, who had known her since they shared an office at Internal Affairs in the early 1940s, 'but I seem to be getting more and more anti-Trust. I have said to Ormond Wilson bluntly that until the Trust publishes research reports, complete with documentary references, for each of its projects, I do not feel people can have much confidence in the Trust's operations. I can't anyway. Moreover the lack of any full-time research organisation puts you in a very vulnerable position, which I think is most unfair.'

Within three months of writing this letter, however, Ruth Ross changed her mind, accepted a place on the committee and wrote to reassure John Pascoe. 'I promise you I won't do a bull-in-the-china shop act at committee meetings. You've just no idea how tactful and retiring I can be!' But less than a year later, she demanded that 'the Trust refrain from acting on the Northland Regional Committee's approval of the inscription proposed for Kaiwaka, and instead furnish the committee with a fully documented research report on the battle of Te Ika a Ranganui'. If the trust did not agree to her demand to ignore its own committee's recommendation, 'I will resign', she told Pascoe.

'I have sent you a letter from Ruth Ross to me, which I felt too sick to answer, tho of course I shall have to do so,' Pascoe confided to Wilson. 'What a prima donna she is, and how exasperating are all her cross-purposes and misconceptions.' When he did finally reply, Pascoe concluded, 'I hope you calm down and respect what there is to be respected about struggling organisations such as ours without creating dragons out of dragon-flies or storm clouds out of morning dew.' This response simply riled Ross even more, as he may have intended, in the hope that she might resign. But Ruth Ross, whom Pascoe privately described to Ormond Wilson and others as 'La Belle Ross Sans Merci', was not so easily cast aside. 'The only reason my resignation did not immediately follow your irresponsible reply is that I consider it is in the interests of the Northland committee that someone, here and now, has a showdown with the Trust over research.'[49] Pascoe understood her concern, but with only a part-time clerical assistant and an overworked part-time researcher to help him, the trust was unable to satisfy everyone's expectations.

In addition to liaising with the 17 regional committees of the 'Hysteric Places Trust' (as Pascoe sometimes called it), he was also required to mediate between members of the board as, for instance, when Ken Melvin (a businessman whose political appointment was made without consulting the trust) complained that he felt 'completely smothered by Beaglehole and his satellites'. 'Frankly, John, I am tired of Beaglehole's assumption of omniscience, and

In 1958 the eminent high country expert, Professor Lance McCaskill, suggested to the National Geographic Board (of which John Pascoe was a member) that the prominent peak near Arthur's Pass, known as the Dome, be renamed Mount Greig in honour of the Director General of Lands, D. M. Greig. Pascoe knew Greig as a member of the Historic Places Trust board. Nevertheless, Pascoe was implacably opposed to McCaskill's suggestion: 'However revered the name it is not likely to be accepted by the Geographic Board, by the users of the [Arthur's Pass National] Park or by the newspapers,' he told McCaskill. 'There has been such a revulsion against personal names for peaks that it is a firm policy of the Geographic Board to resist all attempts to impose them.'

The matter of names was a passionate concern for Pascoe who had steadfastly refused to acknowledge the achievements of his youthful contemporaries by naming peaks after them. 'I have included in my principles my right to reject names proposed to mark the work of my own generation or my own friends; in fact, all personal names. Sorry, Lance, but that is the story. I regret that in this case it has to be against the name of a man whom I regard as the best type of civil servant, and one of the most impressive characters and wisest men I have ever met.'

disturbed that the board should have allowed any single member to dominate its discussions. I must serve notice that I am not prepared to accept this, and if this means stress and tension, so much the worse for those who find themselves stressed.' Pascoe stoutly defended Beaglehole: 'When you know him better I think you will find that he is a very modest, and often humble man. I have never thought him arrogant in any way. He has never worn a mantle of omniscience, so much as have it thrust on him when a blast of scholarship comes around the corner. If he dominates discussion it is usually because it is a topic within his field.' But Pascoe did concede that he, too, once had reservations about Beaglehole. 'Looking back 20 years I think he did annoy me for the first 12 months; after that I counted myself as a grateful if lesser colleague. I number him among the men whose influence I count as good in my life: Joe Heenan, Oliver Duff, Eric McCormick, General Kippenberger.'[50]

Pascoe was also involved with New Zealand's small archaeological community, whose internecine feuds added to his work. At the same time as having to deal with all these problems he was busy producing the trust's first set of publications about particular historic buildings and sites. The trust's first monograph, on Samuel Butler's buildings at Mesopotamia, had been written by Peter Maling, whose experience as an author meant editing and arranging its publication was relatively straightforward, but the second of the series, written by Ormond Wilson about Te Kooti's fighting pa at Te Porere, was far too long. Although Wilson himself agreed that it was 'of inordinate length', getting him to rewrite it required considerable tact and diplomacy.[51]

In this matter, Pascoe might have been more tolerant if Wilson had been mindful of his secretary's heavy workload, but he seemed oblivious of it. This was apparent at board meetings when Pascoe not only took part in discussions, but also had to record them in shorthand. After five years of being a secretary-cum-stenographer he lost patience: 'You are closer to the perfect chairman than I have ever had', Pascoe began a letter to Wilson in 1960, 'only this worries me':

John Pascoe had always thought a party of four the ideal number for transalpine travel. A small group could move more quickly than a larger expedition and, if there was an accident, one person could remain with the casualty while the other two walked out to get help. Some years earlier, when two Tararua trampers were killed at the head of the Matukituki, Pascoe told Ray Chapman 'main moral is that a two man party is not big enough'. So it is curious that John Pascoe and Stan Conway chose to cross the Southern Alps in the summer of 1959–60, without asking Ray Chapman and Bill Hannah, who had accompanied them on all their previous transalpine trips, to join them.

Conway and Pascoe's planned route was an ambitious variation of their Arawata excursion eight years earlier. From the Matukituki Valley they climbed to Hector Col, from where they hoped to climb Mount Aspiring. Persistent bad weather prevented their ascent and they continued westward, descending to the headwaters of the Waipara, a tributary of the Arawata. Progress down the Waipara was difficult and slow. Ten days after their departure from the Matukituki road end, while deep in the heart of the wilderness, Stan Conway become seriously ill. Pascoe's diary entry records that soon after making camp, Conway suffered an internal haemorrhage.

'At the worst part of Stan's illness he had every appearance of dying,' John Pascoe noted. 'Abnormally low body temperature, grey pallor, every part of his facial skin creased like crocodile skin and extreme weakness — he could only lie inert and helpless'.

ALEXANDER TURNBULL LIBRARY

'This left him very weak. I got his wet boots and socks off him and when he was in his sleeping bag and in the tent I slept at the entrance fitfully. There was no point in my leaving Stan to get help; he needed me more where he was.'

Next day Conway coughed up congealed blood which to Pascoe looked 'like lumps of liver'. Despite this, Conway managed to get to the river, 'where I tried it with the rope, but it was no go and he settled down to rest and recuperate in the shade' while Pascoe lit fires in the riverbed, hoping the smoke might be noticed from afar. 'There was little else I could do,' he later told his daughter, Anna, 'except pray.' After two days rest, the pair slowly made their way further downstream until they found a place where, with difficulty, they crossed the Waipara. Conway was exhausted and Pascoe 'marvelled how he had kept going. His energy may have been at a low ebb but never his resolution.'

On the 17th day they reached the confluence of the Waipara and the lower Arawata where they hoped they might find Nolan's Hut occupied. Their luck was in: four deer hunters there were about to be flown out in a small plane. In the past John Pascoe had always railed against aircraft in the hills, but on this occasion he was delighted to be able 'to hitch-hike in a Cessna'. Back in civilisation Conway slowly recovered and later went into hospital for an operation. Pascoe's account of their journey in the Canterbury Mountaineer did not address the obvious question of why he and Conway undertook such a trip without adequate numbers in their party.

Stan Conway and John Pascoe at the end of their transalpine journey, January 1960.

DOROTHY PASCOE COLLECTION

I must bring forcibly to your comprehension the anxiety and strain you caused by not pausing at the end of each resolution at the meeting yesterday. Because you brushed aside my verbal protests, I feel that I must do all I can to convince you that your staff need this breathing space. When a resolution is put, let it be recorded without permitting, or encouraging an immediate cross-fire of talk that makes concentration very difficult.

I felt humiliated at having publicly to protest to you time after time, but if I had not done so I would have had to rely for full precision entirely on memory the following day. I am sure that the very least a secretary (not being a tape recorder) can expect is that the chairman, regarding the resolutions as the guts of a meeting, will phrase them or ask the proposer to phrase them, and not drown them in a babble, leave them unfinished or mutilated. Today we will sweat out what we tried to get down under such nightmare circumstances. The unfortunate result of your haste was not that it helped progress (because in fact I had to plead with you to slow down for a minute at each resolution) but it held up the overall pace and created a state that need not have existed.[52]

Pascoe was soon to discover, however, that Wilson had his own, rather personal reason for proceeding apace during board meetings: the bowel condition colitis. A few months later, Wilson was forced to withdraw from a planned trip to Blenheim with Pascoe: 'After each of these expeditions – Wellington or elsewhere – I find myself more or less laid up for a day. I think it is a question of diet more than exertion but one can't keep to a strict diet when travelling. Anyway, you can cope with cobhouses and earthworks, so there is no need for me to come at all.'[53]

During 1960 Ormond Wilson withdrew increasingly from trust affairs, leaving still more of the work to Pascoe. Understandably, he began to look for a new job. He had accepted the appointment as trust secretary because of his interest in history yet, in the end, he realised that the historical aspect was secondary to all the correspondence, travel and mediation. Any historical writing had been done in the evenings at home, when overtime and travel permitted. Nor did Pascoe see himself as a historian. In 1959 a *Listener* caption of a group of writers at a PEN conference described him as a 'historian and biographer' but, as he told Ruth Ross, 'such bull is not my fault. The more I write my own works, the more I realise their merely modest place in New Zealand affairs, and I would never claim such a title as "historian" when, so far as I am concerned, there are only Sinclair, Beaglehole, Morrell and Phillips worthy of the title.'[54]

But if not an historian, what was he? At the age of 52 it was time to find a new job or he would be trapped in the trust until retirement. Ted Fairway, the chief executive officer of Internal Affairs, had helped Pascoe when he was tired of war history work by suggesting he apply for the secretaryship of the Historic Places Trust. Now, at the end of 1960, Fairway told Pascoe that the position of Controller of the Wildlife Service was about to become vacant. Would he be interested?

CHAPTER NINE

Administrative Man

In 1961 John Pascoe wrote to his brother-in-law, Peter Harding: 'having made a success of the Historic Places Trust I was eager for even greater responsibilities'. At the trust 'I revelled in what is generally termed administration: keeping relatively calm when tension was in the air, being forceful when someone had to give a strong lead on policy and principle, and patiently planning attacks so that the ground was to my advantage and I had prepared possies into which to dig; the holding of arguments in reserve and so on. So far as Internal Affairs was concerned my type of classification changed from specialist to administration.'

Pascoe's new job as Controller of the Wildlife Service was an opportunity to implement this approach. 'My main tenets,' he told Harding, 'are delegate authority, make decisions without delays, don't fight on forlorn issues unless great principles are involved; cut all red tape to shreds unless it is needed as a protection against the wicked and the very foolish.'

Pascoe usually wrote to Harding, who lived in Sydney, only once or twice a year, but his letters always gave a comprehensive account of his life. 'Let me say that I find it far harder to be wise at home than at work,' Pascoe continued. 'I find that whatever are the complexities and problems of official life they are far easier to solve than some of the ones of a growing and partly adolescent female family. This is not to say that things are not well at home; they are. But the struggle of a man in his home is continually for one of potency, so far as authority over his family is concerned, and also a struggle for oneness with his wife; a condition that can never be taken for granted, is perhaps one of the most cherishable of human ambitions, the most blessed and unselfish state of grace, and the best equilibrium in the turmoil of living.'

Prophetic words. In the 1960s John and Dorothy Pascoe, like Peter Harding and his wife Barbara, struggled to cope with a succession of crises involving both families, which added poignant meaning to Pascoe's phrase 'the turmoil of living'.

DOROTHY PASCOE COLLECTION

BEFORE TAKING UP HIS NEW JOB in December 1960, John Pascoe sought out the five other men who had also aspired to be Controller of the Wildlife Service. 'I know you are disappointed not to have the job,' he told them. 'I now give you the all-clear to tell me face-to-face how disappointed you are, and you can now say things that once I am your boss you cannot. Three of the men had no growl or grudge,' he reported to Peter Harding. 'Another man felt badly and got it off his chest in 5 minutes. The last man harangued me with overstatement and perhaps what could be called abuse; so much so, that I said to him "keep calmer, and let me comment on your overstatements paragraph by paragraph, so there is no misunderstanding". Thus I drew their fire and dissolved their rancour so far as it was possible to do so.'[1]

Pascoe started work as Controller of the Wildlife Service on 13 December 1960, but with the Christmas holidays imminent, he could do little more than introduce himself to the staff in Wellington. From Christmas Eve all places of employment closed for several weeks and everyone dispersed to baches and beaches. The Pascoes were no exception, spending their summer holiday on D'Urville Island where they camped in bush beside a sheltered bay in Port Hardy on land owned by the Renes, a Maori family whose forebears had lived there since Ngati Toa conquered much of the South Island in the 1830s. From the stronghold of Kapiti Island, Te Rauparaha, Te Rangihaeata and other Ngati Toa chiefs had led a succession of war parties

'The early morning bird chorus on D'Urville Island was the most wonderful we ever heard,' Dorothy Pascoe later recalled. 'At first light one bellbird started up and gave the key, then gradually the chorus built up and up until there was a great sound all round and the whole family would wake up, and we lay curled up in our sleeping bags listening.'
DOROTHY PASCOE COLLECTION

to Te Wai Pounamu, and after each successful campaign relatives of the warriors settled in newly acquired territory, including Rangitoto (D'Urville Island).

Te O ('Joe') Rene, a descendant of Te Rangihaeata, met John Pascoe when they were Army Bush Guides during the war. Rene appreciated Pascoe's friendship at a time when many Maori, of whatever lineage, were often treated condescendingly by Pakeha. After the war, Rene and his family left Takapuwahia, the Ngati Toa settlement at Porirua, to return to their family land on Rangitoto. At Allman Bay they cleared a few acres, sufficient land to run a few sheep and grow vegetables, but most of the extensive property was left in forest – much to the annoyance of some neighbouring Pakeha farmers who were busily clearing their land for farming.

On earlier excursions to D'Urville from Te Towaka, the Pascoes had been guests of the Leov family. The Leov brothers had two large properties: Harold farmed at Patuki on the northern tip of the island, Len at Greville Harbour on the west coast. He worked hard breaking in the Greville Harbour farm, burning the bush, draining wetlands and bulldozing tracks across the steep hillsides which, when dosed with superphosphate, soon became productive pasture. Len Leov's new house, on a rise looking out over Greville Harbour, symbolised their prosperity and the effectiveness of a pastoral system (encouraged by generous government subsidies) that was transforming marginal hill country throughout New Zealand. Len Leov could not understand why his neighbours, the Renes, did not follow this example. Why did they live in an old house and exist on deer, pigs, fish and vegetables while their land was left untouched? It was incomprehensible and he could not accept it. Ill-feeling occasionally flared between the two families, who shared a common hilltop boundary, and erupted into skirmishing and fighting.

It was against this background that the Pascoes came to stay with the Renes. They crossed Cook Strait in a ketch, the *Saint Michael*, skippered by Ned and Tudor Atkinson of York Bay, who dropped the family off in Port Hardy with their supplies and arranged to return in three weeks to collect them. While John explored the island on foot, Dorothy and her daughters went fishing with Joe Rene's son, Te Momo. On shore, Joe took them into the forest and told them 'tales of the birds and trees – everything had some significance'. Through his stories about the many distinctive rocks in the harbour, the Pascoes came to realise that 'Port Hardy was no longer just a harbour that had sheltered sailing ships waiting for the wind to ease so they could sail into Port Nicholson'. For Dorothy 'it was a place of myth and magic'. Her sense 'of being a stranger in my own land' was

Te Momo 'would row us towards the entrance to Port Hardy where he knew the best fishing areas,' Dorothy Pascoe remembered. 'I noted the extraordinary elegance in the way he baited the hooks, then dealt with the blue cod, scaling and cleaning them before tossing us a liver to eat.'
DOROTHY PASCOE COLLECTION

accentuated by an elaborate dinner at the Renes' house at which the Pascoes ate pork and puha served with the furled heads of ponga fronds while their hosts waited on them. Afterwards Joe took John and Dorothy aside to show them the family's taonga, which included a greenstone mere once owned by Te Rangihaeata. As the only Pakeha to have seen them, John and Dorothy understood the respect the Renes were according them.[2]

The Pascoes had not long returned to Wellington when they received several agitated letters from the Renes who were deeply disturbed about the Hunn Report, a government inquiry into the state of, and prospects for, the Maori people. They had not read the recently released report itself, but were alarmed by newspaper accounts of its recommendations: 'Reforms for the social and economic development of the Maori people are to be welcomed,' wrote Joe Rene, 'but they should not be used as a cloak to disguise the point of a dagger aimed at annihilating the spirit of a race.'[3] His daughter, Ruta, reiterated this concern in more detail:

> The Hunn report actually aims at doing away with Maori. The excuse being to make him into a progressive New Zealander, etc, etc. There is or seems to be a real fear that one day the rising Maori population would jeopardise the white population of New Zealand – hence a policy of consolidating the white superior race by absorbing an inferior one. Well, John, you know what it is with stock – only the best is acceptable. To get that you must have a good strain coming into your flock all the time. The white man has that superior strain – absorb the Maori, and there will be no racial problems such as in Africa – you'd have a better New Zealander who would be progressive enough to see that he is better housed, have better health and would strive for a better education.
>
> Underneath all this business of racial fears there is the question of Maori lands – little tho it is. However, they want to get their hands on it. The report is as good an excuse as any.

Ruta's letter concluded 'Well, John, the answer to the Hunn report lies with you. People like you, your wife and your family. It is only through people like you that the Maori race can look for some hope of survival.'[4]

In his response to these letters, Pascoe first summarised the Renes' arguments, then he made himself thoroughly familiar with the Hunn Report, as well as sending a copy to the Renes. Only then did he reply:

> I regard the Hunn Report as a real attempt to help Maoris as well as Pakehas and I ask you to tell me if you would really prefer the state of present things to continue as they are. I realise that all matters of land policy come very close to the heart of both races and I personally think that the creation of trusteeships is better than a multiple fragmented ownership.
>
> I have read the letters from you and Ruta very many times and I have tried to understand a lot of the Hunn Report, but I don't find any statement in that report that the Maori threatens the security of the Pakeha. Nor do I find the Maori condemned of any crime. I honestly believe that the administrators of Maori Affairs are making an honest attempt to combine (not fuse) 'the Maori and Pakeha elements to form one nation wherein Maori culture remains distinct'.

Finally, I think that I could understand your main anxiety is that by hastening integration, Maoridom is destroyed. It can well be that there is a risk of this, but don't we all live in a world of insecurity?[5]

Forty years on, with the benefit of hindsight and a resurgence of all things Maori, the Renes' view seems less extreme than it did in 1961 when the corrosive consequences of city life had yet to take their toll on recently urbanised Maori. Pascoe's view of Maoridom was relatively enlightened, and if he did show some bias towards 'the administrators of Maori Affairs', that was understandable given his own administrative experience. However the final line of his letter — 'don't we all live in a world of insecurity' — was far more revealing of his own experiences than the Renes', for he had returned from holiday to find that Frank Newcombe, one of the unsuccessful applicants for his job, had lodged an appeal against his appointment.

Newcombe had a strong case. He had joined the Wildlife Service as a teenage trainee and had spent all his working life with it. By 1960 he had reached the senior level of management and was familiar with many of Wildlife's varied functions. Paradoxically, it was probably this familiarity that had cost him the job. Wildlife had been hampered in the past by internal rivalries which, Pascoe had been told, 'threatened the health of two of my predecessors in the job and had caused their premature retirement'.[6] Pascoe,

DON MERTON PHOTO, DEPARTMENT OF CONSERVATION

REDISCOVERY OF THE KAKAPO

By the 1950s, many New Zealanders thought the kakapo, or flightless bush parrot, was extinct because none had been seen for decades. The Wildlife Service, encouraged by the rediscovery of takahe in Fiordland in 1948, hoped a few might have survived. In the late 1950s search parties scoured Fiordland without success but in January 1961, only a few days after John Pascoe had returned from D'Urville Island, a kakapo was found in the Tutoko Valley by two young Wildlife trainees. 'The public generally, and nature lovers and ornithologists in particular, will welcome the news of the rediscovery of the Kakapo,' the Controller of Wildlife, John Pascoe, told the Evening Post. In the following few weeks, three more birds were found in the vicinity. Their rediscovery was a major event and was given prominence by the press. For Pascoe, it was an exciting start to his new job.

Later, more kakapo were found and a few were transferred to a farm near Mount Bruce, in the Wairarapa, where it was hoped they might breed in captivity. This was an unprecedented opportunity to study the birds at close quarters. Pascoe had to decide which scientist should lead the research on the kakapo. 'It is clear that each biologist hopes to have plums and the more personally ambitious a man is,' Pascoe observed, 'the more limelight and publicity he wants.'

on the other hand, was an outsider who knew little about the Wildlife Service except what he had learnt from his friend Major Yerex who headed its deer control operation and from deer cullers he met in the hills. His neutrality, as well as his experience at the Historic Places Trust in dealing with disparate and sometimes quarrelsome people, suggested to Internal Affairs that he might be ideal for the job. That he had established and successfully managed relations with the trust's 17 regional committees meant he would probably be able to gain the confidence and respect of the many acclimatisation societies whose vexatious attitudes had worn down his predecessors Priestley Thomson, who had been with Pascoe on the inaugural ascent of Evans and was now a senior manager in the Forest Service, thought the appointment 'good and imaginative': in his view, Pascoe had the objectivity and skills to do the job.[7]

Pascoe was very disappointed to learn that his new position was threatened. After two months he had told Peter Harding 'I find the job a fascinating one. Firstly because there is so much variety in the work I am constantly on my toes to comprehend quickly new problems, and secondly because the staff is a fine one and the field men particularly have a dedication and devotion to their work that lifts them from any normal civil service rut or pattern'. The real challenge was not in the field, however, but in Wellington where Pascoe's experience of the process of government was useful. 'My predecessors fell down in part of their job in that they were mostly at loggerheads with other departments and often with their own permanent heads of department,' he explained to Harding, adding:

> I have found and must constantly remember that I have some ability at negotiating on a basis of mutual respect and reasoning. By using both tact and frontal attacks, moderation and sympathy for an opponent's dilemma, I can get wildlife projects accepted by people who before have been suspicious and obstructive. That is my main justification for taking the job. I have said these sort of things at my staff meetings:
> 'There is a hell of a lot I don't know that you specialists do know. I will always come to you for advice, and I will give you credit for your knowledge not take it for myself. But remember that no matter how great your knowledge, how intense your enthusiasm, and however important your objectives, you cannot succeed unless I can convey your knowledge, your enthusiasm and your objectives to the head of our department of Internal Affairs to be translated into practical policies that will be accepted by other branches of government, such as town planning, lands and survey, agriculture, forestry and Maori Affairs.'

Unfortunately for John Pascoe, the appeal board was less likely to be interested in matters such as his negotiating skills than in the appropriateness of his appointment in the first place, in the light of the grading and entitlement conventions of the civil service at the time. Here Pascoe's position was precarious and he knew it. Furthermore, Newcombe was to be represented by a lawyer, an expense Pascoe could not afford. Nevertheless, he remained enthusiastic. 'I am not worrying about it because if I get tipped out of this job the experience I have had in it has fortified my need to get similar responsibilities, and will in fact make it easier to get them,' he told

Frank Newcombe resting on Porter's Rock, Takaka Hill.

In 1944 Joe Heenan sent John Pascoe and a young *Wildlife* trainee, Frank Newcombe, to explore the *Abel Tasman* area after its designation as a National Park. Pascoe was fit and seasoned in bushwork; Newcombe, on the other hand, had recently returned from the war, which had affected him badly.

Pascoe led Newcombe on a challenging cross-country bush-bash from the top of the Takaka Hill to the sea, via the Falls River. For much of the time it rained; Pascoe took a few photos but Newcombe had little time to botanise. In improving weather they walked round the coast to complete an arduous appraisal of the area.

Sixteen years later, Newcombe successfully appealed Pascoe's appointment as Controller of *Wildlife* and was awarded the job.

WAR EFFORT COLLECTION,
ALEXANDER TURNBULL LIBRARY

Peter Harding. 'The chap who is appealing is a friend and a chap whom I respect and I have told him that if he wins there will be no hard feelings on my part.'[8]

The case was heard in April 1961, five months after Pascoe had started the job, and Newcombe's challenge was successful. In spite of what he had written, Pascoe found it hard not to be bitter because the whole process seemed poorly managed and unfair. In response to a sympathetic note from Priestley Thomson, John Pascoe wrote: 'One of the disturbing features in my case was that many people knew about the result before I did'. Although Newcombe's lawyer had known the outcome three days after the hearing, for example, Pascoe himself was not officially advised until 12 days later. In the interim rumours were rife. 'It was a tense and disturbing business to have to stand up to all the rumours and I now suspect that even people in Rotorua and Taupo [Wildlife offices] knew the news before I did.'[9]

Pascoe was immediately reassigned to legal and research work in Internal Affairs at a considerably reduced salary. One of his colleagues, John Daniels, who had known Pascoe at the Historic Places Trust, later recalled that Pascoe was 'devastated' by the loss of his Wildlife job. 'He seemed shattered.'[10] Old friends offered sympathy and support. Priestley Thomson, who was about to go through the same appeal process himself, said 'it is iniquitous

that you should have been so long in the job and kept waiting so long for the appeal result'. Ormond Wilson wrote to say 'how terribly upset and distressed Rosamund [his wife] and I have been about your affairs, and about the shocking way in which they have been handled. I hardly know which is worse. The only thing I can hope is that this unfortunate and wretched business will lead to a revision of the whole procedure – but that won't help you. I am very sorry.'[11] A week later, Wilson rang to offer Pascoe his old job at the trust. Although Pascoe was pleased to be asked, he had no interest in a return to the past. Besides, he was confident another challenging administrative job would come his way in the next few months, and he felt that 'the Trust should have a permanent executive officer and not one who is restless for promotion and must always have his eyes open for another main chance'.[12]

As it transpired, Pascoe's time in the wilderness of the Internal Affairs legal division was far longer than he had hoped. It would be almost two years before he succeeded in securing 'another main chance'. In the meantime, he threw himself into his new work, nebulous as it was, with typical enthusiasm. Mountain life had taught him to make the best of any situation. 'I do not pretend not to be disappointed at losing a fascinating job but, now that I have lost it, I must accept that fact and not get embittered or overwhelmed by it,' he told Patricia Whitmore, a family friend.[13]

Within a few weeks he was sufficiently recovered to recognise that his relatively undemanding job left him with enough vitality at the end of the day to resume his old routine of writing at home in the evenings. While he had been in charge of Wildlife, any spare time had been spent reading files and reports; now he returned to work on his neglected encyclopaedia and started several new projects.

The Oxford University Press had approached him in November 1958 asking him to produce an encyclopaedia 'for those around school leaving age, the near adults, who are a bit young to know a lot about their own

In October 1961, John Pascoe returned to the Rakaia mountains. In middle age, he had lost little of the fitness and stoicism required for mountaineering. He and Michael Clark retraced Butler and Baker's route from Erewhon Station to the saddle above the Rakaia from where the pair had first seen what was later called the Whitcombe Pass.

Despite unseasonably heavy snow, Pascoe and Clark saved weight by not taking a tent or a primus. They spent a cold night on Butler Saddle waiting for the clear light of morning so that Pascoe could photograph the pass (in the distance, on the right), a crucial image for his photo essay 'Erewhon Illustrated', which he was then preparing for publication. He was unable, however, to interest a publisher in the work, which remains among his papers.

JOHN PASCOE PAPERS,
ALEXANDER TURNBULL LIBRARY

Black and white photography was John Pascoe's preferred medium. He rarely used colour film as the newspapers, magazines and books which featured his photos could only print in black and white. But the advent of colour printing in the early 1960s spawned a new genre of books such as New Zealand in Colour *illustrated by the Blenheim photographers, Kenneth and Jean Bigwood, with a text by the poet, James K. Baxter. It was so successful that the publishers produced a second volume in 1961 for which John Pascoe wrote the text 'in 5 weeks, rising at 5 a.m. each morning' to get the work done on schedule.*

It was a revelation to Pascoe, who was accustomed to selling perhaps 3000 to 5000 copies of his books, to find that Reeds had printed 40,000 copies of New Zealand in Colour – Volume Two, that it was published in five countries and that 'there is talk of it being translated into foreign [language] editions'.

country'. He had agreed, even though he really did not have the time for such an onerous task, because he enjoyed the prospect of doing something for young people – and the money Oxford offered was simply too good to refuse. Now that he again had free time in the evenings, he set to work to create an encyclopaedia. But where to start? 'First of all, I made a list of headings in the index of a 12 volume junior encyclopaedia. Then I consulted the indexes of books I respected about New Zealand. I accumulated on small cards, well over 500 headings.' The next step, ordering the cards, was vintage Pascoe:

> One night when the rest of the family was out, I spread them all over the living room floor and built myself a little 'mountain' of chairs. I had printed the headings large enough to read from a distance. By climbing up and down my 'mountain' from which I could study the 'plains', I was able to pick out and collate all the related topics.
>
> By the end of the evening, the mass of cards had been sorted into distinct groups. I removed any redundant headings, and the shape of the volume was formed.

Pascoe then contacted more than 100 specialists in various fields and commissioned them to write entries for the encyclopaedia. Some declined. Most accepted. 'In some cases I had years of nagging ahead to screw contributions from my writers,' he later recalled. 'In other cases they died, went abroad or went cold on their promises. In other cases they wrote promptly and well.'[14]

With the encyclopaedia under way, Pascoe could consider new projects. The centenary, in 1961, of Butler and Baker's discovery of the Whitcombe Pass at the head of the Rakaia rekindled his interest in an illustrated version of *Erewhon*, an idea he had contemplated since the 1930s. In October 1961 he returned to the Rakaia with Michael Clark, an Eastbourne friend, to take photos for it. The following March he wrote the text for *New Zealand in Colour – Volume Two*, a coffee table volume of scenic shots. Whatever reservations Pascoe may have had about this genre were more than offset by the publisher's fee and the pleasure he gained from returning to writing, which he found far more satisfying than work on the encyclopaedia. He told a friend it was 'an awful job as my fellow kiwis are the most slap-happy and dilatory people I know and as for kiwi scientists they are prickly and sensitive beyond reason'.[15]

John Pascoe also took the opportunity to spend more time with his family. In January 1962 he, Dorothy, Anna, Sara and a friend of Anna's travelled to Tapawera in the hills behind Nelson to spend three weeks picking raspberries. In the past, Pascoe had often spent most of January in the Southern Alps, but now he needed to supplement his salary. He and Dorothy also recognised that their older daughters were growing up and would soon leave home. Their work was described in Pascoe's account, 'Six Acres of Raspberries', which finished with the following flourish:

> On the positive side we had more than the pay that varied in our gang from £17 to £20: a close identity with soil and sweat, an experience that had tested us for stickability and tolerance, an appreciation of the qualities that emerged

in other pickers, and memories of the Woollaston-like landscape where sometimes clouds and ridges would whorl into each other in arabesques of sultry green and grey, where tobacco plants were cross-lit by low sunlight and peas shrivelled by high sunlight, where patches of snow on Mount Arthur gave thoughts of the snowless scrub-ridden wilderness of the Karamea headwaters beyond, and where a long running rapid and pool of the Motueka would wash away grime and soreness.[16]

John Pascoe also now had time to revive a correspondence with his sister, Alice, in London. He had not seen her for more than 20 years: 'I don't write to you much, so this one is high time,' he began. 'As we get older bonds

Rasberry canes, Tapawera.

THE PICKERS

John Pascoe's account of picking raspberries at Tapawera included the following description of his fellow workers on Tom and June Killalea's farm:

The pickers came from far as well as near; five Australians, of whom three folded up under the work and left; a mother and daughter from Whangarei; an elderly woman from Westport; some student teachers; high school girls from Hamilton and Wakefield; two farm girls from the Owen branch of the Buller, and June Killalea. Whether picking in sunshine or after rain the clothes were colourful, unconventional and raspberry-stained. Hats were wide-brimmed straw from sombreros to dilapidated high crowns, or handkerchiefs. Coats were plastic or parkas. Shirts were most important; long-sleeves needed for Antwerp jungles. Feet were bare or jandalled; all muddy or, at the best, dirty. By the end of the day most pickers were slouchy with drooping tiredness, scratched in places, waiting for the results of the final weighing-up, and ready for a feed and bed.

Picking was sometimes sociable for a pair would start some discussion that focused into argument. This would spread like fire in the fern and straw hats would bob up and down vehemently as points were made. Then again a song could be taken up, till it became something of a cats' chorus as the groups could not concentrate on keeping time with each other. Other times a picker would be hidden as she burrowed in the bushes and it was impossible not to eavesdrop on personal sidelights of school, home, gossip, boy friends or mention of fellow pickers.

And so to hot tired nights, with midges bizzling round the light, some huts in darkness, others with giggles and natters; all knowing that another dawn would bring the call to work.

of friendship and kin seem far closer.' His letter included a detailed description of his family:

Anna is now 19. She has a boy friend who went back to his home in Austria recently, and she pines for him, but tho he writes to her the most revealing and honest letters she finds it difficult to be regular in her replies to him, and spends hours debating what she shall say. He might come back — we don't know. When she has finished her art schooling here in say 4 years she will be anxious to get across to the old world, but will have to make her own money to do so because my family commitments will not leave any surplus with which to help her. Her art work and sense is good but she is a nervous type when it comes to exams.

Sara has grown into a well-built beauty at 16½ years. She plays the flute well, is good at biology and languages, and most certainly will need to go to university for a degree. She is a good worker too, expresses herself well whether in conversation or writing and I am sure she will make an interesting life. She has a New Zealand boy friend studying in the south of France who will be back later this year. She too will want to travel and I think she will be more practical than Anna in overcoming the obstacles.

Martha, now 14, has horse fever endemic, does not do well at school because she is restless, and we have an uphill job to get her to work well — never any difficulty about Anna and Sara in that respect. Jane is 11, plays the violin well, and studies well, has a gentle and nice nature, and is very fond of nature study.

Dorothy is well tho overworked like all mothers of four; does silk screen printing in an effort to get more cash for family affairs, and paints Maori rock drawing designs on wooden bowls and platters. I am still very much in love with her, which is good, and responsive to her. Like many New Zealand men I am sometimes taciturn, which she finds hard, as she lives for stimulating talk about creative things, world affairs and so on. She is a wonderful mother.

I am reasonably fit and frisky for my 53 years, weigh 10 st 4 lbs and can climb hills without puffing. Still want to do more climbing than opportunity allows and because we live from one pay day to the next and have no spare cash I cannot get away to Ruapehu snows this winter. However the main thing is to keep in condition so that I can climb well when I do get a chance of returning to the snows.[17]

There was one correspondence John had never allowed to lapse no matter how busy he was. He wrote to his mother each Sunday evening, as he had done ever since he moved to Wellington in 1937. If for some reason he failed to write, within a few days Effie would be on the phone wanting to know what had happened. She lived in a small house in Cranmer Square in the centre of Christchurch and Paul visited her regularly. Suddenly, in May 1962, the redoubtable 81-year-old seemed to falter. Paul alerted John to the change:

If you or Dorothy come to Christchurch to see Eff can you stay with us and see her by the day? She is so frail and gets so fussed. She seems to cling to her routine, precisely, she is literally crawling and the thread is slender. It is difficult to explain but I can read her so clearly seeing her so often. She is so pathetic and she really is plucky. You might be wise to come reasonably soon.[18]

A week later John was in Christchurch and spent several days with his mother. On his return to Eastbourne, it was arranged that Dorothy should also visit, which was fortunate because Dorothy was with Effie when she was admitted to hospital. She died soon afterwards. 'My abiding and final memory of Eff is of her absolute courage, like a bonny fighter who will neither take the count nor retire from the ring,' John wrote to Alice. 'Having been a nurse yourself you will be familiar with brave old people with tired hearts; how they alternate between plucky fighting, with spasms of resignation but other spasms of "why can't I leave my exhausted old body; what is to become of me ...?"'[19]

When John next wrote it was to describe their mother's funeral.

> I have been so used to writing Eff my weekly letter of family news and routines that I found it quite difficult not to rush to my typewriter last night and tell her what a moving funeral she had had. It was good that Paul and I and his three sons could be pallbearers and Jack Denham. The service was so short and noble that I will carry that with me too for a long time; the Cathedral serene; the graveside service short and dignified; Eff being lowered to Daddy, and the crisp winter sunlight. Lots of friends turned up: old harrier ones, mountaineering ones, as well as the family streams that reunite only at weddings and funerals, giving a sense of fitness and purpose to living, and some acceptance of the inevitable changes.[20]

A month later, John Pascoe was back in Christchurch for a very different reason, to deliver the inaugural W. A. Kennedy memorial lecture at the request of the CMC. It was a great honour that acknowledged Pascoe as the spokesman for his generation of climbers, and he was well aware of it. Months of thought and careful preparation culminated in an address punctuated by humour and illustrated by slides. He first sketched New Zealand's history of mountaineering, then recounted his epic transalpine trip in 1952 from Wanaka to the West Coast with Stan Conway, Ray Chapman and Bill Hannah. He concluded with an excerpt from his own poem, 'Arawata Bill'.

The lecture was well received. Afterwards he received a letter from Norman Hardie, a Canterbury climber. 'I don't know of any other talk I have heard where the speaker's personality emerged so clearly and fitted so well into the subject matter and delivery,' observed Hardie. 'The intermingling of quotations, bawdy wit, cracks at the Alpine Club, musical associations and matters of real historical value were beautifully handled. It was a memorable occasion in every way.'[21]

John Pascoe understood the deeper meaning of the event. It was held in the main hall of the Canterbury Museum, next door to Christ's College where, 40 years earlier, he had been a small, stammering schoolboy who was the frequent target of bullies. At the time, few would have placed him among 'those most likely to succeed', yet here he now stood, an acknowledged alpine authority, confidently speaking to a large audience. Paul Pascoe was present and he too recognised the significance of his brother's success. A few days later he sent John a letter:

Lecture: I wish to evaluate your lecture to be helpful to you. I was glad to be there because I could see myself there too and it made me wish to appraise virtues and faults.

WILL KENNEDY

S.P. ANDREW COLLECTION, ALEXANDER TURNBULL LIBRARY

Christchurch schoolteacher, W. A. Kennedy, introduced many young people to the mountains. As a young man, Will Kennedy was a keen cyclist and climber. In 1896 he led the first bicycle trip from Christchurch to the Hermitage. Later, he also cycled to Otago to climb, and pioneered climbing in the Godley area where he made a number of first ascents. Some years before the railway reached Arthur's Pass in 1914, he built the first hut in the vicinity. It soon became a base for exploration of the surrounding peaks. For many young men and women a trip to Arthur's Pass with Kennedy was their first experience of alpine life.

In 1925, when the Christchurch Tramping Club was formed (later to become the CMC), Will Kennedy was its inaugural vice-president, then its president and patron. As he became less physically active, he gave frequent illustrated talks on the mountains and built up an extensive collection of lantern slides taken by himself and others. He died in 1950. Kennedy's photographic collection (held by the Canterbury Museum) is an invaluable record of a particularly dynamic period in the development of Canterbury climbing.

In 1962 the CMC, as a memorial to him, introduced the W. A. Kennedy lecture. John Pascoe, who had known Kennedy well and greatly respected him, gave the inaugural address.

Virtues: – very very good order of slides, pauses, talks, contrast etc
- presence
- naturalness
- directness
- very very good sense of humour (I was crying with laughter at one stage)
- mystique very good

Faults: – speak slower. Ann tells me I have the same fault. Occasional semi stutter does not matter. If someone laughs and you are speaking slowly you can be heard, if quickly, literally you cannot.

Also throw your voice to the back wall and to do this you must have chin up and never speak down, the floor in front reflects to the front half but it is the back half you need to get and the ceiling is the best acoustic reflector for that (and upper part of side walls).

Sum up: The applause accorded you showed the appreciation of all those present, a lovely lecture.[22]

Paul's appraisal suggested a self-assurance born of professional success. By 1962 he was one of New Zealand's leading architects and his acclaimed design for Christchurch International Airport had led to further commissions for air terminals in Rarotonga and Wellington. He was also kept busy with residential and ecclesiastical work. But Paul had not always prospered. When he returned from England in the late 1930s full of modernist fervour, commissions had been few and far between, and it was not until the 1950s that he had finally become established. During that earlier period it was John who enjoyed the limelight as a photographer and author. But John's career suddenly stalled when he lost the Wildlife job, at the very time when Paul was becoming successful. 'Paul pays in taxes what I get in wages,' John observed. Paul's prosperity was soon evident in his expanding middle-aged waistline, while John remained the same weight he had been for years, kept trim by his energetic life, limited income and a degree of anxiety that became more apparent in the 1960s.

He had plenty to worry about. Soon after the Pascoes returned from raspberry picking in Tapawera, Sara began to show signs of disturbing behaviour, caused apparently by romantic disappointment. Her first serious boyfriend, Hugo Manson, was about to return after a year's study in France and she was understandably 'tensed up about Hugo's return'. When Sara and Hugo met again, they found the easy companionship they previously enjoyed had changed. Hugo went to Victoria University and Sara, who had planned to spend a final year at Hutt Valley High, suddenly decided to go too. It was an unfortunate decision because Hugo now had another girlfriend and Sara 'felt terrible about seeing them arm-in-arm in Victoria University corridors'. Gradually, the daughter John had felt most confident about started 'to shrivel into a core of indecision'.[23] John was sufficiently concerned to warn Anna, now an art student in Christchurch, that she would find a different Sara when she returned to Eastbourne for the holidays:

> Sara (who has always been a fluent and perceptive reader of books that have often included good ones and sometimes abstruse ones) has got a peculiar kind of blockage that seems to make it very difficult for her to read quickly a set book of the classic type such as George Eliot's *Middlemarch*. Result – she cannot write an essay for English. Result – it is unlikely that she will get terms. Result – she won't be able to sit her English exam? We don't know.[24]

Unfortunately, Sara's problems came at a time when other matters demanded her parents' attention. First, John's mother died. Then he was preoccupied with preparing the W. A. Kennedy lecture. Dorothy, as always, was busy running the home and family, and was also starting a business. They did not see much of Sara, whose days were usually spent at the university, and as she 'seldom came home until the evening we did not realise how deeply stressed she had become,' Dorothy later recalled. When Sara was at home, her parents found 'she was hard to communicate with and impetuous in her decisions'.[25]

It did not help Sara's vulnerable state when, in August 1962, the Pascoe household gained another member. Peter Harding and his wife, Barbara, were worried about their eldest daughter, Jenny, aged 20. Could she come and stay with the Pascoes for a few months? After a family meeting the Pascoes agreed. Five years earlier, Barbara Harding had dropped

everything to come to their rescue when Dorothy had a nervous breakdown and John was fully occupied with setting up the Historic Places Trust. John and Dorothy had appreciated her help; now it was time to reciprocate. At first, Jenny seemed to benefit from life with her cousins. After she had been with the Pascoes for two months John reported to Paul 'we are making progress with Jenny Harding'.

> The first 2 weeks were awful as she tried us out in every way imaginable but she has now settled down and tho' she is a hypochondriacal problem girl she is helpful and considerate in many ways and is getting on well with the young ones of the family. It is of course a strain for Dorothy having her and I get the backwash of such strain, but the effort is needed and may pay off, in that Jenny will get better confidence and health.

John was even more positive in a letter to Jenny's parents. She now had a part-time job, was doing some fine drawings and even helped to prepare meals: 'In short, she is fitting into her new life and is making positive and effective efforts to help herself'.[26] John's optimism was shortlived. Within a few weeks Jenny had lost her job and it worried him that she was intending to come with them on a family holiday at Arthur's Pass:

Dorothy Pascoe recovered after her nervous breakdown in 1957, partly because she looked beyond home and family to her own creativity. She enrolled at Wellington Polytechnic, learnt screen printing and established a business making cards and scarves. She also painted Maori rock drawing designs on wooden platters, boxes and trays which she sold through Stockton's craft shop in Woodward Street, Wellington.

DOROTHY PASCOE COLLECTION

Things get a bit grim with Jenny here sometimes; it really is an awful uphill struggle. She seems to want to go to Arthur's Pass, but would be useless there and could hate it; she is fussy about food, cannot lift a weight of over 4 lbs (her phobia), is allergic to sandflies, won't try to get fit, wants Dorothy's company as much as possible, etc. etc.[27]

The holiday was saved by Dorothy's sister, Judy, who had Jenny to stay while they were away. At Arthur's Pass they enjoyed a white Christmas and a family foray up the Crow Valley before John left them to make a transalpine crossing from the Waitaha to the Rakaia with Stan Conway and Michael Clark. It was a tough trip, but John's diary clearly showed his joy and relief at being back in the mountains, far from the challenges of his everyday life.

Sara was so much better while on holiday that John and Dorothy realised just what a destabilising influence Jenny Harding was. Back in

(8) There is much to rejoice in for this trog (= bivi rock). It has good shelter, a bevy of 12 keas, water handy, dracophyllum + leatherwood scrub, a corker fireplace contrived by Michael, +, above all a view to the S.E. with spurs of Blomfield + Antisto Dome with intricately designed patches of snow on schist sheen. The outlook recalls early Chinese art, with delicately pastelled ridges of spiky rock softened to their fraternity of velvety snowgrass: these modulate as + harp in a Mozart variation to steeper land, with Grieg waterfalls for undertone, Wagner growls of the river for overtone, and finally these musical + antistic felicities change to Beethoven grandeur of cliffs + bluffs to demodulate to the simplicity of a Beethoven minor theme in the form of fern fronds dropping regularly with clear rain water.

On 8 Jan it cleared again & we

While contemplating a proposed trip from the *West Coast* to the *Rakaia*, John Pascoe wondered whether, at the age of 55, he was still robust enough to withstand the rigours of such a journey. In anticipation, he consulted a cardiologist who gave him an electrocardiogram. Pascoe was delighted with the result, telling his brother that the cardiologist had said 'my heart is 10 years younger than my age because of the regular exercise, and that if I keep training I can give it the violent exertion of a transalpine trip'.

In January 1963 Pascoe set out, accompanied by his old friend, Stan Conway, and the younger Michael Clark. Their journey began with an arduous traverse of the *Smythe Range* which led to tough terrain at the head of the *Waitaha*, where loose rock hidden under snow made the climb out of the valley dangerous.

Their fourth day was one of relentless exertion. At one stage Stan Conway slipped and was lucky to stop himself. 'I had a sinking feeling in the guts as I belayed Michael who belayed Stan; neither belay was worth a tin of fish,' Pascoe noted in his trip diary. Soon afterwards, while negotiating steep bluffs shrouded in mist, Conway slipped again, damaging an ankle. After a gruelling 14-hour stint, wearing crampons, they were relieved to find a rock bivouac. Here they stayed for several days in the rain, while Conway rested his ankle. Pascoe wrote his diary to pass the time and included this description of the view from their shelter.

JOHN PASCOE COLLECTION,
ALEXANDER TURNBULL LIBRARY

The terminal moraine of the Ramsay Glacier, source of the Rakaia River. In the early 1930s, when John Pascoe made several trips up the Ramsay Glacier to reach the snowfield below Mount Evans, there was no lake. Since then, the glacier has retreated almost 2 kilometres leaving behind an expanse of icy water.

The caption for this photo in John Pascoe's album of his 1963 transalpine trip reads: 'Henry Moore meringue on Evans Glacier'. Five years earlier, when Pascoe was secretary of the Historic Places Trust, he received three autographed photos of Henry Moore sculptures set in the Scottish countryside.

In writing to thank Moore, whose work he admired, Pascoe suggested 'that the most inaccessible moraines of New Zealand glaciers could be the ideal setting for your work. But think of the disadvantages of the sites! The rain would be nearly 200 inches annually; the barrier gorges and icefalls would prohibit all but a few fanatics like myself from visiting them; the moraines themselves move as the glacier ice moves; one year your bronzes might be erect; another year they might be prostrate, as though drunk with beneficent solitude.'

DOROTHY PASCOE COLLECTION

Eastbourne, Sara 'suffered considerably with tension at the prospect of Jenny's return and the incompatibility was quite distressing to realise,' John wrote to Peter Harding. 'I think Sara sees the neurotic in Jenny, and fearing the neurotic within herself, gets very alarmed.'

Sure enough, when Jenny did return tensions in the Pascoe household began to increase and were made worse by a growing disagreement between John and Dorothy over how best to deal with the situation. Dorothy was resolute that Jenny should remain in their care – 'we have taken on a job and must go through with it' – while John thought Jenny should go back to Sydney. Her parents, however, were reluctant to have her back as their eldest daughter was now also starting to show signs of instability and they feared Jenny's return would make Susan worse.[28]

The situation in Eastbourne became even more desperate in February 1963 when Dorothy's older brother, Eric Harding, came to stay. Eric was no ordinary guest, for he had recently had a stroke that at first left him immobilised and unable to write or speak. Still a relatively young man in his late 40s, Eric was now entirely dependent on his wife, Kyra, who also had their four children to look after. Kyra's life was difficult and Dorothy was keen to give her a brief respite. She was also determined to help her brother learn to speak again. But it was hard work and she was already exhausted from dealing with Jenny and Sara. John feared all these demands on Dorothy would eventually endanger her own physical and mental health – and he was determined that would not happen. Jenny must go. Finally, John gave Dorothy an ultimatum that shocked her: 'Either Jenny goes, or I go'.[29]

They agreed to put the matter to Dorothy's psychiatrist, John Hardwick-Smith, but as he was ill it was some weeks before they could see him and in the meantime Jenny remained at Eastbourne. When Dorothy finally saw Hardwick-Smith he was adamant 'that Jenny must not live with our family and that she should get back to Aussie where her own psychiatrist can

Ian Gilmour *met Anna Pascoe in 1962 in Christchurch; she was at the School of Art, he was studying to be a chemical engineer. Her parents were relieved she had a new suitor because her previous boyfriend, Rudi, a self-styled 'existentialist', had returned to Austria and hoped Anna would join him.*

Ian enjoyed the Pascoes, with whom he stayed during the summer of 1962–63 while he had a holiday job in Lower Hutt. He lived in a tent on their lawn because the household was crowded with all four daughters and Jenny Harding.

DOROTHY PASCOE COLLECTION

continue the treatment that she needs badly,' John wrote to Anna as soon as he heard the verdict.[30]

Suddenly life at Eastbourne became more tolerable. Sara was at teachers' training college and Dorothy had made sufficient progress helping Eric to recover his speech that she felt he could leave. Then, quite unexpectedly, John was given a new job. 'It will shortly be announced that the new Acting Chief Archivist of the National Archives is J. D. Pascoe,' he told his brother. 'I did not seek the job, but the applicants for it were not (apparently) as good as me. National Archives has suffered the deaths of 2 of its key men and is falling to bits, so there are immediate problems for me and the first few months will be very exacting.'[31] When he started at Archives in March 1963, he found it 'very hectic' and was faced with 'immediate struggles for more staff and struggles to hold what accommodation we have, as well as plans for expansion. There is a lot of technical stuff that is new to me that I have to assimilate as quickly as possible. The days pass as though they were only 5 minutes.'[32] Within a few months John's job was made a permanent one, a clear indication that Internal Affairs was happy with his performance.[33]

Further good news came with the distribution of Effie Pascoe's estate. John and Dorothy had never been able to afford a car, as these were extremely expensive in post-war New Zealand, but could now buy one. This would, however, take time as John was not prepared to gamble his legacy on a second-hand vehicle, and a new one could only be purchased immediately if partly paid for with overseas funds, of which they had none. The alternative was to join a waiting list. In the meantime, they built a drive from the road to their house and a garage underneath.

At last it seemed that the horrors of the past 18 months were receding. The change in their fortunes was capped by Anna's announcement in May 1963 that she and Ian Gilmour were to marry. 'We like him a lot,' John wrote to Alice, 'and we feel we really know him because he stayed with us for three months last Xmas holidays while he was working at a local paint factory as

Anna Pascoe and her father on her wedding day, January 1964.

In the months before their wedding, Anna and Ian sometimes went to church in Eastbourne. Although John Pascoe was not a churchgoer, he often accompanied them but would not say the creed. However, he enjoyed singing, especially his favourite, Psalm 121, which begins: 'I will lift up mine eyes unto the hills, from whence cometh my help'.

DOROTHY PASCOE COLLECTION

one of his student assignments. They are both very happy and will be married next January.'[34]

Sara Pascoe's response to Anna's news was, however, quite unlike her parents'. During the previous year, several brief romantic relationships had left Sara upset and, according to John, 'in a droopy state'. Now Anna's engagement 'seemed to shake her equilibrium,' Dorothy told her brother, Peter Harding. 'I don't think she has ever quite got over her first love affair with Hugo and those fearfully dramatic entanglements she has had since, have been her way of obliterating her feelings for him.' John noticed Sara was 'all to hell and nervy' in the days after hearing of the engagement. In the next few weeks her condition did not improve. Then, one morning when Sara refused to get up and instead remained in bed 'inert and hostile', her parents took her to see Dr Hardwick-Smith who immediately admitted her to Wellington Hospital. But as she continued to deteriorate she was soon moved to Porirua Hospital.

'This has been an awful ordeal and Sara's plight was pathetic,' John told Peter Harding. 'Dorothy and I have taken it hard.' To make matters worse they were not allowed to visit her for a fortnight. When they finally did see her, Dorothy told Peter how relieved they were that:

> Sara seems to be responding well to the treatment she is having at Porirua. We have seen her twice there and she has pulled out of the dreadful catatonic state she was in amazingly well. We had gone out there braced to meet just anything so it was a wonderful surprise when we were ushered into a small room and Sara came to us and was obviously so pleased to see us. With the shock treatment she has those blockages of memory that go with it, but she seems to be accepting that reasonably calmly. She now looks back at the strange fantasies of her awful few days with a certain awe tempered with amusement and says 'can that have been me?' [35]

Despite her progress, Sara remained in Porirua for the next six months. She was discharged early in January 1964, a few days before Anna and Ian's wedding.

Sara's nervous breakdown and her long stay in hospital was 'quite the most difficult time John and I experienced as parents,' Dorothy later recalled. Coming on top of the loss of John's Wildlife job and their troubles with Jenny, she felt 'as if I had lost my innocence and certainty in the pattern of life we were leading'. Fortunately they now had a car, a new Humber 90, which made visiting Sara in hospital far easier than making the long journey from Eastbourne to Porirua and back by public transport. With only Martha and Jane still at home, the Pascoe household was now much calmer than it had been for several years. As John and Dorothy recovered, they began to pick up the threads of their own lives again. Dorothy continued her craft business while John, in the evening at home, contemplated new writing projects.[36]

For John Pascoe, writing was a sign of vitality which had its origins in his youth. As young women, his sister Alice and her friends had been interested in writing plays and poetry and their example stimulated John. Alice had trained as a nurse then, after her marriage to Colonel David Morgan, had accompanied him to diplomatic posts in various countries. It was John who

Sara Pascoe, aged 16, by Gwen Knight. Sara showed great aptitude for art, languages and music. She was also interested in archaeology. Her youthful promise was, however, jeopardised in 1963 by the onset of a mental illness, later diagnosed as a bi-polar disorder. At the time, knowledge and treatment of this condition, then known as manic depression, were relatively limited. She received shock treatment and anti-psychotic drugs. Despite her illness, Sara continued to paint and in the late 1970s and early 1980s she won several art awards. In 1986 she was prescribed a more effective medication (lithium carbonate) which has enabled her to manage her illness and fully resume her creative life.

DOROTHY PASCOE COLLECTION

became a writer, but his prolific stream of articles and books stopped abruptly in the early 1960s when the loss of his Wildlife job and 'the turmoil of living' dented his confidence. Then, in December 1964, just as the Pascoe family had become more settled and John was beginning to think about writing again, Alice suddenly died. 'I was very upset,' he told David Morgan, 'to hear that Alice had died. I have not seen her for 28 years and it was one of my dearest ambitions – to see her again.' In January 1965, while climbing at Arthur's Pass with his family, they were joined by Anna and her husband

JOHN PASCOE PHOTO, DOROTHY PASCOE COLLECTION

A SENSE OF HISTORY

The Pascoes gathering firewood near Carrington Hut at the head of the Waimakariri, January 1965. From left: Dorothy, Jane, Martha, Anna and Ian. On their return, John Pascoe wrote the following account of their climbing holiday for the New Zealand Alpine Club's Bulletin:

I find it consistent with a sense of history to look forward as well as backward. I study the future as much in contrast to the past as in terms of it. What will the Waimakariri Valley hold for young mountaineers in the year 1999? Will it be so full of heliports or autobahns that even the sandflies will feel themselves to be displaced insects?

I first tramped up the Waimakariri River in Easter, 1930, and bounced over the boulders with some excitement. This was home territory for Canterbury mountaineers; we cherished Sir Arthur Dudley Dobson as our patron; we had our first club hut in the valley; with unfledged zeal, we were eager for experience. Sir Arthur and his fellow-explorers had sought routes across passes. We now sought peaks above those passes. The result of that first holiday was satisfying: three peaks and the gain of confidence.

Thirty-four years passed. I had progressed from the Waimakariri to more remote and tougher valleys. When I had returned to the Waimakariri, it had been for other reasons; interludes such as an alpine honeymoon in 1940 or snatches of leave in which to climb some mountains which I had not visited before. In January,

1965, I returned to the familiar Waimakariri pastures, chosen for their accessible suitability for a mountaineering family. With my wife, my eldest daughter Anna and her husband Ian Gilmour, and my daughters Martha (16 years) and Jane (15 years), I laboured once again with a heavy pack up the well known trails. We had some bad weather, some river trouble, some good weather for climbing, and some time enjoying the shelter of good huts. Only one daughter, Sara, was not there; she was on an archaeological expedition at the Bay of Islands.

One of the most enjoyable wet days at the Carrington Hut was enlivened by a friendly visit from four fellow NZAC members: Don Whitfield, Don Campbell, Dave Allely, and Mike Breen. They slung my rope from the rafters and showed us in turn how to use the latest method of climbing out of a crevasse using prusik loops. It was great fun, and we got laughs as well as instruction. Later in the holiday, four of us climbed Mount Armstrong, and the whole party (two ropes of it) Mount Carrington. The wheel was turning its circle, and in training my family I was fulfilling my sense of history and paying my respects to the pioneers.

Dorothy Pascoe's business, Kotuku Crafts, thrived. She became so busy that her friend, Jill Henderson (left), regularly helped her by preparing surfaces for painting and packing finished items. As they worked, they talked: 'Jill saved my sanity,' Dorothy recalled. 'She was a big talker. I would work. She would talk and it got me through that difficult period with Sara.'
DOROTHY PASCOE COLLECTION

Ian Gilmour, and John 'had time to think a lot about Alice in appreciation of our early life'. He was often reminded of Alice when he looked at his oldest daughter: 'I have always thought Anna is very like Alice whether as a 2 year old or as a 22 year old,' he told David Morgan, warning him that if Anna visited England as she intended, 'you must be prepared for a shock because there are times that the Aliceness of Anna is marked'.[37]

Throughout this difficult period, John Pascoe concentrated on his job and his family. Getting through each day was his objective, and his camera and typewriter often lay idle. His anchors were Dorothy and his work at National Archives which, he told Harold Leov, 'is going quite well, and I like it as much as ever. Had a very interesting time in Hokitika as one of my staff and I dug out records of Magistrates Court going back 99 years which will be good material for future historians.'[38] Handling the raw material of history fascinated Pascoe, who understood its value. He was less familiar, however, with archival systems and protocols, but was willing to learn. Nevertheless, his appointment to Chief Archivist was controversial because

Self-portrait by Samuel Butler.

John Pascoe found comfort and strength in Samuel Butler's exploration of the Rakaia, which he had been the first to publicise. In the aftermath of Edgar Russell's unfortunate death on Avalanche Peak in 1933, for example, Pascoe had written 'Samuel Butler in the Rakaia – The Pass to Erewhon' which was published in the Press. Years later, when he lost his job at Wildlife, Pascoe returned to the Rakaia and marked the centenary of Butler and Baker's discovery with an article in the Listener. Two years later, in the wake of Sara Pascoe's breakdown, he again returned to the Rakaia mountains, this time to gather photos for his 'Erewhon Illustrated'. At the same time, Pascoe wrote a profile of Samuel Butler for the Listener to promote his radio play, The Way to Erewhon, which was broadcast on the YC network in July 1963.

ALEXANDER TURNBULL LIBRARY

he was not a trained archivist and it was widely believed that the appointment was an expedient solution to Pascoe's predicament after losing the job of Controller of Wildlife. This is the view of Michael Bassett in his history of Internal Affairs, *The Mother of all Departments*, and also of Ian Wards, one of the unsuccessful applicants for the job. Pascoe was 'a loose cannon', according to Wards, who could not continue forever as the department's legal officer as he was not a qualified lawyer; he was therefore given the job of Chief Archivist. Wards did not think it 'a good appointment'.[39]

The position of Chief Archivist became vacant in 1962 when the incumbent, Michael Standish, suddenly died at the age of 41 from a heart attack, after visiting his minister to put the case for more funding. Standish and Wards were close friends who shared a common vision for the development of Archives. At the time, Wards was a research officer in the War History Branch of Internal Affairs, and a regular user of Archives. On Standish's death, Wards thought he should succeed him because he was familiar with what his friend had hoped to achieve and, according to Wards, had been told by the Group Executive Officer of Internal Affairs, Ted Fairway, that he had the job. Then, at the last minute, it was given to Pascoe, and Wards could not appeal the appointment since it did not involve a change of Pascoe's grading. 'I felt bloody annoyed,' Wards recalled, even though his later appointment as Chief Historian, a post he held for many years, meant his career was barely interrupted.[40]

Nevertheless, Wards did not forget or forgive Pascoe, whom he never regarded as an equal. Wards and Pascoe had worked together at the War History Branch in the early 1950s, but they were not friends. Wards was a refined, university educated scholar who considered Pascoe rather crude because of his swearing and bawdy stories. Furthermore, Pascoe's work as illustrations editor was 'not full-time, hard work like research and writing... his role wasn't as pressing'. A detached observer, John Daniels, remembers that some former Historical Branch people such as Ian Wards and Bob Burnett had 'a precious attitude towards Pascoe' because he did not have a degree and had not been on active service during the war.[41] When Pascoe became Chief Archivist, it meant his performance in the job would always be rigorously scrutinised by Wards. His subsequent verdict has persisted, through repetition, despite being at variance with the facts.

> I'll say something about John as Chief Archivist. You are entitled to regard it as prejudiced as you wish, but he wasn't a good Chief Archivist. The only way he got through was because he had an excellent number two, Judith Hornabrook. She, as number two, was first class but she didn't have the makings to be number one, not altogether uncommon. She certainly got John through the role of Chief Archivist. During that period his typewriter was very busy and he did a lot of his writing at that time.[42]

In reality, Pascoe did far less writing while Chief Archivist than at any other time in his career. He was simply too busy with problems at home and at work, and he had also lost some of the indomitable energy and confidence that had made him such a prolific writer in the past. What he clearly understood, however, was that he was appointed as an administrator, not as an

DOROTHY PASCOE COLLECTION

KEEPING UP WITH THE PAST

Graham Bagnall, Chief Librarian at the Turnbull Library, and John Pascoe examine the original sheets
of the Treaty of Waitangi. Alexander Turnbull looks on.

The New Zealand Company's plans for the settlement of Wellington included a public records office, although it was never built. Nor did Wellington immediately become the centre of political power, as the Wakefields had hoped. Instead Auckland became the capital. The Treaty of Waitangi was kept there, but it was lucky to survive an 1841 fire in the cottage where it was stored with other official records. When the capital was moved to Wellington in 1865, government records were also moved, but some were lost in the shipwreck of the White Swan.

In 1907 the need for a safe system for storing government records became apparent after fire destroyed Parliament Buildings. All the Native Department's records were lost except the Treaty of Waitangi, which survived only because it was thrown out of a window. Two years later, Dr Thomas Hocken, a book collector with a keen interest in Maori culture, found the Treaty lying forgotten and damaged in the basement of a nearby building.

In the first decades of the 20th century government records were kept at the Alexandra Barracks then, after the First World War, in the basement of the General Assembly Library. In 1926 the Librarian, Guy Scholefield, was also appointed Dominion Archivist. He collected government records throughout the country and established the principle that no records should be destroyed without his permission. In 1936 Scholefield was succeeded by Eric McCormick, who combined his duties as Dominion Archivist with work for New Zealand's centennial celebrations. On 6 February 1940 the Treaty was publicly displayed for the first time, at Waitangi.

During the Second World War, McCormick established a War Archives section within the New Zealand Army. After the war he drew up plans for the management of government records under the control of the Department of Internal Affairs. In 1947 Michael Standish succeeded him and travelled overseas to study archives in other countries. While he was away, a fire in the Hope Gibbons building in central Wellington destroyed departmental records. On his return, Standish laid the foundations for a modern system of record keeping which was codified in the 1957 Archives Act. Based on South African legislation, the act made provision for a Chief Archivist to run National Archives with responsibility for the storage and discretionary disposal of all government records.

The intent of this act was admirable, but hard to achieve while records were stored in 26 separate sites around Wellington, as well as in other regional centres. Standish died in 1962 and was succeeded by John Pascoe who initiated plans for a new Archives building in Wellington where all records could be kept together. He did not live to see the new building, however, as a lack of government support stymied progress for many years and National Archives was not properly housed until 1990 when an existing building in Mulgrave Street, previously the Government Printing Office, was converted and refurbished. When the new building opened, the Treaty of Waitangi, which had earlier been held at the Alexander Turnbull Library, was put on permanent display at National Archives.

expert archivist. He quickly realised that his priorities should be 'to get a better deal for the grossly neglected staff; and then if National Archives is to take full responsibilities under its act, it must have a new building in Wellington'.[43] Within 18 months Pascoe had won substantial salary increases for himself and most of his staff.[44] After three years, he had convinced Internal Affairs to increase the number of staff from seven to 12.[45] At the same time he persuaded the government to buy a block of land on Thorndon Quay for the site of a new Archives building. Another Pascoe initiative was the introduction of yearly reports on the state of National Archives. In his 1966 report he wrote 'site investigations are now being made and planning is making some headway for a new building of five stories for the storage of archives and their administration'.[46] The same year he travelled to the United States to study new archive buildings in several states. In the meantime, while waiting for the new building, he organised temporary premises for Archives (then scattered all round Wellington in a number of buildings) under one roof in Borthwick House on The Terrace.

John Pascoe also made Archives an enjoyable place to work. His deputy, Judith Hornabrook, had first noticed his willingness to welcome and befriend new staff when she worked with him in the War History Branch and he continued this practice at Archives. 'Here was this chap who was interested in me and my family, just as he was in everybody else. The more junior you were, the more he wanted to make you feel at home.'

> We were his family. He was very much a family man but he extended the family. He was interested in anything you were doing. I got to know all his family too. He would tell me all the latest news about the children and they would come in sometimes. And we had a wonderful Christmas 'do' at the Pascoes'. All the staff came.[47]

Pascoe also took an interest in the researchers who visited Archives. In 1964, for instance, the Australian writer Geoffrey Dutton did some research there. On his return to Australia, he wrote to Pascoe:

> A thousand thanks for all your help and hospitality to Nin and myself while we were in Wellington. Having already had experience of the amiability and industry of NZ archives and libraries, I nevertheless never expected to find someone like yourself running the archives. Apart from the documents you provided, you opened up several new avenues of thought on my subject.[48]

Pascoe's achievements at Archives helped to restore his confidence, as did the publication in 1965 of the *Oxford New Zealand Encyclopaedia*. After six years, he was relieved to be rid of it, but had also enjoyed the challenge. 'When I started I knew it was a graunchy job. But then I've always liked long graunchy jobs,' he told the *Listener*:

> It's tied in with my youthful experiences of long distance running, later translated into mucking about in the mountains. I rather like long, slow, patient plodding. This is a gorge and here I am standing on one side of it. This bit in the middle is unknown, with all types of hazards and anxieties. Like marriage and almost anything else. It's part of the interest and justification in the job. This one was helluva sticky now and then, but now it's finished.[49]

The Oxford New Zealand Encyclopaedia bears the unmistakable imprint of its editor, John Pascoe. The cover photo shows cattle being driven across the Arawata River, and the 200 topics covered include 'Mountains', 'National Parks', 'Search and Rescue' and 'Mountaineering'. It also features many photos taken by John Pascoe as well as an aerial view of the new Christchurch International Airport terminal, designed by Paul Pascoe.

John Pascoe spent six years working on the encyclopaedia in his spare time. He determined its contents and scope, commissioned the specialist authors, then edited their contributions. The revised copy was then sent to England where the Oxford University Press's general series editor, Laura Salt, co-ordinated production of the volume.

In December 1965 Martha Pascoe moved to the Wairarapa to become a groom on the Te Parae thoroughbred stud farm. Now that all their daughters but Jane had left home, John and Dorothy were free to go out in the evenings to films, concerts or ballet, which they particularly enjoyed. Dorothy introduced John to ballet, although he was at first sceptical because, as he told her, 'where I was brought up in Christchurch, I was taught that ballet was utterly unmanly and wretched. So I thought: "Well, I'll try anything once, even if I am the only male in the audience. What do I care?" I went along and I was charmed by the combination of the decor, the gymnastics and the music.' John became so keen on ballet that he would sleep on the pavement outside the booking office to get tickets when it first opened. On one occasion he was told to move on by a policeman, who let him stay only after Pascoe had explained, 'But I'm a queue!'[50]

Their only serious concern was Sara, now flatting in Roseneath, who was still having bouts of disturbed behaviour, was disinclined to take her medication and did not often contact her parents. '<u>Do</u> please Sara dear get in touch with me or Dorothy,' John wrote:

In May 1966, John Pascoe attended an archivists' conference in Washington DC. He stayed in a hotel where the laundry was slow and expensive so, like many a traveller, he washed minor items of clothing in the handbasin. Later, while attending a reception for archivists at the White House, he hung his socks up to dry on a tree in the garden.

'I was photographed holding Lady Bird Johnson's hand in a long hold while I told her of my admiration for Eleanor Roosevelt,' John later wrote to his family. 'Got my first and only good cuppa at the White House. It is an awful, vulgar house in its furnishings, all explained to us by a guide from the White House police, but an original Whistler and Monet redeemed one room.'

DOROTHY PASCOE COLLECTION

It is all very well cutting yourself off, but you are adding strain to our lives that we should not have to take. I have been deeply and really anxious about you. It has been a worry without any relief. If you are okay – let us know; if you aren't, at least keep some kind of contact. None of us can live in a vacuum.[51]

In September 1965 Sara was readmitted to Porirua Hospital where she stayed for six months. On her discharge, John got her a job as an illustrator at the New Zealand Geological Survey where the Chief Palaeontolgist, Charles Fleming, kept an eye on her. After several months, however, he reported to John Pascoe that Sara 'would never be a satisfactory illustrator. As I have told her, she is too much (and I think too good) an artist to be an illustrator in science, and the sooner she either finds a job she can put her heart into, or if necessary, a job that merely serves to earn money (keeping her art as her spare time creative outlet) the better for her.'[52]

For the first time in six years, John Pascoe began work on a book, a history of South Westland – at the request of the publishers A. H. & A. W. Reed – to mark the opening of the new Haast Pass highway. In January 1966 he drove the new road in the company of Anna and Ian Gilmour and his youngest daughter, Jane. Then they returned to Haast Pass where they stayed in a roadman's abandoned cottage.[53] As Sara was still in hospital Dorothy was

Construction of the Haast Pass road began on the West Coast at Paringa in 1929 but it was not until 1955 that work began at Makarora, on the Otago side. In 1965, after more than three decades of persistent effort in the face of considerable difficulties, the two roads met at Clarke's Bluff (pictured), near the confluence of the Haast and Landsborough Rivers.

DOROTHY PASCOE COLLECTION

unable to accompany them, although she later joined them and they made a number of ascents in the vicinity before John returned to Wellington to be with Sara. Meanwhile Dorothy took the others to Wanaka where they made several further ascents, and to Lake Wakatipu where they climbed Mount Earnslaw. John was 'tickled pink' when he received the following telegram from Dorothy: 'RAIN SNOW SUN FOG CLIMBED LEARY EAST PEAK EARNSLAW ROCK BIV AT SIX HALF THOUSAND ALL WELL AND FRISKY'. He immediately wrote to Martha and Sara with the news and also rang Stan Conway and other climbing friends.[54]

It was an energetic start to a year that looked promising for John and Dorothy. Jane was about to move to Auckland to study music, and for the first time in their marriage, they could glimpse a life together without children. In December, Dorothy and John celebrated their new freedom by travelling to Christchurch where they stayed with Paul Pascoe, then to Otago to climb Mount Aspiring. On the first day they reached the Colin Todd Hut, above the Bonar Glacier. Next morning they set out very early by torchlight for the top. At 11 a.m., as they neared the summit, Paul Pascoe, who was working in his Christchurch office with his son, Simon, said: 'Can we have quiet for a moment. John is just approaching the summit of Mount

Mount Aspiring from Rolling Pin, a neighbouring peak. After John and Dorothy's ascent of Aspiring, which John considered to be 'the most beautiful mountain', they returned to the Colin Todd Hut. During the descent they were roped together. Dorothy later recalled in a radio programme, Mum, Dad and Mount Aspiring, that she 'had to keep an eye on her husband' who was 'chortling exuberantly' and taking big strides which almost pulled her off her feet.

DOROTHY PASCOE COLLECTION

Dorothy, aged 49, and John
Pascoe, aged 58, after their
ascent of Rolling Pin.
DOROTHY PASCOE COLLECTION

Aspiring.'[55] Their ascent and return took 15 hours, because an ice bridge
across a crevasse they had crossed in the morning had become unsafe in the
afternoon sun and a detour was necessary. Back at the Colin Todd Hut, John
and Dorothy celebrated with a whisky.

Two days later, they climbed a neighbouring peak called Rolling Pin.
A few days afterwards they set out to climb Plunket Dome on which they
encountered a beautiful alpine meadow full of flowers and soft mosses. John
had sudden reservations about completing the climb. 'Who was Plunket anyway? Just another English governor whose name should never have been
given to a mountain!' Instead they spent a romantic day relaxing in the sun.[56]

It was the first time in John Pascoe's life that he had willingly abandoned a peak. All his life he had striven for the top, both literally and
metaphorically. Some who knew him saw this as a sign of an inferiority
complex. Now, for the first time, he chose to relax, content to be with
Dorothy at the start of a different kind of life together.

CHAPTER TEN

When I'm Sixty-Five

The late 1960s were a time of protest, civil unrest and social change. In Paris students built barricades and battled police, in the United States race riots left cities looted and burning, and throughout the western world marchers took to the streets to oppose the war in Vietnam. Others eschewed activism and chose instead to follow the advice of the advocate of LSD (lysergic acid), Dr Timothy Leary, to 'tune in, turn on and drop out'. Popular music, particularly the songs of the Beatles, Bob Dylan and the Rolling Stones, exemplified the new mood.

John Pascoe, aged 60 in 1968, could remember horses and carts on the streets of Sumner. As a child, he was taken to a neighbour's place to hear the new wonder, radio, and playing the banjo encouraged an interest in music. His adult taste was eclectic; he enjoyed Bach, Mozart and Schubert, the sensual black American singer, Eartha Kitt, and the Beatles. In the late 1960s, the Pascoes bought a stereo and on Saturday nights when Dorothy and the girls were out, John would turn up the volume and listen to his favourites. John and his daughters also enjoyed playing music together.

Some of Pascoe's contemporaries objected to the Beatles. They disliked the long hair, psychedelic clothes, obvious disdain for authority and loud new 'electric' music. Yet there was no denying the influence of this group, especially their imaginative 1967 album Sergeant Pepper's Lonely Hearts Club Band. John Pascoe's favourite track, 'When I'm Sixty Four', had particular meaning for him. After 40 years behind a desk, he had his sights firmly fixed on his retirement in 1973, at the age of 65.

In anticipation, he and Dorothy were learning Spanish and saving so they could travel to and climb in South America.

From left: Sara (flute), John (banjo), Jane (violin) and Anna (recorder), Christmas 1968.

IAN GILMOUR PHOTO
DOROTHY PASCOE COLLECTION

I N THE 1972 RADIO PROGRAMME *Mr and Mrs Reminisce*, John and Dorothy Pascoe discussed their favourite music. John described the melding of music and the mountains in his mind: 'You've got these immense, almost timeless mountains all around you, and you feel the urge to climb them, and the exuberance and joy of life which, to me, would be expressed in musical terms by the vigour of a Haydn trumpet concerto. It opens with a terrific scale of triumph that, to me, is overcoming your tiredness and your fear.'[1]

As young mountaineers, John Pascoe and his CMC companions had their triumphs and their fears. Above all, they had the satisfaction of climbing and naming virgin peaks. Pascoe himself had 25 first ascents.[2] By the 1960s, however, most of New Zealand's notable mountains had been climbed and the more dangerous ridges traversed. Young climbers looking for new challenges turned instead to face climbing.

In the 1960s John Pascoe's role also changed. He climbed less frequently and became better known as an alpine authority and commentator. This was apparent in 1966 in the aftermath of a climbing disaster on the Otira face of Mount Rolleston. It was a popular climb, but even in fine weather it was a demanding ascent. On a fine Sunday in June four young men set out to climb the face. One was aged 18, the other three were 19. Two of them were New Zealanders from Christchurch, two from England. As they expected to be on the mountain for about six hours, they only had clothes for the climb and enough food for the day. When they had not returned to Arthur's Pass by the following morning the alarm was raised. At the same time the weather suddenly deteriorated. The wind rose. It began to snow. The blizzard continued without respite for days while dozens of searchers tried to rescue the young climbers in conditions that, as one searcher put it, 'no sane mountaineer would venture into'. After three days rescuers were heartened to hear cries from the face which suggested that at least some of the climbers were still alive, but with no prospect of reaching them, hopes for their survival began to fade.[3]

The alpine drama was front-page news. In Wellington the *Dominion* and *Evening Post* used photos of the Otira face supplied by John Pascoe, who also provided daily comment on the situation. Then the tragedy was compounded when an avalanche in the upper Otira Valley struck the tents of sleeping searchers. Rescuers rescued each other. But as they clawed through the freezing snow, they found that one of their number, John Harrison, was dead when he was pulled free. At this point further attempts to rescue the climbers were abandoned.

The Otira deaths, especially John Harrison's, shocked the New Zealand alpine community and revived perennial concerns about mountain safety. A New Zealand Alpine Club appeal for his wife and children, launched by Ed Hillary, raised £5,000 in less than a week. John Pascoe, who had known Harrison as a boy in Days Bay and had watched him develop into one of New Zealand's leading mountaineers, wrote a tribute in the *Evening Post*. After noting Harrison's achievements in Antarctica and the Himalaya, Pascoe argued that he would not have supported calls for the regulation of young climbers.

The Otira face of Mount Rolleston, from Mount Philistine, one of John Pascoe's earliest colour photographs.

DOROTHY PASCOE COLLECTION

Without knowing the full facts of their attempt, John Harrison would not have been over-critical of the youth and experience or inexperience of the four young climbers who came to climb the Otira Face of Mt Rolleston.

He would not have been crying for regulations to keep them from adventure or hazard. He had been taught years before as a young climber all about safety in the mountains. He took part in such courses as an instructor himself. He would have agreed that education and not prohibition is the answer to those who criticise the freedom with which the youth of New Zealand may approach mountaineering problems.[4]

In the years after the Otira tragedy, John Pascoe's increasing role as an alpine authority led to greater demands on his time and patience. He had always enjoyed his correspondence with a wide range of climbers, historians and writers, but his mail now also included numerous letters from strangers wanting to know some item of historical information or the best way to climb this or that mountain. The requested material was often already available in a Pascoe book. Nevertheless Pascoe always replied, although he could be sharp in referring enquirers to already published sources. Others sought advice about publication, or permission to use Pascoe's photos in their own books. These were the most time-consuming requests: Pascoe sometimes had to spend an evening finding a particular negative which he then had to have printed. All this took time that might otherwise have been spent on his own writing.

In March 1967, A. H. & A. W. Reed asked Pascoe to write the text for a sequel to the highly successful *New Zealand in Colour* books. The photographer, R. J. Griffith, had travelled throughout the country taking photos from the air and when Pascoe saw the results he agreed to write the accompanying descriptions. To do so, however, he had to curtail his correspondence. 'I have put personal letters aside for three months to write another book,' he explained to Harold Leov as the reason for a belated reply to a letter. 'I spent a month planning my research, a 2nd month doing it and a 3rd month writing it. I had meant originally to do only 3 nights a week on it and thus take about 5 months. But I got so interested in it I was doing an average of 6 nights a week and so finished ahead of schedule.'[5] The format of *New Zealand – From the Air* allowed Pascoe the freedom to write what he wanted. As each colour photo occupied a full page there was plenty of space opposite it for his commentary. He saw this as an opportunity to combine historical quotations with excerpts from a wide range of New Zealand poets, and also to include passages from one of his own poems, 'Aerial Mapping', which he had written in 1953 soon after his debut as a poet with 'Arawata Bill'. It was a bold move. On the opening page, for instance, a Pascoe stanza is included among lines from Fleur Adcock, Allen Curnow, Ursula Bethell and Ruth Dallas. 'I am keeping my fingers crossed that the publishers like it,' he confided to Leov, 'because I have not yet heard their verdict.' Fortunately they did. *New Zealand – From the Air* appeared the following year with Pascoe's verse intact.

It was several years since John Pascoe had written a book and it rekindled his enthusiasm. 'I enjoyed writing it so much,' he told publisher, Janet Paul, and immediately began planning another book. Its title, 'The Mountains The Mighty The White Ones', came from Ursula Bethell's poem 'Southerly Sunday' which he had used in *New Zealand – From the Air*. Poetry was

---

AERIAL MAPPING

Aircraft have flown, you say, with camera eye observing
All ridges, gulleys, rock, bush, gorge recorded
From constant height. Inconstant depth will flow into
   deception
till photographic image fixed on paper
Breeds contours, features.

Soar high above the hoary shoulders
Of mountain massif and let the wispy tarns emerge
As spots on spurland. Roar of engine
Blots out the blue of river noise
So far below in mask of forest.

The photographic strips will join.
Expert eyes and expert lenses
Contrive mosaic of patchwork quilt
To hide the land with new found knowledge.

Down there we forced a way through scrub
To gulfs of screes. The heavy loads
Were bloody heavy.
Blue mountain ducks knew no man
Till we disturbed their water frolic.

We camped and slept on mossy flat,
Boiled rice, saw starlight calm our sleep.
The dawn struck clear like limpid gaze of limpid lover.
Tired muscles crossed the pass where a profusion
Of flowers, gorges, despairing rivers
Spurred progress.

Sweaty work on glum red mountain
Crossed the unmapped Westland wastes.
But now the sky has aircraft song
To make the maps and tell the courses.
Of rivers, ranges, gorges, passes.

to play an even greater role; in fact, the entire text was written in free verse which described accompanying photos of Pascoe's transalpine trips of the 1950s and 60s. At times the subject matter suited verse, but at others it might have been better in prose. 'The Mountains The Mighty The White Ones' was written during the summer of 1967–68 and then sent to Reeds for publication. To Pascoe's surprise they rejected it, as did Whitcombe & Tombs. 'Bloody but unbowed', Pascoe then sent it to a literary agent in London but he, too, was unable to interest a publisher.[6] Despite these rebuffs Pascoe remained convinced of its value. 'It is the best thing I have done,' he told another alpine author, Paul Powell, 'and will have to be published posthumously if not in my lifetime.'[7]

At the age of 60, Pascoe had clearly decided it was time to realise his long-held ambition to win recognition as a poet. The attempt to broaden his literary persona occurred at a time when his distinctive identity as a mountaineer was unexpectedly threatened. For 40 years John Pascoe, or 'Johnny' as he was called by many of his climbing friends, had a unique image that made him a familiar figure both in the mountains and on the streets of Wellington. But in 1967, when Paul's son Jonathan made several ascents in the Mount Cook area, it seemed that John's identity might be confused with that of his nephew. John Pascoe was proud of Jonny's alpine achievements, but he worried that the subtle distinction between 'Johnny' and 'Jonny' was not made clear in an alpine journal. In a letter to Paul, John raised the issue and offered some suggestions as to how it might be resolved.

Paul Pascoe's second son, Jonny, on the summit of Mount McClure, in the Godley area, November 1969.

IVAN MACDONALD PHOTO,
JONATHAN PASCOE COLLECTION

Tell Jonny he and I will have to come to some gentleman's agreement about how we are referred to in alpine bulletins. The latest CMC one refers to Jonny's fine winter climb on Lendenfield and Haidinger, but as 'Johnny Pascoe'. Now that is confusing, because although I have not made such climbs they would not be impossible for me if I decided to for some reason. All my old cobbers know me as 'Johnny Pascoe' rather than John Pascoe and 'Johnny Pascoe' was even a newspaper headline in the Mount Evans days. So I think it should be 'Jonathan', 'Jonny' or whatever variant he prefers. After all he is not my son and we cannot very well adopt an expedient such as Johnny Pascoe Jnr or Johnny Pascoe II or Johnny Pascoe the second. Perhaps we should both combine in some big climb before I get too decrepit and then we could startle the alpine world by crediting the climb to 'Johnny Pascoe squared' or 'Johnny Pascoe plus' or something.[8]

John Pascoe's identity was further threatened the following year when Paul Pascoe began making regular trips to Wellington to work on plans for a new airport terminal at Rongotai. John was delighted to see his brother so regularly – 'we nibble a beer together once a week' – but Paul's presence also led to one twin being mistaken for the other. Neither enjoyed it. On earlier visits to Wellington, Paul had been abrupt when greeted by strangers on the street as John, and John was irritated when people mistook him for Paul. 'If I was wearing a Hereford Street suit and a pork pie hat [as Paul often did] it might be alright. But I don't. I'm not Paul. I'm John bloody Pascoe!'[9] When it started to happen again, John came up with a novel strategy. 'I get so fed up with people confusing us that I organised a *Town & Around* interview on TV with Paul and me, and tho brief it went quite well and has realised the purpose of telling many people there are two of us,' he wrote to Anna. 'Strangers say to me in the bus "which one are you today, dear; John or Paul!" ' For good measure, he also invited a local paper, the *Photo News*, to do a story on 'the general confusion about the Pascoe twins'.[10]

John Pascoe had always been happy to appear in the papers, on the radio and now on television. This willingness was described by his friend, Peter Maling, as 'a propensity for self-advertisement'.[11] Yet, as he understood very well, there were strict limitations on what a senior civil servant could discuss in the media. Nevertheless, he had strong opinions which he shared with some correspondents, in particular Harold Leov. He also worked behind the scenes to support Dorothy, whose activism was unfettered. In 1966, for example, John helped her to organise a Hiroshima Day anti-nuclear 'teach-in' at Victoria University and a similar event about anti-war poetry the following year. In 1968 he and Dorothy attended every session of the Peace, Power and Politics in Asia conference at Victoria University. 'It has been an eventful time all over the world,' he wrote to Leov. 'The USA is in for a lot of racial trouble, and if they spent less on Asian wars and more at home on

In January 1970 Jonny Pascoe and two friends made a traverse of the Silberhorn and Mount Tasman, the same climb that his uncle, John Pascoe, had twice attempted in 1936. Jonny Pascoe had read John's account of the ascent in Unclimbed New Zealand and felt that 'climbing Tasman was in a way unfinished business'.

During the traverse Jonny Pascoe 'thought of John a lot, and was pretty impressed that his party had descended the East face. It did not look appealing, particularly if one did not have ice screws and front point crampons.'

To climb Tasman was an ambition Jonny Pascoe had nurtured since he was a boy. 'I remember even as a 10 year old in Standard Four I would look with wonder and excitement at the mountain books and journals in Paul's bookcase. I often gazed longingly at the photo in John's book Great Days in New Zealand Mountaineering taken by H. E. L. Porter of Marcel Kurz on the summit of the Silberhorn looking out with the knife-like ridge to Tasman beyond, and thinking what an incredible place to be.'

Jonny always regretted that he never had an opportunity to climb with his uncle, 'but there was a definite mountain bond between us.'

JONATHAN PASCOE PHOTO

DOROTHY PASCOE COLLECTION

In 1968 John Pascoe (on the right in both photos) invited a local paper, the Photo News, to do a story on 'the general confusion about the Pascoe twins' and supplied the following notes:

THE PASCOE TWINS

Similarity	The difference with John	The difference with Paul
born 1908	3 hours older	
appearance identical in youth	left-hander	right-hander
	long distance runner	swims most of the year
both appreciate mountains and music	transalpine mountaineer and minor exploration	lower ranges
both deal with government at many levels	law clerk, later with Department of Internal Affairs as photographer, editor, Historic Places, Wildlife, chief archivist of National Archives	pioneer in contemporary design — special interest in churches and terminal buildings of airports
both have an interest in New Zealand history	some 15 books and non-books including unpublished verse	NZ Institute of Architects and art societies
	Geographic Board	
travel	only in USA for Archives	twice round the world for airports
domesticated	4 daughters pipe smoker a good peasant	3 sons non-smoker
long term view	preserve raw material for NZ history; access for scholars	leave good buildings behind

social welfare they could do better.' Nor did he think much of the Russians, who would soon invade Czechoslovakia. 'I don't think there is much to choose between the two great powers: America burning and bombing and shooting swathes of large peasant populations and the as great Russia threatening the whole basis of Czech industrial and intellectual life.' As the United States war with Vietnam became bogged down, opposition in the States and elsewhere grew and street protests were common. 'Dorothy marched along with some 4,000 other protestors in the Wellington streets a few weeks ago,' John Pascoe told Laurie Walker. 'I would march too but my worry is that if I got labelled it could be awkward at National Archives where I often have to negotiate things at fairly high government levels. Still, I think it is a great pity that we tag along in Vietnam and we have no right to be there. When I have retired I will then be able to stand up and be counted as one of the protestors against this unjust war.'[12]

One issue Pascoe was prepared to discuss publicly was compensation to authors for the use of their books by libraries. As a member of the writers' group, PEN, Pascoe did newspaper and radio interviews about the proposal (known as the Public Lending Right) in an effort to win public support. Paradoxically, one of the scheme's harshest critics dined at the Pascoes' table most weekends. Dorothy's elderly father had a particular envy of his son-in-law's success as a writer. 'John is a great one for advertising himself,' Guy Harding wrote to Elsie Locke. 'In the Dominion's "Letters to the Editor" he had one boosting an author's claim to a percentage for library books lent out. Ridiculous, I think, although he says it operates in Sweden.' In a later letter, Harding revealed the depth of his dislike. 'John P. is everlastingly impressing his importance as a writer, a mountaineer, a know-all. I got fed up and cancelled my visits for the last 8 weeks. Have heard that he is a joke in literary circles and most likely not taken seriously as a mountaineer. Ain't I horrid!'[13]

Pascoe was probably relieved to have a respite from Harding's weekend visits, especially since it was often he who drove into Wellington to collect Harding from the Harry Squires Hostel and repeated the journey to return him in the evening. At the time, Pascoe was so busy at Archives that he was working on Saturdays as well as weekdays dealing with the papers of the late Sir Walter Nash. During Nash's long political career he had kept much of the paper that crossed his desk and most of it ended up in his house in Lower Hutt. Soon after his death in 1968, Pascoe and other government officials gathered at the house to decide how to deal with the 14 tons of paper. 'The discussion was long and discursive,' Pascoe reported to Internal Affairs. 'It was stimulated by a glimpse of the great accumulation, in an orderly though cramped manner, in the garage, the study and a bedroom at the Nash home.' In the following weeks, books and periodicals were removed to the National Library; the remaining 8 tons was shifted to Archives in a single Saturday. 'It was a long, hard graunchy day,' John wrote to Dorothy in Hawke's Bay, 'and I was not worth a tin of fish at the end of it.'[14]

The arrival of the Nash papers exacerbated an already critical lack of space at National Archives. The temporary premises in Borthwick House on the Terrace were full within two years of moving there, and no progress had been made on the proposed new building because of the government's lack of interest. By May 1968, shortly before Nash's papers were acquired, the corridors of the two floors leased by Archives were clogged with Marine Department files awaiting appraisal. Pascoe arranged to lease two floors in an adjacent building, but his application for the necessary additional funds was not approved. Consequently, more piles of records were stacked in hallways creating 'a fire hazard, hindering reference staff and cleaners and attracting vermin'. To make matters worse, the Marine Department repeatedly refused to cooperate. For example, some indication of the importance (or otherwise) of each file was required before a decision could be made to keep it or destroy it, but no one in the Marine Department bothered to keep appointments with Archives staff. After a year of being ignored, an archivist demanded of the department: 'Either these records are important or they are not important and Archives appraisal could then lead to their disposal'.[15]

A similar situation threatened the efficacy of the Records Centre in Lower Hutt, an outpost of National Archives, where recent departmental records were stored for speedy retrieval, if required. In 1968 the Social Security Department dumped a huge amount of non-archival material at the centre, then refused to shift it. Pascoe protested. But like the Marine Department, Social Security simply did not care. Only after Pascoe had complained to the State Services Commission did it agree to remove some items and allow others of limited archival value to be destroyed. In his regular 'Activity Report' to Internal Affairs, Pascoe noted that 'the area at the Records Centre occupied by dead or duplicate material (as though it was a warehouse and not a place in which to store or hold semi-current records or public archives) could thus be cleared in a few months to the great benefit of National Archives and the Records Centre.'[16] Ironically there are archivists, working today in far better conditions, who have criticised Pascoe for approving the destruction of some departmental records.

Although these problems took up much of Pascoe's time, he also endeavoured to develop National Archives. For instance, he tried to persuade the Statistics Department to allow Archives to keep (or at least to microfilm) data collected in the 1966 census for future use by researchers, but this was opposed by the Government Statistician on the grounds that the information must remain confidential. Nor was Pascoe successful in his attempt to establish an oral history archive. The recent deaths of the influential trade union leader Fintan Patrick Walsh and the businessman Sir Charles Norwood prompted Pascoe to make a list of significant public figures whose recollections should be recorded. He also lined up a political science graduate to do the interviews, but Internal Affairs declined to approve the $8,000 that would be required.[17]

As always, John Pascoe found relief and renewal in the mountains. In January 1969 he and Dorothy joined Anna and Ian, who had recently returned from several years overseas, on a climbing holiday in the Ahuriri Valley, between Lakes Ohau and Hawea. The holiday was a great success and was notable for two reasons: first, for climbing Mount Barth by a face route rather than a ridge (this was John's first face climb apart from his dramatic and unintended descent of the east face of Tasman in 1936), and second, for marking John Pascoe's debut as a colour photographer. During the 1950s and 1960s his tramping friends had gradually switched to colour film, but Pascoe had persisted with black and white because photos in books, newspapers and magazines were rarely printed in colour. This began to change in the 1960s and his involvement with books such as *New Zealand in Colour – Volume Two* and *New Zealand – From the Air* encouraged him to consider colour

Ian Gilmour took this photograph of John Pascoe in the Ahuriri in 1969. Later it was used for the author's portrait in Exploration New Zealand. In a letter to his daughters, John commented that 'you can just about smell the sweat in the photo'.

DOROTHY PASCOE COLLECTION

photography. In the United States in 1966 he had bought a new Rolleicord and he now carried two cameras in the mountains: one for black and white, and one for colour.

The Ahuriri was his first real opportunity to take colour photos. On his return to Eastbourne, he sent some to the *Auckland Weekly News*, which had a colour section. 'I have of course a large selection of monochrome negatives but I thought you would be more interested in colour,' he told the editor, who chose six of his photos for a double-page spread entitled 'Family Mountain Climb'. Pascoe was pleased. 'I liked the good bold layout, and also the reproduction. Many people spoke favourably about the feature. I was greatly encouraged by their publication.'[18]

Further good news followed. Mike Gill, who had led the climb of the Ramsay face of Mount Whitcombe in 1962, wrote to explain that Pascoe's *Unclimbed New Zealand* had inspired the epic ascent, which was to be described in Gill's forthcoming book *Mountain Midsummer*. Gill's letter included the following excerpt from the text: 'It was from Pascoe's book we had the idea of climbing the face for the cover photo shows, on a jagged rock ridge, two climbers, one with ice-axe aloft, against the backdrop of the Ramsay Face. In an earlier guidebook to the region he [Pascoe] thought the face was "likely to remain inviolate", but in a later edition he spoke of "new challenges awaiting the coming generation". That was us.' Gill also described how *Unclimbed New Zealand* had been a model for his own volume. 'A letter such as yours is a good reward for writing a book,' Pascoe replied. 'Not that one needs a reward, and many people take it for granted that a writer will know that they like his work, but how will he ever know unless they tell him?'[19]

In his reply, Pascoe also mentioned a special accolade. 'Recently Denis Glover wrote some unpublished verse to me; that is the sort of event that makes me feel good.' The poem, 'To John Pascoe', is typical Glover verse; its deceptive simplicity skilfully evokes a time (the early 1930s) when both Glover and Pascoe were members of the CMC. But whereas Pascoe was at the forefront of the club's alpine adventures, Glover was only an occasional mountaineer for whom 'the Rubicon snow' of the Torlesse Range was about his limit. During a winter traverse of Mount Rolleston in 1932, for example, Glover found himself climbing the mist-shrouded summit ridge (with the more experienced Rod Hewitt), which left him feeling 'green and terribly frightened'.[20]

'To John Pascoe', first published in the *Listener* in 1969, has since become Pascoe's memorial.

> Johnny, Johnny,
> I stumbled many a mile
> While you wafted on ahead
> With a twitch of a smile.
>
> You whistled in the dawn,
> Johnny, Johnny:
> The keas waddled off in scorn
> And I produced a mighty yawn.
> Johnny, Johnny.

You left me in the Rubicon snow,
Johnny, taciturn Johnny,
While you poked round for
A corn-cob pipe
You had left there years ago.

You taught me to cross a river,
Johnny,
In a way crafty and clear.

What more can I say of the mountains,
Johnny,
What more of the mountaineer?

Glover wrote this poem when he was at a low point in his life. His long-time partner, Khura Skelton, had recently died, he had lost his job and was in financial difficulty.[21] He and Pascoe met regularly at PEN meetings and sometimes enjoyed a few drinks afterwards. Pascoe had always liked Glover, understood him, and was not perturbed, as some of the literati were, by the poet's antics. Glover's poem was an appreciation of that long and steady friendship.

At this time Pascoe's life, by contrast, was going exceptionally well. He and Dorothy enjoyed being on their own. Anna and Ian had bought a house in Christchurch and were expecting their first child. Sara had recently gone to Burma (Myanmar) where she had a married a Burmese, Than Tun, whom she had met while he was a Colombo Plan student in Wellington. Martha was immersed in her job on a thoroughbred stud in the Wairarapa and Jane was making good progress as a music student in Auckland. At last, John and Dorothy were free to concentrate on their own lives.

In August 1969, John travelled to Salt Lake City to attend a conference on the preservation of records. 'We have documents in Wellington that we can't let people use until they're properly repaired,' he told the *Christchurch Star*. 'Early maps of the Lands and Survey Department and immigration lists, for example.'[22] As it happened, the most useful and stimulating aspect of his trip was meeting Willa Baum, an oral history expert at the University of California at Berkeley. The feeling was mutual, leading to a regular correspondence after the conference. On his return, he was inspired to have another go at setting up an oral history project. But, as he told Baum, it was ultimately a political matter: 'I won't be able to do much about oral history archives here till after our general election in November, but once the new range of politicians has settled down and modulated their tail feathers into the straw on their non-brick making nests I shall reintroduce the subject to my department to get authority for such a programme.'[23] It was not, however, approved.

In the meantime, John Pascoe had plenty of other things to think about. If his work at National Archives was difficult and sometimes unproductive, the rest of his life was creative and rewarding. In September 1969, Reeds asked him to write 'a heavily illustrated book about New Zealand exploration'. He accepted the commission with delight and began planning and researching immediately. Later that month, Anna gave birth to a daughter, Dorothy and John's first grandchild. 'You have no idea how good it was to

'When Sue Harding used my camera to take a photo in colour of Dorothy and me and Melissa [the Pascoes' first grandchild] she got an absolute corker,' John told Anna and Ian. 'Beaut bush background. Dorothy shimmering with joy. Me patriarchially-proud. Melissa looking sweet and long as long with her length and legs dangling from Dorothy's expert hold.'

DOROTHY PASCOE COLLECTION

hear the news,' he wrote to Anna. 'It was evocative of that unforgettable day when you arrived and I was jumping for joy around Wellington and telling the tram-driver I was a father. I hope Ian is as proud a father as I was; it was a great feeling, and now I know you have produced your own Ian-and-Anna girl I feel so glad for you both.'[24]

Six weeks later a birth of a different kind also gave John Pascoe pleasure. Mike Gill sent him a copy of his newly published book, *Mountain Midsummer*, which had the following dedication on the title page: 'To John Pascoe, with thanks for your help – and in admiration of what you have written about New Zealand mountains and mountaineers'. Thanking Gill, Pascoe recalled the publication, 30 years earlier, of *Unclimbed New Zealand*: 'I can well remember the pride and joy I felt when I actually saw and handled my first book. My mother was annoyed with me when I emphasised that the experience was analogous with childbirth. All the pangs of proof-reading-gestation; you know the jazz I mean.'[25]

In Mandalay, Sara Pascoe was about to follow Anna's example. 'Sara is expecting a baby in May,' John told Willa Baum. 'She writes long, interesting and loving letters. She has only seen three Westerners since March last, so she must be making good progress with the Burmese language and her letters are full of honest and clear observations: the Buddhist attitude to death; her life and times in Asia.' At last it seemed to John Pascoe that 'the turmoil of living' involved in rearing a teenage family was well and truly behind them. 'Raising four daughters had its moments and months,' he reflected in the same letter, 'but as they got past the teens they came right.' With an empty nest and no family worries, he and Dorothy had their evenings free. One night a week they studied Spanish at a University Extension class and they also went

John Pascoe enjoyed reading books by the New York author, Tom Wolfe, including his portrait of the hippy world, The Electric Kool-Aid Acid Test, and his account of a meeting between Manhattan socialites and black American activists in Radical Chic and Mau-Mauing the Flak Catchers. In a letter to his daughters Martha and Jane, Pascoe described Wolfe as a 'SUPERDAG'.

to concerts and the cinema. 'The Wild Bunch is my pick of the best American films lately,' he wrote to Willa, 'it blows the frontier piety miles high and is bloody and violent, but what a beaut film for country, people, Spanish-speaking Indians and sheer excitement alternating with quiet places, like a Beethoven symphony with the pastoral bits modulating from orgiastic climaxes.' He was as enthusiastic about 'Thomas Wolfe's superb evocation of the hippy world, The Electric Kool-Aid Acid Test, which he admired for its vigour and writing style.[26]

For the Pascoes, however, the peace was brief. Six weeks after writing to Willa, John and Dorothy were again facing a challenging family situation. In April 1970 John told a friend, Hans Bohny of Arthur's Pass, that Martha 'has surprised us and probably herself by getting herself engaged. As we have only met the young fellow once we don't know much about him.' When Dorothy and John did get to know him, they were not impressed. 'He does his best to be nice, and in another context, could pass muster, but he seems to have little respect for Martha and it grates,' John told Anna. Unfortunately, their concern about Martha came at a time when Dorothy was at a low ebb and the anxiety made her worse. 'Dorothy had a pretty tough patch to get through this last weekend,' he continued, 'but after a visit to John Hardwick-Smith and some solid tranquillisers plus effective sleeping pills she is now getting along in low gear. The Martha business hit her hard — harder than me; and add to this the change-of-life business and a state lower-than-usual (because she had not been sleeping or eating well) the result was some anxiety.'[27]

As always, John was candid in writing to Dorothy's brother, Peter Harding. 'Now Dorothy has been to near-illness I am nowhere as anxious or bewildered as last time,' he said, referring to her 1957 breakdown. This time he was convinced that Martha's engagement had been the last straw. 'She is of course vulnerable to extra strain; the Martha impetuosity just added too much of a tip to the scales. As to Martha: I can just accept her kind of life tho I don't like it, but I'm damned if I want to see her tied by marriage. She and the boy are both a bit "wet", have the sad mask of gaiety of the marionette, have not found themselves or their values, and, in rejecting society, want to have some of its fortuitous benefits, but not to the point of study or understanding.'[28]

Nor was Dorothy's situation helped much by her father. 'She had rather an exhausting session with Chief Curmudgeon Harding who was being very nasty about me and fortuitously nasty about Judy [Dorothy's sister], Marjorie Farrant [a family friend] and others,' he wrote to Anna. A trip to see Butch Cassidy and the Sundance Kid was restorative, although John thought it was not as 'punchy or taut or purposeful or symphonic or symbolic or historic-epic-in-silhouette as The Wild Bunch'.[29]

With exquisite bad timing, of which she was not aware, Willa Baum chose this moment to ask the Pascoes if one of her teenage children could come to live with them for a year 'in a nice staid place where girls still wear dresses'. 'Rachel,' Willa wrote, 'is horse crazy and would like to help your horse-caretaker daughter. She is a good student, fairly helpful around the house, a very good hiker, and swimmer.' John was quick to reject the idea.

Martha Pascoe and Arakhan.

'I must say I was flabbergasted when you said you had bought a racehorse, and more so when I realised you want to race him,' John Pascoe wrote to Martha in Christchurch where she was working as a stablehand on a thoroughbred farm. 'This is a great hobby for a rich farmer or an industrialist like one of the Fletchers or the Watties but for a working girl with no capital how the hell do you pay for things over and above essentials of feed and grazing? Such as registration fees, riding fees, jockeys clothes, vet services and transport.

'If in retirement I told you that I proposed to set up as a publisher of books,' he continued, '(publishing books is the quickest way I know to lose money even if the author and bookseller get a bit of money sometimes) I hope that you would have me on and say "don't be a goat". Similarly I want to have you on. Dorothy is writing for herself. I am writing for myself. Whether we say the same thing I don't know because our letters will be independent of each other. But if I squawk like this now it is because it gives me the horrors.'

DOROTHY PASCOE COLLECTION

'I hope you find a place for Rachel for a year,' he replied. 'I am sorry that we cannot provide such. We have no daughters living at home now, and Rachel needs, I imagine, a lively family including people of her own age group. It would be awful to be stuck with us and no young ones around.' He also explained that 'Dorothy was getting dangerously near a breakdown'.[30]

On a wet evening in September 1970 Dorothy was driving along Thorndon Quay when she had to slow down for a double-parked truck. Without warning, a van behind her crashed into her car, shunting it under the tray of the truck. Fortunately, the car's windscreen stopped just short of the truck's tray, otherwise she would have been seriously injured or killed. Even so, the Pascoes' car was a write-off. Dorothy remained calm, but in the weeks afterwards her sleep was disrupted night after night by the slow motion replay of the accident. Unfortunately, the event coincided with a change in her medication. In a letter to Martha, who had ended her unsatisfactory relationship and was now driving a horse float in Westland, John explained the situation:

> Dorothy has had a bad time as the new drug did not take as expected, and the withdrawal from the old one was in itself an upset. Added to that, the sleeping pills did not hold their efficacy. So after visits to Dr Hardwick-Smith and

at times after telephoning him when we thought the distress call was essential he finally decided that the best way out was a modified course of ECT, ie Shock Treatment.

This differs from the similar treatment that Dorothy had in 1957. The number of treatments is less; the after effects (such as having to walk the same day 2 miles to avoid muscle cramps) are far less; the effect on Dorothy's memory will be nothing like last time when the treatment put a lot of her then-anxieties blurred and into recess but messed up her other memory as well.

When the series of treatments is over (which will probably be soon) Dorothy will be able to drive again.[31]

John Pascoe's confidence was further challenged by bad news from elsewhere. The deaths of two climbing companions from his early days were just the beginning of a succession of deaths of people who had been important to him. Writing to tell Stan Conway that their old friends Arthur Pearson and John Clegg had died, John Pascoe admitted, 'To have lost John and Arthur in the same month has rather knocked me.'[32] Two months later Monty McClymont, the historian of exploration who had helped John with *Mr Explorer Douglas*, also died. In a letter to his widow, John recalled, 'My own father died of angina in a few minutes when he was only 48 years old and I was 18 years (I was playing Rubinstein's Melody in F on the banjo at the moment when he died). But I remember so well how it took my mother an awful long time to pick up the pieces. I know it is easy for me to be consoling when I am lucky to have Dorothy with amity and love still with me after 30 years of marriage,' he continued,

> But I have also faced up to the thought of what I would do without Dorothy, and its corollary, what would she do without me. My twin brother Paul's wife died last year but he recovered from that with relative facility because he and she had grown far apart in most ways. But Dorothy is so much more a close part of me now that I can understand how black your world is without Monty.
>
> I was glad that Monty was spared a long illness and pain. Of course you had good plans ahead, as everybody must have when they are happy in near-retirement. I hope to do many things with Dorothy, but whether we are spared to do them together is another matter and one which I cannot take for granted.[33]

In October 1970, John's old friend, David Hall, wrote from Dunedin that he had recently had an operation for cancer. 'I hope the deep ray treatment is very beneficial,' John replied. 'You sound quite philosophical about your illness.' He added that he also had been in hospital — to have all his teeth removed — because 'the roots are all tangled up like macrocarpa stumps'.

> I had 3 nights in Calvary myself and although I looked a mess and my face was swollen it was not too bad a performance. I hope to have the falsies in 2 weeks from now. I have got on quite well as the fangless man; have trained myself to give Paul's mysteriously benign smile instead of a wide and toothless grin. Have been able to enunciate okay without fangs and even had to give a vote of thanks at the NZAC.

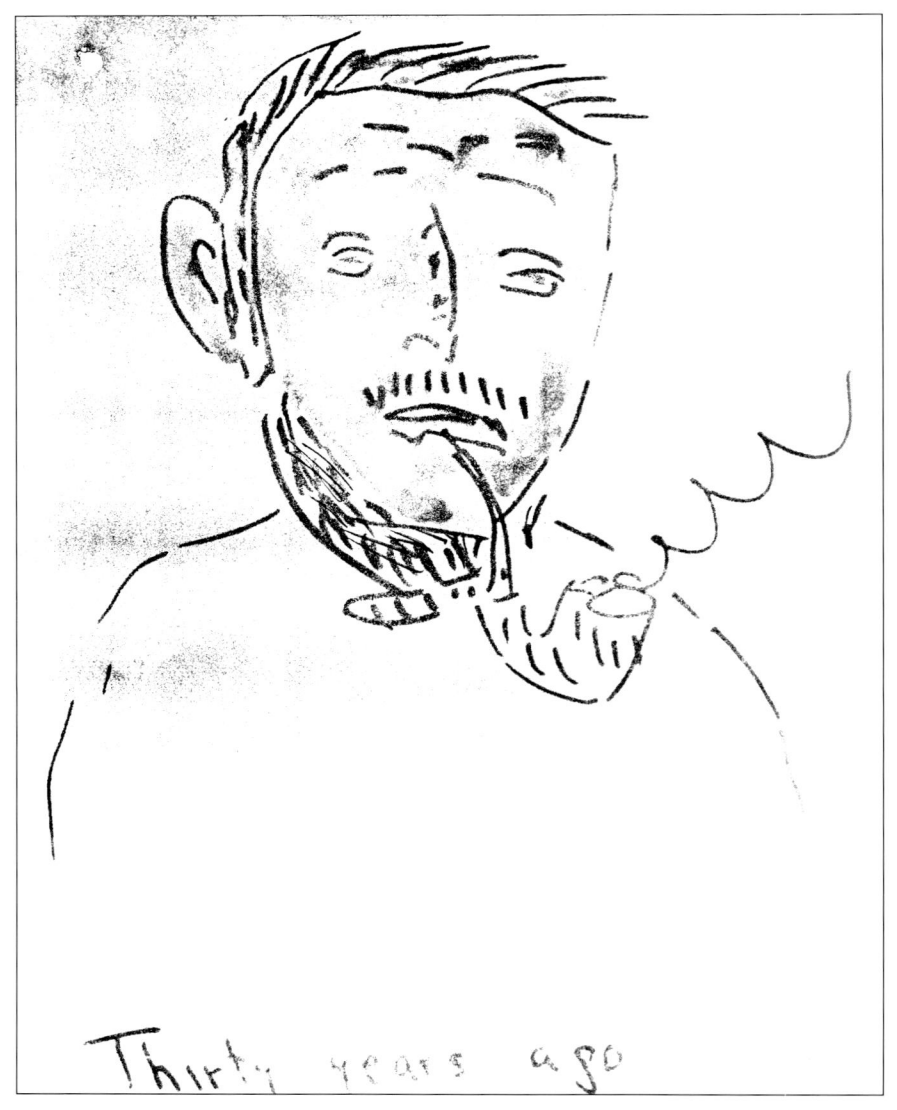

Thirty years ago

'A Cambridge Primary School has asked many non-artists (the crypto-famous, the famous, the pseudo-famous, the very famous, the non-famous and the infamous) to do a painting to be auctioned for school funds. They asked me (I don't label myself as which famous),' John Pascoe told Anna in April 1970. 'I was all set to "do my thing" but found alas that Martha had decamped with Dorothy's poster colours. So I will have to buy marking pens to assure my fame in artists' Valhalla.'

DOROTHY PASCOE COLLECTION

> As I get older I realise we all live on borrowed time. At my present age of 62 years it rocks me to think that my father died when he was only 48. Also I think the knowledge of the borrowed time spurs me along to try to do things with what I have left.[34]

'Things', of course, included writing more books. At the time John had three in different stages of production. 'I have now passed all the proofs etc. of the enlarged revised *National Parks of New Zealand* (colour photos and text) for the Government Printer; in this edition I emerge on the title page as editor,' he told David Hall. He was also pleased to report that after being rejected by five publishers, his book of transalpine photos and free verse had been accepted by John McIndoe Limited. 'Of *Unknown New Zealand* (this title has superseded 'The Mountains The Mighty The White Ones') is very close to my heart. Furthermore I am now writing diligently in my spare time on a new photo exploration book for Reeds which has taken me a year and a half to plan and a long time on research.'

During the worst of Dorothy's breakdown John was distracted from his writing, but as she improved he returned to his typewriter. 'I am managing to write about an hour in the evening till I get tired and have to lapse into reading light thrillers or looking at TV,' he told Anna and Ian. 'But at 5 am I write like a bird on the wing and fly freely.'[35] By December 1970 *Exploration New Zealand* was finished. This was fortunate, because the brief period of calm that had enabled him to complete it was soon followed by more family problems. One of them was Guy Harding. 'Pop's fight at the hostel recently damaged an optical nerve set and blinded one eye, so that is an additional problem with him now; little sight in one eye and nearly deaf in two ears,' John informed Anna, wryly observing, 'Perhaps he may feel less like having a punch-up if he cannot see his opponents. But Samson fought when he was blind in the Temple!'[36]

Sara, in Burma, was of even greater concern. In May 1970 she had given birth to a daughter, Melinda, and at first she seemed to be flourishing but soon her letters changed. Before Melinda's birth, her correspondence had been detailed and observant and she had also recorded a regular 'Burma Report' for Jessica Weddell's National Radio programme. Now her letters were brief notes devoid of description, and there were no more tapes. In December 1970 the Pascoes received a cable from Sara's husband: SARA IS VERY ILL. SHE WANTS BOTH OF YOU TO COME AND TAKE HER BACK BRINGING BABY. John tried to telephone Sara, but as Burma was not linked to the international network he was unsuccessful. The Pascoes then decided to fly to Burma, but it was virtually closed to foreigners, and entry visas were difficult to arrange, especially at short notice. After three days of hectic preparations John and Dorothy left for Burma via Bangkok where they were luckily able to obtain visas to enter the country. When they eventually reached Sara and Than's flat in Mandalay 'Sara was at the head of the stairs; wan and listless,' John recalled in his 'Notes on a Journey'. 'The baby, seven months Melinda (Ma Khin Mu), was in fine condition. An Indian girl was cooking. Than, we found, was on leave without pay to nurse Sara. He was due for an operation himself, the call for our arrival had been a necessary one, and now we had time both to get the flavour of Mandalay and the need to work out the drill for getting Sara and Melinda out of Burma.'[37] With persistence John and Dorothy got the necessary papers to allow Sara and Melinda to leave the country. On Christmas Eve they all arrived in Sydney and spent the next few days with Peter Harding and his family.

Safely back in Eastbourne, John reflected that 'Dorothy and I certainly had had a pipe-opener for our overseas travel'. But as the costs of 'the Burma Rescue' were tallied up, they realised it had wiped out their savings, intended to pay for their trip to South America when John retired. Furthermore, they now had Sara and Melinda living with them which added to the household expenses. Nevertheless, John hoped that future royalties might still enable them to travel. 'Dorothy won't be able to do any [screen] printing while she is nursing Sara and practising her Dr Spock

BURMA RESCUE

When John and Dorothy Pascoe visited Burma in 1970
they stayed with Sara Pascoe and her husband, Than Tun.
Once they had arranged permits and air tickets for Sara and
her baby daughter to leave Burma, John and Dorothy
climbed the Mandalay Hill. In his 'Notes of a Journey' John
recalled the experience:

> From the flat balcony we could see a pagoda on a spur of
> the hill, but I realised we were looking at the gable end of
> a ridge which would climb higher still. This was the hill
> of many pagodas and two thousand (or more) steps. We
> did not take any short cuts but we memorised landmarks.
> It was not unlike climbing a mountain when each new
> bump on the ridge seems like the top — till you get there;
> then, inexorably, the ridge goes up to yet another top, and
> so on. After some twelve pagodas, and some giant and
> impressive golden Buddhas, we did reach the highest point,
> when we looked out across plains to the Irawaddy and
> north-east to the hills and the coffee planting country.

> Chipmunks rattled around the roof, occasionally girl
> flower sellers sang intoned songs, a few monks passed one
> way or another and we scampered down the way we had
> come, not wishing to cause Than anxiety by coming home
> in the dark. We heard a series of staccato shouts that we

DOROTHY PASCOE COLLECTION

> took for monkish chants but learnt later they were at a
> police barracks where men were taught crowd control. We
> both felt that the experience of climbing the Mandalay
> Hill had been worth coming a long way; the pilgrim
> atmosphere was paramount; the sincerity of the friendly
> people undimmed.

refresher course on Ma Khin Mu but my books will help later and I hope
we can travel again on retirement when I get 5 months leave on full pay,'
he told Anna.[38]

Within a few months, however, Pascoe seemed less certain of his
future and his correspondence had a new, harder tone. In response to one
of the many requests he received for photographs, which he normally
treated kindly, he wrote: 'Don't think I am being too ungracious when I
say that this is the last time I will be able to help anyone else illustrate a
book. In my spare time I have three books going through the press, and,
believe me, they get me up early in the mornings for weeks at an end
sometimes. I feel my own books must now take precedence.' Then, as a
postscript, he added:

> Will send the photos when they are done. If you want to see what I mean about
> illustrating other people's books as well as my own look at the Porter's book
> *Under the Nor'West Arch*, Sutherland's *Hunting Guide to Westland*, many of Peter New-
> ton's mustering books, Mike Gill's mountain book, *School Journals*, and
> post-primary bulletins, *New Zealand Geographer*, Banwell's stalking books, New-
> ton, McConochie's stalking books, and many others.[39]

Pascoe's new attitude was also apparent when he declined an invitation to write a biography of the alpine guide, Frank Alack. 'While I am
flattered that you have entrusted your manuscript to me,' he replied to

Alack, 'and that you consider I would be capable of editing your work and writing your biography, I am sorry to have to refuse both tasks.'[40] In the past Pascoe had been an enthusiastic helper on similar projects, for example assisting the daughter of Gerhard Mueller to edit her father's letters, which were published as *My Dear Bannie* in 1958. Five years later, while recovering from a hernia operation, he also helped Mrs H. B. Hewitt finish the autobiography of the alpine guide, Peter Graham, who had died while the work was incomplete. Pascoe wrote a wide-ranging foreword and an extensive epilogue.

John Pascoe had never thought of writing an autobiography himself, at least until 19 May 1971 when he 'went on camera in WNTV1 studio for about 10 minutes with Judy somebody [Fyfe]. She asked me questions about my writing and my books. I liked her and the interview went well,' he told Laurie Walker. Additional filming was done at the Pascoes' home in Eastbourne: 'the background of the house and bush and Dorothy and Melinda added a necessary perspective and dimension to my work'. When the programme was shown a few weeks later Pascoe was delighted with the result. 'Our *On Camera* on WNTV1 rolled for twenty minutes yesterday and it was lively and came over well,' he told Anna and Ian. 'There was a very natural shot of goodwife Dorothy, a glimpse of Sara, a close-up of lush, limpid lambent glowing Melinda and enough of me to make even me think it was high time I stopped talking.' A month later, in a letter to Jane, John revealed that once he had his three books currently being prepared for publication out of the way, 'Then I will leave authorship alone for 2½ years as I want a fallow period in case I want to write an autobiography one day.'[41]

Thoughts of chronicling his life may also have been a response to the deaths of two friends who had greatly influenced Pascoe's intellectual interests in earlier times. In October 1971 Dr John Beaglehole died. Pascoe attended his memorial service which was 'without any religious rites which I personally found bleak. After the quasi-service we went up to the home and talked of him lovingly. He was a great prose writer, a poet, an appreciator of music, a historian (Cook) and in all senses a man of great integrity and humanity whom I am so proud to have known and worked with.'[42] The same sentiments applied to David Hall who died a few weeks later. Hall had been a loyal friend for more than 30 years and a perceptive and helpful critic of Pascoe's prose and verse. Now Pascoe had the sad task of writing Hall's obituary for the *New Zealand Alpine Journal*, which he began with one of Hall's own poems, 'On Holiday Thinking of the Dead'.[43]

Grief and reflection were soon assuaged, however, by the publication of Pascoe's three books at the end of 1971. His cherished *Of Unknown New Zealand* was the first to appear. As usual, reviewers were enthusiastic about his photography but less so about his free verse. The *Christchurch Star*, for instance, remarked that 'Mr Pascoe has written short prose poems. These are an interesting innovation but difficult to get used to, and the limitations of the form seem greater than its advantages.' The *Press* was less charitable. 'All in all the verse is a sad mistake. For the photographs' sake, it is better to treat the text as mislineated prose, extract the information it offers, and forget the rest. For it is the photographs that count; the photographs and the climbing

OF UNKNOWN NEW ZEALAND

John Pascoe's book of free verse and alpine trip photos was dedicated to 'Sara and Than Tun of Mandalay and their daughter Melinda (Khin Mu)'. It begins with the following poem:

Of Unknown New Zealand
Where transalpine ways
Give more than ice and rock.
Transalpine ways give bush and river;
Less alpine achievement;
But more travel;
Less fame but more variety.
Explorers' sweat has fused into mist.
Footprints of men have been covered
By ragged deer trails,
In the pages that follow.
Here is the land where no tourist goes;
Consider the landscape
Primeval.

Of Unknown New Zealand
JOHN PASCOE

'I was thrilled because an advance copy of Exploration New Zealand has now turned up,' John Pascoe wrote to his daughters in November 1971. 'It is good from the dustcover by Heaphy [of explorers canoeing on the Pelorous River] to the gold leaf block design by Sara of an explorer [on the hardcover] to the 8 pages of colour and the many photos and monochrome sketches. Ian's portrait of me in the Ahuriri in 1969 looks well on the inside of the dustjacket flap.'

In August 1971 Exploration New Zealand was one of eight finalists in the Wattie Book Awards. 'This is a great thrill for me because it is public recognition by my fellow countrymen,' he wrote to Jane. 'I am very happy to be in the eight, irrespective of whether I get any higher than that. It is a big lift for me and my publishers that I am in the list of eight when 32 of the 40 had to be eliminated.' When the three prizewinners were announced, Pascoe's book was not among them.

achievements that they record.'[44] Perhaps the saddest mistake of all was the publisher's choice of a cheap, rough-surfaced offset paper which made all but the strongest images dull and dark. But a positive response from Peter Harding bolstered Pascoe. 'Peter has been very appreciative of my free verse,' he wrote to Martha. 'He is a frank and honest critic and has never hesitated to tell me if I have not pulled something off. So when he says I have succeeded I take that at face value, as genuine. Hooray.'[45]

Next published was *Exploration New Zealand*. Pascoe had a particular hope for its release. 'Could I please make bold and suggest that if the publication date proves feasible before Xmas, that you consider my having a "launching party"?' he asked Reeds. 'This is my 16th book and I can honestly say that I have never had such an affair. I further consider that this book is worthy of an event or happening.'[46] Reeds obliged with a function at which the speaker was Priestley Thomson, who had been with Pascoe on the first ascent of Mount Evans. He told the gathering that Pascoe 'knew the New Zealand landscape, the wilderness and back country probably better than anyone else'.[47] Critics and reviewers agreed, universally praising *Exploration New Zealand* for its imaginative accounts of early exploration and its excellent illustrations. The *Evening Post* noted that 'John Pascoe has worked for so long among the records and writings of the men whose tales he relates in *Exploration New Zealand* that he dreams he is with them'.[48]

Pascoe's third book to be published that year and his second to be launched in December, *National Parks of New Zealand*, was also well received, although as a revised edition rather than a new book it did not attract the same attention as either *Of Unknown New Zealand* or *Exploration New Zealand*. He was

This popular volume, first published in 1965, was written by John Pascoe and others. Six years later he revised the second edition and in 1972 he was asked to edit the third edition, but never completed the work.

relieved to see all three finally published. 'Man is mortal and I wrote as tho each weekend was my last and I did not want to die with unfinished work,' he wrote to Alan Bibby, a filmmaker and family friend. 'Now they are finished I can live another twenty years – perhaps.'[49]

Pascoe had written to Bibby to congratulate him. 'Your film of Patagonia was superb – lyrical and everything was right. Good commentary; guitar music just perfect; backlit shots and halation of colour wizard. A beautiful film and one of the best I have ever seen.' Little did Pascoe realise that he, too, would soon be involved in making a film. In November 1971, Peter Coates, a promising young television producer making documentaries for the NZBC, asked Pascoe to appear in a programme about kea. Coates was fascinated by kea, especially people's responses to them. They either loved them or hated them. Every back-country person Coates consulted had a story about kea. Tony Nolan, a veteran tramper and raconteur, was a typical example. Coates filmed him describing his recipe for cooking a kea:

> Keas are protected now but for many years they were fair game. Mountaineers used to eat them but only when they were really desperate because the keas, like the mountaineers, were as tough as old boots.
>
> To cook a kea you first pull out all its feathers then put it in a pot about half full of water. On top of the kea, place a large round stone to stop it bobbing about. Bring the water to the boil then simmer it for about 5 to 6 hours. Then throw away the kea and eat the stone![50]

Another contributor was John Kendrick, who worked for the Wildlife Service and had a pet kea. Left at home on his own the kea was lonely, so Kendrick took him to work each day. Coates filmed the kea hopping about in Kendrick's office. He also made trips to Nelson Lakes and Arthur's Pass to film kea. On his return, Coates asked John Pascoe to introduce and conclude the documentary. With typical enthusiasm, Pascoe accepted the invitation and spent a day filming his part. The programme was screened on national TV in May 1972. Pascoe was delighted with the result, as were the reviewers. In the *Evening Post*, Catherine de la Roche commented that 'there has never been anything like the *Survey* documentary about the kea, *Prince of Nosey Parkers*. For me the marvellous pictures of this clownish – in some ways dangerous and constantly entertaining – mountain parrot with the witty and realistic comments add up to the best animal film I've seen since Lord Snowdon's "Love of a Kind".' The *Dominion* was also impressed. Beneath the headline 'An outstanding documentary', the television critic noted that in 'opening *Survey*'s *Prince of Nosey Parkers* John Pascoe charmingly left the kea to introduce himself. This made me realise that nothing I could put in a review would begin to convey the quality of kea performances so beautifully caught by the cameras.' The *Christchurch Star* thought that 'hard-case climber Tony Nolan probably stole the show with his detailed recipe for cooking kea', and the *Press* provided a lengthy description of how the documentary was made. The media attention was justified: *Prince of Nosey Parkers* was the NZBC's first foray in the field of natural history, and it was also Coates' first experience of working in colour.[51]

By a rather remarkable coincidence John Pascoe had to share the limelight with his brother. The same week the kea documentary was screened,

PRINCE OF NOSEY PARKERS

In December 1971, John Pascoe spent a day's leave filming his part of the Prince of Nosey Parkers, then tentatively titled 'Folk Lore of the Kea'. Soon afterwards, he described the experience in a 'round robin' letter to his dispersed daughters.

I got up at 5 am, my usual time these days, and tidied up my work a bit, then clocked in at TV House where producer Peter Coates and Tony Nolan (fellow victim) had a good gander at the 900 ft of film 'Folk Lore of the Kea' in colour. I had to provide an opening and some of the links; Tony had to do some links but not as many as mine; Tony and I had to provide the climax. To do this we went out to Wilf Wright's pottery at Reikorangi near Waikanae. We had Roger, a cameraman, Keith a sound man, and Robyn, a clapper-girl + Peter Coates as head sherang.

It was a hard graunchy day. Everything has to be just right for colour TV and each of the five filmings with which I was concerned had to be done perhaps ten or more times. You can imagine how weary and tired and browned off you get, but you have to rise above it and to get full of vim and spontaneity even the 12th time. I will tell you what the troubles were. For example, my intermission about Anna and the keas in the Waimak and the recorder music. I began by quoting Douglas, saying the cry of the kea was like the "wail of a lost spirit" and my own description of it as a sad haka of curiosity and triumph; my account of the Waimak episode; my reference to keas as composers "in the modern idiom, ie electronically". Well, you must realise it went like this:

first time — all went well till half way thru when a passing car noise messed up the sound; began again;

second time — an aeroplane messed up the sound; began again;

third time — I forgot an essential few lines (you had to memorise, not to read off scripts) — began again;

fourth time — a fly got in the tape recorder — began again;

fifth time — I stammered over a word badly — began again;

sixth time — cameraman ran out of film and had to change a reel;

seventh time — sound track man, ditto;

eighth time — a puppy rushed on the scene and barked perfection away;

Anna Pascoe plays her recorder to kea outside the Waimakariri Falls Hut, 1965.
DOROTHY PASCOE COLLECTION

ninth time — a child howled at its mum when she did not know we needed quiet;

tenth time — a tractor noise came across a field;

eleventh time — the wind rustled the trees too noisily;

twelfth time — quite good;

thirteenth time — a retake, "just in case". This went on from 1 pm to 5 pm and we did not get home till 7.30 pm. Boy was I tired.

This Survey programme 'Folk Lore of the Kea' will come on schedule sometime next year BUT we have to keep our fingers crossed that nothing will go wrong with the processing in Aussie. Ian MacDonald of Nelson is composing the music specially for this feature. Let us hope it is good.

I hope I haven't bored you with this account. It really was a very funny performance in retrospect; the funniest way I know of spending a day's leave.

Christchurch TV viewers saw a profile of Paul Pascoe on their regional programme. Paul described his and other people's responses in a letter to John.

> One lawyer was really moved to tears, one lady client said I was just 'acting',
> most said it was 'YOU' and humble. My own reaction was I felt a bit of a prick
> (excuse the language) it was so very personal. What came across well was the
> homespun philosophy. For example as I walked across the street into the office
> building here, I was taped as saying 'Lord Kelvin said when you are faced with
> a difficulty you are faced with a discovery'.
>
> What was good was that Brian Phillips the compere said 'like his well-
> known mountaineer brother and twin John Pascoe he has a great love for the
> mountains.[52]

John and Paul Pascoe's willingness to embrace the relatively new
medium of television was typical. Both had the same drive. Both were comfortable with publicity about their achievements and had what Dorothy
Pascoe called a 'sense of destiny'.[53] Dorothy herself was more reticent, as she
demonstrated in the radio interview, *Mr and Mrs Reminisce*. John described the
experience to Anna:

> Some 5 weeks ago a young woman from the NZBC (ie your age) rang me
> and asked if I would do a radio feature with Dorothy about the impact in
> our lives of MUSIC. Stupidly I did not get Dorothy in on the ground floor
> to learn all about it, but said "yes" we would do such a talk. Inevitably
> Dorothy got worried (a) because tho she is a fine talker she gets bothered
> by a mike; (b) she thought our knowledge of the subject was too thin to be
> interesting to anyone else. Eventually I got her more acquiescent, in degree,
> but she thought I did not take it seriously enough and had not thought
> enough about it, etc etc.
>
> In the event the operation was done at home on Saturday in (to me) a relaxed
> atmosphere and it was fun (for me). Dorothy was not quite so sure. But she
> really did very well, I thought. Today (Monday) a chap at work happened to
> have met the young woman who told him yesterday what a good effort we had
> turned on. I hope I don't sound too vain or smug or self-satisfied. My point is
> that we were ourselves, and while I don't count us entertainers-de-luxe, I reckon
> we can hold people's attention if only by the daggy way in which we interrupt
> each other and there is light and shade in our fun and borax.[54]

The previous year John Pascoe had had three books on his mind, but
following their publication his only writing in 1972 was occasional articles
for *New Zealand's Heritage*. 'They pay $25 a thousand words so I find it worth-
while,' he told Martha.

> So far I have written 2,000 words on 'The New Zealand Death' (ie drowning
> in the rivers; historical article); 3,000 words biography of Charlie Douglas;
> 3,000 words on Mount Cook; 3,000 word history of mountaineering from
> the 1880s to 1940; 2,000 word history of the end of the exploration era =
> 1905 to 1935. I still have 1,500 words to write on General Kippenberger;
> 3,000 words on National Parks.
>
> Now that I am not writing any book it amazes me to look back; I wonder
> how I ever found the time and energy to write some. After a day's work I find
> it quite easy merely to read or look at TV.[55]

Two of John Pascoe's companions climb towards Gunn's Pass during their 1972 transalpine trip from the Rangitata to Whataroa.
DOROTHY PASCOE COLLECTION

He also had a holiday and several alpine adventures during 1972. In January, John and Dorothy spent two weeks with Anna and Ian and their two small children exploring the beaches of Golden Bay. In February he made 'a very tough high hairy and difficult transalpine trip' from the Rangitata to Whataroa via Gunn's Pass with Ian Gilmour, Michael Clark and the painter, Austen Deans, whom John had known for many years. They were only the second party to have crossed the pass since a group of goldminers pioneered the route in 1875. John Pascoe was heartened that, at the age of 63, he was still able to cope with such rugged terrain.

Soon after returning to Wellington he had a comprehensive medical examination. 'I had a good heart and liver and lights and other organs check in May by a good physician as I wanted to make sure it was still okay to do an occasional hard transalpine trip,' he wrote to Laurie Walker.[56] Reassured, Pascoe made plans for the future. 'When I retire in September 1973 I hope to begin a biography of Heaphy,' he confided to Peter Maling, who was also interested in Heaphy. 'If I live long enough I may be able to do it. If I don't live long enough I will leave my researches to future users of the Turnbull Library.'[57]

In the meantime, John Pascoe had plenty to occupy him at work. It seemed, at last, that the government was prepared to pay for a long-term solution to the chronic lack of space at National Archives. The planned new building had failed to materialise, but there was now an alternative that was almost as satisfactory. 'I am very busy at work planning the tenancy of 54,400 square feet (a lot of space) by National Archives in the proposed new National Library building,' he told Anna and Ian. By August 1972 detailed planning was complete. 'It has been an interesting exercise,' he wrote to Martha, who was now a postie in Christchurch and entirely restored in her father's affections. 'I only hope I am alive (tho retired) to see a new National Library arise

Work on the foundations for the National Library began in 1974, but building was stopped and it remained a hole in the ground for many years. It was not completed until 1987. Even then, plans for National Archives to occupy one and a half floors did not materialise. Instead, archivists had to wait until 1990, when they moved into a dedicated facility in the refurbished former Government Printing Office in nearby Mulgrave Street (right).

one day on the corner of Hill Street and Molesworth Street opposite the Wellington Cathedral.'[58]

Ten days later he suddenly felt ill at work. 'My taking crook was a silly business,' he explained to Martha:

> After lunch last Tuesday I felt so giddy that the room spun around and I had to grab a chair to stop myself falling. I lay on the floor for a bit and squawked for one of my staff who did not hear me. I knew it was not 'heart' because I had no pain. But I was worried. When Judy Hornabrook of my staff turned up I got her to drive me home. Dr Ken Paterson came round at one stage and took my blood pressure which was normal. Possibly this was a tummy upset or a flu virus (but we don't know) but even the next day I could not keep my balance on my feet nor could I hold down food easily without a slight vomit. So I had two days off work virtually sleeping all the time.
>
> It is rather humiliating when something like that happens. However better a live dog than a dead lion.

The live dog did not allow this episode to slow him down. 'We are making a huge vegetable garden,' he continued:

> I have to line a back wall (a clay bank) with beech spars so that the bank does not slip. Last two weekends I have collected the spars and now have to dig post holes and fix the spars which I hope Dorothy and Sara will help me with. It has been quite a job felling the dead trees for spars, getting them clear with a crowbar from neighbouring trees, then tugging them down the hill over and past obstacles. However I have quite an impressive array now.[59]

He was also looking forward to getting into the mountains again. The dizzy episode, which had been diagnosed as an ear infection, had caused him to miss a weekend on the snow with the Tararua Club, but he was now ready to resume teaching snowcraft. 'My middle ear attack was a month ago. As I have not had a dinkydie re-occurrence of it, I am not too worried,' he told

For more than 30 years John Pascoe typed letters and manuscripts using only one finger on each hand. Despite this he was a prolific writer. Sara Pascoe's painting, 'The Tiredness of the Peasant Soul', is visible in the background.

DOROTHY PASCOE COLLECTION

Anna. 'I expect to be going to alpine instruction on Ruapehu next weekend (23–24 September) and certainly expect to be okay for a good high snowy traverse with Ian [Gilmour] and Bill [Kennedy, a friend of Ian's] on the Craigieburns next month.'

Despite his optimism, John Pascoe was suddenly impatient with impediments at work and the fetters of family. 'I will be glad when I leave this job in about a year; it is a very wearing one, but I suppose all jobs higher up are that,' he continued before describing to Anna why he now found it difficult to be tolerant at home:

Mostly we adjust to the Sara-Mindy life with us. The part that I find very hard to take is that sometimes Sara is so rude (crudely rude) to Dorothy in a way that turns my stomach sour and in a way that none of you other daughters could. Sara sometimes seems to find reaffirmation of her independence in this rudeness, whereas I find it a burden of the spirit; all the heavier because if I try to have her on about the need for respect and courtesy I get told I am taking sides (and why not). Sara is undoubtedly the most difficult of our daughters to live with. Fortunately Melinda makes up for such a lot. It is a pity that Sara has lost the capacity to read. I am sure she has never read any of my books from end to end. She does not really read novels or anything else continuously. But she often wants to prattle and natter when Dorothy and/or I want to read. If we try to involve her in a TV programme she sometimes finds this a threat to her independence (that bloody independence) so that is friction too. She has become voluntarily helpful to me in the heavy peasant work, such as digging, and that is very good to have the extra pair of strong hands.

Above all, John wanted to be free to enjoy life with Dorothy. He concluded his long letter to Anna with a reflection on marriage. 'Where I am lucky is having Dorothy for a wife and after 32 years of married life (I say life, there is a difference; it is not bliss that binds us, it is life) to have the same sense of pride, thrill, duality (here again words are tricky; I say duality because that is the concept of an individual plus another individual, not a fusion of two people into a jellied amorphosity).'[60]

Dorothy, for her part, was worried. 'I feel John is still being affected by this middle ear trouble – he seems so tired. He insists he feels OK and goes on in much the same way doing his outdoor jobs but lacks zest and drops off to sleep very easily,' she wrote in a separate letter to Anna and Ian. 'I try to persuade him to have early nights when he looks droopy. We are not used to John not being 100% and I feel quite insecure in an odd way.'[61] A similar letter to Jane in Auckland caused her disquiet. Although she had music exams in a few days and virtually no money, she spent what she had on an air ticket to Wellington to see her parents. When she departed, John was in tears.[62]

'One evening I came into the living room where John sat with his typewriter on his knees – his hands were still – a look on his face that startled me – not that searching expression as if looking for an appropriate word or phrase – but a deep inward look as if reaching into the depths of one's being,' Dorothy later recalled. 'My first impulse was to go to him – put my arms around him – but that seemed an intrusion. This seemed an essentially private moment not to be intruded on. The moment when one faces one's own mortality. I walked away.'[63]

Whatever presentiments of death John may have had were relegated to the back of his mind by his preparations for his forthcoming Craigieburn traverse with Ian. Since their successful climbing holiday with Dorothy and Anna in the Ahuriri three years earlier, their relationship had deepened. If Ian was the son John never had, John was the father Ian had hoped for but never found in his own. 'He was all the things I wanted my own father to be,' Ian later recalled. John had introduced his son-in-law to the mountains he had longed to explore since he was a boy in Tokaanu, but never had.[64] Similarly, once Ian became a proficient climber he, in turn, introduced John

The Arrowsmith Range and Rakaia River from Mount Oakden at dawn.

In March 1971 John Pascoe, Ian Gilmour and a friend of Ian's climbed Mount Oakden at night. *'We set out at 1 am and reached our summit just at dawn so got glorious views of much of the main divide — we were looking up the Wilberforce, Mathias and Rakaia and back at Lake Coleridge,'* John told Peter Harding. *'We stayed on top for 5 hours and ran down steep screes.'* He also wrote to Laurie Walker, whose station lay directly below Mount Oakden on the hilly ridge between the Rakaia and Mathias Rivers. *'We saw your Manuka Point country from dawn and I felt sad I could not fly down like a bird and have tea in your kitchen. It was a good trip though and I enjoyed sweating up that hill — I first went up it on 1 February 1930.'*

to new mountaineering ideas such as face climbing and its requisite hardware of pitons and ice screws. John and Ian were also bound by testing times, for example their 1971 climb of Mount Olympus (in the Craigieburn Range) when the wind was so strong that they had to crawl. As conditions grew worse the pair used psychology to aid survival. 'Ian and I revelled in our difficult and stormy climb,' John told Jane a few days later. 'It is good to feel you can still meet the elements. When I got really cold and nearly frightened I remembered my own kind of philosophy — "when you are enmeshed in a storm don't get frightened by it but get in tune with it as a part of it how-

John Pascoe at Anna and Ian's house in Christchurch, a few days before his death on 20 October 1972.

IAN GILMOUR COLLECTION

ever violent and you will survive". So I stopped sniffling to myself that I was 63 years old and old enough to know better and said I was lucky to be able to enjoy such an experience.'[65]

They had also made easier, fair weather climbs together: Castle Hill Peak in the Torlesse Range (with Paul Pascoe), Ben More in deep snow and a night climb of Mount Oakden to catch the views at dawn. Now they were to cross the length of the Craigieburn Range where John had made many ascents as a young man, camping on the tops along the way.

The night before their departure from Christchurch, John Pascoe slept badly and was up and down all night. In the morning Dorothy persuaded him to see a doctor and he was admitted to the Princess Margaret Hospital in Cashmere. The diagnosis was a mild stroke. That afternoon Dorothy thought John seemed to be recovering and he asked her to bring him some paper, envelopes and stamps, as well as his pipe 'for morale, not for use'.[66] She visited him again in the evening and left after John said, 'I can sleep now'.

A relieved Dorothy returned to Anna and Ian's house where she was staying. Later that evening Dr Jonny Pascoe phoned and warned her to be cautious. He had visited his uncle and considered his condition was still a matter of concern. Soon afterwards the hospital rang. John Pascoe had suffered a second, much more severe stroke and died.

Two days later, Dorothy wrote a poem prompted by his last words to her:

> 'I can sleep now'
> so saying your farewell
> holding last words
> close – so close
> their imprint on my breast
>
> I left you then
> fruit hangs heavy
> from the branches
> giving all in the
> dying harvest
>
> but you gave no sign
> just a gentle smile
> 'I can sleep now'
> freeing my fingers
> from your encasing hand
>
> I left you then
> an animal dying
> falters to the hills
> to its known death lair
> waits in isolation
>
> you left me then
> night follows night
> finger tips trace
> the contour of your smile
> my body reaches
> to enfold your memory

John Pascoe died on 20 October 1972. Two days later the poet James K Baxter also died. Although the two had known each other only slightly, they were linked in death by Baxter's poetry. In a letter to the *Dominion*, a correspondent, Bill Keir, wrote:

Man of the mountains

Sir

This week two prominent New Zealanders died, James K Baxter and John Pascoe. The following poem was written by James K Baxter. I feel it expresses something about himself and also about John Pascoe, the man of the mountains.

> *High Country Weather*
> Alone we are born
> And die alone;
> Yet see the red-gold cirrus
> Over snow-mountain shine.
> Upon the upland road
> Ride easy, stranger;
> Surrender to the sky
> Your heart of anger.

Not everyone, however, appreciated the association. Denis Glover, who had known both Baxter and Pascoe, was irritated by the 'canonisation' of Baxter (whom he had seen in many revealing moments) and thought the prominence given to Baxter's death obscured that of Pascoe.[67]

Two years before his death, John Pascoe had written 'Notes on Funeral Items' and given a copy to his solicitor. He had hoped for a service in Old St Paul's in Wellington. He also suggested several hymns and listed possible pall-bearers. 'There could be a real wake or tangi. Cremation. Ashes scattered into a nor'wester in the mountains somewhere.' His final request was for the music which, to him, symbolised 'overcoming your tiredness and your fear', Haydn's trumpet concerto in E flat major.[68]

The reality was different. His funeral service was held in Holy Trinity Church, at Avonside in Christchurch, where his grandfather had been vicar for 32 years. The service was conducted by the Reverend David Taylor, a contemporary of John's at Christ's College, who remembered him as 'a very slightly built boy, who showed great determination as he plodded round the football field, finding it impossible to keep up with speedier contemporaries over a short distance. But by perseverance and staying power over a longer distance he left others behind. As we looked at John then,' Taylor recalled, 'we had no idea that in the years to come he would be the first man to climb to the summit of 25 of the peaks of the Southern Alps.'[69] John Pascoe got the hymns he wanted, but not the Haydn trumpet concerto (although it was played at the crematorium). Many mourners remember, however, his daughter Jane playing the andante of Bach's partita for solo violin (No. 2 in D minor). The service was attended by family and friends as well as government officials who flew down from Wellington.

As the hearse left the church for the crematorium at Harewood the officials followed in a line of black cars. At the head of the cortege were Dorothy and her family in Anna and Ian's Volkswagon Kombi van, an incongruous sight, but curiously appropriate, perhaps, in its suggestion that John Pascoe was something of a maverick within the civil service. Although he had spent most of his life working for the government he had neither conformed to the popular image of a civil servant, nor behaved like one. Nevertheless his considerable contribution as author, administrator, archivist and photographer was always understood and appreciated by his superiors.

John Pascoe died on a Friday. The following Sunday, National Radio broadcast *Mr and Mrs Reminisce* as a tribute to him. At the end of the programme it was announced that he had died. For some listeners this was the first news of his death. David Galloway, the editor of the *New Zealand Alpine Journal*, wrote to Dorothy:

> This morning I listened to the programme built around you and John with a mixture of surprise and delight, and was so charmed with your imaginative choice of music that I felt I must write to express appreciation and thanks. I was, however, unprepared for and quite shattered by the news of John's death which came later.
>
> Like so many of my age the first taste of mountains that we had were vicarious ones, lived through the pages of *Unclimbed New Zealand* or *Land Uplifted High*. Much better men than I have been introduced to our hill country in this way and it pleases me to know that John knew that.

Personally I had grown to accept John as something rather timeless; like the mountains themselves 'always there'.[70]

Several weeks after John Pascoe's death his brother led a group of family members to the top of Peak Hill, above Lake Coleridge, in the Canterbury foothills. There, on a windy day, they scattered the ashes of the man for whom the mountains had always been, in his words, 'the bread and passion of life'. Among them was Ian Gilmour. 'I think I felt more emotional about John dying than my own father,' he later recalled.[71] Not long afterwards Ian and three friends climbed the Otira face of Mount Rolleston. Ian took John's pipe with him and carefully buried it in the cairn on the summit.

Pascoe family members, photographed by Jonny Pascoe, gather on the summit of Peak Hill to scatter John Pascoe's ashes, 26 November 1972. From left: Paul Pascoe, Ian Gilmour, Luke Pascoe, Anna Pascoe, Simon Pascoe (holding baby Dominic) and Nell Pascoe.

The following day, Anna Pascoe described the occasion in a letter to her mother in Wellington. 'It was very moving on top, a terrific nor-wester was blowing. We sang All people that on earth do dwell, said the Lord's Prayer and then we scattered John's ashes.'

JONATHAN PASCOE COLLECTION

While filming Prince of Nosey Parkers, John Pascoe told the producer, Peter Coates, that kea were the embodiment of the spirits of dead explorers and mountaineers, an idea that might have come from Charlie Douglas likening the cry of the kea to the 'wail of a lost spirit'.

At Easter 2001, my partner Pauline Rodgers and I climbed Mount Oakden, and camped on the summit to take photos at dawn. Later, while descending scree slopes near the adjacent Peak Hill, we were accompanied by four kea. Three soon left, but one with a slight resemblance to John Pascoe stayed and allowed me to photograph it at close range, on the ground and in flight.

One of the pleasures of researching and writing this book has been meeting, and receiving help from people who knew John Pascoe. I am grateful to Andy Anderson, Roger Ballantyne, Ray Chapman, Peter Coates, John Daniels, Mavis Davidson, Frank and Betty Fitzgerald, Anna and Ian Gilmour, Bernie Greig, Ray Grover, Janet Holm, Stephen Howell, Judith Hornabrook, Liz and Harry Leov, Daphne Logan, Mary Lough, Peter Maling, Deryck Morse, Dorothy Pascoe, Jonathan Pascoe, Martha Pascoe, Nell and Simon Pascoe, Sara Pascoe, Janet Paul, Ian Powell, Jane Shaw, Laurie Stratford, Priestley and Prue Thomson, Ian Wards and Allan Willis.

To have conviction, the story required a degree of familiarity with some of the areas John Pascoe visited so often, especially the Southern Alps and the Marlborough Sounds. For their good company, ideas and interest I thank Paul Bradshaw, Phillip Harper, Susan Harper, Geoff Norman, Jock Phillips, Pauline Rodgers and Paul Thompson. I also thank Scott Wilson for providing sea-kayak transport to and around D'Urville Island, Don and Julie Patterson of Manuka Point for access to the upper Rakaia Valley, and Marie Robertson for permission to cross Mount Oakden Station.

Many others helped me with information and encouragement including John Ahradsen, Shaun Barnett, Ruby Chapman, Chris Cochran, David Crighton, Peter Daniel, Austen Deans, Paul Edwards and Debbie O'Connor (Archway Books), Arnold Heine, Jim Henderson, Janet Holm, Michael King, Alan Knowles, Jennifer Leahy, Julie Liebrich, Bryony and Fiona Macmillan, Keith Matthews, Graeme Maxwell, Colin Monteath, Bobby Porter, John Osborne, Ron Pynenburg, John Rundle, George Silk, Barry Smith, Geoff Spearpoint, Paul Thompson and Redmer Yska.

Successful research often depends on the staff of libraries, government departments and independent agencies. My task was made easier by the help I received from staff of the Alexander Turnbull Library: David Colquhoun, Margareta Gee, Sean McMahon, Valerie Morse and David Retter (Manuscripts and Archives); Diane Woods (Field Librarian); Joan McCracken, Tim Corballis, Heather Mathie and Betty Moss (Turnbull Library Pictures); John Sullivan, Walter Cook and Kirsty Willis (Photographic Archive); Marian Minson and Barbara Brownlee (Drawings and Prints); Jocelyn Chambers (Oral History Centre); Jill Goodwin (Reference) and Margaret Calder (Chief Librarian).

I am also grateful to David Cornick (DAC Group; Elaine Marland and Paul Thompson (New Zealand Historic Places Trust); and Bronwyn Dalley, Fran McGowan and Jock Phillips (Ministry of Culture and Heritage).

John Pascoe would never have been completed without the support of the organisations listed at the front of the book. Among the individuals who helped to arrange grants were Shaun Barnett, Caroline Duggan (New Zealand Alpine Club – Wellington); Christine Hardie, Arnold Heine and John Wheeler (Federated Mountain Clubs – Mountain and Forest Trust); Wanda Hall; Peter Strang (New Zealand Alpine Club – Otago); and Richard Wesley (New Zealand Alpine Club – National Office).

A number of readers suggested changes or pointed out errors; any that remain are mine. Joan Maclean read the first draft; her suggestions made the text clearer and more concise. The following people read and improved part, or all, of the initial typescript: Ray Chapman, Chris Cochran, Margaret Cochran, John Daniels, Anna and Ian Gilmour, Judith Hornabrook, Peter Ireland, Peter Maling, Dorothy Pascoe, Jonathan Pascoe, Martha Pascoe, Sara Pascoe, Simon Pascoe, Pauline Rodgers and Jane Shaw. I am particularly indebted to Graham Langton who took a strong interest in this book from the outset and provided invaluable additional information. His extensive knowledge of alpine history and his careful scrutiny of the text have greatly improved it. Most of the final version was typed by Bronwyn Wynn with assistance from Kath Petrie and Janet Suter; their patience and perceptive suggestions clarified the text. Anna Rogers skilfully edited the final draft. *John Pascoe* was designed by Margaret Cochran and Geoff Norman. Margaret's ideas and understanding of design have improved both the content and appearance of this book. I am equally grateful to Geoff, not only for his patience and good humour throughout the long process of layout and adjustment, but also for his company in the mountains and steadfast friendship. I also thank Robbie Burton and Phillippa Duffy of Craig Potton Publishing for their interest and encouragement as well as their professional handling of the final phase of production. Like many others involved with this book, Robbie's interest reflects both his love of the mountains and esteem for John Pascoe.

My greatest debts are to the organisations who generously provided grants, without which this book could not have been written; to my mother, Joan Maclean, for her perceptive reading of the initial draft, to my partner, Pauline Rodgers, whose generous support gave me time for writing, and to Dorothy Pascoe whose determination to see this biography published never wavered.

I am grateful to the following people who provided illustrations: Shaun Barnett, Anna and Ian Gilmour, Bryony and Fiona Macmillan, Dorothy Pascoe, Jonathan Pascoe, Simon Pascoe, Eric Saggers, Geoff Spearpoint and Rosemary Watt. I would also like to thank Mrs E. M. Bensemann for permission to reproduce the late Leo Bensemann's drawing of Denis Glover, the New Zealand Historic Places Trust for permission to include an example of the Waipapa rock drawings and Land Information New Zealand for permission to include excerpts from its maps.

I acknowledge the interest of Janet Bayly who curated the exhibition *Songs of Innocence — Photographs of New Zealand Childhood by John Pascoe* held in conjunction with the publication of this biography and, in particular, the enthusiasm and encouragement of Gerald Barnett, Director of the Mahara Gallery, Waikanae, the exhibition organiser.

Except where otherwise stated, all black and white photographs were taken by John Pascoe. His photos can be identified by their attribution; for example, Pascoe Collection, Alexander Turnbull Library or Dorothy Pascoe Collection. Colour photographs without any attribution were taken by the author using a Yashica FX-3 Super 2000 SLR camera with 28 mm, 50 mm, 35-70 mm and 70-210 mm lenses, on Fujichrome 100 ASA film.

Images from various photographic collections are identifiable by reference numbers. The relevant page number precedes the reference number. Unless stated otherwise, all images belong to the Alexander Turnbull Library.

Bibliography

ABBREVIATIONS

ATL Alexander Turnbull Library
CM   *Canterbury Mountaineer* (annual)
DPC Dorothy Pascoe Collection
MS   Manuscript Papers
NZAJ *New Zealand Alpine Journal* (annual)
NZAC New Zealand Alpine Club
NZBS New Zealand Broadcasting Service
NZHPT New Zealand Historic Places Trust
NZIA New Zealand Institute of Architects
TTC Tararua Tramping Club

PRIMARY SOURCES

General

Christchurch Tramping Club, Minute Book No. 1, 1925–1927, Deryck Morse Collection.

Fenwick, C. E., 'A Brief History of the Canterbury Mountaineering Club, 1925–1930', 1982, CMC Collection, Canterbury Museum.

von Haast, H. F., Haast family papers, MS-0037 (302 – reel 23), ATL.

Harding, Guy, letters to Elsie Locke, 1940s–1960s, DPC.

Heenan, J. W. A., papers, MS-1132 (60, 134), ATL.

Isaac, Skye, 'Pencarrow' [unpublished typescript], DPC.

Langton, Graham, 'A History of Mountain Climbing in New Zealand to 1953', PhD thesis, University of Canterbury, 1996.

McLean, Gavin, 'Archaeology and the New Zealand Historic Places Trust – An Outline History', 30 November 1995, NZHPT.

New Zealand Alpine Club, 'Copies of correspondence relating to criticism by NZAC of Government Centennial publication "The Mountains" and clippings of letters to newspapers regarding the abovementioned publication, February – April 1940', NZAC 101/85, Hocken Library.

Pascoe, Paul, 'College Days' [scrapbook 1922–1927], Simon Pascoe Collection

Pascoe, Paul, diaries 1924–1925, 1932, Simon Pascoe Collection.

Pascoe bach [at Kowai Bush], Visitors' Book, Simon Pascoe Collection.

State Literary Fund, Correspondence about *Mr Explorer Douglas*, I.A. Series 1, 86/1/22, Archives New Zealand.

Taylor, David, Notes for funeral of John Pascoe, undated, c.24 October 1972, DPC.

Ussher, R. M., 'The Modern Movement in Canterbury – The Architecture of Paul Pascoe', MA thesis, University of Canterbury, 1986.

John Pascoe – Unpublished Writing

(The following articles, diaries, radio scripts and speech notes have been selected from Dorothy Pascoe's extensive collection of her late husband's papers, and from an equally large amount of material held by the Alexander Turnbull Library. Neither collection has been fully catalogued and described. The list below is, therefore, not a complete record of John Pascoe's unpublished writing.

Both collections also include photo albums as well as numerous loose photographs and negatives. As with his papers, only some of Pascoe's photos have been catalogued and described.)

'College Days' [scrapbook 1922–27], DPC.

'Photos and Notes of a trip in the region of the Snowy Tyndall Mountains', 1934–35, Erewhon Tramping Club Collection [Ashburton].

'Southern Tourabout – from Nelson to Milford Sound', October 1941, DPC.

'Fifteen Hundred Cattle can't be Wrong', c.1948, DPC.

'Notes on a holiday in Pelorus Sound', January 1949, DPC.

'Illustrate the text – the use of illustrations in books raises old issues and new problems', c.1950, DPC.

'The Wicked Witch of Ruapehu', c.1952, DPC.

'East is East and West is West – Mount Earnslaw', c.1952, DPC.

'Notes on a holiday, Te Towaka, Pelorus Sound, Marlborough', January 1952, DPC.

'Beyond the Arawata – Personal Notes on an Overland Journey', c.January 1953, DPC.

'Memorial Hut' [poem], April 1953, DPC.

'Names' [poem], May 1953, DPC.

'Bushman' [poem], February 1954, DPC.

'On the Marae' [poem], March–April 1954, DPC.

'Journal of a Change', 3 September 1955, DPC.

'Many Roots and Branches' [satirical account of NHPT], c.1955, DPC.

Landsborough diary, December 1955–January 1956, MS 75-241 (3), ATL.

'Beyond the Main Divide – From Lake Ohau to the West Coast', c.February 1956, DPC.

'Lady Traveller', c.1957, DPC.

'Lake Pukaki and its inn', c.1957, DPC.

'Jim, Jim, The Tide is in' [poem], 1958, DPC.

'Historic Journeys' [a series of unbroadcast radio scripts
    including 'The Bush and the Rain – Brunner in the
    Buller', 'Lord Latymer in the Landsborough' and 'To the
    Mackenzie Country on Bicycles in 1895'],
    MS 75-241 (7), ATL.

Mahitahi diary, December 1957–January 1958,
    MS 75-241 (4), ATL.

'New Zealand has Good Mountains', c.1959, DPC.

'Impressions of New Zealanders' [a series of unbroadcast
    radio scripts c.1959, including profiles of Eric
    McCormick and Paul Pascoe among others],
    MS 75-241 (7), ATL.

Waipara diary, December 1959–January 1960,
    MS 75-241 (11), ATL.

'Erewhon Illustrated' [unpublished booklet], c.1961–63,
    MS-7-241 (4), ATL.

'The Huts at the Rakaia Mouth', August 1961, DPC.

'Six Acres of Raspberries', January 1962, DPC.

'Mountain Life in New Zealand' [article commissioned by *The
    Times*, for a special supplement on New Zealand, February
    1963, but not used], 24 November 1962, DPC.

Waitaha diary, December 1962–January 1963,
    MS-75-241 (3), ATL.

'Report on a visit to d'Urville Island', c. July 1963, DPC.

'The Way to Erewhon' [radio script], 23 September 1963,
    MS-75-241 (7), ATL.

'Bearings and Blazes in our mountain history' [text of address
    to Manawatu Tramping Club], 30 October 1964, DPC.

'The Haast Road is an adventure – Based on History',
    c.January 1966, DPC.

'The Mountains and the Sea – A Family Holiday and a
    Pilgrimage', 29 September 1966, DPC.

'Origins', biographical notes, c.1968, DPC.

'Notes on a Journey' [to Burma], December 1970, DPC.

'Hail to Farewell', 16 January 1972, DPC.

'Beyond the Rangitata', c.February/March 1972, DPC.

'One man's prejudices' [speech notes], 28 April 1972, DPC.

Notes for discussion about musical memories and favourites,
    with Dorothy Pascoe, broadcast as *Mr and Mrs Reminisce*,
    26 October 1972, DPC.

Dorothy Pascoe

*(The following unpublished typescripts were written at the request of the
author. Copies are held by Dorothy Pascoe and the author.)*

'Adventures', September 2000.

'My First Mountain', September 2000.

'On First Meeting J. D. P.', 26 September 2001.

'Our Various Houses', 19 May 2000.

'John and Children', April 2000.

'The Spanish Civil War and World War Two', 13 November
    2001.

'Letters from William Guy Harding to Elsie Locke',
    [explanatory notes] undated.

'Acceptance', October 2002.

'Snow and Rivers – Sun and Sea', 22 April 2002.

'The Dark Days', 12 February 2002.

'Came the Sixties', 17 October 2002.

'When the Bell Tolls', 11 December 2002.

SECONDARY SOURCES

Articles

Anderson, Andrew, 'The Earlier Years', CM, 1975.

Anon, 'Deep Affection for Mountains – John Pascoe Chats
    about their Interest', *New Zealand Free Lance*, 27 December
    1939.

Begg, Neil; Wilson, Ormond (and others), 'Beginnings –
    30 years of historic preservation', *Historic Places in
    New Zealand*, June 1985.

Blackman, Gary, 'My Century of New Zealand Photography',
    NZ Journal of Photography, May 1999.

S. C. [Conway, Stan], 'John Pascoe (1908 – 1972)', CM,
    1972.

Farmer, Diane, 'A Long Graunchy Job', *New Zealand Listener*,
    27 August 1965.

Foley, Roger, 'John Pascoe's Greatest Sporting Thrill –
    Conquest of Mount Evans after being repulsed twice',
    Sports Post, 2 October 1972.

K. F. G., 'National Trust has much of Historic Interest to
    record and preserve', *Freedom*, 25 February 1958.

Guiney, Jack, 'John Pascoe's Spare Frame Packs Great
    Vitality', *Evening Post*, c.1969.

Heine, Arnold, 'The Garden of Eden', *Hills and Valleys*,
    August 1967.

Henderson, Jim, 'Mum, Dad and Mount Aspiring', NZBS,
    Feminine Viewpoint, June 1967; *Open Country*, September
    1967; Oral History Archive No. 2616, TS184, ATL.

Herron, D. G., 'The 1914 Revival of the New Zealand Alpine
    Club and the Membership Controversy', *NZAJ*, 1958.

Holm, Janet, 'A Man For All Seasons', CM, 1999.

Hornabrook, Judith, 'John Dobree Pascoe, Chief Archivist',
    New Zealand Archivist, Summer, 1972.

Hornabrook, Judith, 'John Dobree Pascoe', *New Zealand
    Libraries*, February 1973.

Knox, Ray, 'Mountain Pilgrim: John Dobree Pascoe
    1908–1972', *NZ Listener*, 27 November 1972.

Langton, Graham, 'Early Climbing at Arthur's Pass', CM,
    1997.

Langton, Graham, 'Mates in the Mountains', CM, 1999.

Meares, S. D., 'The Canterbury Mountaineering Club', CM,
    1932.

Newick, Leah, 'Encyclopaedia for inquiring young New Zealand minds', *New Zealand Woman's Weekly*, 30 August 1965.

Newth, Tom, 'Johnny Pascoe Remembered', CM, 1999.

Noble, Jo, 'The National Archives – Raw Material for the Story of New Zealand', *New Zealand Woman's Weekly*, 26 September 1966.

Pascoe, Paul, 'The Quality of Charm in Architecture', *NZIA Journal*, June 1932.

Powell, Paul, 'John Dobree Pascoe – A Tribute', NZBS, 29 November 1972.

Retter, David (ed.), 'A Chronology of archives keeping in New Zealand to 1996', *New Zealand Archivist*, June 1996.

Sim, J. A. (ed.), 'A False Page of Mountain History', *NZAJ*, 1940.

Swain, Pauline, 'These People Don't Just Write for Fun', *NZ Listener*, 12 July 1971.

Thomson, Priestley, 'John Pascoe', *NZAJ*, 1973.

Walker, Howell, 'The Making of an Anzac', *National Geographic Magazine*, April 1942.

Willis, Allan, 'First Ascent of Mount Whitcombe and crossing of the Strachan Pass', *NZAJ*, 1932.

Willis, Allan, 'Johnny Pascoe Remembered', CM, 1999.

Wilson, G. B., 'Reviews in Brief – New Zealand Mountain Writers', *Tararua Tramper*, December 1955.

Wilson, J. G., 'The Mount Rolleston Tragedy', *NZAJ*, 1966.

Books

Alpers, Antony and Baker, Josephine, *Confident Tomorrows – A Biographical Self-Portrait of O. T. J. Alpers*, Godwit, 1993.

Allington, Margaret, 'Old St Pauls and Bishopscourt', in *Historic Buildings of New Zealand – North Island*, Cassell New Zealand, 1979.

Anderson, Betsy, *Story of My Life*, Graham Langton, 2000.

Bassett, Michael, *The Mother of all Departments*, Auckland University Press and the Historical Branch of Internal Affairs, 1997.

Bayly, Janet and Athol McCredie, *Witness to Change*, Photoforum, 1985.

Beaglehole, Ann and Alison Carew, *Eastbourne – a history of the eastern bays of Wellington harbour*, Historical Society of Eastbourne, 2001.

Bobrick, Benson, *Knotted Tongues – Stuttering in History and the Quest for a Cure*, Simon & Schuster, 1994.

Butler, Samuel, *Erewhon*, Golden Press, 1973 (first published 1872).

Cooke, Robin, *Portrait of a Profession*, A. H. & A. W. Reed, 1969.

Dreaver, Anthony, *An Eye for Country – The Life and Work of Leslie Adkin*, Victoria University Press, 1997.

Flecker, J. L., *Hassan*, William Heinemann, 1922.

Flower, Geoff, *The CMC and Me*, 1990.

Galbreath, Ross, *Working for Wildlife – A History of the New Zealand Wildlife Service*, Bridget Williams Books and the Historical Branch of Internal Affairs, 1993.

Glover, Denis, *Arawata Bill*, Pegasus Press, 1953.

Glover, Denis, *Hot Water Sailor*, A. H. & A. W. Reed, 1962.

Greig, B. D. A. (ed.), *Tararua Story*, TTC, 1946.

Hagedorn, Judy W. and Janet W. Kizzair, *Gemini – The Psychology and Phenomena of Twins*, Centre for the Study of Multiple Births, 1983.

Hamilton, Don, *College! A History of Christ's College*, Caxton Press, 1996.

Hewitt, H. B. (ed.), *Peter Graham, Mountain Guide – An Autobiography*, A. H. & A. W. Reed, 1965.

Jonas, Gerald, *Stuttering – The Disorder of Many Theories*, Farrar, Straus & Giroux, 1976.

Logan, Hugh, *Great Peaks of New Zealand*, John McIndoe and the NZAC, 1990.

Logan, Robert, *Waimakariri*, Logan Publishing Co., 1987.

McCormick, E. H. (ed.), *Making New Zealand*, Department of Internal Affairs, 1939–40.

McCormick, E. H., *An absurd ambition – autobiographical writings*, edited by Denis McEldowney, Auckland University Press, 1996.

Mahoney, Michael, *Harry Ayres – Mountain Guide*, Whitcoulls, 1982.

Main, William and John B. Turner, *New Zealand Photography from the 1840s to the present*, Photoforum, 1993.

Maling, P. B., *Samuel Butler at Mesopotamia*, Government Printer and National Historic Places Trust, 1960.

Ogilvie, Gordon, *Denis Glover – His Life*, Godwit, 1999.

Porter, Grace and Ted, *Under the Nor'West Arch – A High Country Story*, A. H. & A. W. Reed, 1970.

Rundle, John and John Gordon, *Mountains of the South*, Random House, 1993.

Sandford, Kenneth, *Mark of the Lion*, Hutchinson, 1962.

War History Branch, *Introduction to New Zealand*, Department of Internal Affairs, 1945.

War History Branch, *Official History of New Zealand in the Second World War 1939–1945*, (Episodes and Studies), Department of Internal Affairs, 1945–1954.

Wilson, Ormond, *An Outsider Looks Back*, Port Nicholson Press, 1982.

Woodman, Howard (ed.), *Year Book of the Arts in New Zealand*, Wingfield Press, 1948.

John Pascoe – Published Writing
(compiled with Graham Langton)

(Book titles in bold type)

'Climbing at the Headwaters of the Mathias River, Canterbury', *NZAJ*, 1931.

'Alpinists', Letter to the Editor, *The Press*, 28 September 1931.

'Climbers and Guides. A Plea for the Amateur', *The Press*, 14 November 1931.

'First Ascent: Mt. Kinkel Climbed', *The Press*, 12 January 1932.

'Exploring the Alps – No. 1. Memorable Journey – Ascents of Rakaia Peaks', *New Zealand Herald*, 27 January 1932.

'Exploring the Alps – No. 2. Inaccessible Mt. Evans – Failure of First Ascent', *New Zealand Herald*, 28 January 1932.

'Climbs in the Rakaia Hills', *Christ's College Register*, April 1932.

'The Reconnaissance of Mt. Evans', *NZAJ*, 1932.

'The Rakaia Valley', *CM*, 1932.

'Particulars of Mathias Pass–Hokitika Trip', *CM*, 1932.

'The Rakaia Pioneers – A Seventy Years' History', *NZAJ*, 1933.

'Mt. Evans (8612 feet), Westland (Further Reconnaissance)', *NZAJ*, 1933.

'Mt. Evans – Another Attempt', *NZAJ*, 1933.

'The Waimakariri Invasion', *CM*, 1933.

'Mt Evans (8612 feet), Westland', *CM*, 1933.

'In Memoriam: S. E. Russell', *CM*, 1933.

'Samuel Butler in the Rakaia – The Pass to Erewhon', *The Press*, 16 September 1933.

'Contentions IX – That in the Ranges Glory is to the Conquered', *The Press*, 13 January 1934.

'Mt. Evans (8612 feet), Westland (First Ascent and Traverse)', *NZAJ*, 1934.

'The Siege of Mt Evans – A Trek and a Traverse', *CM*, 1934 (republished as 'Success on Mount Evans', *CM*, 1975).

Review: *NZAJ*, No. 21, *CM*, 1934.

Review: *In Search of New Zealand*, No.1, *CM*, 1934.

Letter to the Editor: 'The Reconnaissance of Mt. Evans', *NZAJ*, 1935.

'The Mingha-Edwards-Hawdon Valleys, Arthur's Pass National Park', *CM*, 1935.

'The Perth Glaciers', *CM*, 1935.

Reviews: *NZAJ*, No. 22; *Alpine Sport*; *CM*, 1935.

'The Rakaia Ranges', *Victoria League Monthly Notes*, 1 September 1935 (republished *CM*, 1975).

'The Spirit of the Pilgrim – The Golden Journey to Samarkand', *Canterbury University College Review*, No. 85, October 1935.

'Butler in the Mountains – Early Canterbury Exploration', *The Press*, 5 December 1935 (republished *CM*, 1975).

'Fording Rivers – Addendum – A Canterbury River Technique', *NZAJ*, 1936.

'Exploration of the Adams Glaciers and Valley', *CM*, 1936.

'In Memoriam: Maxwell Geith Townsend 1911–1935', *CM*, No. 1936.

'Relief Expeditions in the Mountains', *New Zealand Railways Magazine*, 1 May 1937.

'Memorable Nights above the Snowline', *Monocle*, May 1937.

'Various Expeditions – Hawdon District, Wilberforce District', *NZAJ*, 1937.

'In Memoriam: Sir George Harper', *NZAJ*, 1937.

Letter to the Editor: Revision of Alpine Material, Observations, and Corrections, *NZAJ*, 1937.

'A "Look-See" at Mt. Tasman', *CM*, 1937.

'A Canterbury River Technique', *CM*, 1937.

'Tobacco in the Mountains', *Tobacco*, 1 November 1937.

'First Ascent of Mount Evans, Southern Alps of New Zealand', *Blue Peter – An Independent Magazine of the Sea, Travel, Yachting and Motor-Boating*, No. 189, December 1937.

'Evolution – Anti Clockwise', *Tararua Tramper*, May 1938.

'Route Guide for the Three Passes', *CM*, 1938.

'A Traverse of the Torlesse Range December 1st 1929', *CM*, 1938.

' "The Wilds of Karamea" – Aorere-Heaphy Watershed. The "Gouland Downs" where the tussocks devour the miles', *CM*, 1938.

'Note on River-Crossing technique, based on a letter received from R. R. ("Boney") Chester', *CM*, 1938.

'Norman Arthur Dowling', *CM*, 1938.

'Ascents and Explorations – Canterbury Ranges', *CM*, 1938.

'Mt. Cook Again', *CM*, 1938.

'All the Little Ducks – in the Duck-Pond', *Tararua Tramper*, September 1938.

'Mountaineering Epic in New Zealand Alps', *Pix*, 15 October 1938.

'Plus Snow – Minus Rock. The Search that Failed', *Tararua Tramper*, November 1938.

'The Idle Speculations of an Idle Marathon Runner', *Tararua Tramper*, January 1939.

'Egmont Without Tears. Taranaki, what of the Night?', *Tararua Tramper*, March 1939.

Letter to the Editor: 'Centennial Rendezvous', *Tararua Tramper*, April 1939.

'Take to the Hills – Beyond the Beaten Track', *New Zealand Youth*, No. 1 (1), 14 July 1939.

Review: 'A Mystery Hike into the Realm of Literary Criticism', *The Mountain Way* by R. L. G. Irving, *NZAJ*, 1939.

'Skyline on Ruapehu. The Pinnacle Ridge', *Tararua Tramper*, September 1939.

Unclimbed New Zealand, George Allen & Unwin, 1939 (reprinted in smaller format and with fewer illustrations, 1950, 1954).

'Taranaki Triple', *Tararua Tramper*, November 1939.

The Mountains: Making New Zealand, No. 10, Department of Internal Affairs, 1939.

'A Waimakariri Mountain', *Tararua Tramper*, March 1940.

'By Boot and By Cycle', *Tararua Tramper*, June 1940.

'The Uses of Ice-Axe and Rope', *Tararua Tramper*, July 1940, August 1940.

'Over the Hill to Greenlaw', *CM*, 1940.

'Club Notes – Traverse of Mt. Marion', *CM*, 1940.

'Book Chat: *Peaks and Lamas* by Marco Pallis', *CM*, 1940.

'The Adams Valley and Glaciers, Southern Alps of New Zealand', *Geographical Journal*, No. 6, Royal Geographical Society, December 1940.

'The Waimakariri, Three Pass Trip, Xmas 1940', *Tararua Tramper*, May 1941.

'Wellington' [branch notes], *CM*, 1941.

'Club Notes Christmas 1940', *CM*, 1941.

'South Island Skyline', *Journeys*, August 1941.

'High Nooks – Low Crannies: New Corners in Westland', *Journeys*, November 1941.

'In Memoriam: Brian Tyrwhitt Wyn Irwin, 1905–1942', *NZAJ*, 1942.

'Notes on the Harper Pass Track', *CM*, 1942.

'Retrospect in Pictures – An Inquest on a History Quest', *National Education*, October 1942.

'Return to the Mountains', *CM*, 1943.

'Camera Cautions', *Tararua Tramper*, November 1943.

'A New Zealand Sheep Muster', *Sport and Country*, 9 June 1944.

'Back to the Rakaia', *CM*, 1944.

'Coal from the Mountains', *Tararua Tramper*, December 1944.

'Wool from the Mountains', *Picture Post*, 9 December 1944.

'Canterbury High Country: The Sheep and Sheepmen of the Mountains', *New Zealand Geographer*, Vol. 1, No. 1, April 1945.

'Boulders, Altitude and Waterfalls. Easter on Tapuaenuku, Inland Kaikouras', *Tararua Tramper*, July 1945.

'A New National Park', *CM*, 1945.

'From the Sounds to the Kaikouras', *CM*, 1945.

'Journey Above Nine Thousand Feet', *Journeys*, February 1946.

'Back to the Rakaia', *Tararua Tramper*, March 1946.

'Climb of Mt Whitcombe, and First Ascent of Mt Wanda', *NZAJ*, 1946.

'Names above the snowline', *NZ Listener*, 19 July 1946.

'Up the Rakaia', *CM*, 1946.

'A New National Park', *Journeys*, August 1946.

'Back to the Mountains', *Journeys*, November 1946.

'The Orongos Look on Marathon'; 'Through Tinted Snow-Glasses: Impressions of the Tararua Club'; *Tararua Story*, B. D. A. Greig (ed.), TTC, 1946.

'The Outer Ranges of Canterbury', *Journeys*, February 1947.

'The Pass', *Journeys*, May 1947.

'From the Deception to the Waimakariri', *Tararua Tramper*, May 1947.

'The High Country Run', *New Zealand Post-Primary School Bulletin*, Vol. 1, No. 10, c.May/June 1947.

'Mount Russell is No. 35', *Journeys*, August 1947.

'The Last Round-Up', *CM*, 1947.

Book Review: *The Delectable Mountains* by Douglas Busk, *CM*, 1947.

'Photography in New Zealand', *Landfall*, Vol. 1, No. 4, December 1947.

'Family in a Forest', *New Zealand Design Review*, No. 2, 1948.

'In the Spenser Ranges', *Tararua Tramper*, February 1948.

'Memorial for a Mountaineer', *Journeys*, February 1948.

'Along the Spenser Range', *Journeys*, May 1948.

'Spenser Scrambles', *CM*, 1948.

'Photogeography: A Pictorial Survey of New Zealand – 1. SVP: Marketing Gardening in Wartime', *New Zealand Geographer*, Vol. 4, No. 1, April 1948.

'From Faerie Queen to Enid', *Tararua*, 1948.

'The "Three Pass" Trip', *Journeys*, No. 30, 1 August 1948.

Book Reviews: *Alpine Tragedy* by Charles Gos; *Mount Everest 1938* by H. W. Tilman; *CM*, 1948.

'Photogeography: A Pictorial Survey of New Zealand – 2. Coal from the Buller', *New Zealand Geographer*, Vol. 4, No. 2, October 1948.

'Some Summer Trips', *Journeys*, November 1948.

'Other Trips – A Mountaineer's Range', *Tararua*, 1949.

'Remembering the Rakaia', *Journeys*, February 1949.

'Exploring the South Island's Back Country on Skis', *Journeys*, May 1949.

'Late Spring Snow', *Journeys*, August 1949.

'The Arrowsmiths – An Unfinished Postscript', *CM*, 1949.

Book Reviews: 'Two Biographies': *The Life and Times of Sir Julius von Haast* by H. F. von Haast; *The Splendid Hills – The Life and Photographs of Vittorio Sella* by Ronald Clark; *CM*, 1949.

The Ngarimu Hui, (John Pascoe photographs; text by I. L. G. Sutherland), Polynesian Society, 1949.

'Family Holiday', *Journeys*, No. 35, 1 November 1949.

'A Rangitata Return', *Tararua*, 1950.

'Take your Camera', *Journeys*, May 1950.

'Havelock Glacier, Rangitata Headwaters', *NZAJ*, 1950.

'It Turned Out (N)ice Again', *CM*, 1950.

'Adventure in New Zealand: a Tramper's Diary', *New Zealand Post-Primary School Bulletin*, Vol. 4, No. 3, March 1950.

'Was Wicky Lazy?', (illustrations by Juliet Peters), *School Journal*, 44 (2–6), March–July 1950.

'Shapes for Shelters in the Mountains', *Design Review*, May–June 1950.

The Mountains the Bush and the Sea, Whitcombe & Tombs, 1950 (2nd edition, 1958).

Unclimbed New Zealand, George Allen & Unwin, 2nd edition 1950 (reprinted in smaller format with fewer illustrations, 1954).

'The Arrowsmith Range', *Journeys*, August 1950.

'A New Three Pass Trip', *CM*, 1950.

Book Reviews: 'Alpine Trials and Human Strength': *A History of Mountaineering in the Alps* by Claire Engel; 'A Quartet From Snowy Mountains': *Two Mountains and a River* by H. W. Tilman; *Song of the High Hills* by Charles Gos; *The Early Alpine Guides* by Ronald Clark; *Fourteen Men* by Arthur Scholes; *CM*, 1950.

'Here's My Comfort' (radio talk), NZBS, 13 April 1951.

'The Whitcombe Pass – Samuel Butler's Discovery', *The Press*, 1 September 1951.

'Holidaying in the Sounds', *The Mirror*, October 1951.

'Women in the Mountains', *Journeys*, November 1950.

The Southern Alps (Part 1) – From the Kaikouras to the Rangitata, Pegasus Press, 1951 (revised edition, 1956).

Land Uplifted High, Whitcombe & Tombs, 1952 (2nd edition, 1961).

'Arrowsmith Peaks', *NZAJ*, 1952.

'An Arrowsmith Easter', *CM*, 1952.

'Obituary: Matt Grant', *CM*, 1952.

Book Review: *Aspiring* by W. Scott Gilkison, *CM*, 1952.

The Great Journey by Thomas Brunner (introduced and edited by John Pascoe), Pegasus Press, 1952.

Review: *Deer Hunter* by Joff A. Thomson, *Tararua*, 1953.

'Lake Wanaka to Jackson Bay', *NZAJ*, 1953.

'Over the Land to the Sea', *CM*, 1953.

Book Review: *They Came to the Hills* by Claire Engel, *CM*, 1953.

'Young Climbers on Egmont', *Tararua Tramper*, December 1953.

'Arawata Bill', *New Zealand Poetry Yearbook*, 1953.

'The Thousand Acres Flat', *Journeys*, February 1954.

'A Trip to Earnslaw', *CM*, 1954.

'In Memoriam: John Wesley Mitchell 1884–1954', *NZAJ*, 1954.

Book Reviews: 'Two New Books About Everest': *Our Everest Adventure* by John Hunt; *Forerunners to Everest* by Rene Dittert; *CM*, 1954.

'The Rakaia Valley – A Topographical and Historical Survey', *CM*, 1954.

'From the Arawhata to the Karakoram', *NZ Listener*, 24 September 1954.

'On Mountain Dew – One For The Road', *Journeys*, November 1954.

'Beyond the Arawata', *The Mountain World*, Swiss Foundation for Alpine Research, George Allen & Unwin, 1955.

'Tribute to an Explorer' (A. P. Harper), *CM*, 1955.

'In Memoriam: John Gavin Malcolmson', *CM*, 1955.

'Return to Pelorus', *Journeys*, August 1955.

The High Country Run, Post-Primary School Bulletin, Vol. 9, No. 7, 1955.

'Men of the Mountains' (13 radio talks), NZBS, September–December 1955.

'F. M. C. Miscellany', *The Tararua Tramper*, October 1955.

'The Maori and the Mountains', *Te Ao Hou*, 11 and 12, 1955.

'How to be happy through camping', *NZ Listener*, 9 December 1955.

'Mount Hooker – From a Cave to a Summit', *Journeys*, May 1956.

'Four Explorers of New Zealand Part One: Thomas Brunner', *School Journal*, Autumn 1956.

'A "Literary Type" in the Mountains', *Tararua Tramper*, June 1956.

'Lake Ohau to Karangarua', *NZAJ*, 1956.

'Four Explorers of New Zealand Part Two: Samuel Butler', *School Journal*, Winter 1956.

'Children on the snows of New Zealand', *New Zealand Free Lance*, 3 August 1956.

'Australians Climb High on South Island Snows', *Journeys*, August 1956.

'A Long Way From Lake Ohau', *CM*, 1956.

The Southern Alps (Part 1) – From the Kaikouras to the Rangitata, Pegasus Press, 1956 [revised edition].

'Four Explorers of New Zealand Part Three: John Carne Bidwill', *School Journal*, Spring 1956.

'First Horses over Broderick Pass', *Journeys*, November 1956.

'Four Explorers of New Zealand Part Four: Arthur P. Harper', *School Journal*, Summer 1956.

'Twain River became the Douglas – Exploration of the Karangarua Valley', *The Press*, 22 December 1956.

'Visit by Swiss who climbed Everest – Promise of treat for N.Z. Mountaineers', *Evening Post*, 6 February 1957.

Mr Explorer Douglas, A. H. & A. W. Reed, 1957 (reprinted 1957, 1969; revised edition by Graham Langton, Canterbury University Press, 2000).

'Journey to New Zealand', *School Journal*, Autumn 1957.

Book Review: *In Highest Nepal* by Norman Hardie, *NZ Listener*, June 1957.

'Bishop on Horseback', *School Journal*, Winter 1957.

'Then and Now', *CMC News*, Vol. 2, No. 12, August–September 1957 (republished *CM*, 1975).

'A Prospect of the Mountains', *New Zealand Holiday*, No. 6, 1957.

'Fifty Years Ago', *School Journal*, Summer 1957.

'18 Day Mountaineering trip in South Westland', *The Press*, 20 January 1958.

'Among Storm-Swept Mountains – Rewarding Journey in South Westland', *Evening Post*, 23 January 1958.

'Camera Traps Rare Views of Westland Territory of "Mr. Explorer Douglas"', *Evening Post*, 1 February 1958.

'Up and Down the Maitahi', *NZAJ*, 1958.

'Memories of the Maitahi', *CM*, 1958.

Great Days in New Zealand Mountaineering, A. H. & A. W. Reed, 1958.

My Dear Bannie – Gerhard Mueller's Letters from the West Coast 1865–6, edited by M. V. Mueller (introduction by John Pascoe), Pegasus Press, 1958.

Great Days in New Zealand Exploration, A. H. & A. W. Reed, 1959 (reprinted in paperback, 1976).

The Exploration of New Zealand by W. G. McClymont (introduction by John Pascoe), second edition, Oxford University Press, 1959.

'Impressions of New Zealanders' (radio talks: Sir Edmund Hillary, General Sir Howard Kippenberger, Syd Brookes, David Hall, Dr J. C. Beaglehole), NZBS, November 1959

Book Review: *The Mountain World 1958–59*, *CM*, 1959.

Over the Whitcombe Pass, (introduced and edited by John Pascoe), Whitcombe & Tombs, 1960.

Book Review: *Mountain Search and Rescue* by L. D. Bridge, NZAC Bulletin, No. 35, June 1960.

'From Otago to Westland', *New Zealand Free Lance*, 13 July 1960.

'Men of My Country' (Sir Edmund Hillary, Charles Watson-Munro, George Lowe, Russell Clark, Syd Brookes, Eric McCormick, Sid Odell), *New Zealand Free Lance*, 1 June to 20 July 1960.

'Obituary: Brian Henry Williams', *Tararua*, 1960.

'To the Waipara – Notes from a Diary', *CM*, 1960.

'Men's Homage to Mighty Makalu', *Evening Post*, 27 June 1961.

Land Uplifted High, Whitcombe & Tombs, second edition 1961.

'Holiday at the Sounds', *School Journal*, Part 1, No. 5, 1961.

Book Review: *Samuel Butler at Mesopotamia* by P. B. Maling, *CM*, 1961.

'The Mountains of Erewhon', *NZ Listener*, 17 November 1961.

Book Review: *Pioneers of Martins Bay* by Alice McKenzie, *NZAJ*, 1962.

'The Mountains of Erewhon', *CM*, 1962.

'Our First Hundred Years: Inaugural Kennedy Memorial Lecture', *CM*, 1962.

New Zealand in Colour – Volume Two, A. H. & A. W. Reed, 1962 (photographs by Kenneth and Jean Bigwood).

'Women fought on the beach at Jacksons Bay', *Evening Post*, 7 May 1963.

'The Way of a Pioneer', *NZ Listener*, 19 July 1963.

'From the Waitaha to the Rakaia', *NZAJ*, 1963.

'Beyond the Waitaha', *CM*, 1963.

'Hazards of the East Ridge of Mount Cook', *Evening Post*, 6 January 1964.

'More on Mr Explorer Douglas', *NZ Listener*, 24 January 1964.

'Some Problems in the Popularity of Tararua Ranges', *Evening Post*, 30 November 1964.

'Problems for climbers in legacy of severe winter', *Evening Post*, 18 December 1964.

'A Family in the Waimakariri', *Tararua*, 1965.

'A Sense of History', *NZAC Bulletin*, No. 45, June 1965.

Book Review: *No Place For Men* by Peter Mulgrew, *NZAJ*, 1965.

'Family Return to the Waimakariri', *CM*, 1965.

The National Parks of New Zealand, Government Printer, 1965 (2nd edition 1971, 3rd edition 1974).

Oxford New Zealand Encyclopedia, edited with Laura Salt, Oxford University Press, 1965.

Peter Graham, Mountain Guide – an autobiography, edited by Mrs H. B. Hewitt (introduction and epilogue by John Pascoe), A. H. & A. W. Reed and George Allen & Unwin, 1965 (reprinted in smaller format, 1973).

'Memorial to a climber who answered call', *Evening Post*, 1 July 1966.

'Children in the Hills', *Tararua*, 1966.

'In Memoriam: John Harrison, A Tribute', *CM*, 1966.

The Haast is in South Westland, A. H. & A. W. Reed, 1966 (reprinted, 1968).

'Beautiful Mount Aspiring is Rewarding Climb', *Evening Post*, 23 March 1967.

'Aspiring was their goal', *Weekly News*, April 1967.

'A Mostest for Aspiring', *NZAJ*, 1967.

'Matukituki and Aspiring', *CM*, 1967.

Book Review: *Dusky Bay* by Charles and Neil Begg, *New Zealand Journal of History*, Vol. 1, No. 2, October 1967.

'William Fox in Westland: the naming of the Fox Glacier', *Turnbull Library Record*, November 1967.

'Into Siberia', *NZAJ*, 1968.

Book Review: *Unkilled For So Long* by Sir Arnold Lunn, *NZAJ*, 1968.

New Zealand From The Air – In Colour, (photographs by R. J. Griffiths), A. H. & A. W. Reed, 1968.

'The Ahuriri to Ourselves', *NZAJ*, 1969.

'Family Mountain Climb', *Weekly News*, c.February 1969.

Book Review: *Jack's Hut* by Grace Adams, *NZAJ*, 1969.

'Grading Climbs', *NZAC Bulletin*, No. 54, December 1969.

'A Holiday on D'Urville Island', *School Journal*, Part 1, No. 4, 1970.

'In Memoriam: Arthur Frederick Pearson 1904–1970', *NZAJ*, 1970.

'Reflections on a Family Holiday', *CM*, 1970.

'Freddie Ambrose, man of the mountains', *The Press*, 12 December 1970.

'National or notional?', *NZ Listener*, 8 February 1971.

The National Parks of New Zealand, Government Printer, 2nd edition, 1971.

'Up on the Mountains so happy and free', *CM*, 1971.

Of Unknown New Zealand, John McIndoe, 1971.

Exploration New Zealand, A. H. & A. W. Reed, 1971 (new edition as *Explorers and Travellers*, 1983).

'Many Mountain Challenges left – Veteran writes about peaks', *Evening Post*, 21 December 1971.

Posthumous

'In Memoriam: David Oswald William Hall 1909–1971', *NZAJ*, 1972.

National Parks of New Zealand, Government Printer, 3rd edition, 1974.

'Aerial Mapping', *CM*, 1975.

'The First Ascent of Gizeh and an Ascent of Carrington Peak Easter 1930', *CM*, 1975.

'Butler in the Mountains – Early Canterbury Exploration', *CM*, 1975 (from *The Press*, 5 December 1935).

'Climbs in the Rakaia Hills', *CM*, 1975 (from *Christ's College Register*, April 1932).

'Success on Mount Evans', *CM*, 1975 (from *CM*, 1934).

'The Rakaia Ranges', *CM*, 1975 (from *Victoria League Monthly Notes*, 1 September 1935).

'Then and Now', CM, 1975 (from *CMC News*, August–September 1957).

'The Whitehorn Pass Accident and Subsequent Search', CM, 1975 (accident on 21 May 1934).

Great Days in New Zealand Exploration, Collins Fontana Silver Fern, 1976 (reprint in smaller paperback format).

Explorers and Travellers, (introduced by Dorothy Pascoe), A. H. & A. W. Reed, 1983 (revised edition of *Exploration New Zealand*).

Mr Explorer Douglas, Canterbury University Press, 2000 (revised edition by Graham Langton).

References

INTRODUCTION
John the Evangelist

1 John Pascoe, *Land Uplifted High*, Whitcombe & Tombs, 1952, p.1.

2 Conversation with Dorothy Pascoe, 30 April 1991 (tape).

3 John Pascoe to Robin Muir, 2 October 1952, MS Papers 75-241 (7), Alexander Turnbull Library.

4 John Pascoe to Rob McCullough, 22 May 1953, Dorothy Pascoe Collection.

5 Conversation with Dorothy Pascoe, 27 September 1999 (tape 1).

6 Frank Fitzgerald to the author, 25 December 2001.

CHAPTER ONE
'A Skinny Stammerer'

1 Conversation with Dorothy Pascoe, 20 January 2000 (tape); John Pascoe to Bill Cox, 29 July 1966, Dorothy Pascoe Collection.

2 Conversation with Joan Maclean (neé Whitcombe), 5 September 1999.

3 Dorothy Pascoe, *op. cit.*

4 Conversation with Anna Pascoe, 8 April 2000 (tape).

5 Conversation with Simon Pascoe, 9 April 2000 (tape).

6 Dorothy Pascoe, *op. cit.*

7 Bobrick, Benson, *Knotted Tongues – Stuttering in History and the quest for a cure*, Simon & Schuster, 1994, p.169.

8 Jonas, Gerald, *Stuttering: The Disorder of Many Theories*, Farrar, Straus & Giroux, 1976, p.10.

9 J. D. Pascoe to Norman Hardie, 18 August 1963, Dorothy Pascoe Collection.

10 Conversation with Dorothy Pascoe, 9 March 2000 (tape).

11 Simon Pascoe, *op. cit.*

12 Jean Bertram to Dorothy Pascoe, 1 November 1972, Dorothy Pascoe Collection.

13 O. T. J. Alpers, 'Guy Dobree Pascoe – An Appreciation', *The Press*, May 1927.

14 J. D. Pascoe to N. S. Odell, 16 November 1955, Dorothy Pascoe Collection.

15 J. D. Pascoe, Album 1, P.A.Coll.1:0:406, Alexander Turnbull Library.

16 John Pascoe, *Great Days in New Zealand Exploration*, A. H. & A. W. Reed, 1959, p.176.

17 Ibid., pp.72–77.

18 Ibid., p.124.

19 John Pascoe, *Unclimbed New Zealand*, Allen & Unwin, 1950 (second edition), p.84.

20 John Pascoe, 'The Huts at the Rakaia Mouth', unpublished article, 22 August 1961, Dorothy Pascoe Collection.

21 O. T. J. Alpers to John Pascoe and Paul Pascoe, undated c.1921, Jonathan Pascoe Collection.

22 Don Hamilton, *College! – A History of Christ's College*, Christ's College, 1996, p.322, 323.
Also: conversations with Dorothy Pascoe, 27 September 1999 (tape), Simon Pascoe, *op. cit.*, Jonathan Pascoe, 8 April 2000 and Sara Pascoe, 29 June 2001.

23 Kenneth Sandford, *Mark of the Lion*, Hutchinson, 1962, p.18.

24 Denis Glover, *Hot Water Sailor*, A. H. & A. W. Reed, 1962, p.49.

25 Gordon Ogilvie, *Denis Glover*, Godwit, 1999, p.36.

26 Hamilton, *op. cit.*, pp.339–396.

27 John Pascoe, 'College Days', Dorothy Pascoe Collection; Paul Pascoe, 'College Days', Jonathan Pascoe Collection.

28 Ibid., (John Pascoe).

29 John Pascoe to David Herron, 16 September 1958, Dorothy Pascoe Collection.

30 Conversations with Dorothy Pascoe, 27 September 1999 (tape), and Simon Pascoe, *op. cit.*

31 R. M. Ussher, 'The Modern Movement in Canterbury: The Architecture of Paul Pascoe', MA thesis, University of Canterbury, 1986, p.10.

32 John Pascoe, 'The Huts at the Rakaia Mouth', *op. cit.*

33 Paul Pascoe, Diaries 1924, 1925, Simon Pascoe Collection.

34 J. D. Pascoe, University of New Zealand – Result Notification, December 1925, Dorothy Pascoe Collection.

35 John Pascoe, 'The Huts at the Rakaia Mouth', *op. cit.*

36 Paul Pascoe, Diary 1925, *op. cit.*

37 Simon Pascoe, *op. cit.*

38 Conversation with Dorothy Pascoe, 26 October 2000 (tape).

CHAPTER TWO
The Intelligence Officer

1 Jean Bertram to Dorothy Pascoe, 1 November 1972, Dorothy Pascoe Collection.

2 Academic Officer, New Zealand Vice-Chancellors' Committee to the author, 29 August 2000.

3 John Pascoe, *Unclimbed New Zealand*, George Allen & Unwin, 1950 (2nd edition), p.30.

4 Academic Officer, *op. cit.*

5 Kowai Bush visitors' book, 1 December 1929 (unsourced, undated newspaper clipping), Simon Pascoe Collection.

6 J. D. Pascoe, 'The Waimakariri Invasion – Easter 1930', *Canterbury Mountaineer*, (2) 1933, p.6.

7 Ibid.

8 John Pascoe, *Unclimbed New Zealand*, p.55.

9 Roger Chester to Dorothy Pascoe, 13 February 1973, Dorothy Pascoe Collection.

10 John Pascoe, *Unclimbed New Zealand*, pp.63–65.

11 Ibid., pp.67-70.

12 *New Zealand Free Lance*, (undated clipping), Dorothy Pascoe Collection; *New Zealand Railways Magazine*, March–April 1931.

13 "Climbing at the Headwaters of the Mathias River, Canterbury', *New Zealand Alpine Journal*, 1931, pp.208–215.

14 John Pascoe, 'Climbs in the Rakaia Hills', *Christ's College Register*, April, 1932.

15 John Pascoe, *Unclimbed New Zealand*, pp.85–86.

16 While editing Jakob Lauper's account of his journey with the surveyor, Henry Whitcombe, John Pascoe's research verified that Lauper, not Louper, is the correct spelling of the Swiss guide's surname. It was misspelt on early maps, an error which has continued to this day, causing confusion. Lauper is used throughout this account. See John Pascoe (ed.), *Over the Whitcombe Pass*, Whitcombe & Tombs, 1960, p.12.

17 Conversation with Dorothy Pascoe, 18 May 2001.

18 John Pascoe, *Unclimbed New Zealand*, p.89.

19 Conversations with Dorothy Pascoe, 27 September 1999 (tape); Simon Pascoe, 9 April 2000 (tape).

20 S. A. Wiren, 'Ascent of Mt Westland', *New Zealand Alpine Journal*, 1932, p.31, as annotated by Brian Wyn Irwin, Graham Langton Collection; John Pascoe to Ian Powell, 22 July and 13 August 1931, Dorothy Pascoe Collection.

21 Pascoe to Powell, 13 August 1931.

22 *The Press*, 14 November 1931. (The author is identified as John Pascoe by Brian Wyn Irwin, see his annotated scrapbook, Canterbury Museum Collection.)

23 John Pascoe, *Unclimbed New Zealand*, p.97; Wiren, *op. cit.*

24 Allan Willis, 'First Ascent of Mount Whitcombe and Crossing of the Strachan Pass', *New Zealand Alpine Journal*, 1932, pp.18, 19.

25 Conversation with Allan Willis, 11 April 2000 (tape); Allan Willis to Sara Pascoe, 3 November 1994.

26 Conversation with Andy Anderson, 9 January 2000 (tape).

27 John Pascoe, *Great Days in New Zealand Mountaineering*, A. H. & A. W. Reed, 1958, pp.60, 61.

28 *New Zealand Herald*, 27, 28 January 1932.

29 Pat Lawlor, *Old Wellington Days*, Whitcombe & Tombs, 1959, pp.142-150.

30 John Pascoe to Evan Wilson, 22 July 1958, Dorothy Pascoe Collection.

31 Conversation with Simon Pascoe, 13 April 2001; Paul Pascoe photo album, Jonathan Pascoe Collection.

32 R. M. Ussher, 'The Modern Movement in Canterbury: The Architecture of Paul Pascoe', MA Thesis, University of Canterbury, 1986, p.11.

33 *New Zealand Institute of Architects Journal*, June 1932, pp.46, 47.

34 Ussher, *op. cit.*, p.17.

35 Conversation with Simon Pascoe, 9 April 2000 (tape), 13 April 2001.

36 Allan Willis to Sara Pascoe, *op. cit.*

37 Ibid.

38 Paul Pascoe, Diary, 11 December 1932, Simon Pascoe Collection.

39 Conversation with Priestley Thomson, 22 September 1999 (tape one).

40 Ibid.

41 John Pascoe, 'Climbs in the Rakaia Hills', *op. cit.*

42 John Pascoe, *Unclimbed New Zealand*, p.103.

43 John Pascoe, *Great Days in New Zealand Mountaineering*, p.63.

44 Conversation with Ian Powell, 12 March 1990 (tape).

45 John Pascoe, *Great Days in New Zealand Mountaineering*, p.64.

46 Ibid., p.65.

47 Conversation with Priestley Thomson, 28 June 2001 (tape).

48 John Pascoe, *Unclimbed New Zealand*, pp.113, 114.

49 Ibid., p.115.

CHAPTER THREE

The Explorer

1 John Pascoe, *Unclimbed New Zealand*, Allen & Unwin, (2nd edition), 1950, pp.203, 204.

2 *The Press*, 16 September 1933.

3 John Pascoe, *Unclimbed New Zealand*, p.76.

4 S. A. Wiren, 'Ascent of Mt Westland', *New Zealand Alpine Journal*, 1932, p.31.

5 M. Townsend, 'The Rakaia-Rangitata-Lawrence: A Round Trip from Rakaia Hut', *Canterbury Mountaineer*, (3), 1934, p.56.

6 John Pascoe, *Unclimbed New Zealand*, p.177; John Pascoe to Ian Powell, 17 September 1933, Dorothy Pascoe Collection.

7 *The Press*, 19 August 1933.

8 G. E. Mannering, 'The Disaster on the Tasman Glacier', *New Zealand Alpine Journal*, 1930, pp.119–129.

9 *The Press*, 2 September 1931.

10 *The Press*, 5, 7 September, 10, 11 November 1931.

11 *The Press*, 14 November 1931.

12 *The Press*, 10, 11 January 1934.

13 Paul Pascoe diary, Simon Pascoe Collection; Paul Pascoe photo album, Jonathan Pascoe Collection.

14 John Pascoe, 'In Mountain Ranges', *The Press Junior*, 1934, 1935, David Macmillan Collection.

15 Jean Bertram (neé Stevenson) to Dorothy Pascoe, 1 November 1972, Dorothy Pascoe Collection.

16 Conversation with Dorothy Pascoe, 30 July 2001.

17 John Pascoe, 'The Spirit of the Pilgrim – The Golden Journey to Samarkand', *Canterbury University College Review*, October 1935, pp.9, 10.

18 John Pascoe, *Unclimbed New Zealand*, p.119.

19 John Pascoe, 'Exploration of the Perth Glaciers, Westland', *Canterbury Mountaineer*, (4), 1935, p.33.

20 Ibid., p.33

21 Ibid., pp.34–36.

22 Conversation with Priestley Thomson, 22 September 1999 (tape one).

23 John Pascoe, *Great Days in New Zealand Exploration*, A. H. & A. W. Reed, 1959, p.177.

24 Conversation with Bernie Greig, 6 March 2000 (tape).

25 Austen Deans to the author, 29 March 2000.

26 John Pascoe, *Unclimbed New Zealand*, pp.45, 46, 48.

27 J. D. Pascoe, 'Exploration of the Adams Glaciers and Valley, Westland', *Canterbury Mountaineer*, (5), 1936, p.47.

28 *The Press*, 10 January 1936.

29 J. D. Pascoe, 'Exploration of the Adams Glaciers and Valley, Westland', p.55.

30 *Ibid*.

31 *Ibid.*, p.49.

32 *Ibid.*, p.61.

33 *Ibid.*, pp.47–63.

34 Secretary, Royal Geographical Society, to John Pascoe, 8 June 1936, Dorothy Pascoe Collection.

35 John Pascoe, *Great Days in New Zealand Exploration*, p.182.

36 N. Barker, 'Names for the Hills', *Canterbury Mountaineer*, (10), 1941, p.23.

37 John Pascoe, 'The Rakaia Ranges', *Victoria League Monthly Notes*, 1 September 1935, reprinted in *Canterbury Mountaineer*, (44), 1975, p.77.

38 Frank Gillett, 'The Best Laid Plans', *Canterbury Mountaineer*, (44), 1975, pp.142–143.

39 Tom Newth to Sara Pascoe, 7 November 1994.

40 Michael Mahoney, *Harry Ayres: Mountain Guide*, Whitcoulls, 1982, p.62.

41 Johnny Pascoe to Ian Powell, 15 October 1936, Dorothy Pascoe Collection.

42 John Pascoe, Album 5, PA Coll 1:0:410, Alexander Turnbull Library.

43 *The Press*, 14 November 1931.

44 Hugh Logan, *Great Peaks of New Zealand*, John McIndoe, 1990, p.25.

45 Tom Newth, 'Johnny Pascoe Remembered', *Canterbury Mountaineer*, (60), 1999, p.74.

46 R. Syme, 'Tasman by a New Route', *New Zealand Alpine Journal*, 1931, pp.176–182.

47 John Pascoe, *Unclimbed New Zealand*, p.137.

48 Hugh Logan, *Great Peaks of New Zealand*, p.30.

49 John Pascoe, *Unclimbed New Zealand*, p.138.

50 John Pascoe, 'In Memoriam' (obituary for David Hall), *New Zealand Alpine Journal*, 1972, p.118.

51 Conversation with Priestley Thomson, 29 April 2001.

52 Tom Newth, *op. cit.*

53 John Pascoe, *Unclimbed New Zealand*, p.141.

54 Tom Newth, *op. cit.*; John Pascoe, *Unclimbed New Zealand*, Chapter 11.

55 Conversation with Priestley Thomson, 25 September 1999 (tape 2).

56 Tom Newth, *op. cit.*

57 Tom Newth to Sara Pascoe, 7 November 1994, Sara Pascoe Collection.

58 *The Monocle*, May 1937, p.26, 27; *New Zealand Railways Magazine*, 1 May 1937, pp.39–43.

59 *Tobacco*, 1 November 1937, pp.49–51.

60 *Blue Peter*, (189), December 1937, pp.600–606.

61 John Pascoe to Eff Pascoe, 10 February 1938, Dorothy Pascoe Collection. [Although she was usually known as Effie, John invariably addressed his mother as Eff in his letters.]

62 Academic Officer, New Zealand Vice-Chancellors' Committee, to the author, 29 August 2000.

63 Conversation with Simon Pascoe, 13 April 2001 (tape).

64 Conversation with Frank Fitzgerald, 29 August 2000 (tape).

65 J. H. Upham, testimonial, c. March 1937, Dorothy Pascoe Collection.

66 P. H. N. Freeth, 8 March 1937; H. G. Denham, 8 February 1937 and C. G. Ellis, c. March 1937; Dorothy Pascoe Collection.

67 H. E. Hart, Provincial Superintendent, Lake Coleridge Power Station, 25 March 1937, Dorothy Pascoe Collection.

CHAPTER FOUR

Love and War

1 John Pascoe to Eff Pascoe, 20 July 1939, Dorothy Pascoe Collection; 'Is not a Patron, my Lord, one who looks with unconcern on a man struggling for life in the water, and, when he has reached ground, encumbers him with help? The notice which you have been pleased to take of my labours, had it been early, had been kind; but it has been delayed till I am indifferent, and cannot enjoy it; till I am solitary, and cannot impart it; till I am known, and do not want it.'

2 *Christ's College School List 1850 – 1935*, Christ's College Old Boys' Association, 1935, p.298.

3 J. F. St. B. Barclay to John Pascoe, 9 June 1937, MS Papers 0138-6, Alexander Turnbull Library.

4 John Pascoe, Manuscripts of *Unclimbed New Zealand* and *Land Uplifted High*, MS Papers 1632, Alexander Turnbull Library.

5 John Pascoe to Barclay, 22 July 1937.

6 Eric McCormick, *An absurd ambition – autobiographical writings*, edited by Denis McEldowney, Auckland University Press, 1996, p.140.

7 *Ibid*.

8 John Pascoe to Eff and Paul Pascoe, 1937–1939, Dorothy Pascoe Collection.

9 John Pascoe to Barclay, 3 September 1937.

10 Michael Bassett, *The Mother of all Departments*, Auckland University Press and the Historical Branch, Department of Internal Affairs, 1997, pp.106–110.

11 Eric McCormick, pp.140–142.

12 John Pascoe to Eff Pascoe, 3 February 1938.

13 *Ibid*.

14 Eric McCormick, pp.140–142.

15 John Pascoe, 'Retrospect in Pictures – An Inquest on a Historical Quest', *National Education*, 1 October 1942, p.297.

16 John Pascoe to Paul Pascoe, 7 February 1938, Dorothy Pascoe Collection.

17 Barclay to Pascoe, 8 February 1938.

18 John Pascoe to Eff and Paul Pascoe, 16 March 1938; to Pete (Paul) Pascoe, 18 March 1938, Dorothy Pascoe Collection.

19 Paradise to Pascoe (cable), 24 March 1938, MS Papers 0138-6, Alexander Turnbull Library.

20 John Pascoe to Eff and Paul Pascoe, 25 March 1938.

21 Barclay to Pascoe, 24 March 1938.

22 John Pascoe to Eff and Paul Pascoe, 29 March 1938.

23 Pascoe to Barclay, 26 May 1938.

24 John Pascoe to Eff and Paul Pascoe, 6 May 1938.

25 John Pascoe, 'Retrospect in Pictures – An Inquest on a Historical Quest', *National Education, op. cit.*

26 Conversation with Janet Paul, 27 March 2000 (tape).

27 *Dictionary of New Zealand Biography*, (Volume Five), Auckland University Press and the Department of Internal Affairs, 2000, p.44.

28 John Pascoe to Pete (Paul) Pascoe, 16 November 1938.

29 Dorothy Pascoe, 'On First Meeting J. D. P.', typescript, 26 September 2001, Collection of the author.

30 John Pascoe to Pete (Paul) Pascoe, 4 April 1938.

31 John Pascoe to Eff and Paul Pascoe, 1 May 1938.

32 John Pascoe to Eff Pascoe, 13 May, 24 May 1938.

33 B. D. A. Greig (ed), *Tararua Story*, Tararua Tramping Club, 1946, pp.76, 82; John Pascoe to Eff Pascoe, 14 June 1938.

34 John Pascoe to Eff and Pete (Paul) Pascoe, 18 July 1938.

35 John Pascoe to Eff Pascoe, 21 July 1938; to Eff and Paul Pascoe, 25 July 1938 and 18 August 1938.

36 John Pascoe to Eff and Paul Pascoe, 8 September 1938.

37 Eric McCormick, *An absurd ambition*, pp.142–147.

38 John Pascoe to Eff Pascoe, 11 August 1938.

39 John Pascoe to Eff Pascoe, 22 and 25 November 1938.

40 *The Scotsman*, 23 January 1939; *New Zealand News*, 31 January 1939, Dorothy Pascoe Collection.

41 *Manchester Guardian*, 14 February 1939; *London Mercury*, 1 February 1939; and *Fortnightly Review*, 1 March 1939, Dorothy Pascoe Collection.

42 Frank Smythe, the well-known British mountaineer and photographer. *National Review*, 1 March 1939, Dorothy Pascoe Collection.

43 John Pascoe, *Land Uplifted High*, Whitcombe & Tombs, 1952, pp.104, 105.

44 *New Zealand Free Lance*, 15 March 1939; *The Press*, 25 March 1939; John Pascoe to Eff Pascoe, 28 March 1939.

45 *Bulletin*, 29 March 1939; *Sydney Morning Herald*, 8 April 1939, Dorothy Pascoe Collection.

46 *Appalachia*, (87) June 1939, p.444; *Geographical Review*, American Geographical Society, January 1940, Dorothy Pascoe Collection.

47 *Alpine Journal*, (258) May 1939, pp.155, 156, Dorothy Pascoe Collection.

48 Chris Bonington, *Quest for Adventure*, Cassell & Co., 2000, p.142.

49 *New Zealand Alpine Journal*, (26) June 1939, pp.124-127.

50 John Pascoe to Eff Pascoe, 18 and 24 July 1939.

51 *Ibid.*, 26 September 1939.

52 Dorothy Pascoe, 'On First Meeting J. D. P.'

53 *Ibid.*

54 Dorothy Pascoe, 'My First Mountain', typescript, September 2000, Collection of the author; John Pascoe to Pete (Paul) Pascoe, 8 January 1940.

55 Conversation with Dorothy Pascoe, 23 October 2001.

56 Extract from letter received from Messrs. Whitcombe & Tombs, 14 December 1939, MS Papers 1132, folder 296, Alexander Turnbull Library.

57 Conversation with Graeme Maxwell, 29 October 2001.

58 *Dominion*, 19 December 1939.

59 A. P. Harper to J. D. Pascoe, 14 November 1939, Dorothy Pascoe Collection; *Dominion*, 20 December 1939.

60 John Pascoe to Eff Pascoe, 20 December 1939.

61 *New Zealand Free Lance*, 27 December 1939.

62 A. P. Harper Scrapbook, Gordon Buchanan Personal Papers, Canterbury Museum.

63 Graham Langton, 'A History of Mountain Climbing in New Zealand to 1953', thesis, University of Canterbury, 1996, pp.191–198.

64 John Pascoe to Doug Knowles, 27 June 1933, Alan Knowles Collection; D. G. Herron, 'The 1914 Revival of the New Zealand Alpine Club', *New Zealand Alpine Journal*, 1958, pp.420–427; John Pascoe to David Herron, 16 September 1958, Dorothy Pascoe Collection.

65 Robin Cooke, *Portrait of a Profession*, Reed, 1969, pp.259–262; *Dictionary of New Zealand Biography*, (Volume Four), Bridget Williams Books and the Historical Branch, Internal Affairs, 1998, p.225.

66 *Making New Zealand*, (10) February 1940, p.22.

67 A. P. Harper to Jock Sim, 14 February 1940, New Zealand Alpine Club Papers 101/85, Hocken Library.

68 Jock Sim to A. P. Harper, 4 March 1940, New Zealand Alpine Club Papers, 101/85, Hocken Library.

69 A. P. Harper to J. D. Pascoe, 26 February 1940, New Zealand Alpine Club Papers, 101/85, Hocken Library.

70 Johnny Pascoe to A. P. Harper, 26 February 1940, New Zealand Alpine Club Papers, 101/85, Hocken Library.

71 John Pascoe to Pete (Paul) Pascoe, 27 February 1940.

72 John Pascoe to Eff Pascoe, 28 February 1940.

73 *Otago Daily Times*, 12 March 1940; John Pascoe to Pete (Paul) Pascoe, 14 March 1940.

74 *Evening Post*, 19 March 1940.

75 A. P. Harper to (Roland) Ellis, 26 March 1940, New Zealand Alpine Club Papers 101/85, Hocken Library.

76 Conversation with Dorothy Pascoe, 17 October 2001.

77 John Pascoe to Eff Pascoe, 16 February 1940.

78 John Pascoe to Pete (Paul) Pascoe, 16 February 1940.

79 John Pascoe to Eff Pascoe, 9 January 1940.

80 John Pascoe to Eff and Paul Pascoe, 23 January 1940.

81 Dorothy Pascoe, 'On First Meeting J. D. P.'

82 Conversation with Dorothy Pascoe, 27 September 1999 (tape one).

83 John Pascoe to Eff Pascoe, 4 April 1940; 9 April 1940; to Pete (Paul) Pascoe, 10 April 1940.

84 A. P. Harper to (Roland) Ellis, 26 March 1940; Roland Ellis to Charles Buchanan, 1 April 1940, New Zealand Alpine Club Papers 101/85, Hocken Library.

85 John Pascoe to Eff and Paul Pascoe, 19 April 1940; John Pascoe to Eff Pascoe, 2 May 1940.

86 Dorothy Pascoe, 'On First Meeting J. D. P.'; 'Our Various Houses', 19 May 2000, typescript, Collection of the author.

87 Conversation with Janet Paul, 27 March 2000 (tape).

CHAPTER FIVE

'Traveller with a Camera'

1 John Pascoe to Pete (Paul) Pascoe, 18 October 1940, Dorothy Pascoe Collection.

2 Dorothy Pascoe, 'The Spanish Civil War and World War 2', typescript, 13 November 2001, Collection of the author.

3 Eric McCormick, An absurd ambition — autobiographical writings, edited by Denis McEldowney, Auckland University Press, 1996, pp.150, 151.

4 John Pascoe to Pete (Paul) Pascoe, 18 October, 1940; Conversations with Dorothy Pascoe, 28 November, 27 December 2001.

5 John Pascoe, Land Uplifted High, Whitcombe & Tombs, 1952, pp.110, 111.

6 John Pascoe to Pete (Paul) Pascoe, 18 October 1940.

7 John Pascoe to Eff Pascoe, 27 January 1941, Dorothy Pascoe Collection.

8 John Pascoe to Eff Pascoe, 20 January 1941.

9 John Pascoe to Eff Pascoe, 31 January 1941.

10 John Pascoe to Eff Pascoe, 26 February 1941.

11 John Pascoe to Eff Pascoe, 16 February 1941; Under-Secretary to Minister of Internal Affairs, 4 February 1941, MS Papers 1132, folder 296, Alexander Turnbull Library.

12 Dorothy Pascoe to Ann and Paul Pascoe, 6 March 1941, Dorothy Pascoe Collection.

13 John Pascoe to Eff Pascoe, 13 June 1941.

14 Conversation with Dorothy Pascoe, 7 December 2001.

15 John Pascoe, untitled typescript, c.1941, Dorothy Pascoe Collection.

16 John Pascoe to Eff Pascoe, 6, 15 July 1941.

17 John Pascoe to Pete (Paul) Pascoe, 4 August 1941.

18 Simon Pascoe to the author, 17 December 2001.

19 John Pascoe, 'History of thermal fisheries', 1941, MS Papers 6523, Alexander Turnbull Library; John Pascoe to Pete (Paul) Pascoe, 21 August 1941.

20 Joe Heenan to Eric McCormick, 7 July 1941, MS Papers 1132, folder 134, Alexander Turnbull Library.

21 Conversation with Dorothy Pascoe, 7 December 2001; Dorothy Pascoe, 'On First Meeting J. D. P.', typescript, 26 September 2001, Collection of the author.

22 Eric McCormick to Joe Heenan, 27 September 1941, MS Papers 1132, folder 134, Alexander Turnbull Library.

23 John Pascoe, 'Southern Tourabout', typescript, c. October 1941, Dorothy Pascoe Collection.

24 John Pascoe, Land Uplifted High, pp.91–96.

25 John Pascoe to Eff Pascoe, 21 December 1941; Dorothy Pascoe to Pete (Paul), Ann and Luke Pascoe, 12 January 1942, Dorothy Pascoe Collection.

26 John Pascoe to Pete (Paul), Ann and Luke Pascoe, 12 January 1942.

27 Dorothy Pascoe to Eff Pascoe, 11 January 1942.

28 John Pascoe to Pete (Paul) Pascoe, 10 March 1942.

29 Dorothy Pascoe to Ann and Paul Pascoe, c.15 March 1942.

30 Jock Phillips with Ellen Ellis, Brief Encounter: American Forces and the New Zealand People 1942–1945, Historical Branch, Department of Internal Affairs, 1992.

31 John Pascoe, Land Uplifted High, p.23.

32 Ibid., pp.14, 15.

33 Ibid., p.13.

34 W. J. Heenan, Notebook recording gifts of Making New Zealand to US forces, MS Papers 1132, folder 134, Alexander Turnbull Library.

35 Conversation with Janet Paul (neé Wilkinson), 27 March 2000 (tape).

36 John Pascoe, 'Photography in New Zealand', Landfall, 1 (4), 1947, pp.301, 302.

37 Gisèle Freund, Photography and Society, Gordon Fraser, 1980, pp.115–140.

38 Leonard Bell, 'Irene Koppel — A forgotten "New" Photographer in New Zealand', Art New Zealand, 101, 2001/2002, pp.70–75.

39 Conversation with Dorothy Pascoe, 27 December 2001.

40 Gisèle Freund, Photography and Society, pp.141–160.

41 Pix, 15 October 1938.

42 Conversation with Dorothy Pascoe, 27 December 2001; John Pascoe, 'In Orari Gorge, Canterbury', S & D, 3 September 1943; Argus Weekend Magazine, 25 September 1943; Illustrated London News, 27 November 1943; Sport & Country, 9 June 1944; Picture Post, 9 December 1944, all in the Dorothy Pascoe Collection.

43 The Ngarimu Hui, Polynesian Society, 1949, p.5.

44 Pix, 23 September 1944; conversation with Janet Paul; conversation with Dorothy Pascoe, 27 December 2001.

45 John Pascoe, Land Uplifted High, p.72.

46 John Pascoe, 'Coal from the Buller', New Zealand Geographer, 4 (2) October 1948, p.168.

47 John Pascoe, *The Mountains, The Bush and the Sea*, Whitcombe & Tombs, 1950, Introduction.

48 'Photographic Collection – Pascoe', File T.L. 6/1/30, Alexander Turnbull Library.

CHAPTER SIX

Family Man

1 Dorothy Pascoe, 'Our Various Houses', typescript, 19 May 2002, Collection of the author; conversation with Dorothy Pascoe, 8 February 2002.

2 John Pascoe to Mrs [Anita] Crozier, 3 September 1951, Dorothy Pascoe Collection.

3 John Pascoe, *Land Uplifted High*, Whitcombe & Tombs, 1952, p.29.

4 John Pascoe, 'Summary of work progress from diary', 1947, Dorothy Pascoe Collection.

5 Dorothy Pascoe, 'Our Various Houses'.

6 Conversation with Dorothy Pascoe, 14 March 2002.

7 John Pascoe, *Land Uplifted High*, pp.125–126.

8 John Pascoe, 'Back to the Mountains', *Journeys*, 1 November 1946, p.13.

9 *Ibid.*

10 John Pascoe, 'Mount Russell is No 35', *Journeys*, 1 August 1947, pp.36–41.

11 John and Dorothy Pascoe , 'Mr and Mrs Reminisce', National Radio, 26 October 1972 (tape).

12 John Pascoe, *Land Uplifted High*, Preface.

13 Johnny Pascoe to Charlie [Cran], 7 June 1945, Dorothy Pascoe Collection.

14 John Pascoe, 'Canterbury High Country: The Sheep and Sheepmen of the Mountains', *New Zealand Geographer*, 1 (1), April 1945, pp.30 31.

15 Charlie [Cran] to Laurie Walker, 18 June 1945, postscript to letter from Johnny Pascoe to Charlie [Cran], 7 June 1945, Dorothy Pascoe Collection.

16 Johnny Pascoe to Charlie [Cran], 7 June 1945.

17 Bob Porter to the author, 1 March 2002.

18 John Pascoe, *Land Uplifted High*, pp.114–120; conversation with Dorothy Pascoe, 14 March 2002.

19 Conversation with Sara Pascoe, 14 March 2002.

20 Joe Heenan to Oliver Duff, 10 October 1949, p.2, MS Papers 1132:60, Alexander Turnbull Library.

21 John Pascoe, 'Illustrate the Text', unpublished typescript, c.1949/1950, Dorothy Pascoe Collection.

22 John Pascoe to Lawry [sic] Walker, 14 April 1948, Dorothy Pascoe Collection. [Pascoe always wrote Lawry rather than Laurie.]

23 John Pascoe to Guy Harding, quoted in Guy Harding to Elsie Locke, undated c. September 1948, Dorothy Pascoe Collection.

24 Dorothy Pascoe, 'Letters from William Guy Harding to Elsie Locke written during the years 1940 to 1950s', undated, collection of the author.

25 *Ibid.*

26 Guy Harding to Elsie Locke, 21 August 1949, Dorothy Pascoe Collection.

27 John Pascoe, *Land Uplifted High*, p.90, pp.130-137.

28 John Pascoe, 'Holidaying in the Sounds', *The Mirror*, October 1951.

29 John Pascoe, 'Notes on holiday in Pelorus Sound, January 1949', unpublished typescript, Dorothy Pascoe Collection.

30 John Pascoe, 'Family Holiday', *Journeys*, November 1949, p.49.

31 John Pascoe, *Land Uplifted High*, pp.127–137.

32 Dorothy Pascoe, 'Acceptance', typescript, October 2002, Collection of the author.

33 Conversation with Dorothy and Martha Pascoe, 27 September 1999 (tape).

34 Conversations with Dorothy Pascoe, 19 May 2000 (tape); 14 February 2002.

35 Laurie Walker to Johnny Pascoe, 2 July 1949, Dorothy Pascoe Collection.

36 Dorothy Pascoe, 'Acceptance'.

37 John Pascoe, *Land Uplifted High*, p.143 (footnote).

38 John Pascoe, 'Was Wicky Lazy?', *School Journal*, 44 (2–6), March–July 1950.

39 John Pascoe, 'The Wicked Witch of Ruapehu', unpublished typescript, 14/15 November 1952, Dorothy Pascoe Collection.

40 John Pascoe to Doug Brown, 27 January 1953, Dorothy Pascoe Collection.

41 *Southland Times*, 3 March 1951.

42 John Pascoe, *The Mountains The Bush & The Sea*, 'Photographic Notes', Whitcombe & Tombs, 1950.

43 *Newsview*, February 1951.

44 Gary Blackman, 'My Century of New Zealand Photography', *NZ Journal of Photography*, May 1999, p.20.

45 *Freedom*, 20 December 1950.

46 John Pascoe to Bob Cawley, 13 December 1950, Dorothy Pascoe Collection.

47 John Pascoe to Robin Muir, 2 January 1951, Dorothy Pascoe Collection.

48 John Pascoe, *The Southern Alps – From the Kaikouras to the Rangitata*, Pegasus Press, 1951, p.96.

49 John Dobree Pascoe, Application for Membership of the New Zealand Alpine Club, 12 September 1951, Dorothy Pascoe Collection.

50 Harry Stevenson to John Pascoe, 14 September 1951, Dorothy Pascoe Collection.

51 J. D. Hanning, Secretary, The New Zealand Alpine Club, to John Pascoe, 10 December 1951, Dorothy Pascoe Collection.

52 Bill Hannah to John Pascoe, 3 July 1952, Dorothy Pascoe Collection.

53 John Pascoe, 'Women in the Mountains', *Journeys*, November 1950, p.24.

54 John Pascoe to Bill Hannah, 12 July 1952, Dorothy Pascoe Collection.

55 Chris Bonington, *Quest for Adventure*, Cassell & Co., 2000, pp.142,143.

56 Earle Riddiford to John Pascoe, 8 January 1951, Dorothy Pascoe Collection.

57 George Lowe to John Pascoe,
31 August 1952, Dorothy Pascoe
Collection.

58 Ed Hillary to John Pascoe,
1 September 1952, Dorothy Pascoe
Collection.

CHAPTER SEVEN

The Re-Explorer

1 John Pascoe to Robin Muir,
4 February, 31 March and
28 November 1952, MS Papers
75-241 (7), Alexander Turnbull
Library.

2 Robin Muir to John Pascoe, 23 July
1952, MS Papers 75-241 (7).

3 Gordon Ogilvie, *Denis Glover: His Life*,
Godwit, 1999, pp.283,284.

4 John Pascoe to Robin Muir,
28 November 1952.

5 Stanley Unwin to John Pascoe,
9 October 1950, as quoted in John
Pascoe to Carl Straubel, 16 October
1950, MS Papers 0138-3,
Alexander Turnbull Library.

6 John Pascoe to Pete (Paul) Pascoe,
16 October 1950, MS Papers
0138-3, Alexander Turnbull Library.

7 John Pascoe to Carl Straubel,
16 October 1950, MS Papers 0138-3.

8 Carl Straubel to John Pascoe,
21 May 1951, MS Papers 0138-3.

9 John Pascoe to Carl Straubel, 7 June
1951.

10 John Pascoe, revised draft of
unpublished, untitled novel,
c.1951, Dorothy Pascoe Collection.

11 John Pascoe, 'Notes on a holiday:
Te Towaka, Pelorus Sound,
Marlborough', January 1952,
Dorothy Pascoe Collection.

12 Conversation with Harold Leov
(Junior), 21 November 2001.

13 John Pascoe, 'Notes on a holiday:
Te Towaka, Pelorus Sound,
Marlborough'.

14 John Pascoe to Carl Straubel,
31 January 1952; John Pascoe to
Stan Conway, 12 May 1952,
Dorothy Pascoe Collection; John
Pascoe, 'In Memoriam – D.O.W.
Hall', *New Zealand Alpine Journal*, 1972,
pp.118, 119.

15 John Pascoe to Doug Knowles,
5 December 1933, Alan Knowles
Collection.

16 John Pascoe, *Mr Explorer Douglas*, A.H.
& A.W. Reed, 1957, pp.301–303.

17 John Pascoe to Robin Muir, 8 July
1952, MS Papers 75-241 (7).

18 John Pascoe to Stan Conway,
1 November 1952, Dorothy Pascoe
Collection.

19 Conversation with Ray Chapman,
10 April 2000 (tape).

20 *Evening Post*, 13 December 1952.

21 *The Alpine Journal*, 286, May 1953,
pp.96–98.

22 Conversation with Ray Chapman.

23 John Pascoe, 'Beyond the Arawata –
Personal Notes on an Overland
Journey', January 1953, Dorothy
Pascoe Collection.

24 John Pascoe, 'Beyond the Arawata',
The Mountain World, 1955, p.191;
John and Dorothy Pascoe, 'Mr and
Mrs Reminisce', National Radio,
26 October 1972.

25 John Pascoe, 'Beyond the Arawata –
Personal Notes on an Overland
Journey'.

26 *The Mountain World*, p.192;
conversation with Ray Chapman.

27 Colin Todd to John Pascoe,
31 January 1953, Dorothy Pascoe
Collection.

28 Conversation with Ray Chapman.

29 John Pascoe, 'Beyond the Arawata –
Personal Notes on an Overland
Journey'.

30 John Pascoe to Stan Conway,
20 January 1953, Dorothy Pascoe
Collection.

31 Gordon Ogilvie, *Denis Glover: His Life*,
pp.276–281.

32 Denis Glover to John Pascoe,
26 January 1953, Dorothy Pascoe
Collection.

33 John Pascoe to Denis Glover,
28 January 1953, Dorothy Pascoe
Collection.

34 John Pascoe to David Hall,
28 January 1953, Dorothy Pascoe
Collection.

35 John Pascoe to Louis Johnson,
9 February 1953, Dorothy Pascoe
Collection.

36 David Hall to John Pascoe,
3 February 1953, Dorothy Pascoe
Collection.

37 John Pascoe, 'Bushman', 'The
Rope' and 'A Welcome', February
1953, Dorothy Pascoe Collection.

38 John Pascoe to David Hall,
8 February 1953.

39 Denis Glover to John Pascoe,
16 February 1953.

40 John Pascoe to Louis Johnson,
14 May 1953, Dorothy Pascoe
Collection.

41 *NZ Listener*, 29 May 1953.

42 Louis Johnson to John Pascoe,
undated, c.1953, Dorothy Pascoe
Collection.

43 John Pascoe to Denis Glover,
5 March 1953.

44 Gordon Ogilvie, *Denis Glover: His Life*,
p.286.

45 Dorothy Pascoe, 'Snow and Rivers –
Sun and Sea', typescript, 22 April
2002, Collection of the author.

46 John Pascoe, Treasure Hunt clues,
c.1953, Dorothy Pascoe Collection.

47 *Evening Star*, 19 January 1953.

48 *New Zealand Alpine Journal*, 40, June
1953, p.300.

49 John Pascoe to Jean Johnson,
4 March 1953, Dorothy Pascoe
Collection.

50 Jean Johnson to John Pascoe,
undated, c.1953, Dorothy Pascoe
Collection.

51 John Pascoe to Jean Johnson,
20 April 1953.

52 John Pascoe to Thelma Maurais,
Editor, School Publications,
23 April 1953, Dorothy Pascoe
Collection.

53 Denis Glover to John Pascoe,
undated, c.April 1953.

54 George Lowe to John Pascoe,
15 February 1953, Dorothy Pascoe
Collection.

55 John Pascoe to Jean Johnson,
8 September 1953.

56 *Evening Post*, 27 July 1953.

57 John Pascoe to Eff Pascoe,
1 September 1953, Dorothy Pascoe
Collection.

58 Secretary, New Zealand Alpine
Club, to John Pascoe, 24 March
1953, Dorothy Pascoe Collection.

59 John Pascoe to Stan Conway,
5 August 1953.

60 John Pascoe to Secretary, Canterbury
Mountaineering Club, 25 September
1953, Dorothy Pascoe Collection.

61 John Pascoe to David Hall, 15 June
1953.

62 John Pascoe, Mr Explorer Douglas, A.H.
& A.W. Reed, 1957, p.304.

63 John Pascoe to Ray Chapman,
30 April 1954.

64 John Pascoe to H. E. L. Porter,
24 May 1954, Dorothy Pascoe
Collection.

65 John Pascoe to Jean Johnson,
21 June 1954.

66 John Pascoe, Mr Explorer Douglas,
p.305.

67 John Pascoe to Jean Johnson,
31 May 1955.

68 Evening Post, 31 May 1955.

CHAPTER EIGHT

The Historian

1 John Pascoe, 'Journal of a Change',
3 September 1955, Dorothy Pascoe
Collection.

2 John Pascoe to Lance Davison,
undated, c.1953, Dorothy Pascoe
Collection.

3 Michael Bassett, The Mother of all
Departments, Auckland University
Press and the Historical Branch of
Internal Affairs, 1997, pp.168, 169.

4 John Pascoe to Edgar Burton,
21 March 1956, Dorothy Pascoe
Collection.

5 John Pascoe to Ray Chapman,
11 October 1955, Dorothy Pascoe
Collection.

6 John Pascoe, 'A Hill Man's Yarns'
Outline of Subjects and Notes,
c.1955, Dorothy Pascoe Collection.

7 John Pascoe to Geoff Flower,
11 October 1955, Dorothy Pascoe
Collection.

8 J.H. Hall, Supervisor of Talks,
NZBS, to John Pascoe, 29 October
1956, MS Papers 75-241 (7),
Alexander Turnbull Library.

9 John Pascoe to Evan Meredith,
Wildlife Branch of Internal Affairs,
10 November 1955, Dorothy
Pascoe Collection.

10 John Pascoe to Dorothy Pascoe,
30 December 1955, Dorothy
Pascoe Collection.

11 John Pascoe to W. P. Packard,
2 February 1956, Dorothy Pascoe
Collection.

12 John Pascoe to Dorothy Pascoe,
30 December 1955.

13 New Zealand Free Lance, 3 August 1956.

14 John Pascoe, 'Four Explorers of
New Zealand', School Journal, 1–4,
1956.

15 John Pascoe to John Harper,
26 January 1956, Dorothy Pascoe
Collection.

16 John Pascoe to Geoff Flower,
11 October 1955, Dorothy Pascoe
Collection; Carl Straubel to
Secretary, Literary Fund Advisory
Committee, 7 July 1955; Secretary,
Literary Fund Committee to A. W.
Reed, 27 March 1956, IA-1,
86/1/22, Archives New Zealand.

17 John Pascoe to Peter Maling,
27 July 1956, MS Papers 75-241
(6), Alexander Turnbull Library.

18 John Pascoe to Ted Lovegrove,
19 November 1956, Dorothy
Pascoe Collection.

19 John Pascoe to John Feeney, 6 June
1956, Dorothy Pascoe Collection.

20 John Pascoe to Len Leov,
13 December 1956, Dorothy
Pascoe Collection.

21 John Pascoe to Judy Evans,
16 December 1956, Dorothy
Pascoe Collection.

22 Dorothy Pascoe, 'The Dark Days',
typescript, 12 February 2002,
Collection of the author.

23 John Pascoe to Paul Pascoe,
19 December 1956, Dorothy
Pascoe Collection.

24 John Pascoe to Peter Harding,
31 December 1956, Dorothy
Pascoe Collection.

25 John Pascoe to Judy Evans,
21 January 1957; John Pascoe to
Barbe Harding, 17 March 1957,
Dorothy Pascoe Collection.

26 Dorothy Pascoe, 'The Dark Days'.

27 John Pascoe to Lance McCaskill,
undated, c. February 1958,
Dorothy Pascoe Collection.

28 John Pascoe to the Supervisor of
Talks, NZBS, 27 January 1957;
Supervisor of Talks to Pascoe,
26 April; Pascoe to Acting Supervisor,
26 April; MS Papers 75-241 (7),
Alexander Turnbull Library.

29 Acting Supervisor of Broadcasts to
Schools to John Pascoe, 24 July
1957; John Pascoe to Supervisor
Broadcasts to Schools, 24 August;
MS Papers 75-241 (7), Alexander
Turnbull Library.

30 John Pascoe, Great Days in New Zealand
Mountaineering, A. H. & A. W. Reed,
1958, p.11.

31 John Pascoe to Arch Scott,
19 November 1957, Dorothy
Pascoe Collection.

32 John Pascoe to Peter Harding,
1 November 1957, Dorothy Pascoe
Collection.

33 John Pascoe to Dorothy Pascoe,
24, 25 and 27 December 1957,
Dorothy Pascoe Collection.

34 John Pascoe, 'Up and Down the
Maitahi', typescript, c.January
1958, Dorothy Pascoe Collection.

35 National Historic Places Trust Annual Report,
1957, Appendix II; John Pascoe to
Ormond Wilson, 24 October 1958,
MS Papers 75-241 (6), Alexander
Turnbull Library.

36 Ormond Wilson, An Outsider Looks
Back, Port Nicholson Press, 1982,
pp.10, 174–177.

37 Michael Blain, Wellington Cathedral of
S Paul 1840 – 2001, Victoria
University Press, 2002, pp.69–81.

38 John Pascoe to Charles Brasch,
7 August 1958, MS Papers 75-241
(6), Alexander Turnbull Library.

39 John Pascoe to Ormond Wilson,
5 October 1958, Dorothy Pascoe
Collection.

40 John Pascoe to Bill Hannah,
14 November 1958, Dorothy
Pascoe Collection.

41 John Pascoe to Eff Pascoe,
19 December 1958, Dorothy
Pascoe Collection.

42 Agreement between the Delegates
of the Clarendon Press in the
University of Oxford and John
Dobreé Pascoe, 6 March 1959,
Dorothy Pascoe Collection.

43 John Pascoe to Monty McClymont, 30 September 1959, MS Papers 75-241 (6), Alexander Turnbull Library.

44 Conversation with Dorothy Pascoe, 19 May 2000, (tape).

45 John Pascoe to Ormond Wilson, 20 August 1959, MS Papers 75-241 (6).

46 John Pascoe to Ruth Ross, 17 September 1959; Ruth Ross to John Pascoe, 4 October 1959; MS Papers 75-241 (6); Trevor Richards, *Dancing on our bones*, Bridget Williams Books, 1999, pp.20–29.

47 Conversation with Janet Paul, 27 March 2000 (tape); conversation with Tim Beaglehole, 17 June 2000.

48 Ruth Ross to John Pascoe, 4 October 1959, MS Papers 75-241 (6).

49 Ruth Ross to John Pascoe, 26 March, 21 July 1959, 4 April, 27 April 1960; John Pascoe to Ruth Ross, 20 April 1960; John Pascoe to Ormond Wilson, 11 April, 13 April 1960; MS Papers 75-241 (6).

50 Kenneth Melvin to John Pascoe, 13 July 1959; John Pascoe to Ken Melvin, 14 July 1959; MS Papers 75-241 (6).

51 Ormond Wilson to John Pascoe, 14 July 1960; John Pascoe to Ormond Wilson, 3 August 1960; Dorothy Pascoe Collection.

52 John Pascoe to Ormond Wilson, 25 February 1960, MS Papers 75-241 (6).

53 Ormond Wilson to John Pascoe, 25 September 1960, Dorothy Pascoe Collection.

54 John Pascoe to Ruth Ross, 17 September 1959, MS Papers 75-241 (6).

CHAPTER NINE
Administrative Man

1 John Pascoe to Peter Harding, 25 February 1961, Dorothy Pascoe Collection.

2 Conversation with Dorothy Pascoe, 8 October 2002; Dorothy Pascoe, 'Came the Sixties', 17 October 2002, Collection of the author.

3 Te O Rene to John Pascoe, 3 February 1961, Dorothy Pascoe Collection.

4 Ruta Rene to John Pascoe, 9 February 1961, Dorothy Pascoe Collection.

5 John Pascoe to Te O Rene, 24 March 1961, Dorothy Pascoe Collection.

6 John Pascoe to Peter Harding, 25 February 1961.

7 Priestley Thomson to John Pascoe, 11 May 1961, Dorothy Pascoe Collection; conversation with Priestley Thomson, 22 September 1999.

8 John Pascoe to Peter Harding, 25 February 1961.

9 John Pascoe to Priestley Thomson, 17 May 1961, Dorothy Pascoe Collection.

10 Conversation with John Daniels, 21 November 2000 (tape).

11 Ormond Wilson to John Pascoe, 3 May 1961, Dorothy Pascoe Collection.

12 John Pascoe to Ormond Wilson, 12 May 1961, Dorothy Pascoe Collection.

13 John Pascoe to Patricia Whitmore, 12 May 1961, Dorothy Pascoe Collection.

14 'Encyclopaedia for inquiring young minds', *New Zealand Woman's Weekly*, 30 August 1965.

15 John Pascoe to Walter Elliot, 29 May 1962, Dorothy Pascoe Collection.

16 John Pascoe, 'Six Acres of Raspberries', typescript, January 1962, Dorothy Pascoe Collection.

17 John Pascoe to Alice Morgan, 21 August 1961, Dorothy Pascoe Collection.

18 Paul Pascoe to John Pascoe, 21 May 1962, Dorothy Pascoe Collection.

19 John Pascoe to Alice Morgan, 29 June 1962, Dorothy Pascoe Collection.

20 John Pascoe to Alice Morgan, 2 July 1962, Dorothy Pascoe Collection.

21 Norman Hardie to John Pascoe, 10 September 1962, Dorothy Pascoe Collection.

22 Paul Pascoe to John Pascoe, 19 August 1962, Dorothy Pascoe Collection.

23 Sara Pascoe, 'My Illness', 22 August 2000, Collection of the author; John Pascoe 'Sara notes' 1962–1964, Dorothy Pascoe Collection.

24 John Pascoe to Anna Pascoe, 30 April 1962, Dorothy Pascoe Collection.

25 Dorothy Pascoe, 'Came the Sixties', typescript, 17 October 2002.

26 John Pascoe to Paul Pascoe, 8 October 1962, Dorothy Pascoe Collection; John Pascoe to Peter and Barbara Harding, 11 October 1962, Dorothy Pascoe Collection.

27 John Pascoe to Paul Pascoe, 30 October 1962, Dorothy Pascoe Collection.

28 John Pascoe to Peter Harding, 23 January 1963, Dorothy Pascoe Collection.

29 Conversation with Dorothy Pascoe, 17 October 2002.

30 John Pascoe to Anna Pascoe, 12 March 1963, Dorothy Pascoe Collection.

31 John Pascoe to Paul Pascoe, 21 February 1963, Dorothy Pascoe Collection.

32 John Pascoe to Anna Pascoe, 12 March 1963.

33 John Pascoe to Paul Pascoe, 17 June 1963, Dorothy Pascoe Collection.

34 John Pascoe to Alice Morgan, 31 May 1963, Dorothy Pascoe Collection.

35 John Pascoe 'Sara notes' 1962–1964; John Pascoe to Peter Harding, 28 June 1963; Dorothy Pascoe to Peter Harding, 8 July 1963, Dorothy Pascoe Collection.

36 Dorothy Pascoe Collection, 'Came the Sixties', typescript.

37 John Pascoe to David, Rosemary and John Morgan, 18 December 1964; John Pascoe to David Morgan, 8 February 1965, Dorothy Pascoe Collection.

38 John Pascoe to Harold Leov, 24 September 1964, Dorothy Pascoe Collection.

39 Michael Bassett, *The Mother of all Departments*, Auckland University Press and the Historical Branch, Internal Affairs, 1997, pp.188, 189; conversation with Ian Wards, 15 March 2000 (tape).

40 Conversation with Ian Wards.

41 Conversation with John Daniels, 21 November 2000.

42 Conversation with Ian Wards.

43 John Pascoe to Ruth Ross, 6 April 1964; John Pascoe to Sam Meads, 24 October 1963, Dorothy Pascoe Collection.

44 John Pascoe to Paul Pascoe, 4 August 1964, Dorothy Pascoe Collection.

45 Michael Bassett, *The Mother of all Departments*, p.189; *National Archives of New Zealand — A Review and a Summary of Work*, 1966, Department of Internal Affairs, p.6.

46 *National Archives of New Zealand — A Review and a Summary of Work*, 1966, p.9.

47 Conversation with Judith Hornabrook, 4 September 2002 (tape 1).

48 Geoffrey Dutton to John Pascoe, 20 April 1964, Dorothy Pascoe Collection.

49 *NZ Listener*, 27 August 1965.

50 *Mr and Mrs Reminisce*, National Radio, 26 October 1972; conversation with Dorothy and Martha Pascoe, 27 September 1999 (tape 1).

51 Dr Evelyn Lind to Mr Pascoe, 2 September 1965; John Pascoe to Sara Pascoe, 14 September 1965, Dorothy Pascoe Collection.

52 Charles Fleming to John Pascoe, 20 December 1966, Dorothy Pascoe Collection.

53 John Pascoe, *The Haast is in South Westland*, A. H. & A. W. Reed, 1966, Chapter One.

54 John Pascoe to Sara, Martha Pascoe, 28 January 1966; John Pascoe to Dorothy Pascoe, 28 January 1966, Dorothy Pascoe Collection.

55 Conversation with Simon Pascoe, 9 April 2000 (tape).

56 Conversation with Dorothy Pascoe, 7 November 2002.

CHAPTER TEN

When I'm Sixty-Five

1 *Mr and Mrs Reminisce*, National Radio, 26 October 1972.

2 John Pascoe, 'Origins', c.1968, MS Papers 75-241 (8), Alexander Turnbull Library.

3 *Evening Post, Dominion*, 23 June 1966; *New Zealand Alpine Journal*, 1966, pp.198-199, 334-336.

4 *Evening Post*, 1 July 1966.

5 John Pascoe to Harold Leov, 23 August 1967, Dorothy Pascoe Collection.

6 John Pascoe to Janet Paul, 17 September 1967; John Pascoe to Ian Gilmour, 8 March 1968; Dorothy Pascoe Collection.

7 John Pascoe to Paul Powell, 10 April 1968, MS Papers 75-241 (8).

8 John Pascoe to Paul Pascoe, 28 September 1967, Dorothy Pascoe Collection.

9 Conversation with Ray Chapman, 10 April 2000 (tape).

10 John Pascoe to Ian Gilmour, 8 March 1968; John Pascoe to Anna Pascoe, 18 June 1968; Dorothy Pascoe Collection.

11 Conversation with Dr Peter (Sam) Maling, 9 January 2000 (tape).

12 John Pascoe to Angus Ross, 4 July 1966, Dorothy Pascoe Collection; John Pascoe to Harold Leov, 12 April, 23 August 1968, MS Papers 75-241 (8); Conversation with Dorothy Pascoe, 13 December 2002; John Pascoe to Lawry Walker, 20 May 1971, Dorothy Pascoe Collection.

13 Guy Harding to Elsie Locke, 20 June 1968, and a later undated letter; Dorothy Pascoe Collection.

14 J. D. Pascoe to GEO (Cultural) Internal Affairs, 9 July 1968; John Pascoe to Dorothy Pascoe; MS Papers 75-241 (8); John Pascoe to Willa Baum, 9 June 1970, Dorothy Pascoe Collection.

15 J. D. Pascoe to the Secretary of Internal Affairs, 30 May 1968; Lyandon Pogson, 'Marine Department' memo, 22 November 1968; MS Papers 75-241 (8).

16 Chief Archivist, 'Activity Report', 7 November 1968, MS Papers 75-241 (8).

17 J. D. Pascoe to Superintendent of Management Services, State Services Commission, 18 September 1968; J. D. Pascoe to GEO (Cultural) Internal Affairs, 18 March 1968; MS Papers 75-241 (8).

18 John Pascoe to the Illustrations Editor, *Auckland Weekly News*, 15 May 1969, Dorothy Pascoe Collection; *Auckland Weekly News*, 14 May 1969.

19 Mike Gill to John Pascoe, 28 January 1969, Dorothy Pascoe Collection; John Pascoe to Mike Gill, 31 January 1969, MS Papers 75-241 (8).

20 Gordon Ogilvie, *Denis Glover: His Life*, Godwit, 1999, p.46.

21 Ibid., pp.374–380.

22 *Christchurch Star*, 11 August 1969.

23 John Pascoe to Willa Baum, 4 September 1969, Dorothy Pascoe Collection.

24 John Pascoe to Anna Pascoe, 15 September 1969, Dorothy Pascoe Collection.

25 John Pascoe to Mike Gill, 21 November 1969, Dorothy Pascoe Collection.

26 John Pascoe to Willa Baum, 26 January 1970, Dorothy Pascoe Collection.

27 John Pascoe to Hans and Pat Bohny, 31 March 1970; John Pascoe to Anna Pascoe, 7 April 1970; Dorothy Pascoe Collection.

28 John Pascoe to Peter Harding, 9 April 1970, Dorothy Pascoe Collection.

29 John Pascoe to Anna Pascoe, 12 April 1970, Dorothy Pascoe Collection.

30 Willa Baum to John Pascoe, 2 June 1970; John Pascoe to Willa Baum, 9 June 1970; Dorothy Pascoe Collection.

31 John Pascoe to Martha Pascoe, 21 October 1970, Dorothy Pascoe Collection.

32 John Pascoe to Stan Conway, 12 April 1970, Dorothy Pascoe Collection.

33 John Pascoe to Diana McClymont, 9 July 1970, Dorothy Pascoe Collection.

34 John Pascoe to David Hall, 1 October 1970, Dorothy Pascoe Collection.

35 John Pascoe to Anna, Ian [Gilmour], Melissa, and Martha Pascoe, 18 November 1970; John Pascoe to Peter Harding, 24 November 1970; Dorothy Pascoe Collection.

36 John Pascoe to Anna Pascoe, 2 December 1970, Dorothy Pascoe Collection.

37 John Pascoe, 'Notes on a Journey', December 1970, Dorothy Pascoe Collection.

38 John Pascoe to Anna Pascoe, 6 January 1971, Dorothy Pascoe Collection.

39 John Pascoe to R. J. Moore, 23 February 1971, Dorothy Pascoe Collection.

40 John Pascoe to Frank Alack, 13 May 1971, Dorothy Pascoe Collection.

41 John Pascoe to Lawry Walker, 20 May 1971; John Pascoe to Anna and Ian Gilmour, 28 May 1971; John Pascoe to Jane Pascoe, 28 June 1971; Dorothy Pascoe Collection.

42 John Pascoe to Anna and Ian Gilmour, 21 October 1971, Dorothy Pascoe Collection.

43 *New Zealand Alpine Journal*, 1972, pp.117–119.

44 *Christchurch Star*, 21 August 1971; *Press*, 14 August 1971.

45 John Pascoe to Martha Pascoe, 27 August 1971, Dorothy Pascoe Collection.

46 John Pascoe to A. H. & A. W. Reed Ltd, 19 October 1971, MS Papers 75-241 (11), Alexander Turnbull Library.

47 *Dominion*, 15 December 1971.

48 *Evening Post*, 20 December 1971.

49 John Pascoe to Alan Bibby, 15 October 1971, Dorothy Pascoe Collection.

50 Peter Coates, *Prince of Nosey Parkers*, NZBC Survey, May 1972.

51 *Evening Post*, 4 May 1972; *Dominion*, 5 May 1972; *Christchurch Star*, 18 May 1972; *Press*, 15 May 1972.

52 Paul Pascoe to John Pascoe, 5 May 1972, Dorothy Pascoe Collection.

53 Conversation with Dorothy Pascoe, 19 May 2000 (tape one).

54 John Pascoe to Anna Pascoe, 15 May 1972, Dorothy Pascoe Collection.

55 John Pascoe to Martha Pascoe, 27 May 1972, Dorothy Pascoe Collection.

56 John Pascoe to Lawry Walker and Harold Leov, 31 July 1972, Dorothy Pascoe Collection.

57 John Pascoe to Dr Peter (Sam) Maling, 23 March 1972, Dorothy Pascoe Collection.

58 John Pascoe to Anna and Ian Gilmour, 7 July 1972; John Pascoe to Martha Pascoe, 9 August 1972; Dorothy Pascoe Collection.

59 John Pascoe to Martha Pascoe, 18 August 1972, Dorothy Pascoe Collection.

60 John Pascoe to Anna Pascoe, 15 September 1972, Dorothy Pascoe Collection.

61 Dorothy Pascoe to Anna and Ian Gilmour, c. September 1972, Dorothy Pascoe Collection.

62 Conversation with Jane Shaw, 8 December 2002.

63 Dorothy Pascoe, 'When the bell tolls', 11 December 2002, Collection of the author.

64 Conversation with Ian Gilmour, 8 April 2000 (tape one).

65 John Pascoe to Jane Pascoe, 28 September 1971, Dorothy Pascoe Collection.

66 John Pascoe, note, c.19 October 1972, Dorothy Pascoe Collection.

67 *Dominion*, 24 October 1972; Gordon Ogilvie, *op. cit*, p.404.

68 John Pascoe, 'Notes on Funeral Items', 20 March 1970, Dorothy Pascoe Collection.

69 David Taylor, notes, c.24 October 1972, Dorothy Pascoe Collection.

70 David Galloway to Dorothy Pascoe, 22 October 1972, Dorothy Pascoe Collection.

71 Conversation with Ian Gilmour, *op. cit.*

Index